GLOBAL RECESSION - CAUSES, IMPACTS AND REMEDIES

REASSESSING TARP: SECOND REPORT FROM THE SPECIAL INSPECTOR GENERAL

GLOBAL RECESSION - CAUSES, IMPACTS AND REMEDIES

Additional books in this series can be found on Nova's website under the Series tab.

Additional E-books in this series can be found on Nova's website under the E-book tab.

GLOBAL RECESSION - CAUSES, IMPACTS AND REMEDIES

REASSESSING TARP: SECOND REPORT FROM THE SPECIAL INSPECTOR GENERAL

GEORGE T. BERNHARDT
EDITOR

Nova
Nova Science Publishers, Inc.
New York

For permission to use material from this book please contact us:
Telephone 631-231-7269; Fax 631-231-8175
Web Site: http://www.novapublishers.com

LIBRARY OF CONGRESS CATALOGING-IN-PUBLICATION DATA

Reassessing TARP : second report from the Special Inspector General /
editor, George T. Bernhardt.
p. cm.
Includes bibliographical references and index.
ISBN 978-1-60741-965-5 (hbk.)
1. Troubled Asset Relief Program (U.S.)--Evaluation. 2.
Finance--Government policy--United States. 3. Financial
institutions--United States--Finance. 4. Corporations--United
States--Finance. 5. Economic stabilization--United States. 6. Federal
aid--United States. I. Bernhardt, George T.
HG181.R296 2009
338.6--dc22
2010016723

Published by Nova Science Publishers, Inc. ✝ New York

CONTENTS

PREFACE

The Troubled Asset Relief Program ("TARP") now includes 12 separate, but often interrelated, programs involving Government and private funds of up to almost $3 trillion — roughly the equivalent of last year's entire Federal budget. TARP has evolved into a program of unprecedented scope, scale, and complexity. This book strives to explain the various TARP programs and how the Department of the Treasury has used those programs through March 31, 2009, as well as set forth a series of recommendations for the operation of TARP.

Chapter 1 - The Troubled Asset Relief Program ("TARP") now includes 12 separate, but often interrelated, programs involving Government and private funds of up to almost $3 trillion— roughly the equivalent of last year's entire Federal budget. From programs involving large capital infusions into hundreds of banks and other financial institutions, to a mortgage modification program designed to modify millions of mortgages, to public- private partnerships purchasing "toxic" assets from banks using tremendous leverage provided by Government loans or guarantees, TARP has evolved into a program of unprecedented scope, scale, and complexity. Before the American people and their representatives in Congress can meaningfully evaluate the effectiveness of this historic program, that scope and scale must be placed into proper context, and the complexity must be made understandable. That is what this report attempts to do.

In this report, the Office of the Special Inspector General for the Troubled Asset Relief Program ("SIGTARP") endeavors to (i) explain the various TARP programs and how the Department of the Treasury ("Treasury") has used those programs through March 31, 2009, (ii) describe what SIGTARP has done since its Initial Report to Congress, dated February 6, 2009 (the "Initial Report"), to oversee this historic program with respect to both audits and investigations, and (iii) set forth a series of recommendations for the operation of TARP.

Chapter 2 - The Office of the Special Inspector General for the Troubled Asset Relief Program ("SIGTARP") was created by Section 121 of the Emergency Economic Stabilization Act of 2008 ("EESA"). Under EESA, SIGTARP has the responsibility, among other things, to conduct, supervise, and coordinate audits and investigations of the purchase, management, and sale of assets under the Troubled Asset Relief Program ("TARP"). SIGTARP is required to report quarterly to Congress describing SIGTARP's activities and providing certain information about TARP over that preceding quarter. EESA gives SIGTARP the authorities listed in Section 6 of the Inspector General Act of 1978, including the power to obtain documents and other information from Federal agencies and to subpoena reports, documents, and other information from persons or entities outside of Government.

The Special Inspector General, Neil M. Barofsky, was confirmed by the Senate on December 8, 2008, and sworn into office on December 15, 2008.

On March 25, 2009, Congress unanimously passed the Special Inspector General for the Troubled Asset Relief Program Act of 2009 (the "SIGTARP Act" or the "Act"), which amends EESA as follows:

- provides SIGTARP the authority, with limited exceptions, to conduct, supervise, and coordinate audits and investigations into any actions taken under EESA
- makes clear that SIGTARP can undertake law enforcement functions without first obtaining Attorney General approval
- gives SIGTARP the responsibility to coordinate and cooperate with other inspectors general on oversight of TARP-related activities
- clarifies that SIGTARP's quarterly reports are due 30 days after the end of a fiscal quarter
- provides SIGTARP with the ability to hire up to 25 Federal retirees, without offset of their pension, and, for six months, the authority to hire Federal employees under 5 U.S.C. § 3161, which gives employees a right to return to their original agencies once SIGTARP no longer exists
- requires the Treasury Secretary to take steps to address de ciencies identified by SIGTARP or certify to Congress that no action is necessary or appropriate
- mandates that SIGTARP shall provide a report to Congress, by September 1, 2009, on how TARP recipients have used TARP funds
- releases SIGTARP's $50 million allocation for immediate use

SIGTARP believes that the Act makes clear that it has the authorities it needs to fulfill its mission and will significantly improve its ability to attract and hire experienced Government auditors and investigators. As of April 17, 2009, the Act had not yet been signed into law.

Chapter 3 - This section provides details of activities that the U.S. Department of Treasury ("Treasury") has conducted under the Troubled Asset Relief Program ("TARP"), including the following:

- a financial overview of TARP initiatives, implemented and announced
- a detailed update on previously described programs
- a program-by-program description of newly announced programs
- the status of executive compensation restrictions for TARP recipients

Chapter 4 - Under the Emergency Economic Stabilization Act of 2008 ("EESA"), Congress has authorized the Treasury Secretary to take such actions as necessary to build the operational and administrative infrastructure to support TARP activities. EESA authorized the establishment of an Office of Financial Stability ("OFS") within the Department of Treasury ("Treasury") to be responsible for the administration of the Troubled Asset Relief Program ("TARP"). Treasury has the authority to establish program vehicles, issue regulations, directly hire or appoint employees, enter into contracts, and designate financial institutions as financial agents of the Federal Government. In addition to using permanent and interim staff, OFS relies on contractors and financial agents in legal, investment consulting, accounting, and other key service areas.

Chapter 5 - One of SIGTARP's responsibilities is to provide recommendations to the Department of Treasury ("Treasury") so that Troubled Asset Relief Program ("TARP") programs can be designed or modified to facilitate transparency and effective oversight and prevent fraud, waste, and abuse. SIGTARP's Initial Report to Congress, dated February 6, 2009 (the "Initial Report"), set forth a series of recommendations, some of which were adopted by Treasury and some of which were not. Appendix J: "Treasury Response to SIGTARP Recommendations" contains Treasury's detailed statement as to what it believes it has done to address those recommendations, and, for some of the recommendations that it has not implemented, why it has not done so. Set forth below are SIGTARP's recommendations, first with respect to implemented TARP programs and then for newly announced programs.

In: Reassessing TARP
Editor: George T. Bernhardt

ISBN: 978-1-60741-965-5

Chapter 1

Executive Summary

The Troubled Asset Relief Program ("TARP") now includes 12 separate, but often inter-related, programs involving Government and private funds of up to almost $3 trillion—roughly the equivalent of last year's entire Federal budget. From programs involving large capital infusions into hundreds of banks and other financial institutions, to a mortgage modification program designed to modify millions of mortgages, to public- private partnerships purchasing "toxic" assets from banks using tremendous leverage provided by Government loans or guarantees, TARP has evolved into a program of unprecedented scope, scale, and complexity. Before the American people and their representatives in Congress can meaningfully evaluate the effectiveness of this historic program, that scope and scale must be placed into proper context, and the complexity must be made understandable. That is what this report attempts to do.

In this report, the Office of the Special Inspector General for the Troubled Asset Relief Program ("SIGTARP") endeavors to (i) explain the various TARP programs and how the Department of the Treasury ("Treasury") has used those programs through March 31, 2009, (ii) describe what SIGTARP has done since its Initial Report to Congress, dated February 6, 2009 (the "Initial Report"), to oversee this historic program with respect to both audits and investigations, and (iii) set forth a series of recommendations for the operation of TARP.

Tremendous Expansion in the Scope , Scale, and Complexity of TARP

TARP, as originally envisioned in the fall of 2008, would have involved the purchase, management, and sale of up to $700 billion of "toxic" assets, primarily troubled mortgages and mortgage-backed securities ("MBS"). That framework was soon abandoned, however, and the program's scope, size, and complexity have dramatically increased. As of the writing of this report, TARP funds are being used, or have been announced to be used, in connection with 12 separate programs that, as set forth in Table 1.1, involve a total (including TARP funds, Federal Reserve loans, Federal Deposit Insurance Corporation ("FDIC") guarantees, and private money) that could reach nearly $3 trillion.

Treasury has announced, as of March 31, 2009, the parameters of how $590.4 billion of the $700 billion in TARP funding authorized by the Emergency Economic Stabilization Act of 2008 ("EESA") would be spent through the 12 programs. Of the $590.4 billion that Treasury has committed, $328.6 billion has actually been spent as of March 31, 2009. This report provides an update on those TARP programs that had been announced as of SIGTARP's Initial Report, as well as descriptions of programs that have subsequently been announced.

Table 1.1. Total Funds Subject to SIGTARP Oversight, as of March 31, 2009 ($ Billions)

Program	Brief Description or Participant	Total Projected Funding	Projected TARP Funding
Capital Purchase Program ("CPP")	Investments in 532 banks to date; 8 institutions total $125 billion	$218.0	$218.0
Automotive Industry Financing Program ("AIFP")	GM, Chrysler, GMAC, Chrysler Financial	$25.0	$25.0
Auto Supplier Support Program ("ASSP")	Government-backed protection for auto parts suppliers	$5.0	$5.0
Unlocking Credit for Small Businesses ("UCSB")	Purchase of securities backed by SBA loans	$15.0	$15.0
Systemically Significant Failing Institutions ("SSFI")	AIG Investment	$70.0	$70.0
Targeted Investment Program ("TIP")	Citigroup, Bank of America Investments	$40.0	$40.0
Asset Guarantee Program ("AGP")	Citigroup, Bank of America, Ring-Fence Asset Guarantee	$419.0	$12.5
Term Asset-Backed Securities Loan Facility ("TALF")	FRBNY non-recourse loans for purchase of asset-backed securities	$1,000.0	$80.0
Making Home Affordable ("MHA") Program	Modification of mortgage loans	$75.0	$50.0
PublicPrivate Investment Program ("PPIP")	Disposition of legacy assets; Legacy Loans Program, Legacy Securities Program (expansion of TALF)	$500.0 – $1,000.0	$75.0
Capital Assistance Program ("CAP")	Capital to qualified financial institutions; includes stress test	TBD	TBD
New Programs, or Funds Remaining for Existing Programs	Potential additional funding related to CAP; AIFP; Auto Warranty Commitment Program; other	$109.5	$109.5
Total		**$2,476.5–$2,976.5**	**$700.0**

Note: See Table 2.1 in Section 2 for notes and sources related to the information contained in this table.

OVERSIGHT ACTIVITIES OF SIGTARP

Since the Initial Report, SIGTARP has been actively engaged in fulfilling its vital investigative and audit functions as well as in building its staff and organization.

On the investigations side, SIGTARP's Hotline is staffed, operational, and providing an interface with the American public to facilitate the reporting of concerns, allegations, information, and evidence of violations of criminal and civil laws in connection with TARP. As of the drafting of this report, the SIGTARP Hotline has received and analyzed nearly 200 tips, running the gamut from expressions of concern over the economy to serious allegations of fraud. Both from the Hotline and from other leads, SIGTARP has initiated, to date, almost 20 preliminary and full criminal investigations. Although the details of those investigations generally will not be discussed unless and until public action is taken, the cases vary widely in subject matter and include large corporate and securities fraud matters affecting TARP investments, tax matters, insider trading, public corruption, and mortgage-modification fraud.

SIGTARP has been proactive in dealing with potential fraud in TARP. For example, to get out in front of any efforts to pro t criminally from the Term Asset-Backed Securities Loan Facility ("TALF"), which, as announced, involves up to $1 trillion of lending by the Federal Reserve backed by up to $80 billion in TARP funds, SIGTARP has organized and leads a multi-agency task force to deter, detect, and investigate any instances of fraud or abuse in the program. In addition to SIGTARP, the TALF Task Force consists of the Office of the Inspector General of the Board of Governors of the Federal Reserve Board, the Federal Bureau of Investigation, Treasury's Financial Crimes Enforcement Network, U.S. Immigration and Customs Enforcement, the Internal Revenue Service Criminal Investigation division, the Securities and Exchange Commission, and the U.S. Postal Inspection Service. Representatives from each member organization participate in regular brie ngs about TALF, collectively identify areas of fraud vulnerability, engage in the training of agents and analysts with respect to the complex issues surrounding the program, and will serve as points of contact for leads relating to TALF and any resulting cases that are generated. The TALF Task Force represents a historic law enforcement effort with an ambitious goal: to redefine the policing of complex Federal Government programs by proactively arranging a coordinated law enforcement response before fraud occurs.

On the audit side, SIGTARP has initiated and is in the process of conducting six audits:

Use of Funds: SIGTARP's first audit examines the use of TARP funds by TARP recipients, and is based upon a survey that SIGTARP sent to 364 TARP recipients that had received funds as of January 31, 2009.

Executive Compensation Compliance: SIGTARP's second audit, also based on SIGTARP's survey, examines how TARP recipients are implementing controls with respect to applicable executive compensation restrictions.

Bank of America: The third audit examines the review and approval processes associated with TARP assistance to Bank of America under three different TARP programs and examines Treasury's decision making related to additional TARP assistance provided in connection with Bank of America's acquisition of Merrill Lynch. Since its commencement, the audit's scope has expanded to examine broadly Treasury's decision making regarding the first nine institutions to be considered for funding under TARP.

External Influences: The fourth audit examines whether, or to what extent, external parties may have sought to in uence decision making by Treasury or bank regulators in considering and deciding on applications for funding from individual banks seeking TARP funds. This audit seeks to determine what procedures are in place to avoid undue outside in uence on the process, whether there are any indications of any undue in uence, and what actions might be needed to strengthen existing processes to avoid such undue in uences in the future.

AIG Bonuses: The next audit examines Federal oversight of executive compensation requirements, with a particular focus on recent payouts of large bonus payments to American International Group, Inc. ("AIG") employees. SIGTARP has undertaken an audit to determine: (i) the extent to which the recent bonus payments were made in accordance with conditions imposed in return for TARP assistance, and (ii) Treasury's monitoring of AIG's executive compensation agreements and whether it was aware of the full range of executive compensation, bonus, and retention payments throughout AIG's corporate structure.

AIG Counterparty Payments: AIG, which has received the largest amount of fi- nancial assistance from the Government during the current financial crisis, reportedly made counterparty payments to other financial institutions, including foreign institutions and other TARP recipients, at 100% of face value. SIGTARP will examine the basis for the counterparty payments and seek to determine whether any efforts were made to negotiate a reduction in those payments.

SIGTARP'S RECOMMENDATIONS ON THE OPERATION OF TARP

One of SIGTARP's oversight responsibilities is to provide recommendations to Treasury so that TARP programs can be designed or modified to facilitate effective oversight and transparency and to prevent fraud, waste, and abuse. In Section 4 of this report, SIGTARP details instances in which Treasury has addressed recommendations made in and since the Initial Report, and makes a series of new recommendations, including:

Use of Funds: SIGTARP continues to recommend that Treasury require all TARP recipients to report on their actual use of TARP funds. This recommendation is particularly important with respect to the potential application of the Capital Purchase Program ("CPP") to large insurance companies that may have purchased banks eligible for CPP in order to access TARP funds, and to Treasury's recent announcement of an additional $30 billion investment in AIG. Simply put, the American people have a right to know how their tax dollars are being used. This recommendation applies not only to capital investment and lending programs involving banks and other financial institutions, but also to programs in which TARP funds are used to purchase troubled assets, including transactions in the Public-Private Investment Program ("PPIP") and surrenders of collateral in TALF.

Expansion of TALF: The announced expansion of TALF to permit the posting of MBS as collateral poses significant fraud risks, particularly with respect to legacy residential MBS ("RMBS"). SIGTARP has made a series of recommendations to mitigate these risks, including, among others, that Treasury should require a security-by-security screening for legacy RMBS; that any RMBS should be rejected as collateral if the loans backing particular RMBS do not meet to be riddled with fraud, including certain undocumented subprime residential mortgages (*i.e.*, "liar loans"); and that Treasury should require significantly higher haircuts for all MBS, with particularly high haircuts for legacy RMBS.

PPIP Fraud Vulnerabilities: Aspects of PPIP make it inherently vulnerable to fraud, waste, and abuse, including significant issues relating to con icts of interest facing fund managers, collusion between participants, and vulnerabilities to money laundering. SIGTARP has made a series of recommendations to address these concerns, including, among others, that Treasury should (i) impose strict con ict-of-interest rules upon Public-Private Investment Fund ("PPIF") fund managers, (ii) mandate transparency with respect to the participation and management of PPIFs, including disclosure of the beneficial owners of the private equity stakes in the PPIFs and of all transactions undertaken in them, and (iii) that all PPIF fund managers have stringent investor-screening procedures, including comprehensive "Know Your Customer" requirements at least as rigorous as that of a commercial bank or retail brokerage operation.

Interaction Between PPIP and TALF: In announcing the details of PPIP, Treasury has indicated that PPIFs under the Legacy Securities Program could, in turn, use the leveraged PPIF funds (two-thirds of which will likely be taxpayer money) to purchase legacy MBS through TALF, greatly increasing taxpayer exposure to losses with no corresponding increase of potential profits. Such an expansion could cause great harm to one of the fundamental taxpayer protections in the original design of TALF by significantly diluting the private party's personal stake, the "skin in the game," and therefore reduce their incentive to conduct appropriate due diligence. Treasury should not allow Legacy Securities PPIFs to invest in TALF unless significant mitigating measures are included to address the dilution of this incentive, which could include prohibiting the use of leverage for PPIFs investing through TALF or proportionately increasing haircuts for PPIFs that do so.

Mortgage Modif cation Program: To prevent fraud in the mortgage modification program, SIGTARP has recommended that Treasury build certain fraud protections into the mechanics of the program, including requiring third-party verification of residence and income, conducting a closing-like procedure in which identities of participants are con rmed, and delaying modification incentive payments to servicers. SIGTARP has also recommended that Treasury proactively educate homeowners about the nature of the program, publicize that no fee is necessary to participate in the program, and collect and maintain a database of the names and identifying information for each participant in each mortgage modification transaction.

REPORT ORGANIZATION

The report is organized as follows:

Chapter 1 describes the activities of SIGTARP.

Chapter 2 describes how Treasury has spent TARP money thus far and contains an explanation or update of each program, both implemented and recently announced.

Chapter 3 describes the operations and administration of the Office of Financial Stability ("OFS"), the of ce within Treasury that manages TARP.

Chapter 4 lays out SIGTARP's recommendations to Treasury with respect to the operation of TARP.

The report also includes numerous appendices containing, among other things, figures and tables detailing all TARP investments through March 31, 2009.

The goal is to make this report a ready reference on what TARP is and how it has been used to date. In the interest of making this report as understandable as possible, and thereby furthering general transparency of the program itself, certain technical terms are highlighted in the text and de ned in the adjacent margin. In addition, portions of Section 2 are devoted to tutorials explaining the financial terms and concepts necessary to obtain a basic understanding of TARP operations.

In: Reassessing TARP
Editor: George T. Bernhardt
ISBN: 978-1-60741-965-5

Chapter 2

THE OFFICE OF THE SPECIAL INSPECTOR GENERAL FOR THE TROUBLED ASSET RELIEF PROGRAM

SIGTARP'S CREATION AND STATUTORY AUTHORITY

The Office of the Special Inspector General for the Troubled Asset Relief Program ("SIGTARP") was created by Section 121 of the **Emergency Economic Stabilization Act of 2008 ("EESA")**. Under EESA, SIGTARP has the responsibility, among other things, to conduct, supervise, and coordinate audits and investigations of the purchase, management, and sale of assets under the Troubled Asset Relief Program ("TARP"). SIGTARP is required to report quarterly to Congress describing SIGTARP's activities and providing certain information about TARP over that preceding quarter. EESA gives SIGTARP the authorities listed in Section 6 of the Inspector General Act of 1978, including the power to obtain documents and other information from Federal agencies and to subpoena reports, documents, and other information from persons or entities outside of Government.

The Special Inspector General, Neil M. Barofsky, was confirmed by the Senate on December 8, 2008, and sworn into office on December 15, 2008.

On March 25, 2009, Congress unanimously passed the **Special Inspector General for the Troubled Asset Relief Program Act of 2009** (the "SIGTARP Act" or the "Act"), which amends EESA as follows:

- provides SIGTARP the authority, with limited exceptions, to conduct, supervise, and coordinate audits and investigations into any actions taken under EESA
- makes clear that SIGTARP can undertake law enforcement functions without first obtaining Attorney General approval
- gives SIGTARP the responsibility to coordinate and cooperate with other inspectors general on oversight of TARP-related activities
- clarifies that SIGTARP's quarterly reports are due 30 days after the end of a fiscal quarter
- provides SIGTARP with the ability to hire up to 25 Federal retirees, without offset of their pension, and, for six months, the authority to hire Federal employees under 5

U.S.C. § 3161, which gives employees a right to return to their original agencies once SIGTARP no longer exists

requires the Treasury Secretary to take steps to address de ciencies identified by SIGTARP or certify to Congress that no action is necessary or appropriate

mandates that SIGTARP shall provide a report to Congress, by September 1, 2009, on how TARP recipients have used TARP funds

releases SIGTARP's $50 million allocation for immediate use

SIGTARP believes that the Act makes clear that it has the authorities it needs to fulfill its mission and will significantly improve its ability to attract and hire experienced Government auditors and investigators. As of April 17, 2009, the Act had not yet been signed into law.

Emergency Economic Stabilization Act of 2008 ("EESA"): A law enacted in response to the global financial crisis. This act created TARP and authorized Treasury to spend up to $700 billion to purchase troubled assets.

Special Inspector General for the Troubled Asset Relief Program Act of 2009: The measure amends EESA and expands the authority of the TARP Special Inspector General to conduct, supervise, and coordinate audits and investigations regarding any action taken pursuant to EESA.

SIGTARP's Mission and Core Values

SIGTARP's mission is to advance economic stability through transparency, coordinated oversight, and robust enforcement, thereby being a voice for, and protecting the interests of, those who fund TARP — *i.e.,* the American taxpayers. SIGTARP does so by promoting transparency in TARP, through effective oversight of TARP in coordination with other relevant oversight bodies, and by robust criminal and civil enforcement against those, whether inside or outside of Government, who waste, steal, or abuse TARP funds.

Transparency

Promoting transparency in the management and operation of TARP is one of SIGTARP's primary roles. Through EESA, the American taxpayer has been asked to fund — through programs now involving up to approximately $3 trillion — an unprecedented effort to stabilize the financial system and promote economic recovery. In this context, the public has a right to know how the U.S. Department of the Treasury ("Treasury") decides to invest that money, how it manages the assets it obtains, and how TARP recipients use these funds. Transparency is a powerful tool to ensure accountability and that all those managing and receiving TARP funds will act appropriately, consistent with the law, and in the best interests of the country.

Coordinated Oversight

SIGTARP plays a vital role in promoting economy and efficiency in the management of TARP and views its oversight role both prospectively (by advising TARP managers on issues relating to internal controls and fraud prevention, for example) and retrospectively (by assessing the effectiveness of TARP activities over time and suggesting improvements). SIGTARP's oversight role also reaches the recipients of TARP funds; in that context, SIGTARP complements Treasury's compliance function to ensure that recipients are satisfying their obligations under the various TARP initiatives. SIGTARP plays a significant coordinating role — formalized in the SIGTARP Act — among the TARP oversight bodies both to ensure maximum oversight coverage and to avoid redundant and unduly burdensome requests on Treasury personnel who run the program.

Robust Enforcement

SIGTARP's third primary role is to prevent, detect, and investigate cases of fraud, waste, and abuse of TARP funds and programs. Through its own audit and investigative resources and through partnership with other relevant law enforcement agencies, SIGTARP is committed to robust criminal and civil enforcement against those, whether inside or outside of Government, who waste, steal, or abuse TARP funds.

SIGTARP's Oversight Activities Since the Initial Report

In light of the size and complexity of TARP and the speed with which TARP has been implemented, it has been imperative that SIGTARP conduct a full range of oversight activities even while it builds its staff and capabilities. Since SIGTARP's Initial Report to Congress, dated February 6, 2009 (the "Initial Report"), SIGTARP has continued to conduct its oversight tasks in multiple parallel tracks, from making recommendations relating to preventing fraud and abuse prospectively, to coordinating closely with other oversight bodies in both the audit and investigative arenas, to auditing aspects of TARP both inside and outside of Government, all the while trying to promote transparency in TARP programs to the American people and Congress.

Maintaining Lines of Communication with TARP Managers

SIGTARP has attempted to establish and maintain regular lines of communications with the personnel primarily responsible for running TARP, including those working within Treasury's Office of Financial Stability ("OFS") and Office of General Counsel ("OGC") and within other agencies who manage TARP-related programs or activities, such as the bank regulators, the Federal Reserve Board, and the Federal Reserve Bank of New York ("FRBNY"):

SIGTARP personnel generally receive briefings concerning each new TARP initiative and new developments in implemented programs when necessary.

The Special Inspector General and Chief of Staff meet weekly with the head of OFS and OFS's Chief Compliance Officer to discuss ongoing issues and new developments.

Staff members communicate regularly with OFS's Chief Compliance Officer, who serves as OFS's day-to-day liaison with SIGTARP.

SIGTARP also meets regularly with Treasury's lawyers within OGC to discuss any legal issues relating to TARP.

Upon request, personnel from OFS's outside vendors have made themselves available to SIGTARP personnel.

SIGTARP has established regular communication with of cials from the Federal Reserve System (staff from the Federal Reserve Board of Governors and FRBNY) in connection with the Federal Reserve TARP-related programs.

Generally, Treasury and the other agencies have been cooperative in making their personnel available to SIGTARP and have responded to SIGTARP's requests for documents and information.

In connection with this open communication between SIGTARP and TARP managers, SIGTARP has endeavored, to the extent it has had an opportunity, to examine the planned framework for TARP initiatives before their terms are finalized and to make recommendations designed to advance oversight and internal controls and prevent waste, fraud, and abuse within the programs. Since the Initial Report, SIGTARP has made such recommendations with regard to TALF and the Mortgage Modification Program, among others.

Asset-Backed Securities ("ABS"): A tradable security backed by a pool of loans, leases, or any other cash-flow-producing assets. For a more detailed discussion of the securitization process, see the "TARP Tutorial: Securitization" discussion in Section 2 of this report.

Financial Stability Plan ("FSP"): A Department of Treasury plan to stabilize and repair the financial system, and support the fiow of credit necessary for economic recovery.

Mortgage-Backed Securities ("MBS"): A set of similar mortgages bundled together by a financial institution and sold as one security — a type of ABS.

TALF

The Term Asset-Backed Securities Loan Facility ("TALF") is a Federal Reserve-led program in which FRBNY makes loans that are designed to be fully secured by collateral — **asset-backed securities ("ABS")**. The loans have terms of up to three years and are non-recourse; that is, if the borrower defaults on the loan, the Federal Reserve will have no recourse against the borrower beyond the collateral for the loan. Surrendered collateral will be purchased by a special purpose vehicle that will be funded in part by TARP funds. As TALF is currently structured, FRBNY will loan up to $200 billion (supported by credit protection of up to $20 billion in TARP funds in the event of default), secured by ABS that are backed by credit card loans, auto financing, student loans, auto fioorplan loans, business equipment loans, mortgage servicing advances, and Small Business Administration ("SBA") loans. A potential expansion of TALF has been announced as part of Treasury's **Financial Stability Plan ("FSP")**, with respect to both the inclusion of additional asset classes, such as newly issued and legacy commercial **mortgage-backed securities ("MBS")** and non-agency residential MBS, and to increase lending to up to $1 trillion, supported by up to $80 billion of TARP funds in the event of default. For a more detailed description of the changes to TALF, see the TALF portion of Section 2: "TARP Implementation."

The Initial Report contained a series of SIGTARP recommendations with regard to the design of TALF. Since the Initial Report, SIGTARP has remained in regular contact with Treasury and FRBNY with regard to oversight and fraud prevention in TALF and has sought greater transparency, explicit oversight access, and assurances regarding underwriting standards on the loans underlying the securities, among other things. SIGTARP's past and new recommendations regarding TALF are discussed in greater detail in Section 4 of this report. Although not all of these recommendations have been adopted, the design of the program, in SIGTARP's view, has significantly improved from an oversight perspective due to SIGTARP's suggestions and FRBNY's willingness to engage on these issues.

Mortgage Modification Program

As discussed in Section 2 in detail, Treasury's FSP includes a program entitled the Home Affordable Modification Program ("HAMP") through which TARP funds will be made available to mortgage loan servicers to encourage them to modify certain existing mortgages in an effort to reduce the rate of foreclosures. SIGTARP had a series of brie ngs with OFS with respect to this program, and, after consultation with mortgage fraud experts at the Federal Bureau of Investigation ("FBI"), SIGTARP made a series of fraud prevention-oriented suggestions for the design of the program. As discussed in Section 4 of this report, some of those suggestions were adopted, including a fraud warning sheet and requiring a signed certification with respect to certain representations under criminal penalty.

Coordination with Other EESA Oversight Bodies

EESA, as amended, is explicit in mandating that SIGTARP coordinate audits and investigations into TARP with the other primary oversight bodies: the Financial Stability Oversight Board ("FSOB"), the Congressional Oversight Panel ("COP"), and the Government Accountability Of ce ("GAO"). Numerous other agencies, both in the Inspector General ("IG") community and among criminal and civil law enforcement agencies, potentially have responsibilities that touch on TARP as well. SIGTARP takes seriously its mandate to coordinate these overlapping oversight responsibilities, both to ensure maximum coverage and to avoid duplicative requests of TARP managers. SIGTARP and its partners have continued to have significant success on this front since the Initial Report. These coordination efforts include:

- bi-weekly conference calls with staff from FSOB
- regular meetings with staff from COP
- frequent interactions with GAO to coordinate ongoing and planned work to avoid any unnecessary duplication of efforts and to better facilitate their individual responsibilities

TARP-IG Council

Due to the scope of the various programs under TARP, numerous Federal agencies have some role in administering or overseeing TARP programs. To further facilitate SIGTARP's coordination role, the Special Inspector General founded and chairs the TARP Inspector General Council (iARP-IG Council"), made up of the Comptroller General and those IGs whose oversight functions are most likely to touch on TARP issues. The Council meets monthly to discuss developments in TARP and to coordinate overlapping audit and investigative issues. Since the Initial Report, the Council was expanded to include the Inspector General for the SBA in light of SBA involvement in a new TARP initiative. The TARP-IG Council currently consists of:

- The Special Inspector General
- Inspector General of the Department of the Treasury
- Inspector General of the Federal Reserve Board
- nspector General of the Federal Deposit Insurance Corporation
- Inspector General of the Securities and Exchange Commission
- Inspector General of the Federal Housing Finance Agency
- Inspector General of the Department of Housing and Urban Development
- Treasury Inspector General for Tax Administration
- Inspector General for the Small Business Administration
- Comptroller General of the United States (head of the GAO) or his designee

Coordination with Law Enforcement Agencies

SIGTARP's coordination role extends not only to audits and oversight but also to investigations; it is the only one of the four primary oversight bodies with criminal law enforcement authority. As a result, SIGTARP has been active in forging partnerships with criminal and civil law enforcement agencies. These relationships are designed to benefit both investigations originated by other agencies, when SIGTARP expertise can be brought to bear, and SIGTARP's own investigations, which can be improved by tapping into additional resources. In this regard:

- SIGTARP has continued to develop close working relationships with the FBI, with the Internal Revenue Service Criminal Investigation division ("IRS-CI"), and with the Securities and Exchange Commission ("SEC"), both with each agency's headquarters and various field offices.
- The Special Inspector General and Chief of Staff recently met with the new Chairman of the SEC, and SIGTARP looks forward to a close partnership with a reinvigorated SEC.
- SIGTARP has continued to develop relationships with the Department of Justice ("DOJ"), both at Main Justice and with United States Attorney's Offices across the country, to discuss criminal and civil enforcement.
- The Special Inspector General and Chief of Staff recently met with the Attorney General and Deputy Attorney General, and SIGTARP is confident that DOJ stands ready to prosecute aggressively TARP-related crimes.
- SIGTARP continues to coordinate with State Attorneys General.
- SIGTARP personnel have given training presentations to DOJ prosecutors and to SEC enforcement attorneys.
- SIGTARP representatives have joined the Mortgage, Banking and Securities, and Commodities Working Groups sponsored by DOJ — bodies in which key information regarding these law enforcement disciplines is shared.

Assistant Inspector General for Investigations TARP Working Group

The Assistant Inspector General for Investigations ("AIGI") TARP Working Group was established by SIGTARP's Deputy Special Inspector General for Investigations. Its objective is to provide an active forum for heads of investigative divisions within the IG community and other law enforcement agencies, whose agency mission is in some way affiliated with TARP, to coordinate and share relevant programmatic and investigative information at the national level. AIGIs from various entities work cooperatively within the Working Group to establish the most efficient law enforcement information sharing protocols; share lessons learned on investigative techniques and operations; and determine training requirements for special agents, attorney investigators, and analysts regarding structures and processes affiliated with existing and new TARP-related initiatives.

TALF Task Force

In a proactive initiative to get out in front of any efforts to profit criminally from the up to $1 trillion TALF program, SIGTARP has organized and leads a multi-agency task force to deter, detect, and investigate any instances of fraud or abuse in TALF. In addition to SIGTARP, the TALF Task Force comprises the Federal Reserve Board IG, FBI, Treasury's Financial Crimes Enforcement Network ("FinCEN"), U.S. Immigration and Customs Enforcement ("ICE"), IRS-CI, SEC, and the U.S. Postal Inspection Service ("US PIS"). Representatives from each agency participate in regular briefings about TALF, collectively identify areas of fraud vulnerability, engage in the training of agents and analysts with respect to the complex issues surrounding the program, and will serve as points of contact within each agency for leads relating to TALF and any resulting cases that are generated.

TALF is an important program that, both because of its complexity and its eventual size (up to $1 trillion), is an enormous challenge to law enforcement. This Task Force, consisting of both civil and criminal law enforcement agencies, with both investigative and analytical resources, demonstrates that the agencies involved are meeting that challenge proactively and before the bulk of the money has gone out the door. The members of the TALF Task Force will combine their shared expertise in securities fraud investigations and maximize their resources to deter potential criminals, to identify and stop fraud schemes before they can fully develop, and to bring to justice those who seek to commit fraud through TALF. Although TALF participants who play by the rules have nothing to fear from this Task Force, Federal law enforcement is ready now to detect, investigate, and bring to justice any who would try to steal from this important program.

The TALF Task Force represents a historic law enforcement effort with an ambitious goal: to redefine the policing of complex Federal Government programs by proactively arranging a coordinated law enforcement response before the fraud occurs.

The TALF Task Force has already received its first substantive brie ng on the mechanics of TALF from FRBNY representatives and has further training sessions scheduled.

Coordination with FinCEN and NY HIFCA

On March 13, 2009, SIGTARP entered into an agreement with FinCEN to augment SIGTARP's data and personnel resources. On March 18, 2009, SIGTARP entered into a similar agreement with the New York High Intensity Financial Crime Area ("NY HIFCA"). The FinCEN agreement provides SIGTARP with direct electronic access to Bank Secrecy Act (31 U.S.C. § 5311 *et seq.*) information, including currency transaction reports filed by financial institutions and casinos, currency and monetary instrument reports, foreign bank reports, and suspicious activity reports filed by depository institutions and participants in the securities and futures industries. This electronic access will assist SIGTARP to develop leads for cases, follow up on leads, and identify investigative targets. The agreement with NY HIFCA complements the FinCEN agreement by providing SIGTARP with two experienced financial analysts who will use FinCEN and other available data resources to identify indicators of fraud associated with TARP recipients and provide analytical support with respect to SIGTARP's ongoing investigations.

SIGTARP Hotline and Investigations

SIGTARP's Hotline is staffed, operational, and providing an interface with the American public to facilitate the reporting of concerns, allegations, information, and evidence of violations of criminal and civil laws in connection with TARP. Reporting may include allegations of fraud, waste, abuse, and reprisals for bringing to light TARP-related concerns.

As of the drafting of this report, the SIGTARP Hotline has received and analyzed nearly 200 tips. These contacts run the gamut from expressions of concern over the economy to serious allegations of fraud involving TARP. The SIGTARP Hotline is capable of receiving information anonymously, and identity con dentiality can and will be provided to the fullest extent possible. The American public can provide information by telephone, mail, fax, or online. SIGTARP honors all whistleblower protections.

Both from the Hotline and from other sources of leads, SIGTARP has initiated nearly 20 preliminary and full criminal investigations to date. Although the details of those investigations will generally not be discussed unless public action is taken, the cases vary widely in subject matter and include large corporate and securities fraud matters affecting TARP investments, tax matters, insider trading, public corruption, and mortgage-modification fraud.

SIGTARP Audits

Since SIGTARP's Initial Report, the Audit Division has continued to focus on recruiting staff while launching an initial set of audits and planning future work. At the same time, the Audit Division has been able to launch a survey of 364 TARP recipients to obtain answers to recurring questions regarding use of TARP funding and actions taken to comply with executive compensation requirements associated with the funding. Efforts are now underway to analyze the results of those surveys which will help facilitate two ongoing audits in areas covered by the surveys and provide a potential base of knowledge from which to examine progress of TARP in the future. Meanwhile, SIGTARP is continuing its efforts to coordinate work with other audit agencies engaged in oversight of TARP and its numerous program areas.

Survey of TARP Recipients

Beginning on February 5, 2009, SIGTARP sent letters to 364 TARP recipients — institutions that had received TARP funds as of the end of January 2009 — requesting that they provide information concerning their use of TARP funding and their compliance with executive compensation requirements. Most of the recipients were financial institutions receiving assistance under the TARP Capital Purchase Program ("CPP"). Recipients were asked to provide their responses within 30 days of the date of the request and to include copies of pertinent documentation to support their responses.

As indicated in Table 1.2, the firms surveyed varied in the amount of funding received, with the majority of funding going to a small number of large institutions. Twenty-six firms had received approximately 93% of the funding through January 30, 2009.[1]

As of March 23, 2009, SIGTARP had received responses from all 364 TARP recipients — a remarkable 100% response rate. SIGTARP's initial look at some of the responses indicates that those responding to the request provided a broad range of answers to the two sets of questions. For example, some identified detailed and specific use of the funds, whereas others provided more general responses. Respondents also provided varying degrees of documentation to augment and support their narrative responses, with some noting that additional documentation had been segregated at their of ce and was available for review as needed.

Although time will be required to assess fully the responses received, SIGTARP can report that, based on a preliminary review of responses received:

Use of Funds: Respondents provided diverse answers on how TARP funds have been used; some common responses described use of TARP funds to: strengthen the bank's capital base to provide a foundation for lending activities; retire debt; purchase MBS; increase credit lines; and make loans.

TARP Impact on Lending: Some respondents spoke to new lending activities in relationship to actual TARP funds received, whereas others spoke of leveraging the funds to achieve greater lending than that related to the face value of TARP funds received. Some, however, noted that, although they were committed to making prudent commercial and consumer loans, growth of new loans had slowed as a result of the economy. Others noted that TARP funds permitted them to preserve an adequate level of capital so that they were able to maintain, or at least not severely reduce, their lending levels.

Segregation of Funds: Some respondents indicated that the TARP equity investment was separately recorded as a discrete component of the bank's capital, but the actual funds associated with the investment were not physically segregated from other cash funds; others cited efforts to segregate physically the funds or to manage them separately.

Executive Compensation Compliance: Responses regarding compliance with executive compensation restrictions varied from simple statements of obvious compliance based on the size of their banks and compensation, to detailed answers regarding extensive efforts to assess compensation practices relative to restrictions associated with their funding agreements, including having retained expert consultants to help with the assessments — the latter not necessarily related to the amount of funding received or the size of the bank.

Executive Compensation Regulation Uncertainty: Some responses related to executive compensation expressed frustration with changing guidance and legislation related to executive compensation requirements, as well as the lack of regulations concerning these changes, which has limited their ability to give a complete answer at this time; nonetheless, others noted actions they were taking at this time based on known requirements, recognizing that final guidelines have not yet been issued.

Given the diversity of the responses and the fact they were asked for and provided in narrative form, it will require some time to (i) analyze the data fully, (ii) identify areas where follow-up contact with respondents is needed, and (iii) identify the degree of commonality of responses in selected areas that may be aggregated for reporting purposes.

To further assess and complete its analysis of the responses during a period when it is still in the process of staffing its Audit Division, SIGTARP has awarded a contract to Concentrance Consulting Group, a Section 8(a) women-owned small business, to help analyze the survey data. The contract with Concentrance calls for it to complete analysis of the survey responses within two months, including identification of potential areas for follow-up work by SIGTARP with respondents. From this analysis and any needed follow-up work, SIGTARP expects to issue a preliminary report in June 2009 summarizing the audit responses. Two additional reports — one on use of funds and the other on executive compensation issues — are targeted for completion by summer 2009.

Audits Underway and Planned

As noted in the Initial Report, SIGTARP's Audit Division will conduct primarily performance audits related to TARP, using generally accepted Government auditing standards. SIGTARP audits emphasize:

ensuring transparency in TARP to the fullest reasonable extent so as to foster accountability in use of funds and program results

testing compliance with the policies, procedures, regulations, terms, and conditions that are imposed on TARP recipients

coordinating actively with other relevant audit and oversight entities to maximize audit coverage while minimizing overlap and duplication of efforts

Table 1.2. Number of TARP Recipients Surveyed by Funding Received

Funding Category	Number of firms	Funding Received ($ Billions)	Percentage of Funding
$10 billion or more	8	$219.3	73.4%
$1 billion to $9.9 billion	18	58.3	19.5%
$100 million to $999.9 million	54	14.6	4.9%
Less than $100 million	284	6.6	2.2%
TOTAL	**364**	**$298.8**	**100%**

Note: The total funding includes $190.5 billion under the Capital Purchase Program, $40 billion under the Targeted Investment Program, $40 billion under the Systemically Significant Failing Institutions Program, $23.3 billion under the Automotive Industry Financing Program, and $5 billion under the Asset Guarantee Program.

Source: SIGTARP analysis of Treasury data.

With these objectives in mind, SIGTARP has initiated the following six audits:

1. **Use of Funds:** SIGTARP's first audit examines the use of TARP funds by TARP recipients, as set forth in the previous discussion about SIGTARP's survey of TARP recipients.

2. **Executive Compensation Compliance:** SIGTARP's second audit, also based on SIGTARP's survey of TARP recipients, and initiated at the request of Senator E. Benjamin Nelson, examines how TARP recipients are implementing controls with respect to applicable executive compensation restrictions.

3. **Bank of America:** The third audit examines the review and approval processes associated with TARP assistance to Bank of America under three different programs, including the Capital Purchase Program, **Targeted Investment Program**, and the announced **Asset Guarantee Program's** loss protection on a pool of troubled assets. The audit also examines Treasury's decision making related to additional TARP assistance in connection with Bank of America's acquisition of Merrill Lynch. Since its commencement, the scope of this audit has expanded to examine broadly Treasury's decision making regarding the first nine institutions to be considered for TARP funding in October 2008.

4. **External Infuences:** Concerns have arisen whether, or to what extent, external parties may have sought to in uence decision making by Treasury or bank regulators in considering and deciding on applications for funding from individual banks. Importantly, the Treasury Secretary announced that Treasury would be implementing new guidelines to prevent such external in uences. Accordingly, this audit seeks to determine what processes and procedures are in place to guide consideration of such applications so as to avoid undue outside in uence on the process, whether there are any indications of any undue in uence, and what actions might be needed to strengthen existing processes.

5. **Executive Compensation Oversight (AIG Bonuses):** The next audit, initiated in connection with a request by Senator Charles E. Grassley, examines Federal oversight of executive compensation requirements, focusing specifically on recent payouts of large bonus payments to American International Group, Inc. ("AIG") employees. These payments have raised questions regarding AIG's compliance with executive compensation requirements imposed as a condition of financial assistance under TARP and the extent of coordination between Treasury and the Federal Reserve. Accordingly, SIGTARP has undertaken an audit to determine: (i) the extent to which the recent bonus payments were made in accordance with conditions imposed in return for TARP assistance, and (ii) the extent of Treasury's monitoring of AIG's executive compensation agreements and to what extent it was aware of the full range of executive compensation, bonus, and retention payments throughout AIG's corporate structure. For a detailed description of Government assistance to AIG, see the "InstitutionSpecific" discussion in Section 2: "TARP Overview" of this report.
6. **AIG Counterparty Payments:** At the request of Congressman Elijah E. Cummings and 26 other Members of Congress, SIGTARP has initiated a review of AIG's payments to counterparties to its various transactions. AIG, which has received the largest amount of financial assistance from the Government during the current financial crisis, reportedly made these counterparty payments to other financial institutions, including some foreign institutions and others that received financial assistance under TARP. Further, according to the request made to SIGTARP, the counterparty claims were paid at 100% of face value. As a result, SIGTARP will examine the basis for the counterparty payments and seek to determine whether any efforts were made to negotiate any reduction in those payments.

Targeted Investment Program ("TIP"): A direct-investment program through which Treasury can invest in institutions whose failure would threaten similar institutions and the economy in general.

Asset Guarantee Program ("AGP"): An insurance-like program which allows Treasury to assume a loss position on certain troubled assets held by the qualifying financial institution.

As SIGTARP's Audit Division staffing capacity increases, it expects to undertake additional reviews in the area of Treasury oversight of TARP, executive compensation, and use of TARP funds. In addition, as Treasury implements new programs, such as TALF and home mortgage assistance, SIGTARP's Audit Division anticipates undertaking audits in these areas in coordination with other audit organizations.

Communications with Congress

One of SIGTARP's primary functions is to make sure that Members of Congress, as the creators of SIGTARP, are kept informed of developments in TARP and SIGTARP's oversight activities. To fulfill that role, the Special Inspector General and SIGTARP personnel meet regularly with and brief Members of Congress and Congressional staff. More formally, since the Initial Report, the Special Inspector General has testified six times before various Congressional Committees.

Senate Committee on Banking, Housing and Urban Affairs: On February 5, 2009, Special Inspector General Barofsky testified before the Senate Committee on Banking, Housing and Urban Affairs, during a hearing entitled, "Pulling Back the TARP: Oversight of the Financial Rescue Program." The purpose of this oversight hearing was to explore how TARP can be made more effective in the areas of: protecting home values, college funds, retirement accounts, and life savings; preserving homeownership and promoting jobs and economic growth; maximizing the returns to the taxpayers for their investment; and enhancing some measure of public accountability.

Senate Judiciary Committee: On February 11, 2009, Special Inspector General Barofsky testified before the Senate Judiciary Committee, during a hearing entitled, "The Need for Increased Fraud Enforcement in the Wake of the Economic Downturn." The purpose of the hearing was, among other things, to examine the issue of fraud in TARP.

House Committee on Financial Services: On February 24, 2009, Special Inspector General Barofsky testified before the House Committee on Financial Services, Subcommittee on Oversight and Investigations, during a hearing entitled, "A Review of TARP Oversight, Accountability and Transparency for U.S. Taxpayers." The purpose of this hearing was to ensure that the TARP oversight organizations created/assigned by EESA (*i.e.,* GAO, SIGTARP, and COP) understand their respective roles, cooperate with each other, and avoid repetitive efforts and inefficiencies. The hearing also examined how S.383 (the SIGTARP Act), which primarily deals with SIGTARP and had already been approved by the Senate, will improve TARP oversight.

House Committee on Oversight and Government Reform: On March 11, 2009, Special Inspector General Barofsky testified before the House Committee on Oversight and Government Reform, Subcommittee on Domestic Policy, during a hearing entitled, "TARP Oversight: Assessing Treasury's Efforts to Prevent Waste and Abuse of Taxpayer Funds." The purpose of this hearing was to assess Treasury's oversight of the use of funds by financial institutions that received funds under TARP. Specifically, the hearing evaluated Treasury's data collection procedures for monitoring the use of TARP funds and examined Treasury's ability to detect and prevent waste and misuse of TARP monies.

House Committee on Ways and Means: On March 19, 2009, Special Inspector General Barofsky testified before the House Committee on Ways and Means, Subcommittee on Oversight, during a hearing entitled, "Hearing on the Troubled Asset Relief Program: Oversight of Federal Borrowing and the Use of Federal Monies." The purpose of the hearing was to review the role of Federal borrowing in TARP, its impact on the national debt, and Treasury's efforts to protect public funds. In the latter regard, the hearing explored Federal tax compliance issues.

Senate Committee on Finance: On March 31, 2009, Special Inspector General Barofsky testified before the Senate Committee on Finance during a hearing entitled, "TARP Oversight: A Six Month Update." The purpose of the hearing was to survey the various TARP and TARP-related programs, and to examine SIGTARP's oversight of these programs.

SIGTARP's Organizational Structure

In addition to the executive staff, SIGTARP pursues its mission through four divisions: audit, investigations, operations, and the Division of the Chief Counsel.

Chief of Staff

SIGTARP's mission is supported by the Chief of Staff, Kevin R. Puvalowski, who is the Special Inspector General's senior advisor. The Chief of Staff and the Deputy Chief of Staff, Cathy Alix, oversee and coordinate the activities of the other divisions and manage cross-divisional projects as necessary.

Audit Division

The Audit Division, led by Barry Holman, the Deputy Special Inspector General for Audit, is tasked with designing and conducting programmatic audits with respect to Treasury's operation of TARP and the recipients' compliance with their obligations under relevant law and contract. The division is designed to provide SIGTARP with maximum flexibility in the size, timing, and scope of audits so that, without sacrificing the rigor of the methodology, audit results, whenever possible, can be generated rapidly both for general transparency's sake and so that the resulting data can be used to improve the operations of the fast-evolving TARP.

A particular focus of the Audit Division is to ensure that appropriate compliance and control mechanisms are in place and are complied with, both by Treasury in its management of TARP and by the recipients of TARP funds. Where controls or compliance are found to be lacking, or where particular aspects or policies are found ineffective at reaching TARP's goals, the Audit Division will assist the Special Inspector General in fashioning recommendations to resolve such issues.

Investigations Division

SIGTARP's Investigations Division is led by Christopher R. Sharpley, the Deputy Special Inspector General for Investigations. Made up of special agents, investigators, analysts, and attorney advisors, the Investigations Division supervises and conducts criminal and civil investigations into those, whether inside or outside of Government, who waste, steal, or abuse TARP funds. The model for the division is to build teams of experienced financial and corporate fraud investigators that include not only special agents but also forensic analysts and, critically, attorney advisors, within the division itself, so that SIGTARP can have a broad array of expertise and perspectives in developing even the most sophisticated investigations. Scott Rebein, the Special Agent-in-Charge, will supervise the Federal agents, and Richard Rosenfeld, the Chief Investigative Counsel, will supervise the attorney advisors.

The Investigations Division will, of course, pursue any wrongdoers within Government, but it will also focus on the recipients of TARP funds — *i.e.,* the institutions that receive TARP investments and the vendors hired to administer TARP activities. Those who make intentional misrepresentations in the TARP application process or in their financial reporting to Treasury may be in violation of several criminal statutes, including securities fraud, wire fraud, mail fraud, and false statements. SIGTARP intends to investigate these potential crimes vigorously.

In the interests of maximizing criminal and civil enforcement, the Investigations Division coordinates closely with other law enforcement agencies to form law enforcement partnerships, including task force relationships across the Federal Government, to leverage SIGTARP's expertise and unique position with respect to TARP.

The Investigations Division will take the lead in responding to referrals made to SIGTARP's Hotline through telephone, email, website, and in-person complaints, abiding by all applicable whistleblower protections. When a full audit or investigation is not possible or advisable due to time or other constraints, the Investigations Division will work closely with the Audit Division to conduct inspection and evaluation projects and may issue public Special Reports.

Operations Division

The Deputy Special Inspector General for Operations, Dr. Eileen Ennis, leads SIGTARP's Operations Division. The Operations staff is built around a core group of experienced professionals with cross-functional backgrounds in human resources, information technology, budget and finance, acquisitions, and facilities and logistics, as well as experience in program and project management. These seasoned veterans include employees detailed or transferred from other departments and agencies as well as former Treasury Department employees.

The Operations Division's strategy is to build SIGTARP's support infrastructure and staff rapidly while maintaining fiexibility in an environment in which SIGTARP's oversight responsibilities can change substantially with each new program. Operations takes the lead on building and managing SIGTARP's physical facilities, technical infrastructure, budget and finance functions, procurement activity, and human resources activities. Operations strives to provide SIGTARP with the ability to expand or shift emphasis swiftly — in size, location, and scope of expertise — while ensuring that internal controls are in place and supported with sound policies.

Division of the Chief Counsel

The Chief Counsel, Bryan Saddler, serves as SIGTARP's chief legal advisor and supervises legal work conducted within SIGTARP. The Chief Counsel plays a crucial role in ensuring that SIGTARP is in compliance with the complex framework of laws and regulations applicable to audit and law enforcement entities. He also provides the Special Inspector General advice on contractual and legislative language central to TARP, which directly impacts SIGTARP's oversight of, and recommendations for, those programs.

In addition to fulfilling these legal roles, the Chief Counsel also manages several other important SIGTARP functions, including communications and press issues, legislative affairs, and Freedom of Information Act inquiries. Supporting him, the Communications Director, Kristine Belisle, assists the Special Inspector General with media relations and inquiries, and the Director of Legislative Affairs, Lori Hayman, assists the Special Inspector General with Congressional relations and inquiries.

Since the Initial Report, SIGTARP's organizational structure has been modified to create the Division of Chief Counsel, and to move the communications and legislative affairs functions into that division. The SIGTARP organizational chart, as of March 31, 2009, is included in Appendix K.

PROGRESS IN BUILDING SIGTARP'S ORGANIZATION

From the day that the Special Inspector General was con rmed by the Senate, SIGTARP has worked to build its organization through various complementary strategies, including hiring experienced senior executives who can play multiple roles during the early stages of the organization, leveraging the resources of other agencies, and, where appropriate and cost-effective, obtaining services through SIGTARP's authority to contract. Since the Initial Report, SIGTARP has made substantial progress in building its operation.

Hiring

Since the Initial Report, SIGTARP has succeeded in substantially completing its hiring of senior staff.

As noted previously, Dr. Eileen Ennis has taken over as Deputy Special Inspector General for Operations. Dr. Ennis comes to SIGTARP with more than 21 years of Federal service, most recently with the U.S. Department of Transportation ("US DOT") where she was the Associate Administrator for Administration and Chief Information Of cer at USDOT's Research and Innovative Technology Administration. Dr. Ennis was asked to serve temporarily as the acting Director of US DOT's Volpe National Transportation Research Center in Cambridge, Massachusetts. After Volpe, Dr. Ennis was invited to provide leadership in USDOT's departmental Of ce of the Chief Information Of cer ("C IO") and led two organizations acting as Associate CIO for IT Enterprise Projects and as Associate CIO for IT Policy Oversight. Prior to joining US DOT, Dr. Ennis was at the Commodity Futures Trading Commission from 2000 to 2007. There, she was a Deputy Director for the Of ce of Information and Technology Services. Dr. Ennis holds a Doctorate in Information Systems from Nova Southeastern University in Ft. Lauderdale, Florida, and a Master's Degree in Information and Resources Management from Webster University.

Each of the divisions has begun the process of filling out their ranks. As of March 31, 2009, SIGTARP had approximately 35 personnel, including de-tailees from other agencies, with several new hires to begin over the coming weeks. SIGTARP's employees hail from many Federal agencies, including DOJ, the FBI, the Department of Defense Air Force Of ce of Special Investigations, GAO, USDOT, the Department of Energy Of ce of the Inspector General, the Internal Revenue Service, the Office of the Special Inspector General for Iraq Reconstruction, the Department of Housing and Urban Development Of ce of the Inspector General, SEC, and the U.S. Secret Service. Hiring is actively ongoing, building to SIGTARP's current goal of approximately 150 full-time employees.

Contracting

EESA gives SIGTARP the express authority to contract for goods and services. Whenever it can do so cost effectively, and without damaging its mission or independence, SIGTARP will use the services of other Governmental agencies and outside vendors to develop rapidly its operational capacity. As discussed in the Initial Report, SIGTARP entered into contracts with the following agencies and outside service providers:

Treasury's Bureau of Public Debt for certain back-office human resources and personnel services and for financial reporting services
The Treasury Inspector General for Tax Administration for the detailing of personnel and for certain technical assistance
Deloitte Financial Advisory Services LLP for program management services in connection with the production of SIGTARP's Quarterly Reports to Congress

Since the Initial Report, SIGTARP has entered into several additional contracts:

Concentrance Consulting Group for assistance with SIGTARP's analysis of a survey sent to 364 TARP recipients seeking information about the recipients' use of TARP funds and executive compensation policies
NY HIFCA initiative (under the auspices of the New York High Intensity Drug Trafficking Area program of the Of ce of National Drug Control Policy) for forensic analysts
FinCEN for multi-source financial intelligence expertise and data access

SIGTARP's Physical and Technical Infrastructure

SIGTARP is moving forward in its development of a physical and technical infrastructure, now occupying several different office spaces within the main Treasury building. SIGTARP is in the process of leasing office space at 1801 L Street, NW, in Washington, D.C., the same office building in which the Treasury of cials managing TARP are located. It is anticipated that SIGTARP will be able to move into that space by the end of 2009. In the meantime, SIGTARP is working with Treasury and the General Services Administration to locate and let temporary quarters.

SIGTARP operates a website on which it posts all of its reports, testimony, audits, investigations (once such investigations are made public), contracts, and more. The website also prominently features SIGTARP's Hotline, which also can be accessed by phone (877-SIG-2009 or 877-744-2009). The SIGTARP Hotline is operating to handle referrals from the general public or from whistleblowers concerning allegations of fraud, waste, or abuse with respect to TARP. SIGTARP is, of course, committed to abiding by all applicable whistleblower protections.

Developing SIGTARP's Internal Systems, Policies, and Procedures

Since the Initial Report, SIGTARP has moved rapidly to begin developing and implementing management and information systems, as well as the policies and procedures necessary to run a complex Federal agency. Among other things, SIGTARP has begun to put into place the following:

- policies and procedures concerning the roles and authorities of SIGTARP executives and divisions, standards of conduct and discipline, travel by SIGTARP employees, and subpoena authorities
- systems relating to human resources, time and attendance reporting, expenditure tracking, and recordkeeping
- a budget framework to plan and manage SIGTARP's initial funding authorization and short-term and long-term budget strategies to address the initial startup as well as the potential expansion of TARP and related financial recovery programs

End Notes

[1] Since January 30, 2009, another 150 banks have received about $7.9 billion in CPP funding.

In: Reassessing TARP
Editor: George T. Bernhardt
ISBN: 978-1-60741-965-5

Chapter 3

TARP Overview

This section provides details of activities that the U.S. Department of Treasury ("Treasury") has conducted under the Troubled Asset Relief Program ("TARP"), including the following:

- a financial overview of TARP initiatives, implemented and announced
- a detailed update on previously described programs
- a program-by-program description of newly announced programs
- the status of executive compensation restrictions for TARP recipients

Financial Overview of TARP

As of March 31, 2009, Treasury had announced the parameters of how $590.4 billion[1] of the $700 billion authorized by the Emergency Economic Stabilization Act of 2008 ("EESA") would be spent.[2] Of the $590.4 billion[3] that Treasury has committed, $328.6 billion[4] has been spent. The $328.6 billion already expended has provided support for U.S. financial institutions and companies through the six previously implemented programs that purchase or guarantee troubled assets.[5] TARP expenditures as of March 31, 2009, account for about 47% of the $700 billion available for TARP implementation.

Subsequent to SIGTARP's Initial Report to Congress ("Initial Report") dated February 6, 2009, and in reaction to the continued deterioration of the credit markets, Treasury announced the creation of the Financial Stability Plan ("FSP"). Treasury explained that the FSP was designed "to protect taxpayers and ensure that every dollar is directed toward lending and economic revitalization" and that it would "institute a new era of accountability, transparency, and conditions on the financial institutions receiving funds."[6] According to Treasury, the FSP will address a number of concerns:

- high home foreclosure rates
- a shortage of consumer credit
- a shortage of small-business credit
- ongoing efforts to stabilize financial institutions

Treasury plans to support U.S. financial institutions, companies, and individual borrowers through a combination of 12 separate TARP programs implemented or announced thus far. A number of the newly announced initiatives are interrelated with existing programs. Complete details on these new programs are not yet available, but summaries of their announced descriptions, along with updates on the previously implemented programs, are provided in the following section.

For more information on the previously implemented programs, refer to SIGTARP's Initial Report to Congress dated February 6, 2009, Section 3: "TARP Implementation and Administration."

Troubled Assets: Includes mortgages, mortgage-related instruments, and any other financial instrument whose purchase Treasury determines is needed to stabilize the financial markets.

Capital Purchase Program ("CPP"). Treasury intends for CPP to provide funds to "encourage U.S. financial institutions to build capital to increase the flow of financing to U.S. businesses and consumers and to support the U.S. economy."[7] As of March 31, 2009, Treasury investments in institutions through CPP accounted for approximately $198.8 billion in TARP purchases,[8] out of a projected funding total of $218 billion under the program.[9] Of the $198.8 billion expended, $0.4 billion has been repaid to the Government by CPP participants. See the "Capital Purchase Program" discussion in this section for more detailed information. Subsequent to SIGTARP's Initial Report, Citigroup announced an offering to exchange up to $25 billion of Treasury's preferred shares, obtained through CPP, for common stock.[10] See the "Institution-Specific Assistance" portion of this section for a detailed discussion of Citibank's exchange offering.

Capital Assistance Program ("CAP"). The mechanics of CAP are similar to those of CPP, and both programs involve injecting capital into the financial system. Under CAP, financial institutions with more than $100 billion in assets will have to participate in a "stress test" to determine if they have enough of a capital buffer to continue lending in worse-than-expected economic conditions.[11] Institutions that are found to need additional capital will have up to six months to raise private capital, after which they will be required to accept Treasury assistance under CAP. In addition to the 19 financial institutions participating in the stress test, all qualifying financial institutions may apply to CAP for additional capital without the stress-test requirement. CAP includes a provision whereby preferred shares issued under CPP and the Targeted Investment Program may be exchanged for convertible preferred shares that provide the issuing institution the option to convert preferred shares to common stock, and thus increase the institution's **tangible common equity ("TCE")**. Treasury expects that most applicants will convert existing TARP preferred shares for CAP convertible preferred shares without seeking additional capital.[12] However, those receiving additional capital will do so in exchange for convertible preferred shares under CAP.

Systemically Signifcant Failing Institutions ("SSFI") Program. Under the stated terms of the SSFI program, Treasury invests in **systemically significant** institutions to prevent their failure and the market disruption that would follow.[13] As of March 31, 2009, Treasury's projected investment through this program accounts for $70 billion in investments in and credit provided to American International Group, Inc. ("AIG"). As reported in SIGTARP's Initial Report, $40 billion was used to purchase preferred stock from AIG.[14] Subsequently, Treasury announced the allocation of an additional $30 billion to the SSFI program for a new equity capital facility that AIG can draw on as needed. In return, Treasury will receive **non-cumulative preferred shares.**[15] See the "Institution-Specific Assistance" part of this section for a detailed discussion of the AIG transactions.

Tangible Common Equity ("TCE"): A measure of a bank's capital adequacy; the amount of money that would be left over if a bank were dissolved and all creditors and higher levels of stock were paid off.

Systemically Significant: A financial institution whose failure would impose significant losses on creditors and counterparties, call into question the financial strength of other similarly situated financial institutions, disrupt financial markets, raise borrowing costs for households and businesses, and reduce household wealth.

Non-Cumulative Preferred Shares: Shares where unpaid dividends do not accrue when a company does not make a dividend payment.

Targeted Investment Program ("TIP"). The stated objective of TIP is to make targeted investments in financial institutions where a loss of con dence would "result in significant market disruptions that threaten the financial strength of similarly situated financial institutions and thus impair broader financial markets and pose a threat to the overall economy."[16] As reported in SIGTARP's Initial Report, Treasury purchased $20 billion of **senior preferred stock** and received warrants of common stock from each of Citigroup and Bank of America, for a total expenditure of $40 billion in TARP funds.[17] As of March 31, 2009, Treasury had made no further funding under this program.

Asset Guarantee Program ("AGP"). Through AGP, Treasury's stated goal is to use insurance-like protections to help stabilize at-risk financial institutions. AGP provides certain loss protections on a select pool of mortgage-related or similar assets held by participants whose portfolios of distressed or **illiquid** assets pose a risk to market con dence.[18] As discussed in SIGTARP's Initial Report, Treasury, the Federal Deposit Insurance Corporation ("FDIC"), and the Federal Reserve agreed to provide certain loss protections with respect to $301 billion in troubled assets held by Citigroup.[19] A similar arrangement with Bank of America was announced on January 16, 2009, but had not yet closed as of March 31, 2009. Treasury's projected TARP investment through this program accounted for $12.5 billion as of March 31, 2009 — $5 billion in protection for Citigroup[20] and $7.5 billion for Bank of America.[21] See the discussion of "Institution-Specific Assistance" in this section for more information on Citigroup's transactions.

Automotive Industry Financing Program ("AIFP"). The stated objective of AIFP is to "prevent a significant disruption of the American automotive industry, which would pose a systemic risk to financial market stability and have a negative effect on the economy of the United States."[22] Under this program, Treasury made emergency loans to General Motors Corporation ("GM"), Chrysler Holding LLC ("Chrysler"), and Chrysler Financial Services Americas LLC ("Chrysler Financial"). In addition to these investments, Treasury purchased senior preferred stock from GMAC LLC ("GMAC"). As of March 31, 2009, Treasury has expended $24.8 billion in AIFP investments,[23] out of an initial projected funding total of $25 billion.[24] Subsequent to the Initial Report, the manufacturers (GM and Chrysler) submitted restructuring plans to Treasury on February 17, 2009, as required.[25] Upon submission, the President's Designee on the Auto Industry determined that these restructuring plans did not meet the threshold for long-term viability. However, on March 30, 2009, both GM and Chrysler were granted extensions to complete the restructuring plans in order to comply with the requirements set forth under AIFP. As a modification to the existing loans, GM will receive up to $5 billion and Chrysler up to $500 million in additional working capital during the extension period.[26] See the discussion of "Automotive Industry Financing Program" later in this section for a detailed discussion of the GM and Chrysler restructuring plans. In addition to the initial $25 billion committed in AIFP, Treasury has recently announced two new subprograms to assist the automobile industry.

Auto Supplier Support Program ("ASSP"). As an expansion of AIFP, the stated purpose of ASSP is to provide up to $5 billion of Government-backed financing to break the adverse credit cycle affecting the auto suppliers and the manufacturers by "providing suppliers with the con dence they need to continue shipping their parts and the support they need to help access loans to pay their employees and continue their operations."[27] See the discussion of "Auto Supplier Support Program" for more information.

Auto Warranty Commitment Program. As another complementary program to AIFP, the Auto Warranty Commitment Program was devised by the Administration with the stated intent to bolster consumer con dence in automobile warranties on GM- and Chrysler-built vehicles. In order to reassure consumers that their auto warranties will be honored during this period of restructuring, the Administration will provide Government-backed financing. Treasury preliminarily discussed potential funding for the Auto Warranty Commitment Program for up to an estimated $1.1 billion.[28] See the discussion of "Auto Warranty Commitment Program" for more information.

Term Asset-Backed Securities Loan Facility ("TALF"). TALF was originally intended to increase the credit available for consumer and small-business loans through a Federal Reserve loan program backed by TARP funds. TALF provides non-recourse loans to investors secured by certain types of asset-backed securities. TALF was originally announced as a $200 billion Federal Reserve loan program under which Treasury provides $20 billion in **credit protection** to the Federal Reserve.[29] Treasury and the Federal Reserve have announced plans to expand TALF to cover additional asset classes, including legacy mortgage- backed securities, which could bring the total facility funding up to $1 trillion,[30] for which Treasury will provide up to $80 billion in TARP funds to absorb losses.[31] An overview of TALF, later in this section, provides more information on these activities.

Public-Private Investment Program ("PPIP"). On March 23, 2009, Treasury announced a coordinated effort with FDIC in an attempt to improve the health of financial institutions holding real estate-related assets in order to increase the fiow of credit throughout the economy. Within two subprograms, PPIP will involve investments in multiple Public-Private Investment Funds ("PPIFs") to purchase real estate-related loans **("legacy loans**") and real estate-related securities ("**legacy securities**") from financial institutions. The program, involving up to $1 trillion in total, will utilize up to $75 billion of TARP funds.[32]

Credit Protection: Security against losses on an investment. For TALF purposes, TARP funding is used as credit protection on the Federal Reserve loans (*i.e.,* losses on the loans are absorbed by TARP funds up to the commitment amount).

Legacy Loans: Underperforming real estate-related loans held by a bank that it wishes to sell, but recent market disruptions have made difficult to price.

Legacy Securities: Troubled real estate-related securities (residential mortgage-backed securities ("RMBS"), commercial mortgage-backed securities ("CMBS"), and asset-backed securities ("ABS")) lingering on institutions' balance sheets due to an inability to determine value.

Unlocking Credit for Small Businesses ("UCSB"). On March 16, 2009, Treasury announced that it will begin purchasing up to $15 billion in securities backed by Small Business Administration ("SBA") loans. As demand has diminished in the **secondary market** for these securities due to adverse credit conditions, there has been a reduction in the volume of new small-business loans written by banks. In connection with this program, the Treasury Secretary also called for the largest 21 banks that have received TARP funds to begin reporting monthly the amount of their small-business lending.[33]

Making Home Affordable ("MHA") Program. On March 4, 2009, Treasury announced its MHA program, which might expend up to $50 billion of TARP funds.[34] MHA is a foreclosure mitigation plan intended to "help bring relief to responsible homeowners struggling to make their mortgage payments, while preventing neighborhoods and communities from suffering the negative spillover effects of foreclosure, such as lower housing prices, increased crime, and higher taxes."[35] Treasury, along with other Federal agencies, "will undertake a comprehensive multiple-part strategy," which will provide for (i) a $75 billion loan modification program for homeowners in default on their payments or facing imminent default; (ii) a streamlined re nancing process for homeowners whose loans are serviced by Fannie Mae or Freddie Mac; and (iii) approximately $200 billion to support Fannie Mae and Freddie Mac.[36] The funds for this effort will be provided from both TARP- and non-TARP-related sources.

The following figures and tables provide a status summary of the implemented and announced TARP and TARP-related initiatives:

total funds subject to SIGTARP oversight (Table 2.1)
projected TARP funding for all implemented and announced programs under TARP (Figure 2.1)
expenditure levels by program as of March 31, 2009 (Table 2.2)
cumulative expenditures over time for implemented programs (Figure 2.2)
expenditures by program snapshot as of March 31, 2009 (Figure 2.3)
summary of terms of TARP agreements (Table 2.3 and Table 2.4)
summary of dividend and interest payments received by program (Table 2.5)

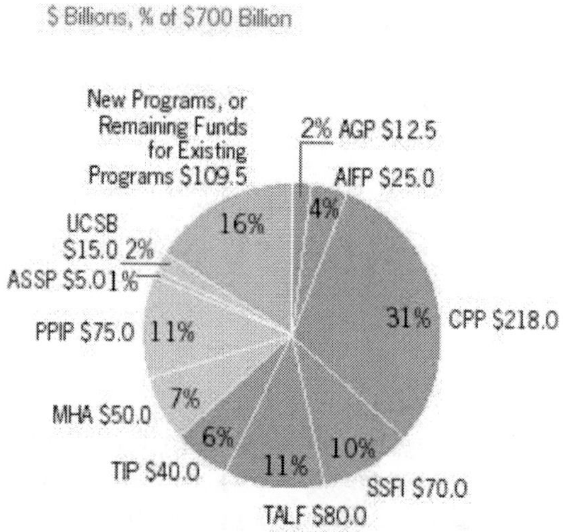

Note: Numbers affected by rounding. As of 3/31/2009, funding for Capital Assistance Program ("CAP") to be determined. Treasury preliminarily discussed potential funding for the Auto Warranty Commitment Program for up to $1.25 billion.
Sources: See final endnote.

Figure 2.1. TARP Projected Funding, By Program

Table 2.1. Total Funds Subject to SIGTARP Oversight, as of March 31, 2009 ($ Billions)

Program	Brief Description or Participant	Total Projected Funding ($)	Projected TARP Funding ($)
Capital Purchase Program ("CPP")	Investments in 532 banks to date; 8 institutions total $125 billion	$218.0	$218.0
Automotive Industry Financing Program ("AIFP")	GM, Chrysler, GMAC, Chrysler Financial	$25.0	$25.0
Auto Supplier Support Program ("ASSP")	Government-backed protection for auto parts suppliers	$5.0	$5.0
Unlocking Credit for Small Businesses ("UCSB")	Purchase of securities backed by SBA loans	$15.0[a]	$15.0
Systemically Significant Failing Institutions ("SSFI")	AIG Investment	$70.0	$70.0[b]
Targeted Investment Program ("TIP")	Citigroup, Bank of America Investments	$40.0	$40.0
Asset Guarantee Program ("AGP")	Citigroup, Bank of America, Ring Fence Asset Guarantee	$419.0[c]	$12.5[d]
Term Asset-Backed Securities Loan Facility ("TALF")	FRBNY non-recourse loans for purchase of asset-backed securities	$1,000.0	$80.0
Making Home Affordable ("MHA") Program	Modification of mortgage loans	$75.0[e]	$50.0
Public-Private Investment Program ("PPIP")	Disposition of legacy assets; Legacy Loans Program, Legacy Securities Program (expansion of TALF)	$500.0 – $1,000.0	$75.0
Capital Assistance Program ("CAP")	Capital to qualified financial institutions; includes stress test	TBD	TBD
New Programs, or Funds Remaining for Existing Programs	Potential additional funding related to CAP; AIFP; Auto Warranty Commitment Program; other	$109.5	$109.5[f]
Total		**$2,476.5 – $2,976.5**	**$700.0**

Note: Numbers affected by rounding.

[a] Treasury announced that it would purchase up to $15 billion in securities under the Unlocking Credit for Small Businesses program.

[b] A new equity capital facility will be created by Treasury allowing AIG to draw down up to $30 billion as needed.

[c] Bank of America's pool of assets has not been finalized.

[d] Bank of America's $7.5 billion of projected TARP funds is preliminary based on the 1/15/2009 Treasury announcement and pending the finalized agreement.

[e] $75 billion is for mortgage modification.

[f] Treasury preliminarily discussed potential funding for the Auto Warranty Commitment Program for up to $1.25 billion.

Sources: CPP, TALF, and PPIP: Treasury, Of ce of Financial Stability, Chief of Compliance and CFO, SIGTARP interview, 3/30/2009; AIFP: Treasury, Fifth Tranche Report to Congress, 3/6/2009, p. 2 states that Treasury will fund an additional $4 billion on 3/17/2009; ASSP: Treasury, "Auto Supplier Support Program: Stabilizing the Auto Industry in a Time of Crisis," 3/19/2009, accessed 3/19/2009; UCSB: Treasury, "Unlocking Credit for Small Businesses: FAQ on Implementation," 3/17/2009, accessed 3/18/2009; SSFI: Treasury, "U.S. Treasury and Federal Reserve Board Announce Participation in AIG Restructuring Plan," 3/2/2009, accessed 3/4/2009; TIP: Treasury, Transactions Report, 4/2/2009; AGP: Treasury, "Treasury, Federal Reserve, and FDIC Provide Assistance to Bank of America," 1/16/2009, accessed 1/16/2009; Treasury, "U.S. Government Finalizes Terms of Citi Guarantee Announced in November," 1/16/2009, accessed 3/30/2009; TALF: Treasury, "Financial Stability Plan Fact Sheet," 2/10/2009, accessed 3/17/2009; MHA: Treasury, "Making Home Affordable: Updated Detailed Program Description," 3/4/2009, accessed 3/4/2009; GAO, "Report to Congressional Committees: Troubled Asset Relief Program — March 2009 Status of Efforts to Address Transparency and Accountability Issues," 3/26/2009; PPIP: Treasury, "Public-Private Investment Program: Fact Sheet," 3/23/2009, accessed 3/23/2009; Treasury, SIGTARP brie ng, 4/14/2009.

For a reporting of all purchases, obligations, expenditures, and revenues of TARP, see Appendix C: "Reporting Requirements."

> **Secondary Market:** Created when banks sell a portion of their loans to a dealer who then pools the loans together and sells portions of the loan pools as securities to investors. The secondary market serves as a source of cash for banks, providing them money to make new loans.

Table 2.2. Expenditure Levels by Program, as of March 31, 2009 ($ Billions)

		Amount		Percent (%)	Section Reference
Authorized Under EESA			$700.0		
Released Immediately		$250.0		35.7%	
Released Under Presidential Certificate of Need		$100.0		14.3%	
Released Under Presidential Certificate of Need & Resolution to Disapprove Failed		$350.0		50.0%	
TOTAL RELEASED			**$700.0**	**100.0%**	
Less: Expenditures by Treasury Under TARP[a] Capital Purchase Program ("CPP"):					"Capital Investment Programs"
Bank of America Corporation[b]	$25.0			3.6%	
Citigroup, Inc.	$25.0			3.6%	
JP Morgan Chase & Co.	$25.0			3.6%	
Wells Fargo and Company	$25.0			3.6%	
The Goldman Sachs Group Inc.	$10.0			1.4%	
Morgan Stanley	$10.0			1.4%	
Other Qualifying Financial Institutions[c]	$78.8			11.3%	
CPP TOTAL		**$198.8**		**28.4%**	
Systemically Significant Failing Institutions Program ("SSFI"): American International Group, Inc. ("AIG")	$40.0			5.7%	"Institution-Specific Assistance"
SSFI TOTAL		**$40.0**		**5.7%**	
Targeted Investment Program ("TIP"):					"Institution-Specific Assistance"
Bank of America Corporation	$20.0			2.9%	
Citigroup, Inc.	$20.0			2.9%	
TIP TOTAL		**$40.0**		**5.7%**	
Asset Guarantee Program ("AGP"): Citigroup, Inc.[d]	$5.0			0.7%	"Institution-Specific Assistance"
AGP TOTAL		**$5.0**		**0.7%**	
Automotive Industry Financing Program ("AIFP"):					"Automotive Industry Financing Program"
General Motors Corporation ("GM")	$14.3			2.0%	
General Motors Acceptance Corporation LLC ("GMAC")	$5.0			0.7%	
Chrysler Holding LLC	$4.0			0.6%	
Chrysler Financial Services Americas LLC[e]	$1.5			0.2%	
AIFP TOTAL		**$24.8**		**3.5%**	

Table 2.2. (Continued)

		Amount		Percent (%)	Section Reference
Term Asset-Backed Securities Loan Facility ("TALF"): TALF LLC	$20.0			2.9%	"Term Asset-Backed Securities Loan Facility"
TALF TOTAL		**$20.0**		**2.9%**	
SUBTOTAL – TARP EXPENDITURES			$328.6	47.0%	
TARP REPAYMENTS[f]			**$(0.4)**	**(0.1)%**	
BALANCE REMAINING OF TOTAL FUNDS MADE AVAILABLE AS OF MARCH 31, 2009			$371.8	53.1%	

Note: Numbers affected by rounding.

[a] From a budgetary perspective, what Treasury has committed to spend (e.g., signed agreements with TARP fund recipients).

[b] Bank of America's share is equal to two CPP investments totaling $25 billion, which is the sum $15 billion received on 10/28/2008 and $10 billion received on 1/9/2009.

[c] Other Qualifying Financial Institutions ("QFIs") include all QFIs that have received less than $10 billion through CPP.

[d] Treasury committed $5 billion to Citigroup under AGP; however, this funding is conditional based on losses realized and may potentially never be expended.

[e] Treasury's $1.5 billion loan to Chrysler Financial represents the maximum loan amount. This $1.5 billion has not been fully expended because the loan will be funded incrementally at $100 million per week. As of 3/31/2009, $1,175 million out of the $1.5 billion has been funded.

[f] As of 3/31/2009, CPP repayments total $353.0 million and AIFP loan principal payments (Chrysler Financial) total $3.5 million.

Sources: EESA, P.L. 110-343, 10/3/2008; Library of Congress, "A joint resolution relating to the disapproval of obligations under the Emergency Economic Stabilization Act of 2008," 1/15/2009, accessed 1/25/2009; Treasury, Transactions Report, 4/2/2009; Treasury, responses to SIGTARP data call, 4/6/2009 and 4/8/2009.

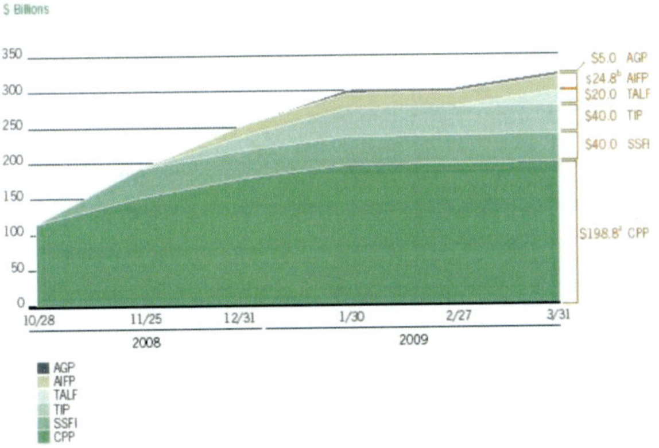

Note: Numbers affected by rounding.

[a] As of 3/31/2009, $353.0 million of CPP funding has been repaid.

[b] As of 3/31/2009, $3.5 million of principal payments related to AIFP loans (Chrysler Financial) has been repaid.

Source: Treasury, *Transactions Report*, 4/2/2009. Treasury response to SIGTARP data call, 4/8/2009.

Figure 2.2. Expenditures, by Program, Cumulative

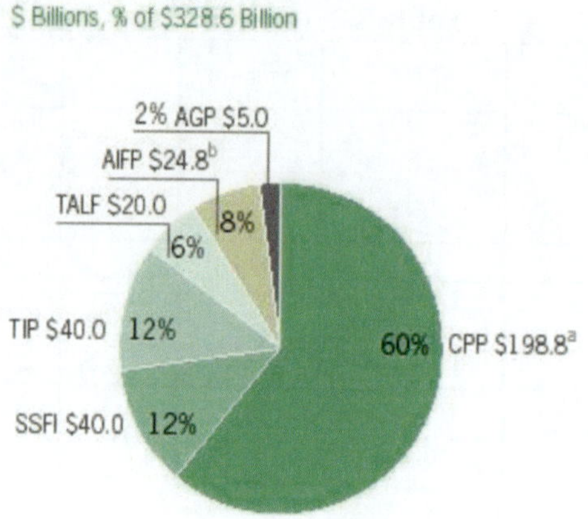

Note: Numbers affected by rounding.

[a] As of 3/31/2009, $353.0 million of CPP funding has been repaid.

[b] As of 3/31/2009, $3.5 million of principal payments related to AIFP loans (Chrysler Financial) has been repaid.

Source: Treasury, Transactions Report, 4/2/2009.

Figure 2.3. Expenditures by Program, Snapshot

Table 2.3. Equity Agreements

TARP Program	Company	"Date of Agreement"	Cost Assigned	Description of Investment	Investment Information	Dividends	Term of Agreement
CPP – Public	280 QFIs	10/14/ 2008[a] and later	$195.6 billion[b]	Senior Preferred Equity	1-3% of Risk Weighted Assets, not to exceed $25 billion for each QFI	5% for first 5 years, 9% thereafter	Perpetual
				Common Stock Purchase Warrants	15% of Senior Preferred amount	—	Up to 10 years
CPP – Private	252 QFIs	11/17/ 2008[c] and later	$3.2 billion[b]	Preferred Equity	1-3% of Risk Weighted Assets, not to exceed $25 billion for each QFI	5% for first 5 years, 9% thereafter	Perpetual
				Preferred Stock Purchase Warrants that are exercised immediately	5% of Preferred amount	9%	Up to 10 years
SSFI	AIG	11/25/2008	$40 billion	Perpetual Senior Preferred Equity	$40 billion aggregate liquidation preference	10%	Perpetual
				Common Stock Purchase	2% of issued	—	Up to 10 years

Table 2.3. (Continued)

TARP Program	Company	"Date of Agreement"	Cost Assigned	Description of Investment	Investment Information	Dividends	Term of Agreement
				Warrants	and outstanding Common Stock on investment date; $2.50 strike price		
TIP	Citigroup	12/31/2008	$20 billion	Senior Preferred Equity	$20 billion	8%	Perpetual
				Warrants	10% of total Preferred Stock issued; $10.61 strike price	—	Up to 10 years
TIP	Bank of America	1/16/2009[d]	$20 billion	Senior Preferred Equity	$20 billion	8%	Perpetual
				Warrants	10% of total Preferred Stock issued; $13.30 strike price	—	Up to 10 years
AIFP	GMAC LLC	12/29/2008	$5 billion	Senior Preferred Membership Interests	$5 billion	8%	Perpetual
				Preferred Stock Purchase Warrants that are exercised immediately	5% of Preferred amount	9%	Up to 10 years

Notes:

[a] Announcement date of CPP Public Term Sheet.

[b] As of 3/31/2009, $353.0 million of CPP funding has been repaid ($338.0 million Public, $15.0 million Private).

[c] Announcement date of CPP Private Term Sheet.

[d] Date from Treasury's *Transactions Report,* dated 1/27/2009. The Security Purchase Agreement has a date of 1/15/2009.

Sources: Treasury, *Transactions Report*, 4/2/2009; Treasury, "TARP Capital Purchase Program Agreement, Senior Preferred Stock and Warrants, Summary of Senior Preferred Terms," 10/14/2008; Treasury, "TARP Capital Purchase Program Agreement, (Non-Public QFIs, excluding S Corps and Mutual Organizations) Preferred Securities, Summary of Warrant Terms," 11/17/2008; Treasury, "Securities Purchase Agreement dated as of November 25, 2008 between American International Group, Inc. and United States Department of Treasury," 11/25/2008; Treasury, "TARP AIG SSFI Investment, Senior Preferred Stock and Warrant, Summary of Senior Preferred Terms," 11/25/2008; Treasury, "Securities Purchase Agreement dated as of January 15, 2009 between Citigroup, Inc. and United States Department of Treasury," 1/15/2009; Treasury, "Citigroup, Inc. Summary of Terms, Eligible Asset Guarantee," 11/23/2008; "Securities Purchase Agreement dated as of January 15, 2009 between Bank of America Corporation and United States Department of Treasury," 1/15/2009; Treasury, "Bank of America Summary of Terms, Preferred Securities," 1/16/2009; Treasury, "GMAC LLC Automotive Industry Financing Program, Preferred Membership Interests, Summary of Preferred Terms," 12/29/2008.

Table 2.4. Debt Agreements

TARP Program	Company	Date of Agreement	Cost Assigned	Description of Investment	Investment Information	Interest/ Dividends	Term of Agreement
AIFP	General Motors Corporation	12/31/2008	$13.4 billion	Debt Obligation with Warrants and Additional Note	Loan is funded incrementally; $4 billion funded on 12/29/2008, $5.4 billion Funded on 1/21/2009, $4 billion funded on 2/17/2009	LIBOR + 3%	12/29/2011
AIFP	General Motors	1/16/2009	$884 million	Debt Obligation	To purchase Class B membership interest of GMAC LLC	LIBOR + 3%	1/16/2012
AIFP	Chrysler Holding LLC	1/2/2009[a]	$4 billion	Debt Obligation with Additional Note	Loan up to $4 billion, available on the closing date; Additional note of $267 million (6.67% of the maximum loan amount)	3% or 8% (if the Company is in default of its terms under the agreement) plus the greater of a) three-month LIBOR or b) LIBOR floor (2.00%)	1/2/2012
AIFP	Chrysler Financial	1/16/2009	$1.5 billion[b]	Debt Obligation with Additional Note	Loan is funded incrementally at $100 million per week; Additional note is $75 million (5% of total loan size), which vests 20% on closing and 20% on each anniversary of closing	LIBOR + 1% for first year LIBOR + 1.5% for remaining	1/16/2014

Notes:

[a] Date from Treasury's Transactions Report, dated 1/27/2009. The Security Purchase Agreement has a date of 12/31/2008.

[b] As of 3/31/2009, $3.5 million of principal payments related to AIFP loans has been repaid.

Sources: Treasury, "Loan and Security Agreement By and Between General Motors Corporation as Borrower and The United States Department of Treasury as Lender Dated as of December 31, 2008," 12/31/2008; Treasury, "General Motors Corporation, Indicative Summary of Terms for Secured Term Loan Facility," 12/19/08; Treasury, "General Motors Promissory Note," 1/16/2009; Treasury, "Loan and Security Agreement By and Between Chrysler Holding LLC as Borrower and The United States Department of Treasury as Lender Dated as of December 31, 2008," 12/31/2008; Treasury, "Chrysler, Indicative Summary of Terms for Secured Term Loan Facility," 12/19/2008; Treasury, "Chrysler LB Receivables Trust Automotive Industry Financing Program, Secured Term Loan, Summary of Terms," 1/16/2009; Treasury, response to SIGTARP draft, 1/30/2009.

Table 2.5. Dividend and Interest Payments, by Program ($ Millions)

Program	Amount
CPP	$2,517.9
SSFI	–
TIP	$328.9
AGP	$26.9
AIFP	$250.6
TOTAL	$3,124.3

Note: Numbers affected by rounding. Data as of 3/31/2009.
Source: Treasury, response to SIGTARP data call, 4/8/2009.

Capital Investment Programs

Treasury has created two TARP initiatives aimed at facilitating the investment of capital in financial institutions. According to Treasury, the Capital Purchase Program ("CPP"), announced in October 2008, was created to stabilize the financial system by providing capital to institutions of all sizes. Treasury announced the establishment of the Capital Assistance Program ("CAP") in February 2009, with the intent to ensure that banks have a sufficient capital cushion to withstand larger-than-expected losses in the future. A comparison of the terms of each program can be found in Table 2.15 in the "CAP Terms" discussion in this section.

Capital Purchase Program

Under CPP, as of March 31, 2009, Treasury anticipated that $218 billion[37] of TARP funds will eventually be invested in **Qualifying Financial Institutions ("QFIs")**, which include private and public U.S.-controlled banks, savings associations, **bank holding companies**, and certain **savings and loan holding companies**.[38] Treasury originally announced that CPP would be a $250 billion program, but, on March 30, 2009, stated that it now forecasts only expending $218 billion. According to Treasury, the intention of CPP is to invest in healthy, viable banks in order to promote financial stability, maintain con dence in the financial system, and permit institutions to continue meeting the credit needs of American consumers and businesses.[39] For a summary of the distribution of CPP funding by participant, see Figure 2.4.

Treasury issued initial guidelines for **public applicants** for CPP on October 20, 2008.[40] Guidelines were released for **private applicants** on November 17, 2008,[41] for **"S" corporations** on January 14, 2009,[42] and on April 7, 2009, guidelines were released for **mutual organizations**.[43] Key dates for each type of institution that may apply for CPP funding are outlined in Table 2.6.

For more information regarding the CPP application process, refer to SIGTARP's Initial Report, Section 3: "TARP Implementation and Administration."

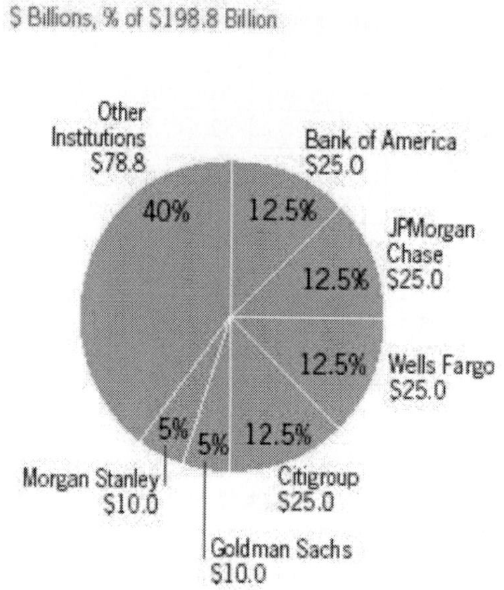

Note: Numbers affected by rounding. As of 3/31/2009, $353 million has been redeemed. Bank of America. Bank of America Corporation; JPMorgan Chase = JPMorgan Chase & Co.; Wells Fargo = Wells Fargo and Company; Citigroup = Citigroup Inc.; Goldman Sachs = The Goldman Sachs Group, Inc.

Source: Treasury, Transactions Report, 4/2/2009.

Figure 2.4. CPP Expenditures, by Participant, Cumulative.

Table 2.6. Key Dates and Deadlines for CPP Application Process, by Applicant Category

Type	Announced Date	Application Deadline
Publicly Held	10/20/2008	11/14/2008
Privately Held	11/17/2008	12/8/2008
"S" Corporation	1/14/2009	2/13/2009
Mutual Organization	4/7/2009	5/7/2009

Note: Private QFIs are those that are non-public QFIs, excluding S corporations and mutual organizations. Data as of 4/7/2009.

Sources: Publicly Held: Treasury, "Application Guidelines for TARP Capital Purchase Program," no date, accessed 1/22/2009; Privately Held: Treasury, "Process Related FAQs for Private Bank Capital Purchase Program," no date, accessed 1/22/2009; "S" Corporation: Treasury, "S Corporation FAQs," no date, accessed 1/22/2009; Mutual Organization: Treasury, "Process Related FAQs for the Capital Purchase Program, Mutual Holding Company FAQs," 4/7/2009, accessed 4/7/2009.

Qualifying Financial Institutions ("QFIs"): Private and public U.S.-controlled banks, savings associations, bank holding companies, and certain savings and loan holding companies.

Bank Holding Company ("BHC"): A company that controls a bank. Typically, a company controls a bank through the ownership of 25% or more of its voting securities.

Savings and Loan Holding Company ("SLHC"): A company (other than a BHC) that controls a savings association.

Public Applicant: A QFI whose securities are traded on a national securities exchange and is required to file, under national securities laws, periodic reports with either the Securities and Exchange Commission or its primary Federal banking regulator.

Private Applicant: Any QFI whose shares are not traded on a national securities exchange, excluding S corporations and mutual organizations.

S Corporation: Any U.S. bank, U.S. savings association, bank holding company ("BHC"), or savings and loan holding company ("SLHC") organized such that it is exempt from most Federal income taxes as they are passed through to the shareholders.

Program Updates

The CPP process remains largely the same since SIGTARP's Initial Report, with the exception being the modifications contained in the American Recovery and Reinvestment Act of 2009 ("ARRA"), which imposed more stringent executive compensation requirements and changed the terms under which a TARP recipient could pay back Treasury investments. The new repayment terms provide greater flexibility by removing time restrictions and no longer requiring the bank to demonstrate that it has received private equity investment in proportion to the funds that it seeks to repay. Under ARRA, EESA's executive compensation provisions were amended to detail the number of employees subject to more stringent guidelines based on level of funding. The amendments also require TARP recipients to create a Board Compensation Committee, submit a certification of compliance, and require the Treasury Secretary to review prior compensation payments.[44] For more information on the amended executive compensation restrictions, see the "Executive Compensation" discussion in this section.

Mutual Organization: A corporation that is owned by depositors which distributes income in proportion to the amount of business that members do with the company.

Status of CPP Funds

As of March 31, 2009, Treasury had purchased $198.8 billion in **preferred stock** from 532 different QFIs in 48 states, the District of Columbia, and Puerto Rico.[45] Closings for CPP purchases generally occur each week on Friday, and information about the transaction is made publicly available by the following Tuesday. For the geographical distribution of all the QFIs that have received funding see Figure 2.5. For a full listing of CPP recipients, see Appendix C: "Reporting Requirements."

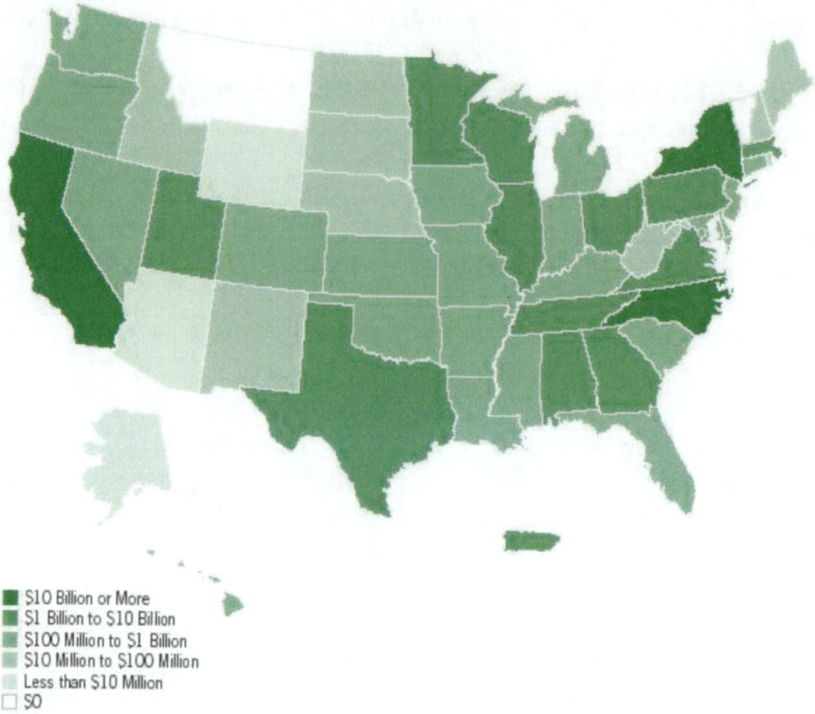

Note: Banks in Montana and Vermont had not received any funds as of 3/31/2009.
Source: Treasury, "Local Impact of the Capital Purchase Program," 3/31/2009

Figure 2.5. Tracking Capital Purchase Program Investments Across the Country.

Preferred Stock: A form of ownership in a company that generally entitles the owner of the shares (an investor) to collect dividend payments. Preferred shares are senior to common stock, but junior to debt.

Market Capitalization: The value of a corporation determined by multiplying the current market price of one share of the corporation by the number of total outstanding shares. This is an important metric because it is often used to determine the aggregate value of a company.

Although the eight largest investments accounted for $134.2 billion of the program, CPP has also had many more modest investments: 206 of the 532 recipients received less than $10 million each. Table 2.7 shows the distribution of recipients based on their **market capitalization**, and Table 2.9 shows the 10 largest firms that received funds. Table 2.8 and Table 2.10 show the distribution of the investments by size. A full listing of all public recipients' market capitalization can be found in Appendix C: "Reporting Requirements."

On February 6, 2009, the Congressional Oversight Panel ("COP") released a report in which it discussed a valuation analysis conducted with respect to Treasury's investments. The report concluded that "Treasury paid substantially more for the assets it purchased under TARP than their then-current market value." The report estimated that for every $100 spent on the eight largest CPP transactions of 2008, Treasury received assets worth approximately \$78.[46] In addition to the COP analysis, on April 4, 2009, the Congressional Budget Of ce ("CBO") issued a new estimate of \$356 billion as the "ultimate cost to taxpayers" for assistance to finan- cial institutions under TARP. In other words, CBO projects that Treasury will only recover \$344 billion, or approximately 49%, of the \$700 billion of TARP funds.[47]

Table 2.7. Public CPP Recipients by Market Capitalization

\$20 Billion or More	7
\$1 Billion to \$20 Billion	29
\$100 Million to \$1 Billion	82
Less than \$100 Million	154

Note: Data accessed 4/1/2009 10:20am.
Sources: Treasury, Transactions Report, 3/31/2009; Capital IQ, Inc., a Division of Standard & Poor's.

Table 2.8. CPP Investment Size

\$10 Billion or More	6
\$1 Billion to \$10 Billion	18
\$100 Million to \$1 Billion	56
Less than \$100 Million	452
TOTAL	**532**

Note: Data as of 3/31/2009. Bank of America Corporation and SunTrust Banks, Inc., each received funds in two separate transactions.
Source: Treasury, Transactions Report, 3/31/2009.

Table 2.9. Top 10 Public CPP Recipients by Market Capitalization (\$ Billions)

Company	Market Capitalization	CPP Funding Received
JPMorgan Chase & Co.	**\$99.9**	**\$25.0**
Wells Fargo & Company	**\$60.4**	**\$25.0**
The Goldman Sachs Group, Inc.	**\$49.0**	**\$10.0**
Bank of America Corporation	**\$43.7**	**\$25.0**
Bank of New York Mellon Corporation	**\$32.5**	**\$3.0**
U.S. Bancorp	**\$25.7**	**\$6.6**
Morgan Stanley	**\$24.6**	**\$10.0**
American Express Company	**\$15.8**	**\$3.4**
Citigroup, Inc.	**\$13.9**	**\$25.0**
Northern Trust Corporation	**\$13.4**	**\$1.6**

Note: Data accessed 4/1/2009 10:20am. Numbers affected by rounding.
Sources: Treasury, Transactions Report, 3/30/2009; Capital IQ, Inc., a Division of Standard & Poor's.

Table 2.10. CPP Investment Summary

Largest Capital Investment	**$25 Billion**
Smallest Capital Investment	**$301,000**
Average Capital Investment	**$372.2 Million**
Median Capital Investment	**$15 Million**

Note: Data as of 3/31/2009. Bank of America Corporation and SunTrust Banks, Inc., each received funds in two separate transactions.

Source: Treasury, *Transactions Report*, 3/31/2009.

Table 2.11. Largest Positions in Warrants Held by Treasury as of March 31, 2009

Participant	Transaction Date	Stock Price as of Transaction Date	Number of Warrants Received	Strike Price as Stated in the Agreements	Stock Price as of 3/31/2009	In or Out of Money?	Amount "In the Money" or "Out of the Money" as of 3/31/2009	Percent Change in Stock Price Since Initial Report
Bank of America Corporation	10/28/2008	$23.02	48,717,116	$30.79	$6.82	OUT	(23.97)	9.3%
Bank of America Corporation	1/9/2009	$12.99	73,075,674	$30.79	$6.82	OUT	(23.97)	9.3%
Citigroup Inc.	10/28/2008	$13.41	210,084,034	$17.85	$2.53	OUT	(15.32)	-27.1%
JPMorgan Chase & Co.	10/28/2008	$37.60	88,401,697	$42.42	$26.58	OUT	(15.84)	9.5%
Wells Fargo & Company	10/28/2008	$34.46	110,261,688	$34.01	$14.24	OUT	(19.77)	-10.3%
Morgan Stanley	10/28/2008	$15.20	65,245,759	$22.99	$22.77	OUT	(0.22)	21.7%
The Goldman Sachs Group, Inc.	10/28/2008	$93.57	12,205,045	$122.90	$106.02	OUT	(16.88)	41.5%
The PNC Financial Services Group Inc.	12/31/2008	$49.00	16,885,192	$67.33	$29.29	OUT	(38.04)	-3.2%
U.S. Bancorp	11/14/2008	$26.30	32,679,102	$30.29	$14.61	OUT	(15.68)	-0.2%
SunTrust Banks, Inc.	11/14/2008	$33.52	11,891,280	$44.15	$11.74	OUT	(32.41)	-21.6%
SunTrust Banks, Inc.	12/31/2008	$29.54	6,008,902	$33.70	$11.74	OUT	(21.96)	-21.6%
Capital One Finan-cial Corporation	11/14/2008	$31.19	12,657,960	$42.13	$12.24	OUT	(29.89)	-36.7%

Note: Bank of America Corporation and SunTrust Banks, Inc., each received funds in two separate transactions.

Sources: Participants and Transaction Date: Treasury, Transactions Report, 3/31/2009, accessed 3/31/2009; Market price data: Capital IQ, Inc. (a division of Standard & Poor's), accessed 3/12/2009 at 11:00am EST and 4/2/2009 at 2:00pm EST; Number of warrants and strike price: Treasury, response to SIGTARP data call, 4/1/2009.

Warrants Received by Treasury

As discussed in the Initial Report, Treasury receives **warrants** of **common stock** from publicly traded CPP participants.[48] Appendix H: "Warrants" includes a full listing and status of all warrants from publicly traded CPP participants. As of March 31, 2009, no warrants of common stock in public companies had been exercised. Table 2.11 outlines Treasury's warrant positions from its 10 largest CPP investments.

For more information regarding the mechanics of warrants, refer to SIGTARP's Initial Report, Section 2: "TARP Overview"

Warrant: The right, but not the obligation, to purchase shares of common stock at a fixed price.

Common Stock: A security that provides voting rights in a corporation and pays a dividend after preferred stockholders have been paid.

Dividends Received by Treasury

As of March 31, 2009, Treasury had received approximately $2.5 billion in dividends from preferred stock investment through CPP. Most CPP recipients made a dividend payment on February 15, 2009; however, eight recipients did not declare dividends due to a lack of necessary regulatory and/or shareholder approvals. According to the CPP terms, six missed payments give Treasury the right to elect two members to the board of directors.[49] For a detailed table of the dividends received by Treasury from all programs under TARP, see Appendix C: "Reporting Requirements."

The top 10 largest dividends paid by CPP recipients since TARP funding began are captured in Table 2.12.

Table 2.12. Top 10 Cumulative Dividends Paid by CPP Recipients Since Program Implementation ($ Millions)

Company	Size of Cumulative Dividends
JPMorgan Chase and Co.	**$427.1**
Citigroup Inc.	**371.5**
Wells Fargo and Company	**371.5**
Bank of America Corporation	**272.9**
Goldman Sachs Group Inc.	**148.6**
Morgan Stanley	**106.9**
US Bancorp	**83.4**
Suntrust Banks, Inc.	**72.9**
Bank of New York Mellon Corporation	**59.2**
The PNC Financial Services Group, Inc.	**47.4**
TOP 10 TOTAL	$1,961.4

Note: Numbers affected by rounding. Data as of 3/31/2009. Bank of America Corporation paid an additional $128.9 million under TIP. Citigroup, Inc. paid an additional $26.9 million under AGP and $200 million under TIP.

Sources: Treasury, response to SIGTARP data call, 4/8/2008; Treasury, response to SIGTARP draft, 4/9/2009.

Federal Banking Agency ("FBA"): One of four agencies:

1) Comptroller of the Currency
2) Board of Governors of the Federal Reserve System
3) Federal Deposit Insurance Corporation
4) Director of the Office of Thrift Supervision

Repayment of Funds

Pursuant to ARRA, repayment of the capital provided by Treasury is "subject to consultation with the appropriate Federal banking agency."[50] Any bank wishing to buy back its shares can contact both Treasury and its **Federal Banking Agency ("FBA")**, at which point Treasury will discuss the request with the FBA. If the FBA con rms that the bank will have sufficient capital after repayment, banks can choose to pay back the entire CPP investment in a lump sum, or they can pay it back over time as long as every payment is at least 25% of the original total investment (unless the last payment is less by default). Banks that repay the CPP investment also have the opportunity to repurchase the warrants received by Treasury at their fair market value. Under ARRA, if the bank does not repurchase its warrants, Treasury is required to liquidate the warrants at the current market price. Additionally, banks are responsible for any unpaid dividends that are owed to Treasury at the time of their redemption. All principal funds that are repaid can be used for other TARP initiatives. However, dividends, interest, and profits from the sale of equity interests must be used to pay down the debt and cannot be reused.[51]

As of March 31, 2009, five banks have repurchased their shares from Treasury. Treasury has received $353 million in principal and an additional $2.3 million in accrued and unpaid dividends.[52] As of March 31, 2009, one of the five institutions had notified Treasury that it intends to buy back its warrants as well. Treasury has indicated that it will give the banks 15 days to exercise this right before Treasury seeks to sell the warrants to a third party.[53] For details of the share repurchases conducted as of March 31, 2009, see Table 2.13.

Table 2.13. CPP Share Repurchases ($ millions)

Repurchase Date	Institution	Original Investment Amount	Principal Amount Repurchased as of 3/31/2009
3/31/2009	Signature Bank	$120	$120
3/31/2009	Old National Bancorp	100	100
3/31/2009	IberiaBank Corporation	90	90
3/31/2009	Bank of Marin Bancorp	28	28
3/31/2009	Centra Financial Holdings, Inc.	15	15
	TOTAL	**$353**	**$353**

Note: Data as of 3/31/2009. Treasury has also received $2.3 million in accrued and unpaid dividends.
Source: Treasury, Transactions Report, 4/2/2009.

Treasury's Snapshots

On January 8, 2009, Treasury launched an effort to begin measuring the lending activities of CPP recipients to "help taxpayers easily assess the lending and other activities of banks receiving Government investments."[54] Treasury is performing both quarterly and monthly data analysis. The quarterly data will illustrate balance sheet changes for all CPP recipients.[55] The first quarterly report will be publicly available on June 30, 2009.[56]

> **Call Report:** Quarterly report of financial condition commercial banks file with their Federal and state regulatory agencies.

Monthly Lending and Intermediation Snapshot

The stated purpose of the monthly snapshot is to provide both Treasury and the public with data regarding the lending activities of the banks that received CPP funding. Treasury originally stated that analyzing the largest banks, which represent over 80% of the total CPP funds disbursed, would "quickly but effectively provide an objective analysis to the public."[57] This survey is intended to report on the potential impact, but not use, of TARP funds.

On January 16, 2009, the Interim Assistant Secretary for Financial Stability sent letters to the 20 largest CPP recipients in which he explained the snapshot process:

> This Monthly Intermediation Snapshot will complement a more thor-ough analysis Treasury will conduct quarterly of all CPP recipient banks using **call report** data. The snapshot is designed to be simple enough to allow Treasury and TARP senior management to draw inferences about intermediation activity generally, but also granular enough to provide insight into patterns by broad category and by institution.[58]

In addition to the snapshots, pursuant to a recommendation made by the Government Accountability Office ("GAO"), Treasury recently requested certain monthly lending data from all CPP recipients. The first CPP Monthly Lending Report is due by April 30, 2009, and is expected to be published in mid-May 2009.[59]

December 2008 Monthly Lending and Intermediation Snapshot

The initial set of responses to Treasury's letters was published on February 17, 2009, and contained data for the time period from October through December 2008. These responses included data looking back for a three-month period; subsequent reports only include data from the prior month. Treasury made the following conclusions from the initial monthly snapshot:

Banks continued to originate, re nance, and renew loans despite significant headwinds posed by unprecedented financial market crisis and economic turn.[60]

Banks reported a general trend of modestly declining total loan balances due to decreasing loan demand and tighter underwriting standards, as well as other factors such as charge-offs, or losses written off on loans.[61]

Month-to-month changes were driven by outside factors, including falling interest rates, loan demand, and the credit crisis.[62] Treasury made the following observations about these changes:

Lending activity decreased from October to November 2008.

Lending activity increased from November to December 2008.
Drivers of this phenomenon varied by loan type.

January 2009 Monthly Lending and Intermediation Snapshot

The next set of responses was published on March 16, 2009, and contained data for the time period between January 1, 2009, and January 31, 2009. Treasury surveyed the top 21 recipients of Government investments through CPP rather than the top 20, due to a large investment on January 9, 2009.[63] Treasury reviewed and analyzed data from December 31, 2008, to January 31, 2009, and came to the following conclusions:

Consumer lending levels increased as a result of increases in originations of residential mortgages and student loans due to attractive interest rates and seasonal demand.[64]
Commercial lending, industrial lending, and commercial real estate lending declined from the prior month due to weak demand for debt.[65]
Renewals of existing accounts and new loan commitments in commercial real estate lending decreased significantly from the prior month as a result of the frozen securitization markets and lack of commercial mortgage-backed securities activity.[66]

Capital Assistance Program

On February 10, 2009, Treasury announced the Capital Assistance Program ("CAP") as part of FSP. CAP follows CPP as the vehicle for Treasury to provide TARP capital to QFIs.[67] CAP has three main components:

a stress test to evaluate major financial institutions' capital buffers
access to capital for QFIs
a Financial Stability Trust to manage the Government's investments in the program

CAP's stated goal is to "ensure the continued ability of U.S. financial institutions to lend to creditworthy borrowers in the face of a weaker-than-expected economic environment and larger-than-expected potential losses."[68]

Risk-Weighted Assets: The amount of a bank's total assets after applying an appropriate risk factor to each individual asset.

Professional Forecasters: The three forecasters used for the purpose of the stress test were the Consensus Fore-casts, the Blue Chip Survey, and the Survey of Professional Forecasters.

Stress Test

According to Treasury, the stress test assesses whether a QFI has enough capital to continue lending under economic conditions that are worse than expected. The test is required for the 19 financial institutions with more than $100 billion in **risk- weighted assets**. These 19 institutions represent roughly two-thirds of aggregate U.S. BHC assets.[69] The tests are designed to determine how much additional capital each institution may need to remain well capitalized in an economic downturn. Regulators have created two forward-looking economic scenarios. The first scenario is a baseline forecast for 2009 and 2010, based on the most recent projections available from three **professional forecasters** prior to the start of the stress tests on February 25, 2009.[70] Although the baseline is intended to forecast likely economic metrics, the unemployment rate in the baseline scenario, 8.4%, has already been eclipsed with the April 3, 2009, announcement of 8.5% unemployment.[71] The second scenario evaluates the institutions under worse economic conditions than those provided in the baseline forecast — an "adverse case" scenario. The assumptions for the baseline and adverse case are found in Table 2.14.

QFIs will be asked to report their estimates of losses and resources to absorb them using a standardized template. The FBAs will then evaluate the estimates by examining the data and assumptions and request additional material, as necessary. The FBAs supervise the process and may revise the estimates that will be used to determine the amount of capital needed to establish the appropriate buffer.[72]

When the stress tests are completed, by the end of April 2009,[73] the institutions that are found to need additional capital will have up to six months to raise private capital. If an institution raises enough private capital, it is not required to take CAP assistance.[74] If it is unable to raise a sufficient amount of private capital, then it must accept CAP assistance.[75]

Access to Capital

The second core component of CAP is "access for qualifying financial institutions to contingent common equity provided by the U.S. Government as a bridge to private capital in the future."[76] In addition to the 19 targeted institutions, CAP will make capital widely available to other QFIs by offering to invest in the QFI in return for shares of mandatory convertible preferred stock. Such securities are considered a higher quality of capital for banks because they have more characteristics similar to common equity than the investments made under CPP and TIP, which can be viewed more like debt. They are riskier investments for the taxpayer, however, because once the shares are converted to common stock, the Government will no longer be entitled to receive a set quarterly dividend and will have a junior right to repayment if the bank were to fail. Existing TARP recipients that decide to apply for participation in CAP will be able to take advantage of this higher-quality capital offered under CAP by exchanging their existing CPP and TIP equity for CAP equity. For more details on the terms of these agreements, see the "CAP Terms" discussion in this section. For a more detailed description of the financial terms used in this discussion, refer to "TARP Tutorial: Capital Structure" later in this section.

On February 25, 2009, Treasury released the terms for public QFIs to apply for CAP funding. QFIs must apply to their appropriate FBA by May 25, 2009. According to Treasury, the process and eligibility determination will be substantially similar to those under CPP.[77] For more information on the CPP process, refer to SIGTARP's Initial Report, Section 3: "TARP Implementation and Administration." As of March 31, 2009, the process details for CAP applications by private QFIs, S corporations, and mutual organizations have not yet been released.

Table 2.14. Economic Metrics under Baseline and More Adverse Scenarios

	2009 Scenarios		2010 Scenarios	
	Baseline	More Adverse	Baseline	More Adverse
Real GDP (% Change in Annual Average)	-2.0%	-3.3%	2.1%	0.5%
Civilian Unemployment Rate	8.4%	8.9%	8.8%	10.3%
House Prices (% Change Relative to Q4 of Prior Year)	-14.0%	-22.0%	-4.0%	-7.0%

Note: As reported by the source document, baseline forecasts for real GDP and the unemployment rate equal the average of projections released by Consensus Forecasts, the Blue Chip Survey, and the Survey of Professional Forecasters in February 2009.

Source: FDIC, "FAQs – Supervisory Capital Assessment Program," 2/25/2009, accessed 3/25/2009.

Financial Stability Trust

As of March 31, 2009, under CPP and TIP, Treasury invested $238.8 billion for preferred shares and warrants of common stock.[78] Similar investments under CAP will be managed in a separate entity called the Financial Stability Trust.[79] As of March 31, 2009, there were no additional details available about this entity.

Convertible Preferred: A preferred stock that is convertible into common stock. In the context of CAP, the conversion is at the option of the QFI until year seven when it becomes mandatory.

Redeem: To buy back a prior obligation. In the case of CAP, the QFI can buy back (redeem) its CPP shares with the funds received from the CAP investment.

CAP Terms

Under CAP, Treasury will provide the QFI with additional capital by purchasing new convertible preferred stock ("**convertible preferred**"). If the QFI already received funds from either the CPP or TIP, the QFI may choose to use CAP to **redeem** the previously issued preferred stock. CAP allows the QFI effectively to exchange one type of equity for another by permitting the bank to convert preferred shares purchased under CPP to CAP convertible preferred shares.

As its name suggests, the convertible preferred shares that will be acquired by Treasury can be converted into common stock. The QFI can choose to convert the stock from preferred to common with the approval of its FBA. If the QFI does not choose to convert, the CAP terms require that the conversion automatically take place seven years after the transaction date. Once converted, Treasury will hold common stock in the QFI as if it had been purchased in the public market. Note that, as such, it will carry voting rights in the institution just like other common stock; Treasury's stake, however, will no longer have the benefit of receiving de ned dividends as would preferred stock. Since Treasury could potentially own a significant percentage of a QFI's common stock, it has stated that it will publish how it will use these rights prior to closing any transactions.[80] Prior to conversion, convertible preferred shares subject the QFI to terms similar to those under CPP. Table 2.15 compares the key characteristics of the convertible preferred terms for public QFIs under CAP to the preferred terms for public QFIs under CPP.

Upon receipt of the CAP investment, the QFIs agree to comply with Treasury's rules, regulations, and guidance with regard to executive compensation, transparency, accountability, and monitoring that are published and effective at the time of the closing.[81] As of March 31, 2009, Treasury has not published any additional executive compensation guidance for this program. For more information on executive compensation, refer to "Executive Compensation" later in this section.

Table 2.15. Comparison of Expected Terms: CAP Convertible Preferred and CPP Preferred Shares

Eligibility	CAP All QFIs	CPP All QFIs
Size	Between 1% and 2% of Risk-Weighted Assets plus amount necessary to redeem CPP and/or TIP shares, or more as per "exceptional assistance" clause	Between 1% and 3% of Risk-Weighted Assets not to exceed $25 billion
Security	Convertible Preferred	Senior Preferred
Term of Conversion to Common Stock	Mandatory at 7 years At option of QFI before 7 years	N/A
Conversion Price	90% of the average closing price for the common stock for the 20 trading days period ending on 2/9/2009	N/A
Dividends Prior to Conversion	9%	5% for the first 5 years9% thereafter
Voting Rights	Voting Rights upon conversion to common (if dividends are not paid prior to conversion)	Non-Voting (unless dividends are not paid)

Notes: Data as of 3/31/2009. The contents of this table have been summarized for readability and highlight differences between the programs rather than provide a comprehensive representation of the programs' terms. As of 3/31/2009, no agreements have been issued under CAP and thus the terms may change.

Source: Treasury, "Summary of Mandatorily Convertible Preferred Stock ("Convertible Preferred") Terms Capital Purchase Program Description," 3/25/2009, accessed 3/25/2009.

Table 2.16. Comparison of Expected Terms: CAP Warrants and CPP Warrants

	CAP	CPP
Warrant	20% of Convertible Preferred amount on the date of investment	15% of the Senior Preferred amount on the date of the investment
Term	10 years	10 years
Exercisable	Immediately, in whole or in part	Immediately, in whole or in part
Voting	Treasury will not exercise voting	Treasury will not exercise voting

Note: The contents of this table have been summarized for readability and highlight differences between the programs rather than provide a comprehensive representation of the programs' terms. As of 3/31/2009, no agreements have been issued under CAP and thus the terms may change.

Source: Treasury, "Summary of Mandatorily Convertible Preferred Stock Terms," 3/25/2009, accessed 3/25/2009.

In addition, the QFI will be required to provide Treasury with warrants of common stock. The terms of the warrants under CAP are similar to the warrant terms under CPP and are summarized in Table 2.16.

The CAP Application Process

In addition to the 19 institutions required to participate in stress testing, CAP, like CPP, is open to applications from all public QFIs. According to Treasury, the pplication process, eligibility requirements, and determination criteria are similar to those under CPP.[82] Note that the 19 institutions do not need to wait for the completion of the stress tests in order to apply for CAP funding.[83] The deadline for public QFIs to submit a CAP application is May 25, 2009. As of March 31, 2009, application deadlines and term sheets had not been released for private QFIs, S corporations, or mutual organizations. A timeline of CAP milestones can be found in Figure 2.6.

For more information regarding the CPP application process, refer to SIGTARP's Initial Report, Section 3: "TARP Implementation and Administration."

Program Considerations

CAP introduces several new considerations relating to Government assistance for the financial industry. Although final details of the program have not been published, the program announcement provided insight into several elements of the program.

Equity Quality: As discussed in "TARP Tutorial: Capital Structure" later in this section, both shares issued under CPP and CAP are considered tier one capital "T 1"). As such, they are part of a bank's cushion against future losses and depositors' demands. However, the market views CAP's convertible preferred shares as also fitting the higher-quality classify-cation of tangible common equity ("TCE"). TCE is the cushion left over if all creditors and higher levels of stock, like preferred stock, were paid off. The convertible preferred under CAP was designed to create higher quality of capital for the banks than the preferred shares under CPP and TIP. This provides a better cushion for the banks in the event of further deterioration of the economy and the banks' balance sheets.

Converting Preferred to Common: According to the Treasury-issued term sheet, CAP participants can convert the convertible preferred to common stock at any point with the permission of the appropriate FBA. This conversion takes place not at the market price, but at a 10% discount to the average price for the 20-day trading period prior to February 9, 2009. Should market prices drop further prior to the conversion, this price is more advantageous to the QFI.[84] On the other hand, if the institution's share price increases, the Government will realize a gain. This concept is demonstrated in Table 2.17 with a select sampling of QFIs chosen for illustrative purposes.

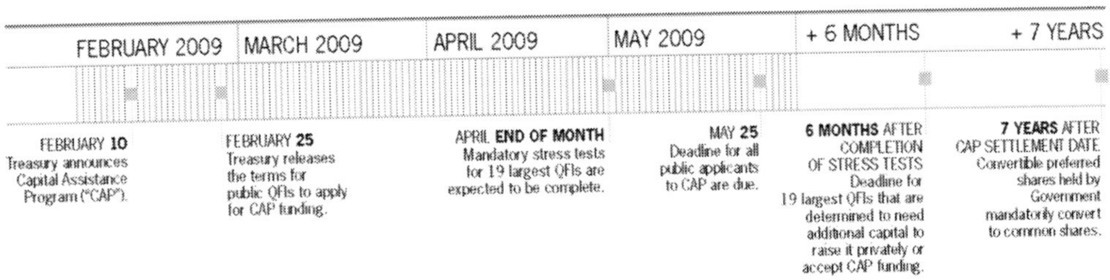

Sources: Treasury, "Secretary Geithner Introduces Financial Stability Plan," 2/10/2009, accessed 3/25/2009; Treasury Press Release, "U.S. Treasury Releases Terms of Capital Assistance Program," 2/25/2009, accessed 3/25/2009; FDIC Press Release, "Agencies to Begin Forward-Looking Economic Assessments," 2/25/2009, accessed 3/25/2009; Treasury, "Application Guidelines for Capital Assistance Program," no date, accessed 3/25/2009; FDIC, "FAQs—Supervisory Capital Assessment Program," 2/25/2009, accessed 3/25/2009; Treasury, "Summary of Mandatorily Convertible Preferred Stock Terms," 3/25/2009, accessed 3/25/2009.

Figure 2.6. Capital Assistance Program Timeline

Table 2.17. Hypothetical Conversion Price Example

Institution	2/9/2009 Value Average Price or the Preceding onth)	Conversion Price (90% f 2/9/2009 verage)	3/31/2009 Market Price	Unrealized Treasury Gain Loss) Per Share
Bank of America Corp	$6.93	$6.24	$6.82	$0.58
Citigroup, Inc.	$3.85	$3.46	$2.53	($0.93)
JPMorgan Chase & Co.	$24.67	$22.20	$26.58	$4.38
Wells Fargo & Company	$18.64	$16.78	$14.24	($2.54)
Morgan Stanley	$19.49	$17.54	$22.77	$5.23
The Goldman Sachs Group Inc.	$79.92	$71.93	$106.02	$34.09
The PNC Financial Services Group, Inc.	$34.01	$30.61	$29.29	($1.32)
U.S. Bancorp	$16.26	$14.64	$14.61	($0.03)
SunTrust Banks, Inc.	$15.23	$13.71	$11.74	($1.97)
Capital One Financial Corporation	$19.84	$17.86	$12.24	($5.62)

Sources: Treasury, Transactions Report, 3/31/2009; Capital IQ, Inc., A Division of Standard & Poor's.

When a QFI is faced with the decision to convert, it must weigh the benefit of not having to pay dividends against the disadvantage of further dilution to its common shareholders' stake. This "dilution" occurs when ownership of the company is spread over more common shares.

Mandatory Seven-Year Conversion: CAP convertible preferred must be converted to common stock after seven years. Unlike CPP, this gives the institutions and the markets a clear date by which the terms attached to the preferred shares expire and when additional common stock will enter the market.

Investment Size: The CAP terms allow a QFI to issue convertible preferred shares totaling between 1% and 2% of the QFI's risk-weighted assets in addition to Treasury's investment under the CPP or TIP. Additionally, Treasury will determine, on a case-by-case basis, if an institution qualifies for "exceptional assistance." In these exceptional cases, Treasury may fund the QFI in excess of the stated limits.[85] Once the stress tests are completed, Treasury will have a better indication of the size of the total investment.

Common Stock Voting Rights: The convertible preferred will generally have no voting rights prior to its conversion. If the QFI chooses to convert the shares to common stock, then Treasury will have the standard voting rights associated with common stock. Prior to closing any transaction, Treasury will publish further guidance as to how these voting rights will be used, although it has stated that the shares will be held in the Financial Stability Trust.[86] The inclusion of voting rights is necessary to maintain the market value of the common shares if, and when, Treasury sells them in the open market.

TARP Tutorial: Capital Structure

The Bank Balance Sheet and TARP

Since the onset of the current credit contraction, the financial industry has expressed concern with the weakening of American banks' balance sheets.[87] In December 2008, Interim Assistant Secretary Neel Kashkari testified before Congress that, "As the markets rapidly deteriorated in October, it was clear to Secretary Paulson and Chairman Bernanke that the most timely, effective way to improve credit market conditions was to strengthen bank balance sheets quickly through direct purchases of equity."[88] This section provides an illustration of the generally accepted accounting principles regarding the balance sheet.

The Balance Sheet Overview

Put simply, the balance sheet is a statement of a bank's financial condition at a single point in time.[89] It provides three fundamental pieces of information: how much the company owns (assets), how much it owes (liabilities), and the amount of the shareholders' position (owners' equity). A financial analyst or regulator will look at the relative levels of certain sub-components of the balance sheet to make judgments as to the financial health of the institution. A summary balance sheet for our hypothetical example bank, Sample Bank, is shown in Table 2.18.

In this example, note that "Assets = Liabilities + Equity" (shareholders' equity is often referred to simply as "equity"). By definition, this equation is always true. It is one of the most important accounting principles and is useful to remember when assessing the effects of bank activity. For example, if a bank experiences losses, those losses will reduce its assets, and equity will have to shrink to keep the equation in balance. At a certain level of losses, the bank's equity will be zero or less, and the firm will then be considered insolvent and potentially shut down by regulators.[90]

Assets

The asset side of Sample Bank's balance sheet shows how it categorizes its income-producing resources — or how it makes money from the resources it holds. Assets are listed by order of liquidity (the easier to convert to cash, the higher on the balance sheet). The asset line item labeled "Loans" represents the bank's **loan portfolio**. Although not particularly liquid, loan portfolios typically represent the majority of a bank's assets. Loans are typically the highest interest-bearing (and also highest risk) investments banks make. Depending on several characteristics of the loans, such as what they are used for (*e.g.*, mortgages, corporate, home equity) and where the assets underlying the loan are located (*e.g.*, economic sector, geographical location), a financial analyst can gain a picture of the relative strength or riskiness of a bank's loan portfolio.

Securities (*e.g.*, stocks, bonds, ABS, MBS) make up the second largest component of assets for Sample Bank. Securities are more liquid than loans, and tend to pay a lower interest rate, especially the safest ones such as Government debt.

Cash is often the smallest component of assets, since holding cash does not make a bank any money. The bank needs to keep a certain amount on hand, however, to satisfy customers' withdrawals.

Other assets, such as the bank's real estate and buildings or intangible assets (such as goodwill, which attempts to capture such factors as the bank's brand value or competitive position), also tend to be a relatively small component of a bank's total assets.

Table 2.18. Sample Bank – Hypothetical Balance Sheet

Assets	**$ Million**	**% of Assets**
Cash	$100	2%
Securities	1,000	20%
Loans	3,500	70%
Other Assets	400	8%
TOTAL ASSETS	**$5,000**	**100%**
Liabilities & Equity	**$ Million**	**% of Liabilities & Equity**
Deposits	$3,200	64%
Debt	1,300	26%
Shareholder's Equity	500	10%
Total Liabilities & Equity	**$5,000**	**100%**

Liabilities and Shareholders' Equity

The liabilities and shareholders' equity portion of Sample Bank's balance sheet summarizes the claims on the company, by both creditors and shareholders. Like most banks, the majority of its liabilities are deposits — customers' savings and checking account balances. This is often the least expensive form of capital. For example, the interest that a bank pays to its customer on a checking or savings account is lower than what a bank charges its loan customers. Deposits are considered liabilities because they represent the amount of money the bank owes to its depositors. In many ways, a deposit is a loan from a customer to a bank.

Loan Portfolio: The total amount of dollars the bank has lent to customers and expects to be repaid.

Securities: A financial instrument that represents debt, such as a bond, or which represents ownership, such as a stock certificate. A security can be assigned value and traded in the financial markets.

Debt also re ects a major source of funds. It includes bonds that the bank sells, loans it gets from other financial institutions, or loans from the Federal Reserve. Debt tends to require a higher interest rate than deposits, and is thus used more as a secondary fund source by the bank.

Shareholders' equity represents the difference between assets and liabilities, and will include such items as initial payments into the bank by the shareholders, and any profits retained by the bank, but equity is reduced by the reserves it has set aside against losses.

Regulatory Capital: The net capital position of a financial institution as determined by the rules of the applicable Federal or state banking regulator.

Insolvent: A condition where a financial institution has liabilities that exceed its assets. By definition, shareholders' equity in such a situation will be negative.

Tier One Capital ("T1") = Common Equity + Preferred Equity + Retained Earnings – Goodwill.

Tangible Common Equity (TCE) = Common Equity – Intangible Assets.

Tier One Capital Ratio ("T1 Ratio") = T1 / Risk-Adjusted Assets.

Determining If a Bank Is Healthy

Banking sector regulators (such as FDIC, the Of ce of the Comptroller of the Currency ("OCC"), and the Federal Reserve) use a variety of measures to enforce compliance with banking regulatory standards. Central to these measures is the notion of capital. The term "**regulatory capital**" is generally used to describe the cushion a bank has against future losses. As a starting point, it is helpful to think of the bank's capital as being roughly equal to the shareholders' equity. If capital is adequate, then theoretically the firm could cover all liabilities by selling all assets, and still have something left over for its shareholders. If, however, losses become greater than the bank's capital, the firm would be **insolvent** — assets could not cover outstanding liabilities.

The solvency of the bank, therefore, depends on how it accounts for losses (which reduce its assets) and how capital is de ned. In practice, there are many different ways of de ning capital, each describing a different level of cushion against losses.

"Tier One Capital" versus "Tangible Common Equity"

Two of the most relevant measures of capital adequacy are **tier one capital ("T1")** and **tangible common equity ("TCE")**. For many TARP recipients, these two measures are signifi- cantly divergent in the current market, capturing different aspects of their health or lack thereof.

T1, often called "core capital," is the measure of bank capital traditionally used by regulators in the United States. It can be described as a measure of the bank's ability to sustain future losses and still meet depositor's demands. T1 is a concept coordinated internationally through an agreement known as the "Basel II Accord."[91] Federal regulators look at T1 to calculate the **tier one capital ratio ("T1 Ratio")**, which determines what percentage of a bank's total assets is categorized as T1 — the higher the percentage, the better it is for the bank. Under traditional Federal regulations, a bank with a T1 Ratio of 4% or greater is considered adequately capitalized.

Tangible Common Equity Ratio ("TCE Ratio") = TCE / Risk-Adjusted Assets.

TCE is a more conservative measure of capital adequacy. Only capital that is "real" and possesses the last claim on the assets of a company can be counted as TCE. It can be thought of as the amount that would be left over if the bank were dissolved and all creditors and higher levels of stock, such as preferred stock, were paid off. TCE is the highest "quality" of capital in the sense of providing a buffer against loss by claimants on the bank. TCE is used in calculating the **tangible common equity ratio ("TCE Ratio")** which determines what percentage of a bank's total assets is categorized as TCE — the higher the percentage, the better it is for the bank. Preferred stock is an example of capital that is counted in T1, but not in TCE.

Why the Selection of Capital Measure Matters

Through TARP, Treasury makes capital investments in banks. The type of security it receives in return for these capital investments depends on the type of bank capital it wishes to support. The difference between alternative definitions of capital is important.

Under CPP, TARP purchased preferred stock, which is included in tier one capital. Going forward, however, under CAP, investments would involve convertible preferred stock. TARP will purchase "convertible" preferred stock, which is effectively common stock, a measure more targeted to TCE.

The stress tests for bank holding companies appear to be targeting more than simply the traditional tier one capital. According to FDIC, regulators will be examining "the composition, level and quality of capital; the ability of the institution to raise additional common stock and other forms of capital in the market; and other risks that are not fully captured in regulatory capital calculations."[92]

In this context, it is clear that the Citigroup exchange offer, which can convert up to $25 billion in Treasury's preferred stock to common stock, had the primary effect of increasing Citigroup's TCE ratio. See the "Institution-Specific Assistance" portion of Section 2 for a detailed description of the Citigroup exchange offer. A comparison of Citigroup's T1 Ratio and TCE Ratio, before and after the exchange, demonstrates this difference. See Table 2.19.

Derivative Instruments: Investments that are valued by reference to the values of other investments. Examples include options and credit default swaps.

As Treasury of cials have recognized, the massive infusion of preferred shares as a result of its CPP investments have altered analysts' views of tier one capital. Analysts have begun to view Treasury's preferred shares investment more as debt than traditional tier one capital, causing investors and analysts to discount tier one capital as a measure and look more closely at TCE as a measure of a bank's health.

When a Bank Gets Into Trouble

The balance sheet problems affecting many banks during the current credit crisis stemmed from losses from two of their primary types of assets. First, many banks saw the value of their loan portfolios (mortgages, home equity, or other loans) decline as some of their loan customers defaulted on their debts. Second, many banks owned MBS or **derivative instruments** that ultimately took their value from mortgages, which also dropped in value as homeowners began defaulting on their mortgage payments.

When a bank forecloses on a property, it must be able to re-sell the property to recover as much as possible of the loan value. Given the nationwide decline in real estate values, many banks faced losing not only the stream of income they had enjoyed from the loans as the homeowner made payments on the mortgage, but also faced being forced to accept losses of cially on the difference in the value of the loan and the value they would get in re-selling the property in a depressed market. Similarly, the market for the mortgage-related securities had also declined and many of the securities the banks held could no longer be sold in the open market for more than a fraction of what they had paid.

These developments affected the banks' balance sheets in various ways. First, the decline of the value of the banks' loan portfolios meant a decline in the value of their assets. As losses occurred, they were subtracted from equity, which resulted in a decline in the banks' tier one capital.

Assuming that the example bank, Sample Bank, suffered similar losses, Table 2.20 demonstrates the deterioration of its balance sheet in three places: the Securities line on the

Assets side, the Loans line on the Assets side, and the Shareholders' Equity line on the Liabilities & Equity side. The shareholders' equity goes down by the amount of the total losses because of the fundamental equation (shareholders' equity = assets – liabilities). In other words, the balance sheet must "balance" by matching any reduction in assets with a reduction in shareholders' equity. The loss in Sample Bank's Securities category represents the decline of the MBS market and the decrease in the value of the bank's securities holdings. Further, if Sample Bank had a large number of subprime mortgages in its loan portfolio, and a portion of those borrowers had defaulted, it would have to **write down** the value of its Loan line. Supposing that the value of securities (the MBS) held by Sample Bank declined by 20%, and the value of its loan portfolio (mortgages) declined by 15%, we can observe that Sample Bank now has negative shareholders' equity, or is insolvent.

This sudden swing in shareholders' equity from +10% to –5% affects the key regulatory ratios — both T1 and TCE are now negative. Sample Bank must take some action to avoid being shut down by the regulators or forced into bankruptcy by its creditors.

Write Down: The act of recognizing the loss on an asset as permanent on a bank's balance sheet.

For more information on CPP eligibility criteria and process, refer to SIGTARP's Initial Report,Section 3: "TARP Implementation and Administration."

Table 2.19. Capital Adequacy Comparison — Effect of Citigroup Exchange Offer

(as of 12/31/08)	No Exchange	If Exchange
Tier One Capital (T1) Ratio	**11.9 %**	**11.9%**
Tangible Common Equity (TCE) Ratio	**3.0 %**	**8.1 %**

Source: Citigroup Inc., Form 8K, 3/10/2009, accessed 4/10/2009.

Table 2.20. Sample Bank — Deteriorating Balance Sheet

	Before		**After**	
Assets	**$ Million**	**% of Assets**	**$ Million**	**% of Assets**
Cash	$100	2%	$100	2%
Securities	1,000	20%	800	19%
Loans	3,500	70%	3,000	70%
Other Assets	400	8%	400	9%
TOTAL ASSETS	**$5,000**	**100%**	**$4,300**	**100%**
Liabilities & Equity	**$ Million**	**% of Liabilities & Equity**	**$ Million**	**% of Liabilities & Equity**
Deposits	$3,200	64%	$3,200	74%
Debt	1,300	26%	1,300	30%
Shareholder's Equity	500	10%	-200	-5%
TOTAL LIABILITIES & EQUITY	**$5,000**	**100%**	**$4,300**	**100%**

Note: Numbers affected by rounding. Values in red re ect changes in balance sheet.

Fixing the Problems

For the bank, taking action to improve its weakening balance sheet boils down to raising more capital. For example, it has to sell enough preferred or common stock (thereby increasing the asset of cash with what it receives from investors for the sale of stock, and therefore enjoy a corresponding increase in its shareholders' equity) to bring its capital ratios above the minimum requirements. By mid-2008, it became very hard for banks to sell bank stock, as prospective investors were concerned that not all of a bank's losses had yet been recognized.

There are other, less effective things a troubled bank can do. For example, the bank can reduce its assets (especially its risky ones) to improve the capital ratio. This is called "shrinking the balance sheet" which has some side effects for the bank, such as reducing the potential for profits. The problem with shrinking the balance sheet is an obvious one for policy makers; it reduces new lending because new loans require capital. As new loans decline, jobs and consumer activity may be adversely affected. A third option is for the bank to seek a merger with a stronger bank. This is an option only if the losses on the losing bank can be quantified and accounted for in the purchase price.

During this crisis, Treasury, through CPP, became the critical outside investor for some banks. It provided the funds needed to increase their capital.[93] This action increased tier one capital for the participating banks by increasing cash and shareholders' equity, thereby helping them to meet or improve their cushion over the risk-adjusted capital ratio.

Institution-Specific Assistance

As of March 31, 2009, the institution-specific programs accounted for $122.5 billion of total TARP funding, having increased $30 billion since SIGTARP's Initial Report.[94] This section provides updates to institution-specific assistance previously reported in SIGTARP's Initial Report, including modifications to existing agreements and any additional funding guidance. The institution-specific programs in SIGTARP's Initial Report included the Systemically Significant Failing Institutions ("SSFI"), Targeted Investment Program ("TIP"), Asset Guarantee Program ("AGP"), and the automotive programs; the automotive programs have since been expanded and are given their own discussion, "Automotive Industry Financing Program" later in this section. TARP institution-specific assistance is focused on three institutions: American International Group, Inc. ("AIG"), Citigroup Inc., and Bank of America Corp.

Figure 2.7 provides the status of TARP institution-specific assistance by institution and program as of March 31, 2009.

American International Group, Inc.

As of March 31, 2009, $70 billion in TARP funding has been allocated to AIG through the SSFI program. The initial $40 billion of TARP funds was used to purchase preferred stock in AIG,[95] and the remaining $30 billion has been committed to create an **equity capital**

facility for AIG in exchange for additional preferred shares.[96] Treasury and the Federal Reserve announced a restructuring of the Government's assistance to AIG on March 2, 2009. According to Treasury, the stated intention of the restructuring is to stabilize AIG and to enhance the company's **capital** and **liquidity** to facilitate the orderly **divestiture** of certain of the company's assets.[97]

According to Treasury, the restructuring plan offers a multi-part approach, which identifies and separates AIG's non-core businesses and provides protection for taxpayers in connection with this commitment of resources. The stated goal of Treasury and the Federal Reserve under the plan is to create an economically viable company for the repayment of taxpayer money as soon as possible,[98] largely from the sale of AIG's non-core businesses.[99]

For more information on the terms and conditions of the programs associated with institution-specific assistance, refer to SIGTARP's Initial Report, Section 3: "TARP Implementation and Administration."

Equity Capital Facility: An agreement between two parties under which one may require the other to make an equity investment.

Capital: Money invested in a company

Liquidity: The ability to convert an asset to cash quickly — characterized by a high level of trading activity.

Divestiture: Disposition or sale of an asset by a company.

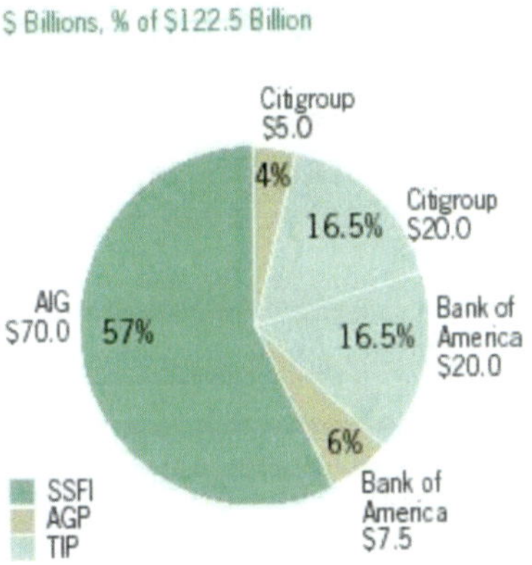

Note: Numbers affected by rounding. For purposes of this report, amounts in the *Transactions Report* are considered committed, and as of 3/31/2009, total $85.0 billion. AIG—SSFI includes an additional projection of $30.0 billion announced by Treasury and Federal Reserve on 3/2/2009. Bank of America—AGP is Treasury's projected guarantee of $7.5 billion announced by Treasury, FDIC, and Federal Reserve on 1/16/2009.

Sources: Treasury, *Transactions Report*, 3/31/2009. Treasury, "U.S. Treasury and Federal Reserve Board Announce Participation in AIG Restructuring Plan," 3/2/2009, accessed 3/4/2009. FDIC, "FDIC Press Release," 1/16/2009, accessed 1/23/2009.

Figure 2.7. Institution-Specific Commitments and Projections, By Participant, Cumulative

The restructuring plan involves the following three key steps:[100]

Preferred Equity Exchange: Treasury will exchange the $40 billion of preferred shares that it originally received under the SSFI program for new preferred shares. These new preferred shares will have revised terms that will more closely resemble those of common equity; these new shares will not receive dividend payments unless declared by AIG's board of directors. However, as mentioned in the following "AIG Preferred Equity Exchange" discussion, repeated failure to pay dividends could result in a change in AIG's governance.[101] The written agreement for the preferred equity exchange had not been finalized as of March 31, 2009.

Equity Capital Commitment: Treasury will create a new equity capital facility in which AIG will be allowed to receive up to $30 billion in return for preferred shares.[102] The written agreement had not been finalized as of March 31, 2009.

Federal Reserve Revolving Credit Facility: The Federal Reserve will make several modifications to the Revolving Credit Facility established in September 2008. The Revolving Credit Facility will be reduced by up to approximately $26 billion in exchange for preferred interests in two special purpose vehicles ("SPVs") created to hold all of the outstanding common stock of two life insurance holding company subsidiaries of AIG. In addition, the total amount available under the Revolving Credit Facility will be reduced from $60 billion to $25 billion. The interest rate payable under the Revolving Credit Facility will be modified by removing the existing fioor (3.5%) on the three-month London Interbank Offered Rate ("LIBOR").[103] As agreed to on September 22, 2008, an additional issuance of preferred stock representing a 77.9% equity interest in AIG was finalized on March 4, 2009. "As a result of the Transaction, a change in control of AIG has occurred"[104] as the 77.9% equity interest in preferred shares has been placed in an independent trust account for the sole benefit of the U.S. Government.[105]

AIG Preferred Equity Exchange

Under the proposed terms of the AIG Preferred Equity Exchange, the original preferred shares issued to Treasury on November 25, 2008, will be exchanged for new preferred shares. The conversion amount will be equal to the amount paid for the original preferred shares, plus any dividends unpaid to Treasury that have accrued since the November 25, 2008, agreement. The original preferred shares paid a 10% annual dividend (paid quarterly) to Treasury.[106] As of March 31, 2009, approximately $733 million in dividends have accrued and gone unpaid to Treasury.[107] The new preferred shares will have features more like common stock; Treasury will only receive dividends from AIG if and when the AIG board of directors, or a duly authorized committee, declares them.[108] In other words, under the original agreement, AIG was required to pay $4 billion a year to Treasury in dividends; under the new agreement, AIG will have no obligation to pay any dividends — but if it declares any dividends, it must pay the Government first. Corporate control provisions were preserved in the new agreement.

Should dividends (under the new agreement) not be paid for four dividend periods (need not be consecutive), Treasury will have the right to elect the greater of:[109]

two directors
number of directors (rounded up) equal to 20% of the total number of directors (currently there are 11 directors)

Once four consecutive dividend payments have been made, the Treasury- selected directors shall resign.[110] As of March 31, 2009, the terms of this proposed transaction have not been finalized. For more information on the original terms of AIG's SSFI agreement, refer to SIGTARP's Initial Report, Section 3: "TARP Implementation and Administration."

AIG Equity Capital Commitment

In addition to the preferred equity exchange, Treasury has announced that it will invest more equity into AIG. Treasury's stated intent is to provide AIG with ready access to capital in order to stabilize its business and/or lower its **leverage**. It will do this through a new equity facility with a five-year duration. Under the terms of the equity facility, AIG will be able to sell to Treasury additional preferred shares for up to $30 billion, as needed, upon the date of each drawdown. According to the term sheet, at the start date of the facility, Treasury will receive a warrant to purchase shares equal to 1% of AIG's issued and outstanding common stock. The warrant will have an initial **strike price** of $2.50, adjusted for future common share issuances.[111] The price of AIG's common stock was $1.00 as of March 31, 2009.[112]

Under the announced terms of the agreement, if AIG files for Chapter 11 Bankruptcy, it may not receive additional funds through the equity facility.[113] As of March 31, 2009, the terms of this announced agreement had not been finalized.

AIG Executive Compensation

On March 15, 2009, AIG paid out $165 million in retention bonuses to employees under one plan in its Financial Products Division. According to the Treasury Secretary, "this is the very division most culpable for the rapid deterioration of AIG."114 Treasury stated its recognition that AIG believed the employee bonus contracts, negotiated in April 2008, to be binding. Treasury stated that its lawyers concluded that it would be "legally difficult to prevent these contractually-mandated payments."[115]

Under the new capital restructuring plan, AIG must comply with stricter guidelines on executive compensation, including those yet to be finalized, and continue to comply with restrictions on expenses and lobbying included in the original SSFI agreement dated November 25, 2008.[116] The modified executive compensation guidelines include the most recent amendment to Section 111 of EESA that is contained in Section 7001 of ARRA.[117] Under ARRA, executive compensation provisions were amended to detail the number of employees that the more stringent guidelines apply to based on the institution's level of TARP funding, but do not apply to any employment contracts entered into prior to February

11, 2009; therefore, they do not apply to the AIG bonuses for its Financial Products Division.[118] As of March 31, 2009, the Treasury Secretary is reportedly working with the Department of Justice to determine "what avenues are available by which the U.S. Government can recoup the $165 million in bonuses paid to AIG Financial Products Division employees."[119]

For more information on the mechanics of warrants, refer to SIGTARP's Initial Report, Section 2: "TARP Overview."

Leverage: The ratio of a company's debt to its equity.

Strike Price: The stated price per share for which underlying stock may be purchased by the option holder upon exercise of the option contract.

For more information on the terms and conditions of the programs associated with Citigroup Inc., refer to SIGTARP's Initial Report, Section 3: "TARP Implementation and Administration."

ARRA legislation requires the Treasury Secretary to publish regulations that implement the executive compensation requirements within Section 7001 of ARRA.[120] As of March 31, 2009, Treasury had not yet released regulations implementing Section 7001. For more information on the amended executive compensation restrictions and SIGTARP's announced audit on executive compensation oversight, refer to "Executive Compensation" later in this section.

Citigroup Inc.

Treasury funding to Citigroup has been pursuant to the following three programs: the Capital Purchase Program ("CPP"), the Targeted Investment Program ("TIP"), and the Asset Guarantee Program ("AGP"). Since SIGTARP's Initial Report, Treasury has made no further funding to Citigroup. According to Treasury, Citigroup is still considered a systemically significant institution, and the AGP agreements — which protect Citigroup against future losses on an asset pool of $301 billion — are "part of a broader effort to support Citigroup as the company executes its restructuring plans."[121] The funding received by Citigroup, as of March 31, 2009, includes:[122]

Capital Purchase Program: $25 billion on October 28, 2008
Targeted Investment Program: $20 billion on December 31, 2008
Asset Guarantee Program: $5 billion loss protection on January 15, 2009

Citigroup Use of Funds Report

Under its TIP agreement, based on SIGTARP's recommendation, Citigroup has a number of requirements including the submission of a quarterly report to Treasury outlining the following information:[123]

how it has used TARP funds
the implementation of internal controls for its use of TARP funds
Citigroup's compliance or non-compliance with restrictions on use of its TARP funds

Citigroup must submit this quarterly report, entitled "TARP Progress Report" until it has accounted for all of its TARP funds.

On February 3, 2009, Citigroup released its "TARP Progress Report for Fourth Quarter 2008." This report describes the actions and results of Citigroup's Special TARP Committee (the "Committee"), made up of senior Citigroup executives for the purpose of reviewing and approving the use of TARP capital. According to the report, the Committee has authorized initiatives to deploy $36.5 billion of TARP funds across various areas in order to expand credit.[124] This represents approximately 81% of the $45 billion in cash that Citigroup received under TARP as of March 31, 2009.

According to the report, Citigroup plans to increase lines of credit in areas such as residential mortgages, business and personal loans, student loans, credit card lending, and corporate loan activity.[125] Details provided by Citigroup on the distributions of the $36.5 billion authorized by the Committee are shown in Figure 2.8.

Status of Citigroup Funds

As of March 31, 2009, Citigroup has been allocated $45 billion in TARP funding including $25 billion in connection with CPP and $20 billion in connection with TIP.[126] Treasury also allocated $5 billion of TARP funds to the AGP "**ring-fencing**" of approximately $301 billion of Citigroup assets, but this amount has not yet been disbursed.[127] A more detailed discussion on ring-fencing occurs later in this section. Although Treasury has not allocated additional funds to Citigroup since SIGTARP's Initial Report, Treasury's investments are expected to be modified. Potential modifications include an **exchange** of a portion of Citigroup's preferred shares held by Treasury as part of CPP funding, and an increased seniority of TIP and AGP preferred shares.[128]

Citigroup's Exchange Offering

On February 27, 2009, Citigroup requested that Treasury participate in an offer to exchange preferred shares for common equity in an effort to strengthen its capital structure and, in particular, its tangible common equity.[129] For more details about a bank's capital structure, see the "TARP Tutorial: Capital Structure" earlier in this section. Citigroup offered the exchange to both its private and public preferred shareholders. Citigroup would exchange up to $27.5 billion of its non-Treasury held preferred securities to common equity. Treasury announced it would match up to $25 billion of non-Treasury preferred securities by exchanging its own preferred stock acquired under CPP, equaling a maximum total conversion, subject to shareholder approval, of $52.5 billion.[130]

On March 19, 2009, Citigroup announced that it had entered into agreements with a portion of its non-Treasury holders of preferred stock. The agreements, so far, provide for the exchange of a total of $12.5 billion in preferred stock that was originally issued in January 2008. As of March 31, 2009, Citigroup is in the process of finalizing definitive documentation of this transaction.[131] The effect of the announced transaction would not increase the total dollar amount of Treasury's investment in Citigroup;[132] however, it would convert up to $25 billion of Treasury's preferred shares to common equity. If all $25 billion of Treasury shares were exchanged, it would increase the percentage of Treasury ownership to "approximately 36% of Citigroup's outstanding common stock."[133] The exchange would also eliminate the 5% dividend on those shares converted by Treasury, which would equal up to $1.25 billion per year.

Ring-fencing: Segregating assets from the rest of a financial institution, often so that the assets' problems can be addressed in isolation.

Exchange: In reference to Citigroup agreement, taking one type of stock (*i.e.*, preferred) and converting it at a specific rate to another type of stock (*i.e.*, common).

Trust Preferred Security: A security that has both equity and debt characteristics. Trust Preferred Security is created by establishing a trust and issuing debt to the new trust. A company would create a trust preferred security to realize tax benefits, since the trust is tax deductible.

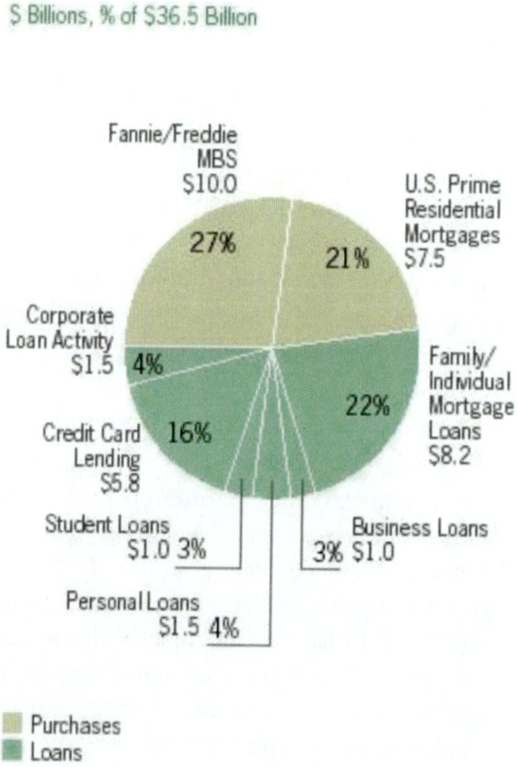

Note: Numbers affected by rounding. MBS = mortgage-backed securities.

Source: Citigroup Inc., "What Citi is Doing to Expand the Flow of Credit, Support Homeowners and Help the U.S. Economy, TARP Progress Report for Fourth Quarter 2008," 2/3/2009, accessed 2/24/2009.

Figure 2.8. Citigroup Use and Intended Use of Funds.

Table 2.21. Proposed Citigroup Exchange of Treasury's CPP Investment

Details	Preferred Shares[a]	Common Shares at Announced Exchange Rate[b]
# of shares	25 million	7,692,307,692 ($25 billion / $3.25)
$ per share	$1,000	$3.25
Total Value	$25 billion	$25 billion
Dividends	$1.25 billion/year (5% annually)	Only if declared by Citigroup's Board of Directors

Note: Numbers are affected by rounding. Agreements and terms have not been = nalized.

Sources:

[a] Citigroup Inc., "Securities Purchase Agreement," 10/28/2008.

[b] Citigroup Inc., 8-K, 3/2/2009.

The $20 billion and $4 billion in preferred shares received under the TIP and AGP agreements, respectively, would be converted into a **trust preferred security** that has greater seniority than Treasury's original preferred shares. Treasury will still be entitled to receive dividends on these shares under the original agreements at 8% annually.[134]

Table 2.21 details an example of Treasury's exchange of Citigroup shares.

Asset Guarantee Program for Citigroup

Under the Asset Guarantee Program, Treasury, FDIC, and the Federal Reserve provided certain loss protections with respect to $301 billion of troubled assets held by Citigroup.[135] In return for the guarantees provided by Treasury and FDIC, the U.S. Government collected $7 billion in premiums in the form of preferred stock plus warrants of common stock; $4 billion of the preferred shares and all the warrants were received by Treasury.[136] For more information on the contractual terms of the preferred shares, refer to SIGTARP's Initial Report, Section 3: "TARP Implementation and Administration." The AGP agreement calls for segregating or "ring-fencing" of the asset pool and lays out which assets will be covered, the loss considerations, and management of the asset pool.

Citigroup Ring-Fencing

In banking, "ring-fencing" refers to the separation of certain assets within a finan- cial institution. This separation does not physically remove the assets from the institution's balance sheet. Instead, the specific assets are identified and tracked for special controls on management, accounting, and measures to contain any losses on those assets.

Ring-fences are often confused with the concept of a "**bad bank**," whereby a bank accumulates its problem loans (or other troubled assets) into a separate entity (the bad bank). In the bad-bank process, the problem assets are taken off the books of the original bank, which is what distinguishes a bad bank from a ring-fence. Having placed its problems into a separate company, management of the original bank will now find it much easier to raise new capital from potential investors. This is because investors will have comfort that they are protected from unexpected future losses on the hard-to-value assets now held by the bad bank.

The AGP agreement with Citigroup creates a ring-fence around $301 billion of Citigroup's assets ("**covered assets**"). These assets are not physically removed from

Citigroup's balance sheet, and therefore do not constitute a "bad bank." The Federal Reserve notes that Citigroup assets "will remain on the books of the institution but will be appropriately 'ring-fenced.'"[137] The covered assets are retained throughout the bank's operating units and are identified for tracking purposes.[138]

Although the covered assets are not removed from Citigroup's balance sheet, investor exposure to future losses on the troubled assets is limited because Treasury, FDIC, and the Federal Reserve have agreed to provide certain loss protections after the first $39.5 billion in losses. Citigroup will then absorb 10% of all additional losses on the pool of assets, and Treasury and FDIC will absorb 90% of further losses up to $5 billion and $10 billion, respectively. At that point, should any further losses be incurred, the Federal Reserve will provide **non-recourse loans** collateralized by these assets with the same 90%/1 0% loss-sharing provision.[139]

Bad Bank: An entity (the "bad bank") that is legally separated from the bank that created it (the "good bank") and into which are placed problem loans (or other troubled assets). Usually created by banks to clean up their balance sheets.

Covered Asset: An asset owned by Citigroup or any of its subsidiaries that is included in the ring-fence.

Non-Recourse Loan: A secured loan whereby the borrower is relieved of the obligation to repay the loan upon the surrender of the collateral.

Equity Security: Any stock or similar security that represents ownership (or the right to purchase ownership) in an organization or asset.

Covered Assets Criteria

Only certain assets on Citigroup's books are eligible for inclusion in the ring-fence. The criteria to determine covered assets are as follows:[140]

The asset must have been issued or originated prior to March 14, 2008, as mandated by EESA.

Equity securities, and securities whose value is derived by reference to equity securities, are excluded.

Foreign assets, subject to limited allowances per the Master Agreement, are excluded (*i.e.,* only U.S. entities and securities are eligible).

Assets guaranteed by any Governmental authority (outside of the Master Agreement) are excluded.

The first announcement regarding the loss protections, dated November 23, 2008, sized the asset pool at a total of $306 billion.[141] After excluding assets not permitted under EESA, the final agreed-upon portfolio was reduced to $301 billion.[142]

From the Master Agreement date of January 15, 2009, Citigroup has 90 days to prepare and deliver a finalized listing of covered assets ("**Schedule A**") to all relevant U.S. Government parties. The Master Agreement includes a preliminary Schedule A, which is a summary of the $301 billion ring-fenced assets. The finalized Schedule A will detail the value for asset categories, reclassifications or corrections to original **baseline values**, and adjustments for **market values**. The Schedule A may be updated from time to time as Citigroup and the U.S. Government mutually agree.[143] The U.S. Government parties (Treasury, FDIC, and the Federal Reserve) have 120 days after the receipt of the finalized Schedule A to object to covered assets that do not meet the covered asset criteria, are improperly categorized, or are improperly baseline valued.[144]

Schedule A: Listing of the covered assets.

Baseline Value: The value of each covered asset on November 21, 2008. For mark-to-market assets, it is the fair market value, and for accrual assets, it is the unpaid principal balance.

Market Value: The price at which an asset can be sold to a willing buyer by a willing seller, in a reasonable amount of time.

Mark-to-Market Assets: An asset being assigned a value based upon the market value as of a specific date.

Accrual Assets: In the context of the AGP agreements, accrual assets are those that are held on the bank's books at accrued value (*i.e.*, earned but not necessarily received), as opposed to "mark-tomarket" value.

The pool of covered assets is divided into two groups for valuation purposes: **mark-to-market** assets and **accrual assets**. The mark-to-market assets are valued at their current market value; those assets totaled $24.63 billion as of November 21, 2008. [145] Accrual assets are valued based on the unpaid principal of each asset, and, together, accounted for $264.96 billion of the covered assets as of November 21, 2008.[146] Blackrock Inc., a financial management company, has been retained by the Federal Reserve to conduct the valuation and pricing of assets.[147] Figure 2.9 shows the breakdown of the types of covered assets included in mark-to-market asset and accrual asset categories.

Management/Administration of the Covered Assets

Citigroup is responsible for establishing a **senior oversight committee ("SOC")**, consisting of senior members of Citigroup's management who are acceptable to U.S. Government parties. SOC responsibilities include, but are not limited to:[148]

- reviewing and approving the overall business and governance strategy for the covered assets
- reviewing a plan for communication with key stakeholders (*i.e.,* board of directors, shareholders, and the U.S. Government) prepared by the Executive Team
- reviewing strategic responses developed by the Executive Team or the business units
- monitoring compliance

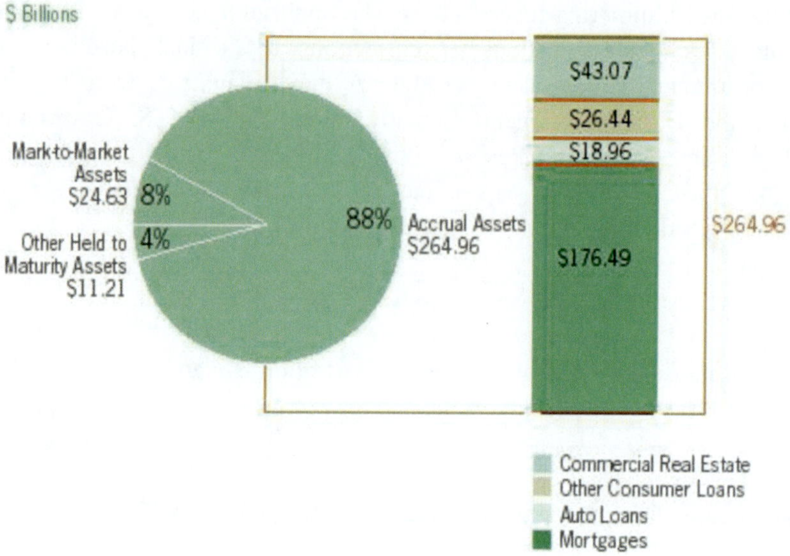

Note: Numbers affected by rounding.
Source: Citigroup Inc., Master Agreement, "Schedule A," 1/15/2009.

Figure 2.9. Citigroup's Ring-Fenced Assets

Additionally, Citigroup has appointed a "Covered Asset CEO," a Citigroup employee. The appointment was subject to approval by the SOC and U.S. Government parties. The Covered Asset CEO is responsible for management and oversight of the covered assets. The Covered Asset CEO reports to the SOC and will be the primary point of contact for the U.S. Government parties.[149] The SOC is responsible for establishing any bonus or incentive components for the Covered Asset CEO. In turn, the Covered Asset CEO is responsible for setting bonus and incentives for the other members of the Executive Team and appropriate portfolio managers. All compensation packages are subject to review and approval by the SOC and the U.S. Government parties.[150] The governance structure for the covered assets is detailed in Figure 2.10.

Senior Oversight Committee ("SOC"): Consists of Citigroup's Chief Financial Officer, Chief Risk Officer, General Counsel, Controller, Chief Accounting Officer, and the Treasurer.

The Covered Asset CEO is supported by the Executive Team, comprising representatives of Citigroup business units, finance, risk, and legal functions. These representatives are to commit substantial time to the management oversight of the covered assets. Each Executive Team representative will manage the covered assets (including monitoring of the performance of the covered assets, modifying processes and procedures as needed, and ensuring compliance by the portfolio managers) from their relevant business unit. Incentives and compensation guidelines, based on the performance of the covered assets, are to be established and overseen by the SOC and Covered Asset CEO, with U.S. Government parties' review and approval.[151]

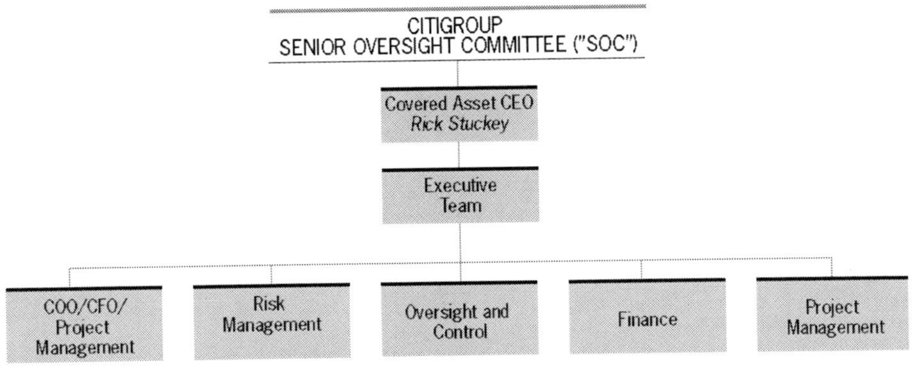

Source: Treasury, response to SIGTARP data call, 4/4/2009.

Figure 2.10. Covered Asset Governance Structure

According to the Master Agreement, the management, administration, and oversight of the covered assets will remain in control of Citigroup. However, the U.S. Government can assume certain management responsibilities over the assets once certain levels of losses are suffered. Specifically, at any time when losses in excess of $19 billion are reached, the U.S. Government parties reserve the right to take actions which include, but are not limited to:[152]

imposing increased reporting, communication, or audit requirements
appointing one or more representatives of the U.S. Government parties as voting members of the SOC
reviewing/revising compensation guidelines

Net Loss: Net loss occurs when total expenses exceed total revenues.

Realized Losses: Loss realized by an investor on a security after it has been finally sold and the costs associated with the security exceed the benefits of the holding.

Impaired: Decrease of value in an asset due to long-term credit deterioration or temporary market disruption.

At any time that **net losses** incurred are in excess of $27 billion, the U.S. Government parties have the right to change the asset manager for all or part of the covered assets. It may also change the fundamental business objective of Citigroup and require Citigroup to provide a business plan re flecting changes in management and business strategy with respect to the covered assets acceptable to the U.S. Government parties.[153]

Determining Covered Losses

At the end of each calendar quarter, Citigroup will calculate its actual losses on the covered assets. The schedule in Figure 2.11 is used to determine if a loss claim is to be paid, and by which agency.[154]

Only **realized losses** are covered under AGP, not "mark-to-market" fluctuations in value. That is, there has to have been some event that caused an actual loss to be incurred. For example, if Citigroup sells an asset at a loss, the loss portion is eligible for coverage. In addition, if an actuary, appraiser, or other valuation expert determines that an asset's value has been **impaired** in such a way that it results in a write-down of the value on Citigroup's books, the drop in value will be eligible for a claim.[155] Variations in asset value that are not realized in these fashions will not create losses.

The definition of "loss" is a net loss concept. Net loss is calculated by accounting for the effects of both gains and losses from across a ring-fence entity, adding provisions for fees and costs of workouts, and any other permanent valuation changes. The net loss is calculated on a quarterly basis. For example, if asset A is sold for a loss of $6, but asset B is sold for a $4 pro t, the net loss on these two assets is $2.

Over time, the potential liability of Treasury, FDIC, and the Federal Reserve may decline as Citigroup experiences excess gains and recoveries on covered assets, and as covered assets progress to maturity. A reduction in coverage could also occur if losses are deemed to be due to the failure of Citigroup to manage and service the covered assets in compliance with the terms of the "Governance and Asset Management Guidelines" set forth in the Master Agreement.[156]

Citigroup is generally prohibited from exchanging assets from its own portfolio in and out of the covered assets pool, but may do so under strict rules regarding equivalent valuation and trading.[157] As an example, two assets that have similar collateral and similar market values may be swapped with the approval of U.S Government parties.

According to Treasury, estimated losses on the ring-fence portfolio through December 31, 2008, were approximately $900 million. Information on losses incurred after December 31, 2008, has not yet been received.[158]

For more information on the guarantees and loss protections to Citigroup, refer to SIGTARP's Initial Report, Section 3: "TARP Implementation and Administration."

$ BILLIONS

	Loss 1	Loss 2	Loss 3	Non-recourse Loan	**Total**
0	$39.5	$45.1	$56.2		$301
Citigroup	$39.5	$0.6	$1.1	$24.5	**$65.7**
Treasury	—	$5.0	—	—	**$5.0**
FDIC	—	—	$10.0	—	**$10.0**
Federal Reserve	—	—	—	$220.4	**$220.4**
	$39.5	**$5.6**	**$11.1**	**$244.8**	**$301.0**

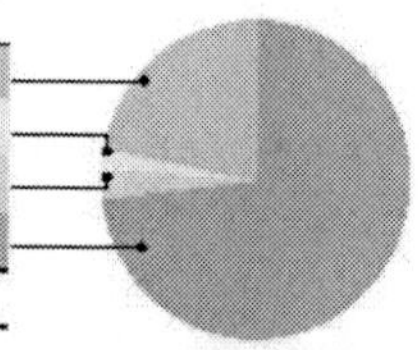

Note: Numbers affected by rounding. According to the Federal Reserve, Citigroup's loss position is "exclusive of reserves."

Sources: Citigroup Master Agreement, 1/15/2009; Federal Reserve, response to SIGTARP draft, 1/29/2009.

Figure 2.11. U.S. Government Guarantees And Loss Protections To Citigroup.

Bank of America Corporation

Since SIGTARP's Initial Report, Treasury has made no further funding to Bank of America beyond that of its CPP, TIP, and proposed AGP agreements. Bank of America has received $25 billion in CPP funding (which includes the $10 billion received with the acquisition of Merrill Lynch).[159] It has also received $20 billion in TIP funding and is projected to receive another $7.5 billion in loss protection from Treasury through AGP.[160] According to Treasury, the previously approved Asset Guarantee Program agreement with Bank of America is currently in the process of being finalized and will contain ring-fencing parameters similar to those detailed in the Citigroup Agreement.

The funding received by Bank of America as of March 31, 2009, includes:[161]

Capital Purchase Program: $15 billion on October 28, 2008
Capital Purchase Program: $10 billion on January 9, 2009
Targeted Investment Program: $20 billion on January 16, 2009

Additionally, Treasury announced Bank of America's participation in the Asset Guarantee Program:[162]

Asset Guarantee Program: $7.5 billion loss protection announced on January 16, 2009

Asset Guarantee Program for Bank of America

On January 16, 2009, Treasury, in partnership with FDIC and the Federal Reserve, indicated the U.S. Government's intention to provide certain loss protection for approximately $118 billion in troubled assets held by Bank of America.[163] In return for the guarantees provided by Treasury and FDIC, the U.S. Government will collect $4 billion in premiums in the form of preferred shares of stock and warrants. Bank of America will also be required to implement a mortgage modification program acceptable to the U.S. Government.[164] As of March 31, 2009, the AGP transaction had not closed, and the description herein is based solely on the intended terms announced by the parties. For more information on the contractual terms of the preferred shares, refer to SIGTARP's Initial Report, Section 3: "TARP Implementation and Administration."

Figure 2.12 shows the announced loss protections provided by the U.S. Government in return for the premiums paid. The preliminary terms of the AGP agreement call for ring-fencing of the asset pool. It also describes which assets will be covered and the loss considerations for those assets.

Description of Covered Assets

According to Bank of America's Annual Report released on February 27, 2009, the asset pool of $118 billion is projected to include approximately $81 billion of **derivative assets** and $37 billion of other financial assets. Assets expected to be covered may generally include pre-market disruption assets (*i.e.*, originated prior to September 30, 2007) and the majority are assets added to Bank of America's books as a result of the acquisition of Merrill Lynch. Types of assets expected in the asset pool may include:[165]

$ BILLIONS

	Loss 1 ▶	Loss 2 ▶	Non-recourse Loan	Total
0	$10.0	$21.1		$118.0
Bank of America	$10.0	$1.1	$9.7	**$20.8**
Treasury	—	$7.5	—	**$7.5**
FDIC	—	$2.5	—	**$2.5**
Federal Reserve	—	—	$87.2	**$87.2**
	$10.0	**$11.1**	**$96.9**	**$118.0**

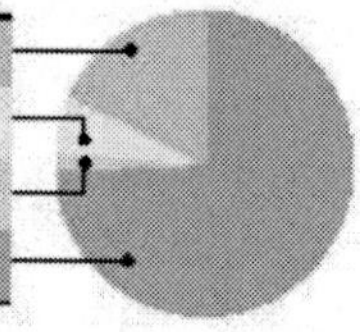

Note: Numbers affected by rounding. The details in this graphic are based on preliminary terms announced by Treasury, the Federal Reserve, and FDIC on 1/16/2009.

Sources: FDIC, "FDIC Press Release," 1/16/2009, accessed 1/23/2009; Bank of America AGP Agreement, "Summary of Terms, Eligible Asset Guarantee," 1/15/2009.

Figure 2.12. Announced U.S. Government Guarantees and Loss Protections to Bank of America

leveraged and commercial real estate loans
collateralized debt obligations ("CDOs")
financial guarantor counterparty exposure
trading counterparty exposure
investment securities

Although an agreement with Bank of America has not been reached, it is expected that assets excluded will be generally similar to those excluded in the Citigroup agreement, other than certain foreign assets that would have not been allowable under the Citigroup agreement, but may be permitted for Bank of America.[166] As of March 31, 2009, the AGP agreement with Bank of America had not been finalized.

Derivative Asset: An asset whose stated value or cash flow is determined by reference to the value or cash flow of another asset (the "underlying asset").

For more information on the guarantees and loss protections to Bank of America, refer to SIGTARP's Initial Report, Section 3: "TARP Implementation and Administration."

The Automotive Industry Financing Program

The assistance provided by Treasury to the U.S. automotive industry comes under the Automotive Industry Financing Program ("AIFP"); the stated objective of AIFP is to prevent a significant disruption of the American automotive industry that could pose a systemic risk to financial market stability and have a negative effect on the economy of the United States.[167] The program requires participating institutions (General Motors Corporation ("GM"); Chrysler Holding LLC ("Chrysler"); GMAC LLC ("GMAC"); and Chrysler

Financial Services Americas LLC ("Chrysler Financial")) to implement **restructuring plans** that will achieve long-term viability, and to adhere to executive compensation standards and other measures designed to protect the taxpayers' interests, including limits on the institution's expenditures and other corporate governance requirements.

On December 19, 2008, Treasury created AIFP, and, on December 29, 2008, signed an agreement to provide assistance to GMAC, followed shortly by an agreement with GM signed on December 31, 2008. The agreement for assistance to Chrysler was signed on January 2, 2009, and to Chrysler Financial on January 16, 2009. TARP funding provided to each institution is illustrated in Figure 2.13. In order to receive assistance, the manufacturers were required to submit restructuring plans by February 17, 2009.

Recent Developments

Since the publication of SIGTARP's Initial Report, there have been several important developments relevant to TARP assistance to the automotive sector. As of March 31, 2009, key developments include:

Release of Restructuring Plans and Viability Determination. On February 17, 2009, both GM and Chrysler released their restructuring plans as required in their respective assistance agreements with Treasury. Treasury determined that the manufacturers had not met the threshold to assure their longterm viability. Treasury granted Chrysler a 30-day extension, until May 1, 2009, and GM a 60-day extension, until June 1, 2009, to resubmit their restructuring plans.

Creation of Presidential Task Force on the Auto Industry. On February 20, 2009, President Obama formed a committee, headed by the Treasury Secretary and the National Economic Council Director, to review issues related to the auto industry and provide recommendations.[168]

Initiation of Auto Supplier Support Program. On March 19, 2009, Treasury announced a program to support auto industry suppliers with up to $5 billion worth of receivables financing. As stated by Treasury, the objective of the program is to address concerns about the auto manufacturers' ability to make payment on parts they buy from their suppliers by providing Government-backed financing to suppliers.

Launch of Auto Warranty Commitment Program. On March 30, 2009, the Administration announced the creation of a warranty commitment program that guarantees consumer warranty obligations on GM and Chrysler vehicles purchased during the restructuring period. Treasury preliminarily discussed potential funding for the Auto Warranty Commitment Program of up to an estimated $1.25 billion.[169]

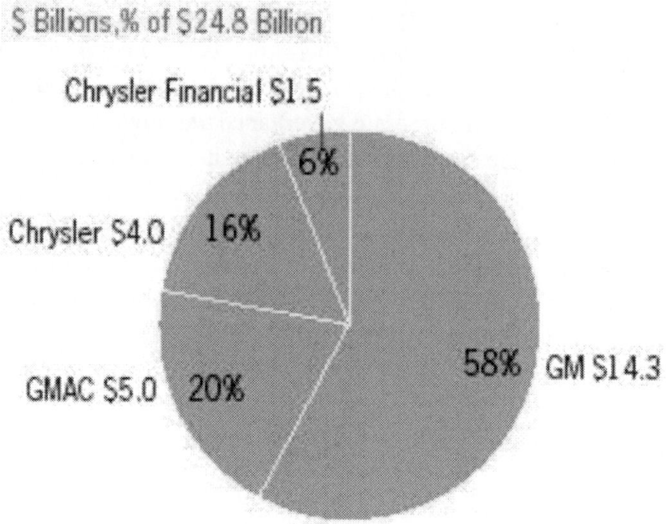

Note: Numbers affected by rounding. As of 3/31/2009. On 3/17/2009, Chrysler Financial made its first principal repayment in the amount of $3.5 million.
Sources: Treasury, Transactions Report, 4/2/2009; Treasury, response to SIGTARP data call, 4/9/2009.

Figure 2.13 AIFP Expenditures by Participant, Cumulative

Presidential Task Force on the Auto Industry

Since SIGTARP's Initial Report, the Administration created a Presidential Task Force on the Auto Industry ("Task Force"), which comprises the heads of several Federal departments and agencies. The Task Force, of cially introduced on February 20, 2009, is headed by the Treasury Secretary and the National Economic Council Director and is responsible for, among other things, coordinating the Administration's response to the restructuring plans submitted by GM and Chrysler.[170] The President named Ron Bloom as Senior Advisor on Auto Issues at Treasury and Steven Rattner as Counselor to the Treasury Secretary to lead Treasury's efforts with regard to the automotive sector bailout.[171] The two will act as day-to-day co-leaders of the Task Force. In addition, on March 30, 2009, Edward Montgomery was appointed the Director of Recovery for Auto Workers and Communities and will work to facilitate economic recovery efforts in areas affected by changes in the auto industry.[172] As of March 31, 2009, the Treasury Secretary was serving as the of cial **President's Designee** until a permanent appointment could be made. The Task Force structure is outlined in Figure 2.14.

The Task Force held its initial meeting on February 20, 2009, to review the restructuring plans of GM and Chrysler. The participants also reportedly discussed financial and operational restructuring, improving competitiveness of wage and benefit structures, and progress toward creating clean, competitive cars. The members were tasked with performing additional analysis and forming initial recommendations in their areas of expertise for presentation at the next meeting. The Task Force members also have reviewed the auto manufacturers' progress reports and issued a report on the viability of both GM and Chrysler on March 30, 2009.

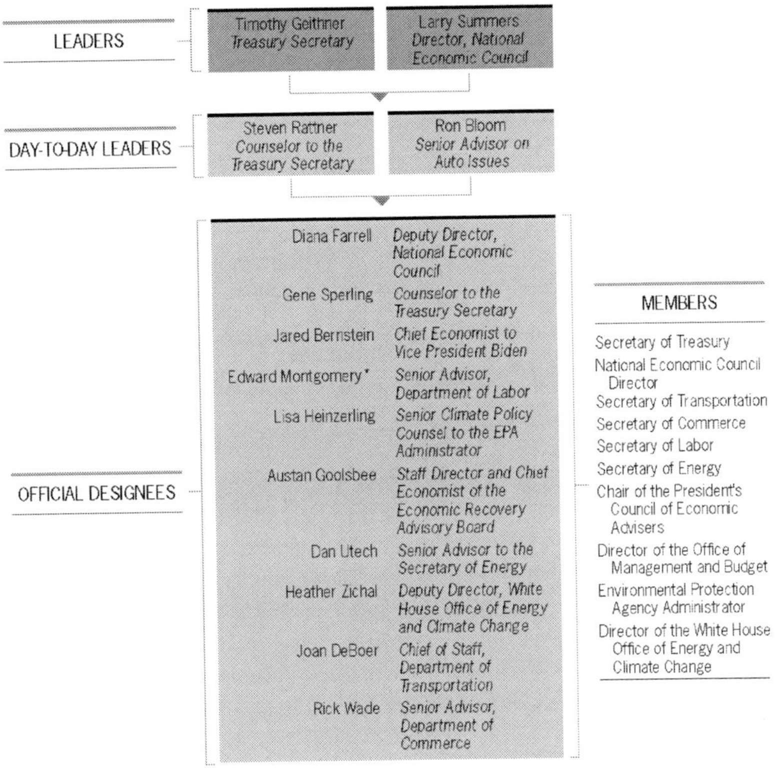

Note: *Edward Montgomery is also serving as the Director of Recovery for Auto Workers and Communities.

Sources: White House Press Release, "Geithner, Summers Convene Official Designees to Presidental Task Force on the Auto Industry," 2/20/2009, accessed 4/13/2009; White House Press Release, "Obama Administration New Path to Viability for GM & Chrysler," 3/30/2009, accessed 3/30/2009.

Figure 2.14 Presidential Task Force on the Auto Industry

President's Designee: One or more Officers from the Executive Branch designated by the President. For the purposes of AIFP, the President's Designee is the Treasury Secretary.

Reporting Requirements

The manufacturers' assistance agreements (virtually identical for both GM and Chrysler) contain a number of strict reporting requirements, ranging from developing viable restructuring plans to the ongoing reporting of key indicators such as liquidity and compliance with executive compensation limitations. Table 2.22 shows a summary of the reporting requirements, as well as the status of the auto makers' compliance. Both GM and Chrysler were given extensions from the original March 31, 2009, restructuring plan progress report due date.

Table 2.22. Reporting Requirements for Auto Makers: Status

Report Type	Due or Start Date	Frequency*
Restructuring Plan	2/17/2009	Once
Restructuring Plan Progress Report	3/31/2009	Once
Cash Forecast Status Report	1/12/2009	Weekly
Liquidity Status Report	1/12/2009	Bi-weekly
Expense Policy Certificate	After closing date	Monthly
Executive Compensation Compliance Certificate	After closing date	Quarterly
Financial Statements	As Reported	As Reported

Note: * Both GM and Chrysler submitted each report, statement, and certificate at the required frequency.

** Initial due date. On March 30, 2009, the date was extended 60 days for GM and 30 days for Chrysler.

Sources: GM Agreement, "Loan And Security Agreement By and Between The Borrower Listed on Appendix A As Borrower and The United States Department of Treasury as Lender Dated as of December 31, 2008." Chrysler Agreement, "Loan And Security Agreement By and Between The Borrower Listed on Appendix A As Borrower and The United States Department of Treasury as Lender Dated as of December 31, 2008;" White House Press Release, "Obama Administration New Path to Viability for GM & Chrysler," 3/30/2009, accessed 3/30/09; Treasury, response to SIGTARP data calls, 4/1/2009 and 4/8/2009.

General Motors Corporation

The key developments relating to Treasury assistance to GM since the issuance of SIGTARP's Initial Report include the following:

release of restructuring plan and viability determination
issuance of the 2008 10-K report

For more information on the terms and conditions of both the GM and Chrysler agreements, refer to SIGTARP's Initial Report, Section 3: "TARP Implementation and Administration."

Restructuring Plan and Viability Determination

The GM restructuring plan, issued on February 17, 2009, attempts to address the key requirements set forth in the Loan and Security Agreement ("LSA") of December 31, 2008. On March 30, 2009, the Treasury Secretary, as the President's Designee, determined that GM had not met the requirements of its LSA, because its restructuring plan failed to demonstrate that GM was on the path to long-term viability. The Treasury Secretary characterized GM's timeframe and industry growth rate assumptions as overly optimistic. He also noted that GM had failed to meet the following conditions of its LSA: reach an agreement on its labor modifications, receive the necessary approvals of the Voluntary Employees Beneficiary Association's ("VEBA's") modifications, and execute a required bond exchange offer.[173]

The Treasury Secretary acknowledged that, although GM has made significant progress on meeting its goals, more progress needs to be made in order for GM to become a viable long-term enterprise. GM was given 60 days to submit a revised plan to demonstrate progress for its long-term viability. If it fails to do so, GM's loan from the Government will become due 30 days thereafter, which will likely force GM into bankruptcy.[174] GM will submit a report on the progress of its restructuring on June 1, 2009. Table 2.23 provides an overview of the program details contained in the February 17, 2009, "General Motors Corporation 2009-2014 Restructuring Plan."

Additional Funding

As part of the February 17, 2009 restructuring plan, GM requested additional funds through a combination of secured term debt, a revolving line of credit, and preferred equity. For the baseline scenario, GM asked for up to $22.5 billion — consisting of an $18 billion investment, plus $4.5 billion in required incremental funding.[175] GM also ran a downside scenario in which GM would require an additional $7.5 billion of funding in the form of a secured revolver facility. This additional funding would bring GM's total Government assistance up to $30 billion.[176] Based on the revised submission date granted to GM, additional funding, estimated to be up to $5 billion, will be provided to GM during the 60-day extension.[177]

Table 2.23. Key Aspects of GM Restructuring Plan

Loan Agreement Requirement	February 17, 2009 Plan Details
Competitive Product Mix and Cost Structure	Reducing the number of brands, nameplates, and retail outlets to focus on "fewer, better" entries with more competitive dealer economics
	Focused on core brands of Chevrolet, Cadillac, Buick, and GMC, with Pontiac playing niche role
	A 25% reduction in number of nameplates by 2012
	Increased focus on cars and crossovers (81% of nameplates by 2014, up from low of 52% in 2004)
	Consolidating dealerships into fewer locations (25% reduction over 4 years)
	Increase use of global architectures (centralized planning, design, engineering, etc.) to develop 50% of GM's U.S. passenger cars by 2012, and approximately 90% by 2014
	Improvements in manufacturing productivity since 2000 show GM competitive with Toyota for North American vehicle assembly
	Lowered cost per vehicle by 26% from 2004 to 2008
	Suspended JOBS program, which provided full income and benet protection in lieu of layoff for indenite period
	Implemented voluntary incentivized attrition program for hourly workforce
	Reached tentative agreement on modifying labor agreement with United Auto Workers (UAW), awaiting ratication by union
	Plans in place to report competitiveness progress to U.S. Secretary of Labor to certify competitiveness relative to foreign manufacturers operation in United States

Table 2.23. (Continued)

Loan Agreement Requirement	February 17, 2009 Plan Details
Compliance with Federal Fuel Economy and Emission Requirements	In 2008, offered 20 models with greater than 30 MPG (highway), up from 8 in 2004; plans for 23 by 2012 and 33 by 2014
	Increased number of alternative fuel models from 6% of sales in 2004 to 17% in 2008; plan calls for increase to 61% in 2012 and 65% in 2014
	Increased number of hybrid and plug-in models from 2 in 2004 to 6 in 2008; plan calls for 14 in 2012 and 26 in 2014
	Stated intention to comply with 2007 Energy Independence and Security Act, which sets mileage targets for 2020
	Plan targets an average fuel efciency of 33.7 MPG for cars and 23.8 MPG for trucks by 2012, and 38.6 MPG for cars and 26.8 MPG for trucks by 2014
Domestic Manufacturer of "Advanced Technology" Vehicles	Increased investment in electric vehicles and lithium-ion battery development (1,000 engineers and technicians), including planned construction of new manufacturing facility for battery packs
	Submitted two proposals for advanced technology vehicle development to U.S. Department of Energy totaling $8.4 billion, with a third submitted on March 31, 2009
Rationalization of Costs, Capitalization, and Capacity	Accelerated efforts at labor cost reductions
	Specics relating to salaried cost competitiveness, restructuring VEBA obligations (VEBA is a tax-free health reimbursement arrangement where GM makes contributions into a trust account for employees and their families to use for eligible out-of-pocket healthcare costs and premiums)
	Negotiating plan with UAW to convert VEBA and retiree "pay as you go" healthcare obligations (present value of $20 billion) into plan whereby GM funds 50% of the obligations, and meets the other half of obligations by paying common stock into the VEBA trust
	Plan anticipates, if negotiations with UAW and regulatory review are successful, to complete conversion in May 2009
	Negotiating bond exchange where 2/3 or more of the unsecured bondholders would receive equity instead
	Plan contains letter of understanding, with anticipated bond exchange scheduled for late March
Financial Viability and Federal Loan Repayment	Signicant short-term negative cash ow for North American and global manufacturing (anticipated negative operating cash ow of $14 billion in 2009)
	Despite reduced sales expectations, plan anticipates positive operating cash ow by 2010 for North American operations, reaching approximately $7 billion by 2013-2014
	Globally, anticipate positive operating cash ow by 2012
	Baseline NPV analysis (assuming reduction of VEBA and conversion of 2/3 debt to equity), shows positive $5 billion – $14 billion; downside analysis is negative NPV; upside analysis is positive $30 billion – $41 billion
	Plan calls for total TARP funding to reach $22.5 billion by 2011, and repayment to begin in 2012
	Estimates for repayment of TARP funds average approximately $3 billion per year beginning 2012 with nal repayment in 2017

Source: General Motors, "General Motors Corporation Restructuring Plan 2009–2014," 2/17/2009.

Auditors' Opinion

Exhibit 23.a of GM's annual report on Securities and Exchange Commission ("SEC") Form 10-K filed on March 5, 2009, contains a declaration from the company's independent auditors that expresses "the existence of substantial doubt about the Corporation's ability to continue as a **going concern**."[178] The auditor provided a detailed statement regarding GM's recurring losses from operations, its stockholders' de cit, and its inability to generate sufficient cash to meet its obligations and sustain its operations. The statement re ects the auditors' concern that GM may not be able to overcome its losses and generate enough cash to stay in business.

Going Concern: Term used by auditors to refer to a company that is able to continue its operations into the foreseeable future.

GMAC LLC

The Federal Reserve approved an application for GMAC to reorganize as a bank holding company in December 2008. As part of this reorganization, the Federal Reserve required GMAC to increase capital by raising $7 billion of new equity. TARP funded $5 billion of this requirement through a purchase of senior preferred equity ("the stock purchase agreement"),[179] and GMAC conducted a rights offering for the remaining capital requirement. As part of this rights offering, GM and Cerberus Capital Management (GMAC's majority shareholder) entered into agreements to purchase new common equity.[180] Treasury loaned GM $884 million through TARP to participate in the GMAC rights offering, which closed on January 16, 2009. Under the terms of its loan agreement, Treasury has the right to exchange its loan for the shares purchased by GM in the rights offering.[181] As of GMAC's 8-K report issued on March 25, 2009, Treasury has not yet exercised that right.

As a condition of the Federal Reserve's approval of the bank holding company status, neither GM nor Cerberus was allowed to maintain a controlling interest in *GMAC. GM* was to reduce its holding to less than 10% and transfer that interest to an independent trust, to be approved by the Federal Reserve and Treasury.

GMAC was also required to make changes to its board of directors no later than March 24, 2009. The new board should include seven members: the GMAC CEO, one representative from FIM Holdings, LLC (a subsidiary of Cerberus), two directors appointed by a trust to be formed by Treasury, and three independent directors selected by the other directors. In addition, GM and FIM Holdings, LLC are each entitled to one non-voting observer on the board. In GMAC's 8-K filed on March 25, 2009, it states that several board members resigned or were removed on March 24, 2009, and lists the names of the new appointments: Stephen Feinberg (FIM Manager), Alvaro G. de Molina (the CEO), and Robert Hull and Samuel Ramsey (the CEO Appointments).

Key Reporting Requirements Performance

Under the stock purchase agreement, GMAC must comply with restrictions on stock repurchase, dividends, executive compensation, and expense policy requirements similar to those required for GM.[182]

Chrysler Holding LLC

Since SIGTARP's Initial Report, Chrysler released its restructuring plan on February 17, 2009, which was also found to be de cient.

Table 2.24. Key Aspects of Chrysler Restructuring Plan

Loan Agreement Requirement	February 17, 2009 Plan Details
Competitive Product Mix and Cost Structure	• Signed term sheet agreeing to work toward a 50% reduction in Chrysler's VEBA Cash Payment Liability (conditioned on satisfactory debt restructuring)
	• Shareholders (Cerberus and Daimler) will (i) relinquish their equity, and (ii) convert 100% of their 2nd lien debt for equity (conditioned on a viable plan and overall restructuring)
	• Signed tentative agreement with the UAW with respect to competitive level compensation, work-rules and severance provisions with U.S. transplants
	• Continue to work with UAW on funding the 2009 healthcare payments out of the existing VEBA, and to modify the terms of the settlement agreement to include the pension pass-through revision and future payment streams
Compliance with Federal Fuel Econ-omy and Emission Requirements	• For the 2009 model year, 73% of Chrysler's products offer improved fuel economy compared with 2008 models
	• An all-new family of fuel-efcient V-6 engines will join Chrysler's lineup in 2010
	• Over the past decade, built more than 1.5 million Flexible Fuel Vehicles capable of running on renewable, American-made ethanol fuel — (E85) — are committed to making 50% of Chrysler's new light-duty vehicles capable of using alternative fuels in 2012
	• In the proposed alliance with Fiat, would gain access to Fiat Group vehicle platforms that would complement current product portfolio and would accelerate the company's plans for the introduction of more environmentally friendly vehicles
	• Plans to launch additional small, fuel-efcient vehicles as well as a breakthrough family of all-electric and range-extended electric vehicles
	• Will have more than 66 ENVI advanced propulsion electric-drive vehicles in fleet service this year
	• First Chrysler electric-drive vehicle will be available for retail customers in 2010, with additional models in production by 2013
Rationalization of Cost, Capitalization and Capacity	• Reduced fixed cost by $3.8 billion (27%)
	• Reduced unit capacity by 1.3 million (35%)
	• Reduced headcount by 35,000 (41%)
	• Completed asset sales of $1.0 billion
	• Nameplate reduction by 7
	• Eliminated retiree life insurance
	• Suspended salary merits and bonuses
	• Suspended 401(k) match
	• Suspended tuition assistance program
	• Fully compliant with all Government executive compensation requirements
Financial Viability and Federal Loan Repayment	• A commitment from the UAW to restructure the VEBA
	• Wage and benet reductions and work-rule modications that are competitive with the U.S. transplant levels
	• Severance benet reductions, incl. elimination of "Jobs Bank"
	• Cerberus and Daimler have agreed to convert their 2nd lien debt
	• Has no public bonds, and has requested its three creditor groups to participate in reducing its debt and debt service by $5 billion

Source: Chrysler Restructuring Plan for Long-Term Viability, 2/17/2009.

Restructuring Plan and Viability Determination

Chrysler issued the "Restructuring Plan for Long-Term Viability" on February 17, 2009. On March 30, 2009, the Treasury Secretary, acting as the President's Designee, determined that Chrysler was not on target to meet the conditions laid out in the LSA dated December 31, 2008, based on its February 17, 2009, restructuring plan. He also determined that Chrysler would not be able to operate as a stand-alone entity in the long term and therefore must formalize a partnership with Fiat SpA ("Fiat") or another external entity to ensure its long-term viability. In addition to producing a non-viable restructuring plan, Chrysler was not able to obtain approval of the required labor modifications, did not receive the necessary approvals of its VEBA modifications, and had not commenced the required debt exchange offer.[183] Table 2.24 summarizes Chrysler's restructuring plan submission that was determined to be non-viable by Treasury.

On May 1, 2009, Chrysler is required to produce an update on its efforts to implement the restructuring plan, which, as a condition to receiving continued Government support, must include a formal partnership with Fiat or another company.[184] Chrysler will be provided with approximately $500 million in TARP funds while it attempts to complete its restructuring plan.[185]

Chrysler Financial Services LLC

As discussed in SIGTARP's Initial Report, Treasury announced on January 16, 2009, a loan under AIFP of up to $1.5 billion to Chrysler LB Receivables Trust ("Chrysler Trust"), a special purpose entity created by Chrysler Financial, to finance the extension of new consumer auto loans. Under the agreement, Chrysler Financial must comply with the executive compensation and corporate governance requirements of Section 111(b) of EESA, as well as enhanced restrictions on executive compensation including the need to reduce its bonus pool for Senior Executive Officers and Senior Employees by 40%.[186] Per the agreement with Treasury, Chrysler Financial has specific requirements related to the loan. In particular, interest, principal, and other proceeds from the repayment of the loan financed with TARP funds must be deposited into a collection account. Disbursements from Treasury to Chrysler Financial under this loan are shown in Table 2.25. Chrysler Financial made its first loan payment to the Government on March 17, 2009, repaying $3.5 million of its principal balance along with interest payments of approximately $932,000.[187]

According to Treasury of cials, Chrysler Financial sought additional funding from TARP beyond the initial $1.5 billion. In response, on April 7, 2009, Treasury asked Chrysler Financial to obtain waivers from the top 25 Chrysler Financial executives that would have waived legal claims against Treasury and Chrysler Financial resulting from the recent changes in executive compensation requirements for TARP recipients. Chrysler Financial's management, however, informed Treasury that it was unable to obtain waivers from all 25 executives, therefore the request for additional funding was denied.[188]

Table 2.25. Funds Disbursed to Chrysler Financial ($ Millions)

Date of Funding	Amount of Funding
1/16/2009	$100
1/22/2009	100
1/29/2009	100
2/5/2009	100
2/19/2009	–
2/26/2009	–
3/5/2009	250
3/12/2009	250
3/19/2009	150
3/26/2009	125
TOTAL	$1,175

Notes: Amount of funding is based on Bank of New York Mellon's Cash Activity Report.
Source: Treasury, response to SIGTARP data call, 4/6/2009.

Auto Supplier Support Program

On March 19, 2009, Treasury announced a new program aimed at supporting the suppliers to the U.S. auto manufacturing industry. The Auto Supplier Support Program ("ASSP") is a renewable one-year program that will provide up to $5 bil-lion in financing that is intended to benefit both suppliers and auto manufacturers. The program provides Government-backed protection to the suppliers against any failure by the manufacturers to make payments on goods that they receive from their suppliers, even if the manufacturers file for bankruptcy.[189]

Program Objectives

As of March 31, 2009, TARP has provided $24.8 billion of support to GM, Chrysler, GMAC, and Chrysler Financial. The auto suppliers, however, are confronted by their own challenges in the face of potentially bankrupt clients. First, the auto suppliers are concerned with whether they will continue to have customers (the auto manufacturers) to purchase their parts. These auto suppliers have developed symbiotic, long-term relationships with the auto manufacturers, frequently developing specialized parts for their use. Secondly, the auto suppliers are uncertain about whether they will receive payments for auto parts that are delivered to the auto manufacturers. On March 19, 2009, the Treasury Secretary stated:

> The Supplier Support Program will help stabilize a critical component of the American auto industry during the difficult period of restructuring that lies ahead. The program will provide supply companies with much needed access to liquidity to assist them in meeting payrolls and covering their expenses, while giving the domestic auto companies reliable access to the parts they need.[190]

Treasury stated that it intends to provide Government-backed financing to break the adverse credit cycle affecting the suppliers and the manufacturers by "giving suppliers the con dence they need to continue shipping parts, pay their employees and continue their operations." The program goals are as follows:[191]

enable access to the program for auto companies and suppliers (upon approval) for a fee based on qualifying terms
provide suppliers with Government-backed protection that money owed to them for products they ship will be paid no matter what happens to the auto manufacturer
permit suppliers to sell their **receivables** into the program at a modest discount, which provides access to funding to pay their workers and support ongoing operations

Receivables: Receivables are amounts of money owed to a company. They include claims to cash or other assets that arise from the sale of goods or services, or other provisions.

Background

The ASSP aims to address three areas of concern:[192]

Tightening Receivables: Because of uncertainties about the manufacturers' abilities to honor their obligations, suppliers are tightening receivables conditions, or the timing of when the manufacturers must pay for their parts. Normally, suppliers allow manufacturers 45 to 60 days to pay for the parts that they deliver. However, currently suppliers are shortening the time that they are giving the manufacturers to pay for the parts, at times requiring cash on delivery, or even advance payment. The suppliers are shortening these time periods because they are concerned that they will not be paid should the manufacturer declare bankruptcy.

Manufacturer Disruptions: More stringent payment terms complicate the manufacturers' attempts to implement their restructuring programs, because they would need significantly more cash on hand to make these payments so quickly. It also complicates their ability to produce automobiles on a normal schedule, which, through a self-reinforcing cycle, further endangers the suppliers.

Tightening Credit for Suppliers: Banks are less willing to extend credit based on the suppliers' receivables, because the banks are not certain that suppliers will be able to collect the funds in the event that the auto manufacturers are unable to pay.

Implementation

All domestic auto manufacturers have been invited to participate in the program, and, as of March 31, 2009, GM and Chrysler have accepted.[193] The auto manufacturer, not Treasury, selects which receivables from which suppliers it wishes to include in ASSP. According to Treasury of cials, once approved into the program, the supplier will pay a fee that is deducted from the purchase price to participate.[194]

Only receivables that are made with normal commercial terms are eligible for participation. Further, only receivables relating to products or services shipped after March 19, 2009, are eligible.[195] The program will not cover the entire industry; only certain receivables from certain suppliers, as selected by the manufacturer, will be included in the program.[196] The ASSP gives SIGTARP, GAO, and Treasury the same inspection rights and access to personnel and information for the suppliers as they currently have for the auto manufacturers. Treasury will also receive periodic certifications from the suppliers to ensure compliance with the program's requirements.[197]

Special Purpose Vehicle

The key operating component of the ASSP will be a special purpose vehicle ("SPV") that will be administered by Citigroup.[198] The participating auto manufacturer will provide an up-front cash commitment to the SPV (to be 5% of the total value of its program). TARP will then provide a loan to the SPV for the agreed-upon amount.[199]

The SPVs will be structured in a way that, in the event of a bankruptcy filing by the participating auto manufacturer, the SPV will be able to continue financing receivables while the company continues to operate under bankruptcy protection.[200]

Operations

Once included in the program, the suppliers will have the option either to allow a receivable covered by the program to run its normal payment term (45 to 60 days) or sell it to the SPV immediately at an additional discount. According to Treasury of cials, the supplier's choice has the following ramifications:

> If they choose the former option, and the auto manufacturer pays the receivable on its due date, the supplier receives that payment less a 2% discount and has essentially paid a fee to insure against default. If the manufacturer fails to pay the receivable, the TARP-funded SPV will fund the payment to the supplier.
>
> If the supplier chooses to sell the receivable before the payment is due, the TARP-funded SPV will buy the receivable at a 3% discount from the supplier, and then will seek payment from the auto manufacturer for the full amount originally due to the supplier.[201]

In either case, if the auto manufacturer fails to make the payment, the SPV (and, as direct result, the American taxpayer) will suffer a loss to the extent that accumulated fees from earlier transactions and the auto manufacturer's 5% contribution are not sufficient to make up the shortfall.[202]

For example, an auto manufacturer anticipates that it will purchase $1,000 worth of auto parts from a supplier this year, so it pays the SPV $50 (*e.g.*, 5% of $1,000) to participate in the program with the supplier. Thereafter, every time the auto company buys $100 worth of auto parts, it owes the supplier $100, giving the supplier a $100 receivable. The supplier can then place the receivable into the program. The supplier then has two possible ways to proceed based on its business needs:

Sell at a Discount: Sell the receivable to the SPV, immediately, at a 3% discount, $97 in this case. Although the supplier receives less than $100 for the goods sold, it has cash in hand for its operations. The SPV will then attempt to collect payment from the auto manufacturer.[203]

Collect on Due Date: Collect the receivable when it is due at a 2% discount, $98 in this case. The SPV will then attempt to collect the full amount from the auto manufacturer.[204]

Traditionally, the private sector has offered similar receivables financing services to suppliers in a variety of industries. However, due to the perceived riskiness of the U.S. auto industry, and the general tightness of credit, the interest rates for these loans have become too high for suppliers to afford. Treasury's stated objective of ASSP is to provide a temporary option to the affected industry and to transition back to the private sector as soon as practical.[205]

Executive Compensation

Although the auto manufacturers that participate in ASSP are bound by the EESA executive compensation limits, Treasury is not requiring the suppliers, even though they are obvious beneficiaries of the program, to be bound by the same restrictions.

Auto Warranty Commitment Program

On March 30, 2009, Treasury announced a new program designed to give consumers purchasing new GM and Chrysler automobiles the con dence that their warranties will be honored.[206] Treasury preliminarily discussed potential funding for the Auto Warranty Commitment Program of up to an estimated $1.1 billion.[207]

Restructuring Period: As it relates to the Auto Warranty Commitment Program, the restructuring period began on March 30, 2009, the announcement date of the Program, and ends the date that restructuring is complete.

Program Objectives

As noted previously, the Administration is working with both GM and Chrysler to develop new restructuring plans that comply with the requirements set out under AIFP. On March 30, 2009, both GM and Chrysler were granted 60- and 30-day extensions, respectively, for submitting revised restructuring plans to Treasury.[208] The Auto Warranty Commitment Program will help provide certainty to GM and Chrysler consumers that if they purchase a new car during the **restructuring period**,[209] their warranties will be valid, even if the manufacturer goes bankrupt.[210]

Background

The **warranty** program will cover all warranties on new vehicles purchased from GM and Chrysler from the date of the announcement, March 30, 2009. Their participation in the program is subject to the same executive compensation and corporate governance provisions that were established for AIFP. Specifically, the program will involve the following activities:[211]

- creation of a separate legal entity that is jointly funded by cash from the manufacturer and a loan from Treasury to pay for warranty expenses on new vehicles sold during the restructuring period
- appointment of a program administrator who will either arrange for the warranty liabilities to be assumed by a third party or use the cash to pay for covered warranty services in the event that an auto manufacturer fails

Implementation

Consumers who buy a new GM or Chrysler car during the covered periods are eligible for the Auto Warranty Commitment Program. Participation in the program is automatic; the consumer does not need to do anything to receive the program's benefits.

Auto manufacturers normally establish an accounting reserve, or funding allowance, for each new vehicle sold to cover expected warranty costs for each vehicle. According to Treasury, future warranty payments will be estimated from historical costs by vehicle type. The warranty program will be funded for 125% of projected future costs — 15% by auto manufacturers and 110% by Treasury; this cash will be placed into a "**special purpose company**" for paying warranty claims. The special purpose company will be able to continue paying warranty claims even if the auto manufacturer discontinues operations. In the event that the auto manufacturer discontinues operations, the program administrator and Treasury will attempt to transfer the warranty obligations to another entity, such as an insurance company, another auto manufacturer, or parts supplier that could fulfill the consumers' warranty claims. If the obligation cannot be transferred, the administrator will use the cash to pay covered warranty claims.[212]

Warranty: A service contract or agreement for a specific duration that is a guarantee of the integrity of a product and details the manufacturer's responsibility for the repair or replacement of defective parts.

Special Purpose Company: Term used interchangeably with special purpose vehicle ("SPV").

TARP TUTORIAL: SECURITIZATION

Securitization: A process whereby afinancial institution assembles pools of cash-ow-producing assets (such as loans) and then sells an interest in the cash fiows as securities to investors.

Subprime Borrowers: Refers to borrowers who do not qualify for prime interest rates because they exhibit one or more of the following characteristics: weakened credit histories typically characterized by payment delinquencies, previous charge-offs, judgments, or bankruptcies; low credit scores; high debt-burden ratios; or high loan-to-value ratios.

Securities Issuer: A separate legal entity that buys cash- flow-producing assets such as loans, pools them together, and sells portions of the pools of loans as securities. ncial institution buys pools of cash-flow-producing assets (such as loans) and then sells interests in the monthly payments by the borrowers as securities to investors.

Basics of Securitization

Securitization is a process whereby a financial institution buys pools of cash-flow-producing assets (such as loans) and then sells interests in the monthly payments by the borrowers as securities to investors.

Securitized assets, which include consumer and business loans, have played a prominent role in the current credit crisis. The weakness in the securitized asset market can substantially be traced back to the individual subprime borrowers whose loans had been securitized. As the **subprime borrowers** began to miss their monthly loan payments, the value of the securities backed by the borrowers' loans began to lose value. Throughout 2008, investors were losing con dence in these securities and therefore stopped buying them. Banks, unable to sell their loans to **securities issuers**, did not have the money to continue making new loans.

In response to these circumstances, Treasury and the Federal Reserve introduced TALF and other programs designed to alleviate the impact of problems in the securities market. A short overview of the subject will help place some of these programs in context.

Conceptually, all securitizations share the same simple timeline:

1. Borrowers take out loans with a lender or bank.
2. The bank sells a collection of the loans to a specialized entity (the "issuer" or "securities issuer").
3. The issuer sells "securities" to investors.

The actual transactions can become extremely complex, but the essential steps in Figure 2.15 will always be present.

The process has the potential to be beneficial to all parties. First, the borrowers may receive lower interest rates as a result of the greater supply of funds available for lending. Second, the bank can sell a large number of loans for cash, which allows it to make more loans. Third, the investors can put their money in a small number of relatively diversified and potentially liquid (*i.e.*, easy to sell) investments (securities), rather than investing in individual loans.

Securitization has become important because it has been replacing the traditional way that banks held loans, *i.e.*, on their books and for the long term. This change has been especially significant for residential and commercial mortgages, which have been packaged into mortgage-backed securities ("MBS"), and for consumer and small-business loans which have been packaged into asset-backed securities ("ABS"). This method of funding had been growing until 2008, when troubles in the securitization market led to a precipitous decline. Treasury has estimated that, prior to 2008, securitization represented 40% of all lending in the United States, with traditional financial institutions such as banks making up the remaining 60%. Figure 2.17 illustrates how significantly securitization has declined as a result of the current crisis. This decline in lending contributed to the crisis that prompted Treasury's creation of TARP.

Major Securitization Participants

An example of a mortgage securitization (see Figure 2.16) will help illustrate the process.

The Borrower. The borrower is the homeowner. The process of creating a mortgage starts with a prospective homebuyer who selects a house to purchase and then applies for a loan.

The Bank. The bank is the lender. The homeowner works with a lender who prepares and approves the mortgage application. Lenders are typically banks, savings and loan institutions, or mortgage bankers.

If the application is approved, funds are loaned to the homeowner for the purchase of the home; at this point, a mortgage is created. The lender or "loan originator" may then sell the newly created mortgage to the issuer. Banks do this in part to "free up" capital, to get more cash and make more loans.

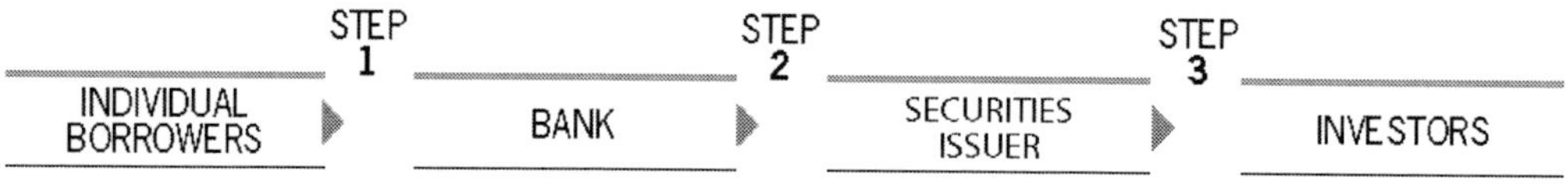

Figure 2.15. Simplified Securitization Process

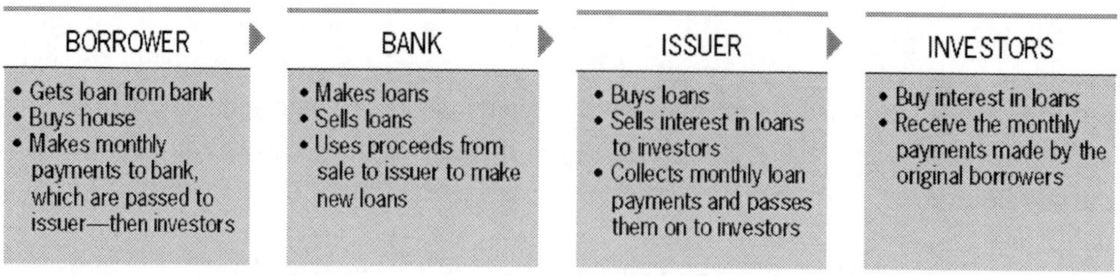

Figure 2.16 Securitization Participants and Roles

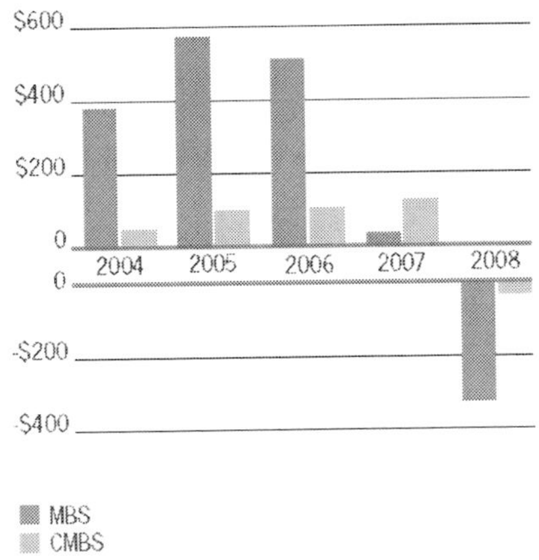

Note: Data as of 3/12/2009.
Source: Federal Reserve, "Flow of Funds Account of the United States," 3/12/2009, accessed 3/31/2009

Figure 2.17 Private-Label Mortgage-Backed Securities Net Issuance in the United States

The Issuer. The issuer is the party that buys loans made by banks and creates a security backed by the pool of loans. The issuers buy the loans from sellers and place them into a company they have created to own a specific collection of loans — such an entity is known as a special purpose vehicle ("SPV") or mortgage trust.

The SPV is a company in its own right. It has its own special collection of assets and its own corporate structure.

Because the securities that the issuer creates are collateralized, or "backed" by the mortgages that make them up, they are called mortgage-backed securities, or MBS. These MBS are like bonds; they pay an interest rate to the investors who buy them. The money to pay the interest comes from the monthly payments made by each one of the homeowners who make their monthly mortgage payments on their loans.

The issuer might sell more than one class of MBS from the same pool of loans. It may, for example, sell the first dollars received from the underlying mortgages to a "class A" security, and the remaining payments to a "class B" security. These various "classes" of securities are sometimes called "tranches."

The Investor. The investors in MBS are almost exclusively institutions: pension funds, insurance companies, mutual funds, and corporations. They buy the MBS from the issuer and can hold the MBS and receive the regular interest payments, or can sell it to others on the open market.

Supporting Securitization Participants

The Loan Servicer. The SPV typically hires a specialty firm to service the loans it buys. These firms collect the monthly payments from the borrowers, follow up on delinquencies, and, when payments are significantly late, arrange foreclosures or negotiate loan modifications.[213]

The Rating Agency. The SPV hires a rating agency to perform an analysis of the pool of loans that have been collected together and assign a rating. Rating agencies consider factors such as the credit scores of the borrowers, the underwriting standards used, and the anticipated cash fiow.[214] The rating re ects the rating agency's opinion as to the likelihood that the borrowers will continue to make the necessary payments on their mortgages. During the current economic crisis, rating agencies often proved to be overly optimistic with respect to the repayment rates of MBS, in particular MBS backed by residential mortgages.

TERM ASSET-BACKED SECURITIES LOAN FACILITY

In November 2008, the Federal Reserve and Treasury announced the Term Asset-Backed Securities Loan Facility ("TALF"), a new facility under which, as initially announced, the Federal Reserve Bank of New York ("FRBNY") would issue up to $200 billion in loans designed to make credit available to consumers and small businesses. As part of the original TALF, Treasury committed to provide up to $20 billion to absorb losses on those loans using TARP funds.[215] Subsequent to the initial TALF announcement, Treasury and the Federal Reserve have announced the intended expansion of TALF, bringing the total facility funding up to $1 trillion, of which Treasury anticipates it will fund up to $80 billion.[216]

In recent years, funds for consumer and small-business loans have frequently come from the sale of ABS. In the ABS market, pools of loans are gathered together and then securitized. Rating agencies rate the riskiness of the pooled loans. Investors, in turn, base their interest rate requirements, or the amount of interest the security will pay to the investor, to a large degree, on the ratings of the security. The ABS market made up almost 25% of the overall funding for consumer and small-business loans prior to the credit market disruptions of 2008.[217]

In 2008, with investors increasingly reluctant to buy AAA-rated ABS, the Federal Reserve proposed TALF as a means of reopening channels of funding for assets that have traditionally been securitized, and, thus, indirectly supplying funds to the end user — the consumer and business borrowers. According to the Federal Reserve, TALF's effect on the market began even before its first transaction: "Recently, consumer loan growth has also reportedly been buoyed by banks' decisions to build inventory in anticipation of issuance into the Term Asset-Backed Securities Loan Facility (TALF)."[218]

The ABS Market Faces Breakdown

In 2008, as borrowers began defaulting on their loans and the ABS supported by those loans depreciated in value, investors stopped buying ABS. Traditional investors exited the market, non-traditional investors were unable to obtain funding, and investors in general were concerned about a deep recession.[219] According to Treasury, "the [market] shock was compounded by the fact that loan underwriting standards used by some originators had become far too lax and by the proliferation of structured credit products, some of which were ill-understood by some market participants."[220]

Lenders that relied on the ABS securitization of their consumer and small-business loans were then unable to make as many loans, because their funding source for such loans — the cash they received from the sale of existing loans — was no longer available. With traditional ABS investors absent from the market, FRBNY and Treasury developed TALF to provide low-cost, non-recourse financing for the purchase of certain types of ABS in an attempt to induce investors to purchase AAA-rated ABS.

For more details on the securitization process and the typical lending process prior to the market breakdown, refer to "TARP Tutorial: Securitization" earlier in this section.

Floorplan: Revolving lines of credit used to finance inventories of items including, but not limited to, vehicles; agricultural, construction, or manufacturing equipment; manufactured housing; large appliances; and electronic equipment.

Servicing Advance Receivables: Receivables related to residential mortgage loan securitizations that grant the servicerfirst priority in any insurance or liquidation proceeds from a loan, and, if those proceeds are insufficient, grants the servicer a first priority to general collections of the related securitization.

Haircut: Difference in the value of the collateral and the value of the loan (the loan value is less than the collateral value).

Primary Dealers: Banks and securities broker-dealers that trade in U.S. Government securities with the Federal Reserve Bank of New York for the purpose of carrying out open market operations. The 16 current primary dealers are listed below.

Primary Dealer List:
BNP Paribas Securities Corp.
Banc of America Securities LLC
Barclays Capital Inc.
Cantor Fitzgerald & Co.
Citigroup Global Markets Inc.
Credit Suisse Securities (USA) LLC
Daiwa Securities America Inc.
Deutsche Bank Securities Inc.
Dresdner Kleinwort Securities LLC
Goldman, Sachs & Co.
Greenwich Capital Markets, Inc.
HSBC Securities (USA) Inc.
J. P. Morgan Securities Inc.
Mizuho Securities USA Inc.
Morgan Stanley & Co. Incorporated
UBS Securities LLC

TALF Mechanics

As of March 31, 2009, TALF could fund up to $200 billion in FRBNY loans, and it has been announced that TALF's funding capacity could increase up to $1 trillion. TALF is divided organizationally into two parts:

lending program: originates loans to eligible borrowers
asset disposition facility: an SPV used by FRBNY if borrowers choose to stop paying interest on their loans and surrender their collateral

FRBNY will manage both the lending program and the asset disposition facility. The funding for the lending program will come from FRBNY. The funding for the asset disposition SPV will first come from interest payments made by borrowers from the lending program, and then from Treasury's use of TARP funds to purchase subordinated debt from the SPV.[221] As of March 31, 2009, TARP participation in TALF had committed $20 billion, but it has been announced that this commitment could increase to up to $80 billion as TALF expands. The funding provided by TARP to the SPV is available to purchase surrendered assets from FRBNY and offset losses associated with disposing of the surrendered assets.

Lending Program

In its current form, FRBNY's TALF lending program makes three-year, non- recourse loans to eligible borrowers. The TALF loans are secured by the posting of collateral in the form of ABS, which may be backed by student, auto, credit card, equipment, auto **fioorplan,** small-business loans, or mortgage **servicing advance receivables.** Both the interest rates and the **haircuts** on TALF loans are based on the type and riskiness of the ABS securing the TALF loan. Since the loan is non- recourse, FRBNY cannot hold the TALF borrower liable for any losses beyond the surrender of any assets pledged as collateral — in this case, the ABS securities.

Eligible Borrowers and Eligible Collateral

TALF's lending program makes secured loans to qualifying borrowers.[222] TALF participants must use a **primary dealer** to access TALF and to deliver the **collateral** to the **custodian bank** (The Bank of New York Mellon ("BNYM")). The type and characteristics of eligible collateral for TALF is detailed in Table 2.26.

Collateral must meet eligibility criteria such as:[223]

The collateral is in the form of U.S. dollar-denominated cash (not **synthetic**) **ABS**.
The ABS must have a short-term and long-term credit rating of the highest investment-grade rating category (*e.g.,* AAA) from two or more major, nationally recognized statistical rating organizations ("NRSROs"). In addition, the ABS cannot have a long-term credit rating less than the highest rating by a major NRSRO. Major NRSROs for purposes of TALF are Fitch Ratings, Moody's Investors Service, and Standard & Poor's.
Substantially all of the loans underlying the ABS were originated in the United States.

The loans supporting the ABS were initially limited to auto, student, and credit card loans, or small-business loans guaranteed by the U.S. Small Business Administration ("SBA"). As of March 31, 2009, permissible underlying loans also include equipment loans, fioorplan loans, or receivables related to residential mortgage servicing advances (servicing advance receivables).

ABS backed by credit card loans and dealer fioorplan must be issued to refinance existing credit card and dealer fioorplan ABS maturing in 2009, and must be issued in amounts no greater than the amount of the maturing security.[224]

Collateral cannot be backed by loans originated or securitized by the TALF borrower or an affiliate of the borrower. In other words, the TALF borrower cannot also be, or be affiliated with, either the institution that is selling the ABS or the original lender.

Collateral: An asset pledged by a borrower to a lender until a loan is repaid. In the case of TALF loans, the collateral is asset-backed securities.

Custodian Bank: The bank that holds the collateral and manages the accounts for FRBNY.

Synthetic ABS: A security that derives its value and cash fiow from sources other than from a physical set of reference assets.

Table 2.26. TALF-Eligible Asset-Backed Securities

Sector	Subsector	Loan Characteristics	Expected Life	ABS Issuance Date
Auto Loans	Retail loans and leases related to cars, light trucks, motorcycles, and other recreational vehicles	Originated on or after October 1, 2007	≤5 years	January 1, 2009
	Commercial, Government and rental fleet leases	Originated on or after October 1, 2007	≤5 years	January 1, 2009
Student Loans	Federally guaranteed (including consolidated) and private	Originated on or after May 1, 2007		January 1, 2009
Credit Card Receivables	Consumer or corporate	Maturing in 2009	≤5 years	January 1, 2009
Equipment Loans	Retail loans and leases	Originated on or after October 1, 2007	≤5 years	January 1, 2009
Floorplan loans	Revolving lines of credit to nance dealer investors	Maturing in 2009	≤5 years	January 1, 2009
Small-Business Loans	Fully guaranteed SBA 7(a) and 504 loans, debentures, and pools	Originated on or after January 1, 2008		January 1, 2008
Servicing Advance Receivables	Principal and interest, tax and insurance, and corporate advances made by Fannie Mae- or Freddie Mac-approved residential mortgage servicers under pooling and service agreements	Originated on or after January 1, 2007	≤5 years	January 1, 2009

Source: FRBNY, "Term Asset-Backed Securities Loan Facility: Terms and Conditions," 3/19/2009, accessed 3/27/2009.

Skin in the game: Equity stake in an investment; down payment; the amount an investor can lose.

Loan Terms by Asset Class

TALF loans are collateralized by ABS, as previously described, and are non-recourse to the borrower with terms of up to three years. The eligibility of the TALF borrower and the TALF collateral is determined through the application process. Once the collateral is deemed to be eligible, a haircut will be assigned to the collateral. Haircuts represent the amount of money put up by the borrower, or the borrower's "**skin in the game**," and are required for all TALF loans in varying amounts. Under TALF, FRBNY will lend each borrower the amount of the purchase price of the pledged ABS minus the haircut, subject to certain limitations. The risk for any borrower is limited to the haircut amount; the Government is responsible for all losses beyond that original down payment. The initial haircuts, as a percentage of collateral value, are shown in Table 2.27.

Some of the underlying assets may have an average life beyond the de ned terms. If the average life of Government-guaranteed ABS (SBA loans) is greater than five years, haircuts will increase by one percentage point for every two years of average additional life. For all other ABS with average lives beyond five years, haircuts will increase by one percentage point for each additional year of average life.

Interest Rates

Interest rates are based on the loan asset class, and most are quoted at a **spread** over the **London Interbank Offered Rate ("LIBOR")** (a generally accepted interest rate standard). Interest payments on the TALF loans are payable monthly. TALF loan interest rates may be fixed or fioating, as determined by the collateral, and are generally below market rate. If the cash fiow supporting the collateral has a fixed interest rate, then the TALF loan will have a fixed interest rate; and if the cash fiow supporting the collateral has a fioating interest rate, then the TALF loan interest rate will also fioat. Table 2.28 illustrates the interest rates for the March 2009 loans.

Table 2.27. TALF Haircut Percentages

		ABS Expected Life (years)						
Sector	**Subsector**	**0-1**	**>1-2**	**>2-3**	**>3-4**	**>4-5**	**>5-6**	**>6-7**
Auto	Prime retail lease	10%	11%	12%	13%	14%	NA	NA
Auto	Prime retail loan	6%	7%	8%	9%	10%	NA	NA
Auto	Sub-prime retail loan	9%	10%	11%	12%	13%	NA	NA
Auto	RV/Motorcycle	7%	8%	9%	10%	11%	NA	NA
Floorplan	Auto	12%	13%	14%	15%	16%	NA	NA
Credit Card	Prime	5%	5%	6%	7%	8%	NA	NA
Credit Card	Subprime	6%	7%	8%	9%	10%	NA	NA
Student Loan	Private	8%	9%	10%	11%	12%	13%	14%
Student Loan	Government Guaranteed	5%	5%	5%	5%	5%	6%	6%
Small Business	SBA Loans	5%	5%	5%	5%	5%	6%	6%

Source: FRBNY, "Term Asset-Backed Securities Loan Facility (Operations for 3/17/2009)," accessed 3/27/2009.

Asset Disposition Facility

FRBNY created TALF LLC, the SPV for the asset disposition facility, to "purchase and manage any [surrendered] assets received by the New York Fed in connection with any TALF loans."[225] TALF LLC will purchase these assets at a "price equal to the outstanding TALF loan amount plus accrued but unpaid interest."[226] Both the Federal Reserve and TARP will fund the purchase of the surrendered assets in the form of a senior and subordinated loan, respectively.

When FRBNY created TALF LLC, TARP loaned TALF LLC $100 million to provide initial funding, of which $1 5.75 million was allocated to cover administrative costs.[227] TARP will continue to fund TALF LLC, as needed, until the full TARP commitment has been invested. If more funds are required, then FRBNY would make a non-recourse loan to the SPV.[228]

Spread: The difference between two interest rates.

London Interbank Offered Rate ("LIBOR"): The interest rate that large banks in London charge each other for dollar- denominated funds.

Basis Points (bps): One one-hundredth of a percentage point. (For example, the difference between interest rates of 5.5% and 5.0% is 50 basis points.)

Federal Funds [Target] Rate: The interest rate that financial institutions charge each other for overnight loans of their monetary reserves. A rise in the Federal funds rate (compared with other short-term interest rates) suggests a tightening of monetary policy, whereas a fall suggests an easing. The Federal Funds Target Rate is an interest rate goal set periodically by the Federal Open Market Committee.

Table 2.28. Talf Interest Rates

Sector	Subsector	Fixed	Floating
Auto		3-year LIBOR + 100 **bps** (2.733% for the March loans)	1-month LIBOR + 100 bps
Credit Card		3-year LIBOR + 100 bps (2.733% for the March loans)	1-month LIBOR + 100 bps
Student Loan	Private	NA	1-month LIBOR + 100 bps
Student Loan	Government guaranteed	NA	1-month LIBOR + 50 bps
Small Business	SBA loans 7(a)NA	NA	**Fed Funds Target** + 75 bps
Small Business	SBA loans 504	3-year LIBOR + 50 bps (2.233% for the March loans)	NA

Source: FRBNY, "Term Asset-Backed Securities Loan Facility (Operations for 3/17/2009)," accessed 3/27/2009.

Please refer to the "Unlocking Credit for Small Businesses" discussion in this report for more information on SBA loans.

Subscription Date: Loan request date. For TALF loans, requests include: ABS collateral expected to pledge, loan amount, and interest rate format (fixed or fioating).

CUSIPs: Unique identifying number assigned to all registered securities (similar to a social security number).

Offering Documents/Prospectus: Documents which disclose and describe a securities offering to the public and private investors, containing information required under Federal and state securities laws as applicable.

Settlement Date: The closing date for the sale of an investment, similar to the closing date for a home purchase. On the settlement date (three days after trade in the case of U.S. equities), funds and securities trade hands and any necessary legal documents are signed.

A portion of the interest rate paid by each borrower for a TALF loan will accumulate in the asset disposition facility and absorb losses on surrendered collateral.[229] Once losses become greater than the accumulated interest, TARP will then provide the additional funding for the SPV until the purchase of surrendered collateral exceeds the amount of committed funds by TARP — currently $20 billion but anticipated to be up to $80 billion. FRBNY will provide any additional funding once the TARP commitment is expended. The funding for the SPV will be in the form of loans to the SPV, with TARP receiving interest at one-month LIBOR plus 3% and the Federal Reserve receiving one-month LIBOR plus 1%.[230]

Treasury's maximum liability is for losses equal to the total amount committed to the SPV. Any residual returns (*e.g.,* proceeds from the sale of the assets or interest earned on the loans) would be shared between FRBNY and Treasury, with Treasury receiving 90% and FRBNY receiving 10%.[231]

TALF Process Example

To start the process of ultimately obtaining a loan under TALF, an eligible borrower contacts a primary dealer about receiving a TALF loan. Prior to the **subscription date** of the TALF loan, the eligible borrower submits to the primary dealer its loan package, which includes the loan request amount, interest rate format (based on collateral), **CUSIPs** of the ABS, and the **prospectus** or **offering documents**. On the subscription date of the loan, the primary dealer submits to BNYM (custodian bank) and FRBNY the loan package of the borrower and the total loan amount from all of the individual borrowers serviced by that primary dealer. BNYM then reviews the loan packages.[232]

Prior to the **settlement date**, BNYM will return to each primary dealer a list containing the borrower's approved loan amount, ABS expected to be delivered, administration fee, and haircut amount. On the settlement date, the primary dealer submits to BNYM the ABS, the administration fee, and the haircut amount, and BNYM credits the primary dealer's account (for further delivery to the borrower) the loan amount.[233]

In making the required monthly payments, any principal and interest that the ABS generates (*e.g.,* the amount of principal and interest to which the security entitles the holder) is received by BNYM and applied to the TALF loan. Given the low interest rate charged by FRBNY, at least initially, the interest earned on the ABS will likely be greater than the interest charged by FRBNY on the TALF loan. Accordingly, as long as the ABS maintains its value, the borrower will likely not need to make any cash payment each month, but will actually receive a monthly interest payment from BNYM (representing the interest paid on the ABS minus the smaller TALF interest rate). If there is not enough interest received from the ABS to cover the TALF loan payments, BNYM requests the balance from the TALF borrower. As long as the TALF borrower makes the regular monthly interest payments, the collateral will be returned when the loan is repaid in full.[234]

Monthly Interest Example

If the TALF borrower owes 3% interest to FRBNY ($2.25 monthly) on a $900 TALF loan, and the TALF borrower receives 6% interest ($5 monthly) on $1,000 of the ABS collateral, then BNYM sends the difference of $2.75 ($5 – $2.25) to the TALF borrower.

If the borrower decides to walk away from the loan, it must submit a Collateral Surrender and Acceptance Notice which signs over the rights to the collateral to FRBNY. Since the loan is non-recourse, there is no further action against the borrower, who can keep the total amount borrowed. If the borrower does not submit the Collateral Surrender and Acceptance Notice, it may be required to repay the entire TALF loan.[235] Should the borrower surrender the loan, the Federal Reserve will sell the surrendered collateral to the Asset Disposition SPV.[236] When the SPV buys the collateral, it pays the outstanding loan amount plus any unpaid interest. For a detailed explanation of non-recourse loans and their application to TALF, refer to SIGTARP's Initial Report, Section 3: "TARP Implementation and Administration."

For further detail on the TALF process, see Figure 2.18.

Fraud Prevention Provisions

SIGTARP identified a number of risks associated with TALF in its Initial Report. Refer to Section 4 of this report for information on SIGTARP's recommendations. Acting on some of SIGTARP's recommendations, the Federal Reserve has announced several fraud-prevention provisions for TALF.

The fraud deterrent and compliance framework announced by FRBNY includes: "a borrower acceptance standard, an assurance program related to borrower eligibility requirements, on-site inspection rights related to the borrower's obligations under the MLSA [Master Loan and Security Agreement] in respect to its borrowings under the TALF and the right to reject a borrower for any reason."[237] To further assist in the borrower screening, "primary dealers are required to apply their internal customer identification program and due diligence procedures to each borrower."[238] "Instances may arise where a borrower will not be eligible on subscription day because the borrower has been previously identified as 'high-risk' and, therefore, subjected to a more in-depth review by FRBNY compliance."[239]

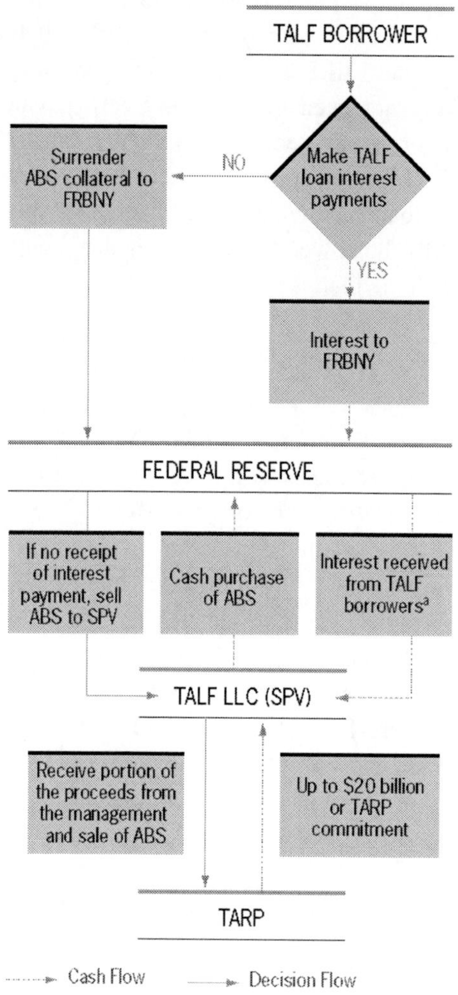

Note:

[a] A portion of the interest rate paid by each TALF borrower will accumulate in the SPV.

Sources: Diagram based on Term Asset-Backed Securities Loan Facility: Terms and Conditions from FRBNY, 3/19/2009, response to SIGTARP draft report, 4/9/2009.

Figure 2.18. TALF Process Flow

Additionally, an ABS issuer must provide a certification that the ABS are TALF eligible, that an independent accounting firm has certified that the ABS are TALF eligible, and the issuer has not made any material misstatements to an NRSRO to obtain a particular credit rating.[240] This certification provides that the loans are made in good faith and in compliance with the standards set forth in the terms and conditions of TALF. Table 2.29 provides the framework set forth for fraud deterrence and compliance.

Table 2.29. TALF Fraud Prevention and Compliance Framework

Issuer/ Sponsor	**Issuer/Sponsor certifies that:** • The terms and conditions have been reviewed. • The ABS have the highest investment-grade rating category from two or more rating agencies; cannot have a rating below the highest rating available from any NRSRO; the ratings depend on no third-party credit enhancement; and they are not on review or watch from downgrade. • The securities are cleared through the Depository Trust Company (DTC). • Substantially all of the underlying borrowers are U.S.-domiciled. • The underlying assets are of a permitted type (auto, student, credit card, equipment, I oorplan, or receivables), and contain no exposures that are themselves cash or synthetic ABS. • All underlying loans were made after their respective eligibility dates. • The accounting firm it uses for FRBNY work on the securities may call the TALF compliance hotline, regardless of client confidentiality rules. • It understands that the securities may not be submitted to TALF by anyone affiliated with originators of the underlying loans. • It will issue a press release if any statements regarding basic eligibility criteria change or become false. • The information provided to the rating agencies was true. • It will cover any losses of the FRBNY and TALF LLC that resulted from relying on the information provided by the issuer/sponsor (*i.e.*, provide "indemnification"). • Should the collateral be proven to be ineligible, the issuer/sponsor agrees to allow Treasury officials, SIGTARP, and GAO to have access to personnel, data, documents, etc. relevant to the breach.
Auditor	**Auditor Attestation Form confirms the issuer/sponsor's eligibility claims:** • Substantially all of the originations of the loans in ABS were made to U.S.-domiciled people or entities. • Underlying ABS credit exposure types are eligible and do not include exposures that are cash or synthetic ABS. • Substantially all of the underlying ABS Loan Characteristics (origination date, maturity date, etc.) meet the criteria.
Primary Dealer	**Primary Dealer represents and warrants that:** • It has the power and authority to enter into the agreements. • It is in good standing under the laws of its jurisdiction. • The agreement is legally binding. • It has made no untrue statement in any document, certificate, or statement related to the Agreement, or omitted any material act. (With respect to the offering materials, this applies only to the Primary Dealer that acted as underwriter.) • It has provided each borrower with a copy of the lending agreement, and that the borrower has authorized the Primary Dealer to act on its behalf. • It is subject to the certain rules, including that it maintains and is in compliance with an anti-money-laundering program under the USA Patriot Act, that it is Federally regulated, that it has implemented a customer identity program enabling it to know the identity of its customers, and that it will annually so certify.

Table 2.29. (Continued)

	• Its customer agreements are in full force. • All written material delivered to the Lender, Administrator, or Custodian is accurate and complete. • The borrower is eligible. • The collateral is eligible.
FRBNY	• FRBNY has limited on-site inspection rights of borrower personnel, data, documents, etc. relevant to the certifications above. • FRBNY can reject a loan application for any reason. • FRBNY may review all loan files held by the custodian related to all of the TALF loans. If the collateral is found to be ineligible, FRBNY has the right of indemnity against the issuer/sponsor in the event damages are suffered in relation to the collateral and further remedy is available if there is evidence of fraudulent activity. If the borrower is ever found to be ineligible, the non-recourse feature of the TALF loan becomes inapplicable and the borrower must repay the entire loan amount. • FRBNY has established a telephone and Internet hotline to report fraudulent conduct or activity related to TALF.

Sources: Issuer/Sponsor: FRBNY, "Term Asset-Backed Securities Loan Facility: Frequently Asked Questions," 3/19/2009, accessed 3/27/2009; FRBNY, "Certification as to TALF Eligibility," 3/24/2009, accessed 3/27/2009. Auditor: FRBNY, "Form of Auditor Attestation," 3/19/2009, accessed 3/27/2009. Primary Dealer: FRBNY, "Term Asset-Backed Securities Loan Facility: Frequently Asked Questions," 3/19/2009, accessed 3/27/2009; FRBNY, "Master Loan and Security Agreement," 3/27/2009, accessed 3/27/2009. FRBNY: FRBNY, "Master Loan and Security Agreement," 3/27/2009, accessed 3/27/2009; FRBNY, "Term Asset-Backed Securities Loan Facility: Frequently Asked Questions," 3/19/2009, accessed 3/27/2009.

Status of Funds

As of March 31, 2009, FRBNY lent $4.7 billion backed by auto and credit card ABS collateral. Since the program's commencement, there has been one group of TALF loans issued. For a breakdown of the loans by ABS sector, see Table 2.30.

As of March 31, 2009, TARP loaned TALF LLC $100 million to provide initial funding, of which $1 5.75 million was allocated to cover administrative costs. As of the drafting of this report, no TALF-related assets had been surrendered. Table 2.31 illustrates the total TARP commitment and total funds disbursed.

Executive Compensation

As of March 31, 2009, no executive compensation restrictions were placed on any of the participants in TALF, including the issuer/sponsor or the borrower. Originally, it was contemplated that the ABS issuers/sponsors and FRBNY would be required to be bound by EESA executive compensation restrictions. After the ARRA changes to EESA, however, Treasury removed the restrictions on TALF issuers/sponsors, because "such a policy would not enhance the effectiveness of the TALF in restoring consumer credit markets."[241]

SIGTARP requested from OFS and Treasury's General Counsel a legal explanation for these changes; the letter from SIGTARP and the responses from OFS and the Treasury General Counsel are contained in Appendix I.

Going Forward

Treasury and the Federal Reserve have announced expansions in TALF. Additional types of collateral have been made eligible for the April 2009 TALF loans. Moreover, in conjunction with the introduction of the Public-Private Investment Program ("PPIP"), a white paper issued by Treasury stated that TALF loans "will be made available to investors to fund purchases of legacy securitization assets," which are expected to include legacy RMBS.[242] Treasury also has announced that it is exploring the possibility of extending TALF to AAA-rated tranches of new securitizations in the form of CMBS, RMBS, and structures backed by corporate debt. To accommodate these additions, TALF may increase its commitments up to $1 trillion, with TARP participation increasing up to $80 billion.[243] Treasury and the Federal Reserve also expect to add **collateralized debt obligations** to the list of eligible collateral.[244]

Collateralized Debt Obligation: A security that entitles the purchaser to some portion of the cash flows from a portfolio of assets, which may include bonds, loans, mortgage-backed securities, or other CDOs.

Table 2.30. TALF Loans ($ Millions)

Sector	Amount	Interest Rates	
		Fixed	Floating
Auto	$1,902.4	2.733%	1.523%
Credit Card	2,804.5	2.733%	1.523%
Student Loan	–		
Small Business	–		
Total	**$4,706.9**		

Source: Numbers affected by rounding. Data as of 3/31/2009. FRBNY, "Term Asset-Backed Securities Loan Facility (Operations for 3/17/2009)," accessed 3/27/2009.

Table 2.31. TARP Loans to TALF LLC

Total Committed	$20 billion
Total Disbursed	$100 million
Interest Received	–

Source: Numbers affected by rounding. Data as of 3/31/2009. Treasury, GAO, and SIGTARP, briefing on TALF, 3/13/2009.

Table 2.32. Additional TALF Interest Rates

Sector	Subsector	Fixed	Floating
Equipment		3-year LIBOR + 100 bps	1-month LIBOR + 100 bps
Floorplan		3-year LIBOR + 100 bps	1-month LIBOR + 100 bps
Servicing Advances	Residential Mortgages	3-year LIBOR + 100 bps	1-month LIBOR + 100 bps

Source: Data as of 3/31/2009. FRBNY, "Term Asset-Backed Securities Loan Facility (Operations for 4/7/2009)," accessed 3/27/2009.

Table 2.33. Additional TALF April Loan Haircut Percentages

Sector	Subsector	ABS Expected Life (years)				
		0-1	>1-2	>2-3	>3-4	>4-5
Auto	Commercial and Government Fleets	9%	10%	11%	12%	13%
Auto	Rental Fleets	12%	13%	14%	15%	16%
Equipment	Loans and Leases	5%	6%	7%	8%	9%
Floorplan	Non-auto	11%	12%	13%	14%	15%
Servicing Advances	Residential Mortgages	12%	13%	14%	15%	16%

Source: Data as of 3/31/2009. FRBNY, "Term Asset-Backed Securities Loan Facility (Operations for 4/7/2009)"

April 2009 TALF Loans

FRBNY has released the terms for the April 14, 2009, TALF loans. Eligible collateral has been expanded to include ABS collateral backed by equipment loans, non- auto fioorplan loans, leases of vehicle fieets, and receivables related to residential mortgage servicing advances (servicing advance receivables). Table 2.32 and Table 2.33 illustrate the additional interest rates and haircuts for the April loans.

Legacy Assets in Public-Private Investment Program

Treasury, the Federal Reserve, and FDIC have announced the creation of PPIP to facilitate the purchase of certain real estate-related legacy assets. The "Public-Private Investment Program" discussion immediately following describes how the elements of PPIP provide leverage to private investors. As part of PPIP, Treasury has announced that certain PPIP investment funds will be eligible to participate in TALF, magnifying the leverage already provided to private capital. As further discussed in Section 4 of this report, SIGTARP has recommended that PPIP funds should not be permitted to participate in TALF without significant additional protections.

PUBLIC-PRIVATE INVESTMENT PROGRAM

On March 23, 2009, Treasury announced a coordinated effort with the Federal Reserve and FDIC that, it has stated, will improve the health of financial institutions holding real estate-related assets in an attempt to increase the fiow of credit throughout the U.S. economy.[245] The Public-Private Investment Program ("PPIP") will make investments in multiple Public-Private Investment Funds ("PPIFs") to purchase legacy loans and legacy securities (collectively "legacy assets") from finan- cial institutions.

Public-Private Investment Program Details

Under the terms of PPIP, Government funds will be invested in varying proportions with private investors to purchase legacy assets. Plans for PPIP call for the use of $75 billion of TARP funds in two new legacy asset subprograms and expansion of TALF.[246] Using significant leverage, either from, or backed by, the Government, PPIP will involve from $500 billion to $1 trillion of capital for the purchase of legacy loans and legacy securities in the Legacy Loans and Legacy Securities programs:[247]

Legacy Loans Program ("Loans Program") — PPIFs in the Loans Program will purchase real estate-related loans using TARP funds and private investment capital combined with FDIC-guaranteed debt.

Legacy Securities Program ("Securities Program") — PPIFs in the Securities Program will purchase real estate-related securities (*i.e.*, MBS) using TARP funds and private investment capital combined with TARP-issued debt.

Expansion of TALF — TALF will be expanded to accept legacy securitized assets, which are expected to include legacy MBS.

> **Legacy Assets:** Also known as troubled assets, legacy assets are real estate-related loans and securities (legacy loans and legacy securities) that remain on banks' balance sheets and that have lost value, but are difficult to price due to the recent market disruption.

Both the Loans Program and the Securities Program have equity and debt financing elements. It is currently contemplated that TARP will be used to fund Treasury's equity position under PPIP.

Figure 2.19 describes the anticipated funding components of PPIP.

PPIP is designed to allow market participants to set the price for legacy assets rather than having the Government or an independent third party determine value. According to Treasury, this mechanism will help establish the highest market value for the assets.[248]

Legacy Loans Program

Treasury has stated that it intends for the Legacy Loans Program to providefinancial institutions of all sizes a mechanism for the disposition of hard-to-value legacy loans through the formation of multiple **special purpose vehicles ("SPVs")** or PPIFs. Under the terms of the Loans Program, FDIC will oversee the formation, funding, and operation of the PPIFs, which in turn will invest in legacy loans in an auction process.[249]

> **Special Purpose Vehicle ("SPV"):** An entity whose operations are limited to the acquisition and financing of specific assets.

Each PPIF will consist of equity made up of private investment capital matched, dollar-for-dollar, with TARP funds and will have access to financing guaranteed by FDIC. FDIC will determine the financing level of the targeted legacy loan pool based on its analysis and with the assistance of a third-party valuationfirm. Given the quality of the pool of legacy loans, FDIC will determine how much of the loan purchase price it is willing to guarantee. According to the Treasury fact sheet, it is contemplated that financing will not exceed a 6-to-1 debt-to-equity ratio.[250] Although FDIC will have an idea of value for the pool of legacy loans, according to Treasury of cials, FDIC will conduct an auction to determine the ultimate price for the loan pools.[251]

The Legacy Loans Program includes a prohibition against private investor participation in the auction process when the sellers of the loans at auction are affiliates of the private investor, or where the seller of the loans at auction represents 10% or more of the aggregate private capital in the PPIF.[252] In other words, the bank selling the loan can invest up to 10% in the fund that is buying the loans that it is selling. The PPIFs must agree to fraud, waste, and abuse protections and provide access to SIGTARP.[253]

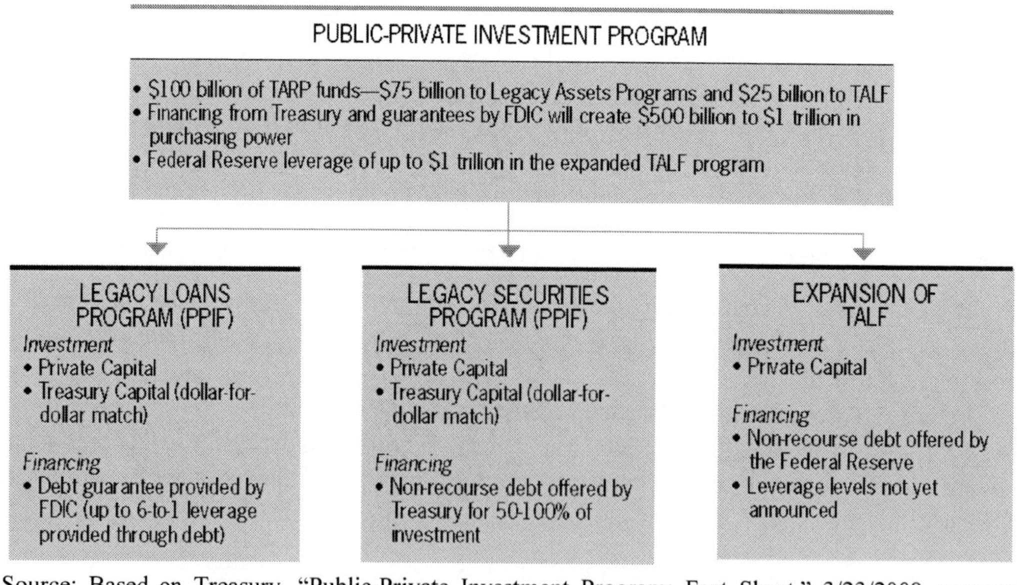

Source: Based on Treasury, "Public-Private Investment Program: Fact Sheet," 3/23/2009, accessed 3/23/2009. Treasury, Of ce of Financial Stability, Chief of Compliance and CFO, SIGTARP interview, 3/30/2009

Figure 2.19. PPIP Overview

How the Legacy Loans Program Works[254]

1. Eligible banks, in conjunction with their primary banking regulators, identify a pool of legacy loans they wish to sell and submit a request to FDIC.
2. FDIC engages a private, third-party firm to analyze and value the loans. Based on this review, FDIC decides how much leverage (in the form of FDIC- guaranteed loans) it is willing to give to the pre-qualified private investors bidding on the asset. This amount may not exceed a 6-to-1 debt-to-equity ratio. In effect, FDIC will guarantee up to $6 for every $1 that the PPIF invests.
3. FDIC conducts an auction, soliciting bids from the PPIFs.
4. Private investors must be pre-qualified and submit a refundable cash deposit of 5% of the bid value to FDIC in order to participate.[255]
5. The seller bank is then presented with the highest bid. If the seller accepts the highest bid, the bidder is granted access to PPIF funding for purchase of the legacy loans.
6. The PPIF debt is fully **guaranteed** by FDIC and collateralized by the purchased loans and the buildings and/or land on which the purchased loans were taken.
7. The remaining capital is invested in the PPIF by private investors and Treasury in equal parts. Therefore, of the $1 invested in the previous example, the private investor would invest $0.50 and Treasury, using TARP funds, would invest the remaining $0.50. In addition, Treasury receives warrants from the PPIF (the SPV created to make the purchase) for its investment.
8. Any profits or losses will be passed on to the private investor and Government in proportion to their investment, i.e., 50%/50%.
9. The guarantee by FDIC is such that the private investor need not pay back the loan. If there are significant losses, the private investor can walk away from the transaction and lose no more than its initial $0.50 investment, using the example noted earlier.

Guarantee: A commitment from a third-party lending institution ensuring that liabilities of a borrower will be met. If the borrower fails to make payments, the guarantor will step in and make the payment on the borrower's behalf. Under the Legacy Loans Program, the FDIC guarantee effectively commits the Government to make up any shortfalls if the PPIF no longer makes payments on the money that it borrows to buy the legacy loans.

Legacy Loans Program Example

Bank A, in conjunction with FDIC, determines that it would like to sell loans with a face value of approximately $100. After analyzing the pool of loans, FDIC determines that the appropriate funding structure of a PPIF for such an investment is a 6-to-1 debt-to-equity structure. FDIC auctions the legacy loans and a private investor makes a $60 winning bid. The private investor who submitted the winning bid is offered PPIF financing. The PPIF subsequently can obtain a loan for $51 that will be 100% guaranteed by FDIC. The remaining $9 of the purchase price is invested in the PPIF in equal parts by the private investor and Treasury — $4.50 each. The seller, Bank A, receives the full price of $60 and the PPIF will be required to make the interest payments on the $51 loan. Under this scenario, Treasury contributes $4.50 and, in return, receives warrants in the PPIF and half of the future profits and losses generated by the PPIF. If the investment fails entirely, Treasury loses $4.50, the private investor loses $4.50, and FDIC loses $51. Figure 2.20 illustrates the example legacy loan transaction funding structure by participant.

Legacy Securities Program

The Securities Program provides a mechanism for the disposition of legacy securities; the program targets securitized interests in mortgages (securities collateralized or "backed" by real estate or residential or commercial properties), rather than the mortgages themselves. The securitized interests include residential mortgage- backed securities ("RMBS") and commercial mortgage-backed securities ("CMBS") that are held by a diverse group of financial institutions.

The Securities Program contemplates two approaches for stimulating private capital investments in legacy securities: through the creation of PPIFs managed by private fund managers and an expansion of the Federal Reserve's TALF Program.

For more details on Securitization, refer to "TARP Tutorial: Securitization" earlier in this section.

PPIF Managers

Under the Securities Program, Treasury will appoint up to five fund managers from a pool of applicants to manage the PPIFs. According to Treasury of cials, after the initial pre-qualification of fund managers, Treasury will consider opening the program to smaller fund managers. Qualified managers must meet the following criteria, "which will be viewed on a holistic basis, and it is anticipated that failure to meet any one criteria will not necessarily disqualify a proposal:"[256]

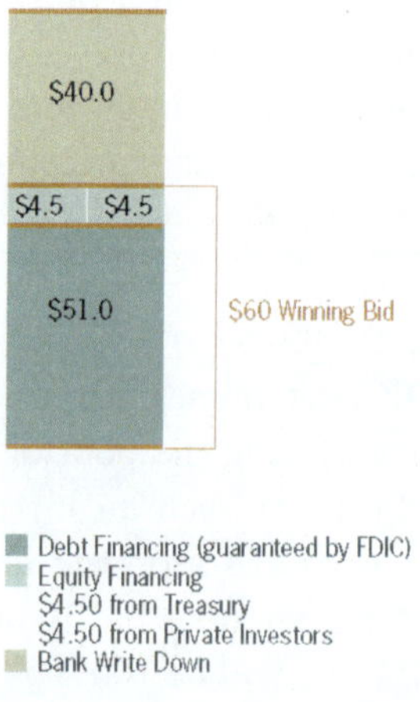

Note: Numbers affected by rounding.

Source: Diagram based on an understanding of Treasury, "Fact Sheet: Public-Private Investment Program," 3/23/2009, accessed 3/23/2009.

Figure 2.20. Legacy Loan $100 Face Value

capacity to raise $500 million of private capital
experience investing in legacy securities
management of $10 billion in legacy securities
ability to manage in a manner consistent with Treasury's investment objective
headquartered in the United States

As in the Legacy Loans Program, PPIFs can only purchase from sellers that are not affiliates of the fund manager, and are also prohibited from purchasing from any private investor who represents 10% or more of the aggregate private capital raised.[257] The PPIFs must agree to fraud, waste, and abuse protections and provide access to the Special Inspector General.[258]

How the Legacy Securities Program Works[259]

1. Fund managers apply to Treasury with a proposed funding structure for the creation of a PPIF.
   The proposal details the appropriate levels of debt and equity financing necessary for the purchase of legacy securities, as well as other structured considerations outlined in the application.
2. Fund managers appointed by Treasury are granted time to raise capital from private investors for the purchase of legacy securities.
3. Treasury matches the capital raised by the fund manager dollar-for-dollar.
   Treasury receives warrants in the PPIF for its contribution in addition to a share of any profits.
4. Fund managers can borrow additional money from Treasury of up to:
   50 – 100% of total equity investments, depending on "restrictions on asset- level leverage, withdrawal rights, disposition priorities, cash- ow priorities, and other factors Treasury deems relevant."[260] The total PPIF fund could thus consist of $1 of Treasury investment, $1 of private investment, and up to $2 of non-recourse Treasury loans. Because the loan is non-recourse, the total amount of exposure of the private investor is $1, while Treasury could lose as much as $3. Furthermore, the fund manager, which will receive fees from both the private investor and Treasury, is not required to have any investment in the fund, and therefore has no risk of loss for its investment decisions.
   Under the current structure, the fund manager can leverage the fund through TALF loans, but, in that case, Treasury financing for the PPIF would be limited to 50% of the total equity.
5. The fund manager purchases legacy securities and has full discretion over investment decisions, including the price at which the securities will be purchased, and provides Treasury monthly reports on the PPIF's activities.
6. The withdrawal rights of the private investors in the PPIF are yet to be determined, but for any PPIF receiving Treasury financing, no private investor can withdraw (or have the voluntary right of withdrawal of) funds until the third anniversary of the first investment made in the PPIF. The stated strategy is to hold the securities for the long term, but not more than 10 years.[261] It has not been announced how Treasury will enforce this goal, or whether it will permit members of the funds to sell or transfer their interests.

For more information on TALF background and mechanics, refer to "TALF" earlier in this section.

Expansion of TALF for Legacy Securities

The Securities Program also expands the terms of the previously announced TALF. Acceptable collateral under TALF, as originally implemented, included newly issued ABS backed by auto, student, credit card, and small-business loans. The Securities Program would expand TALF so that TALF loans could be secured by legacy MBS that were originally rated AAA, although it will not be required that they have that rating at the time of purchase through the TALF program. Haircuts and interest rates applicable to these loans will be determined at a later date.[262]

Executive Compensation

Treasury has not indicated to what extent the EESA executive compensation restrictions will apply to the participants in the legacy loan, legacy security, or expanded TALF programs. According to Treasury, "the applicability of the executive compensation regulations, which have not yet been published, will be fact-dependent. Until Fund Managers make proposals under the TALF program, it is not known whether they will seek to be co-owners of the PPIFs. If they do, they would not be passive investors and could be subject to the executive compensation restrictions."[263]

UNLOCKING CREDIT FOR SMALL BUSINESSES

On March 16, 2009, Treasury announced that it would purchase up to $15 billion in securities backed by pools of Small Business Administration ("SBA") loans in order to encourage banks to extend more credit to small businesses.[264] These securities will be backed by loans participating in two SBA programs: the **7(a) Program** and the **504 Community Development Loan Program**. Banks often sell a portion of these loans in a secondary market to pool assemblers (issuers).[265] This secondary market serves as a source of cash for banks, providing them money to make new loans.[266] Frozen conditions in the secondary market have caused a reduction in the volume of new loans written by banks. According to Treasury, the Unlocking Credit for Small Businesses ("UCSB") program was designed to provide banks the liquidity necessary to start writing new small-business loans again.[267]

In addition to stimulating the secondary markets for SBA loans, Treasury has announced increased tracking of small-business-related lending. On March 16, 2009, the Treasury Secretary called for the 21 largest banks receiving TARP funding to report the monthly amount of their small-business lending. This reporting would begin with participants' April 2009 submissions and include data on average small- business loans outstanding and monthly originations to small businesses. In order to make timely data available, the Treasury Secretary called for every U.S. bank to report their total small-business lending on a quarterly basis instead of once per year. This reporting would be facilitated by bank regulators. The Treasury Secretary "emphasized that all lenders (including those not participating in the FSP) should take a special responsibility for providing the credit that small businesses need to operate, expand and add jobs."[268]

SBA 7(a) Program Securities

The SBA 7(a) Program assists small businesses that cannot otherwise obtain conventional loans at reasonable terms.[269] If a small business meets specific SBA eligibility requirements, it can borrow from a lender approved by SBA, and SBA will guarantee a portion of that loan.[270] Treasury announced that SBA, using non-TARP funds, will temporarily raise its guarantee on 7(a) loans up to 90% from current levels of 75% to 85%, and will also temporarily eliminate SBA loan fees.[271] Loan fees can reach up to 3.7 5% for the largest loans.[272] Treasury announced in its March 16, 2009, press release that, by the end of March 2009, it would begin using TARP funds to purchase securities backed by Government-guaranteed portions of these 7(a) Program loans ("7(a) Program Securities") that were securitized on or after July 1, 2008.[273] The origination date of the underlying loans is not a factor for eligibility.[274] As of March 31, 2009, however, Treasury had not announced the execution of any of these purchases or published any more detailed terms. For a description of the securitization process, refer to "TARP Tutorial: Securitization" earlier in this section. Further details on these programs will be provided in SIGTARP's next report.

7(a) Program: SBA loan program guaranteeing a percentage of loans for small businesses that cannot otherwise obtain conventional loans at reasonable terms.

504 Community Development Loan Program: SBA loan program combining Government-guaranteed loans with private-sector mortgage loans to provide loans of up to $10 million for community development.

Pool Assembler (issuer): A separate legal entity that buys cash- ow-producing assets such as loans, pools them together, and sells portions of the pools of loans as securities.

SBA 504 Program Securities

According to Treasury, SBA's 504 Community Development Loan Program is aimed at economic development in communities through long-term loans of up to $10 million, with approximately 50% of the financing guaranteed by SBA and the remainder provided through private-sector mortgage loans.[275] Like 7(a) loans, these private- sector mortgage loans (the portion of 504 Program loans not guaranteed by SBA) were often pooled as securities ("504 Program Securities") and sold in a secondary market.[276] However, according to Treasury, in the last year, this secondary market has frozen.[277] Under the American Recovery and Reinvestment Act of 2009 ("ARRA"), SBA will begin to guarantee a portion of these 504 Program Securities.[278] Treasury stated that it will begin to use TARP funds to purchase these newly guaranteed 504 Program Securities, once SBA implements the new ARRA guidelines.[279]

Treasury also expects to begin purchasing some non-guaranteed 504 Program Securities beginning in May 2009.[280]

As with 7(a) Program Securities, 504 Program Securities must have been securitized on or after July 1, 2008, with no restriction for the origination date of the underlying loans.[281]

The 504 Program Securities that are not guaranteed by SBA must also meet certain eligibility criteria. However, as of March 31, 2009, these criteria were not yet announced.[282]

Administration

Treasury has hired EARNEST Partners, LLC, an independent investment manager, to assist in executing the program to purchase 7(a) Program Securities and 504 Program Securities. The Bank of New York Mellon will serve as Treasury's custodian for these securities. Treasury has stated that it and its investment manager will analyze current and historical prices of comparable securities to determine reasonable prices aimed at providing liquidity to increase small-business lending while protecting the taxpayers' interest.[283]

Executive Compensation and Warrants

Treasury reported that executive compensation provisions under EESA will apply to pool assemblers (issuers) who sell 7(a) Program Securities to Treasury; however, they may apply differently for each pool assembler, based on the obligations incurred by the pool assemblers. As consideration for the purchase of 7(a) Program Securities, Treasury will also receive warrants from pool assemblers, consistent with EESA. Although warrant terms were still under consideration as of March 31, 2009, Treasury expects that they will be in the form of rights to purchase common stock for public companies or the rights to purchase common stock, preferred stock, or senior debt obligations for private companies. Treasury has also indicated that executive compensation and warrant requirements under EESA may also apply to entities selling 504 Program Securities to Treasury. The full application of these provisions was still under consideration as of March 31, 2009.[284]

Making Home Affordable Program

On March 4, 2009, the Administration announced a new program, Making Home Affordable ("MHA"), which is intended to assist homeowners who are facing foreclosure or having difficulty making their monthly mortgage payments. As of March 31, 2009, MHA funding has not been expended and the program details are largely limited to those contained in the proposed term sheet made public on March 4, 2009. MHA has three major initiatives, one of which involves TARP funds:

Loan modif cation program: The Home Affordable Modification Program ("HAMP") is designed to lower monthly payments of borrowers facing foreclosure, and will be funded by $50 billion from TARP and an additional $25 billion from the Housing and Economic Recovery Act ("HERA").[285] Under HAMP, the $50 billion from TARP will be used for modification of **private-label mortgages** and the $25 billion from HERA will be used for modification of Fannie Mae and Freddie Mac mortgages.

Loan ref nancing program: The Home Affordable Re nancing Program ("HARP") intends to help borrowers re nance their mortgages at lower interest rates and will be limited to homeowners with mortgages owned or guaranteed by Fannie Mae or Freddie Mac.

Actions to lower mortgage interest rates by supporting Fannie Mae and Freddie Mac: This initiative includes investments intended to lower mortgage interest costs for borrowers by increased liquidity at Fannie Mae and Freddie Mac through a $100 billion increase in planned Treasury purchases of both Fannie Mae and Freddie Mac preferred stock. Additionally, Treasury will allow Fannie Mae and Freddie Mac each to hold another $50 billion in mortgage securities on their portfolios, with a corresponding increase in debt outstanding.

Homeownership and Foreclosure Avoidance in EESA

Prior to the formation of the MHA program, Congress directed Treasury to pursue foreclosure mitigation policies "to the extent the Secretary acquires mortgages, mortgage backed securities and other assets secured by residential real estate."[286] Specifically, EESA made Treasury responsible for the following actions if it decided to acquire such assets:[287]

implement a plan that seeks to maximize assistance for homeowners
encourage servicers to take advantage of the Federal Housing Administration's ("FHA") HOPE for Homeowners Plan
use loan guarantees and credit enhancements to facilitate loan modification
coordinate with FDIC, the Federal Reserve, Federal Housing Finance Agency ("FHFA"), and FHA
consent to reasonable loan modifications

Private-Label Mortgage: Loans that are not issued or guaranteed by Fannie Mae, Freddie Mac, Ginnie Mae, or another Federal agency.

Although Treasury has not yet acquired the assets that would trigger these obligations, Treasury contends that the newly introduced MHA program addresses most of these requirements. For a list of how the MHA program addresses the EESA provisions for Treasury, see Table 2.34.

Home Affordable ModifiCation Program

MHA offers the prospect of a loan modification to borrowers who are at "imminent risk of default on their mortgage and can be expected to enter into foreclosure proceedings." The loan modifications offered in HAMP will be funded by up to $50 billion of TARP funds for modification of private-label mortgages, and an additional $25 billion from HERA for modification of Fannie Mae and Freddie Mac mortgages. The Administration believes HAMP may "reach three to four million homeowners."[288] As of March 31, 2009, detailed program guidelines have not yet been released; however, servicers have been given basic instructions so that modification negotiations with homeowners can begin immediately.

Table 2.34. Treasury Responses to EESA

EESA Provisions	Section of EESA	References to Treasury Involvement
Develop a homeo-wner assistance plan	109(a)	According to the "Making Home Affordable: Updated Det-ailed Program Description," MHA provides homeowners the ability to renance or modify their existing mortgage depending on eligibility.
Encourage servi-cers to utilize FHA HOPE for Homeowners	109(a)	According to the "Making Home Affordable: Updated Detailed Program Description," MHA will provide sim-ilar incentives to servicers for modications under the HOPE for Homeowners program.
Use loan guaran-tees to facilitate modica-tions	109(a)	TARP requires loan modication support of certain particip-ants. For example, Exhibit F of the Asset Guarantee Prog-ram ("AGP") requires that Citigroup adopt a loan modica-tion program.[a]
Coordinate with other agencies	109(b)	According to the "Making Home Affordable: Updated Deta-iled Program Description," Treasury is responsible for over-sight and audit of loan modications under the terms of MHA.
Consent to reaso-nable loan medic-ation requests	109(c)	According to the "Making Home Affordable: Updated Detailed Program Description," MHA denes criteria for determining eligibility for loan modication.

Note: MHA refers to Making Home Affordable as proposed 3/4/2009.
[a] Exhibit F FDIC Mortgage Loan Modification Program.

The Administration envisions a "shared partnership" between the Government and private lenders to reduce a borrower's monthly payments to an "affordable" level — de ned as 31% of a borrower's monthly income. The private-sector lender will be responsible for all payment reductions necessary to bring a borrower's monthly payments down to 38% of the borrower's gross monthly income. The additional reductions required to bring the borrower's monthly payment down to 31% of the borrower's gross monthly income will be shared equally between the private lender and the Government.[289]

To meet its portion of the shared program, Treasury will provide the following types of support:

monthly payment reduction payments to servicers
payments to servicers for principal reductions
support for extensions of the borrower's loan term

Loan modification applications under the program will be accepted until December 31, 20 12.[290] Any scheduled subsidy payments on a particular mortgage will be made for a period of three to five years as de ned under MHA.

To encourage wide adoption of the program, TARP will provide funding for incentive payments. These incentives will be targeted toward the three main participants in the loan workout process: the homeowners who stay current on their loans after a modification, the loan servicers who establish successful modifications, and the investors who own loans.

How the HAMP Loan Modification Subsidies Are to Be Determined

The MHA process puts borrowers facing default through a series of tests to see if the loan qualifies for Government assistance and, if so, for how much.[291] If a test is failed at any stage, the loan servicer has the right either to attempt a loan modification, without Government incentives, or to proceed with foreclosure and eviction if the borrower defaults. The first step in the modification process addresses homeowner eligibility. If the homeowner is deemed eligible for modification, the second step determines the appropriate subsidies from the Government.

Step #1: Is the homeowner eligible for loan modification under HAMP?[292]

The servicer must collect documentation that ALL of the following are true:

1. The mortgage was originated before January 1, 2009.
2. The borrower is an "owner-occupant" living in a one- to four-unit home as a primary residence.
3. The borrower is not an "investor" living elsewhere.
4. The home is not vacant or condemned.
5. The borrower is at risk of "reasonably foreseeable or imminent default."
6. The borrower has suffered an adverse event (either income reduction or payment increase).
7. The mortgage has an unpaid principal value of less than $729,750 for one- unit homes.
8. The borrower has limited liquid assets.

There is no minimum or maximum loan-to-value ratio for eligibility; that is, the value of the home is not a consideration for eligibility, although it may affect the calculation of potential subsidies.

Step #2: What is the Federal subsidy?[293]

First, the lender must lower the borrower's monthly payment to 38% of the borrower's documented gross monthly income (by lowering the interest rate, extending the term, reducing the principal, or a combination). Then the U.S. Government will match dollar-for-dollar with the lender any reductions necessary to get the monthly payment to 31% of the borrower's monthly income. For purposes of these calculations, "monthly payment" is de ned as the sum of principal, interest, taxes, insurance, and association fees ("PITIA") related to the mortgage. The ratio of PITIA to gross monthly income is referred to as the Front-End-Debt-To-Income ("DTI") test. In conducting the DTI test, the servicer will perform the following tasks:

1. certify the borrower's income

2. calculate the lender reductions necessary to make monthly loan payments 38% of monthly income
3. calculate the lender reductions and U.S. subsidies necessary to make monthly loan payments 31% of monthly income

In addition to a DTI test, the servicer performs a net present value ("NPV") test. In this test, the servicer inputs the estimated foreclosure value of the home (that is the amount of money left over that the servicer believes it could get if the home is foreclosed upon and sold) into a cash- ow projection to see if subsidizing a loan modification is less expensive to the servicer than letting the home fall into foreclosure. This includes:

1. obtain an estimate of the home value and projected losses should a foreclosure occur
2. compare with estimated present value of cash fiows under a loan modification scenario
3. calculate the results of the NPV test
4. confirm that the test supports modification as the lowest cost alternative (if yes, begin a 90-day trial period)
5. if 90-day trial period of reduced payments is successful (*i.e.,* borrower makes payments), begin monthly subsidies

Example of a HAMP Modification

Mr. Smith owns a single-family home which he bought for $200,000. In order to buy the home, Mr. Smith took out a $160,000 mortgage with a 6.0% interest rate. Mr. Smith pays $960 monthly on his mortgage. Due to recent budget cuts at his company, Mr. Smith was moved to part-time work and may be at risk of defaulting on his mortgage.

Mr. Smith called his mortgage servicer and asked whether he qualified for HAMP assistance. After supplying evidence of his income, Mr. Smith and the servicer determine that his monthly mortgage payment is 43% of his gross monthly income. The servicer calculates that the monthly mortgage payment must be reduced to $848 (or 38% of Mr. Smith's monthly income) in order to qualify for additional Government subsidies under HAMP. To do that, the servicer cuts the interest rate to 4.89%.

Pursuant to the terms of HAMP, the lender further reduces the monthly payment on Mr. Smith's mortgage to $692, which is 31% of his gross monthly income. To do that, the servicer cuts the interest rate to 3.2%. Assuming Mr. Smith makes three payments at this new rate during a trial period, Treasury will then pay the lender $78 monthly for five years (as long as Mr. Smith stays current on his mortgage) for half the difference between the modified monthly mortgage payment (38% of monthly income) and the lower modified monthly mortgage payment (31% of monthly income) ($848 – $692). Mr. Smith will be able to keep this new, lower mortgage payment for five years.

HAMP Incentive Payments

HAMP creates a series of incentive payments designed to encourage loan modifications.[294]

To Loan Servicers[295]

"Pay for Success" Up-Front Payments: An up-front payment of $1,000 will be made to loan servicers for each eligible modification they successfully implement and bring through the 90-day trial period.

"Pay for Success" Ongoing Payments: Additional payments of $1,000 per year will be made for each year that the borrower stays current on their loan modification. This payment will be payable for up to three years.

Responsible Modification Incentive Payment: A one-time payment of $500 will be made to a loan servicer who modifies a loan that is still current (less than 30 days delinquent).

Second Lien Release Success Payment: Delinquent loans are frequently accompanied by a **second lien debt** (such as a second mortgage or a home equity line of credit). In order to reduce the overall monthly mortgage payments of the borrower, servicers will be encouraged to contact second lien holders and attempt to negotiate the extinguishment of the second lien. Servicers will receive a success payment equal to $250 per second lien extinguished, plus an additional amount based on a schedule to be published by Treasury.

To Mortgage Holders[296]

Responsible Modification Incentive Payment: Mortgage holders will receive $1,500 for making loan modifications made while a borrower at risk of imminent default is still current (less than 30 days delinquent).

Home Price Decline Payments (up to $10 billion): The Administration, working with FDIC, has announced a cash payment that provides lender compensation to offset partially the losses from failed modifications when home prices decline. The payment is not fixed; rather, it is linked to declines in the home price index.

Second Lien Holder Incentives: Treasury will publish a schedule detailing incentive fees that may be paid to junior lien holders who extinguish their junior liens. This is intended to reduce the borrower's overall monthly mortgage payments.

To Homeowners[297]

"Pay for Success" Payment: Payments of up to $1,000 per year, for five years, will be made to borrowers who remain current under their loan modification. This payment will be applied directly to the reduction of their principal balance

Total TARP-funded HAMP Incentives

In addition to the $78 monthly subsidy for the modification of Mr. Smith's mortgage payments from the HAMP modification example, TARP is responsible for funding a number of the HAMP incentive payments; if a delinquent loan like Mr. Smith's is modified under HAMP, and Mr. Smith makes all of his monthly payments for five years, at least $9,000 of incentive payments will be funded by TARP:

$1,000 to loan servicers for upfront "Pay for Success" incentive
$3,000 ($1,000/year for 3 years) paid to loan servicers for ongoing "Pay for Success" incentives
$5,000 ($1,000 annually) of principal reductions for borrowers

Second Lien Debt: Is subordinate to a senior claim on the same collateral.

Mortgage Holders: Lender or investor (depending on whether the mortgage is securitized) who owns the right to the borrower's monthly payments. For more information on how a securitization process works, refer to "TARP Tutorial: Securitization" earlier in this section.

If the loan was current at the time of the modification, TARP would also be responsible for the following incentive payments:

$500 Responsible Modification payment to the loan servicer
$1,500 Responsible Modification payment to the mortgage holder

In total, TARP would expend $15,680 to modify Mr. Smith's mortgage — $9,680 toward paying Mr. Smith's mortgage and $6,000 in incentives to the servicers and investors.

Other HAMP Provisions

In addition to the monetary initiatives of HAMP, the Administration announced other actions to assist with homeowner loan modifications.

First, it released a set of standardized loan modification guidelines to be used as an industry standard. These guidelines were developed by an interagency working group of Federal agencies with housing interests, including Federal banking regulators, FDIC, National Credit Union Administration, FHA, and FHFA.

Second, all TARP recipients will be required to use these guidelines for loan modifications.

Finally, the Administration announced that it will seek statutory changes to the bankruptcy code to facilitate the goals of its loan modification program. Specifically, its proposal would permit bankruptcy judges "to reduce the outstanding principal balance of a primary residence loan to current fair market value."[298] Further statutory changes would provide FHA and the Veterans Administration with the authority to make partial payments of claims on insured mortgages in the event of bankruptcy or voluntary modification.

HAMP Administration

Treasury has retained Fannie Mae as financial agent to manage the payment program and Freddie Mac as compliance agent for monitoring of the program administration. Ongoing reviews will be necessary to ensure continued eligibility, to manage cash, and to monitor and track changes in status, such as a subsequent delinquency.

Executive Compensation

Section 7002 of ARRA specifically exempted mortgage modification efforts from EESA's executive compensation restrictions. As such, no executive compensation restrictions will apply to this program.

EXECUTIVE COMPENSATION

Any financial institution directly participating in TARP and under an ongoing obligation to Treasury, other than in the mortgage modifications programs, must abide by a set of executive compensation provisions set forth under EESA legislation and regulations mandated by Treasury. Since October 14, 2008, shortly after the original requirements were first enacted in Section 111 of EESA, there have been additional regulations, amendments, and notices that will replace previously existing guidelines. On February 17, 2009, Section 111 of EESA was amended by Section 7001 of the American Recovery and Reinvestment Act of 2009 ("ARRA").[299] This legislation, which will be implemented by regulations promulgated by Treasury, replaces the executive compensation guidelines in Section 111 of EESA. As agreements are finalized and funding is issued, executive compensation restrictions may also continue to be tailored more specifically for each institution. Figure 2.21 describes the changes in executive compensation restrictions set forth by Congress and Treasury regulation over time. Information regarding each set of restrictions on the timeline is detailed in this section.

On February 5, 2009, SIGTARP announced an audit of controls over executive compensation. The audit has requested that recipients of TARP funds provide "specific plans and the status of implementation of those plans, for addressing executive compensation requirements associated with the funding."[300] Additionally, after AIG paid out $165 million in bonuses on March 15, 2009, SIGTARP announced a review of Federal oversight of executive compensation. This includes the bonus payments made by AIG.[301] For more information on these audits, refer to "SIGTARP Oversight Activities" in Section 1 of this report.

EESA Restrictions

Section 111 of EESA, as originally enacted, required any financial institution that sells troubled assets to Treasury under TARP to abide by certain executive compensation rules. These rules have been replaced by Section 7001 of ARRA, which will be implemented by Treasury regulation. All TARP executive compensation restrictions have their basis in the initial restrictions set forth by EESA:[302]

Excessive Risk: Incentive compensation for **Senior Executive Officers ("SEOs")** must not encourage unnecessary and excessive risks that threaten the value of the financial institution.

Clawback: Mandatory clawback of any bonus or incentive compensation paid to an SEO will be enforced if based on statements of earnings, gains, or other criteria that are later proven to be materially inaccurate.

Golden Parachute: Certain severance payments (golden parachute payments) to SEOs are prohibited when Treasury purchases troubled assets directly from the firm.

Tax Deductibility: Executive compensation in excess of $500,000 or more for each SEO may not be deducted by the TARP participant for tax purposes.[303]

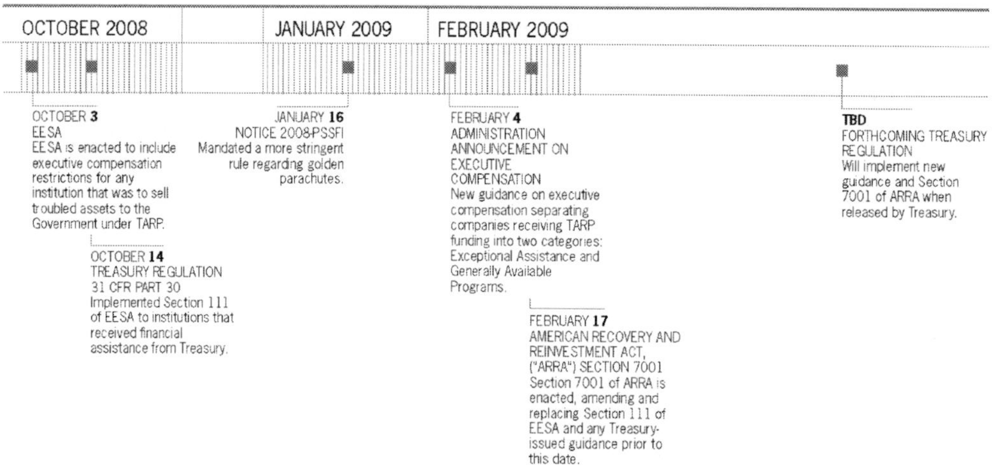

Sources: EESA, P.L. 110-343, 10/3/2008; Treasury, "Treasury Regulation 31 CFR Part 30," 10/14/2008; Treasury, "Notice 2008 - PSSFI," 1/16/2009, accessed 1/19/2009; Treasury, "Treasury Announces New Restrictions on Executive Compensation," 2/4/2009, accessed 3/20/2009; ARRA, P.L. 111-5, 2/17/2009.

Figure 2.21. Executive Compensation Restrictions Timeline.

Treasury Regulation 31 CFR Part 30

On October 14, 2008, Treasury provided guidance on executive compensation through Treasury regulation 31 CFR Part 30. The regulation implemented Section 111 of EESA on executive compensation restrictions to those institutions that received financial assistance from Treasury. This included all institutions participating in CPP and institutions participating in other TARP programs with language in their contracts requiring them to do so. In addition, according to the regulation, all institutions that received financial assistance through TARP must meet Treasury restrictions for as long as they are participants in the program (*i.e.,* as long as Treasury holds the shares).[304]

Senior Executive Officers ("SEOs") (as de ned in original Section 111 of EESA): The top five highly paid executives.

Clawback: Recovery by the company of bonuses or incentive compensation paid to a senior executive.

Golden Parachute (as de ned in original Section 111 of EESA): Compensation to (or for the benefit of) a Senior Executive Officer made upon severance from employment that exceeds specified thresholds. Under EESA as originally enacted, such compensation is limited to three times the executive's annual base salary.

Notice 2008-PSSFI

On January 16, 2009, Treasury released Notice 2008-PSSFI which mandated a more stringent rule for SSFI participants with respect to golden parachute payments and a clarified definition of SEO.[305] Currently, AIG is the only institution subject to this guidance; under the terms of Notice 2008-PSSFI, AIG must comply with the following:

Golden parachutes: Agree to the restrictions regarding golden parachutes established under EESA and the Capital Purchase Program Interim Final Rule (31 CFR Part 30) where senior partners, de ned as employees who participate in the company's "senior partners plan," are prohibited from receiving golden parachute payments beyond three times their base salary amount. In addition, under Notice 2008-PSSFI, the definition of golden parachutes is expanded to prohibit the payment of all severance payments to the company's top five SEOs, which include its Principal Executive Officer ("PEO"), Principal Finance Officer ("PFO"), and its next three highly compensated executives, according to the guidance.[306]

Citigroup and Bank of America are following similar guidance on golden parachutes according to their Securities Purchase Agreements under the Targeted Investment Program. According to new agreements between AIG and the Government, AIG will be following the executive compensation restrictions detailed in ARRA's Section 7001 when it is implemented by Treasury.[307]

Administration Announcement on Executive Compensation

On February 4, 2009, the Administration announced new guidance on executive compensation restrictions. According to Treasury, these new restrictions would support the need to monitor and hold accountable institutions receiving Government funding. The announcement contemplated requiring TARP recipients to complete, annually, a certification of compliance with executive compensation guidelines. It also noted that there would be differences in restrictions for institutions receiving "**exceptional assistance**" (*i.e.,* AIG, Citigroup, and Bank of America), and those involved in **generally available programs** (*i.e.,* CPP and CAP) within TARP.[308]

For more information on the executive compensation restrictions for AIG, Citigroup, and Bank of America, refer to SIGTARP's Initial Report, Section 3: "TARP Implementation and Administration."

Exceptional Assistance: Increased assistance to an institution that needs more than allowed under a generally available program (*i.e.,* CPP and CAP).

Generally Available Programs: Programs having the same terms for all recipients, with limits on the amount each institution may receive and specified returns for taxpayers (*i.e.,* CPP or CAP).

The Administration's announcement contemplated that companies receiving exceptional assistance from the Federal Government would have to comply with the following restrictions:[309]

Compensation Cap: The cap limits senior executives from receiving more than $500,000 in total compensation (excludes restricted stock).

Restricted Stock: Any pay over $500,000 must be in restricted stock that cannot be sold or transferred while the company is still receiving TARP assistance.

Say on Pay: Executive compensation and strategy must be fully disclosed and subject to a "**Say on Pay**" shareholder vote.

Clawbacks: Mandatory clawback of any bonus or incentive compensation paid to an SEO will be enforced if based on statements of earnings, gains, or other criteria that are later proven to be materially inaccurate.

Golden Parachutes: Any form of severance payment to the top 10 senior executives is prohibited, as are golden parachute payments greater than one year's compensation to the next 25 executives.

Luxury Expenditures: TARP recipients' boards of directors must adopt company-wide policy on expenditures related to aviation, facility renovations, entertainment and parties, and conferences.

Additionally, prior to the amendment of EESA, pursuant to the Administration's announcement, Treasury contemplated issuing guidance (subject to public comment) on executive compensation requirements for institutions receiving Government assistance through newly created generally available programs, such as the Capital Assistance Program, and were to include the following:[310]

Say on Pay: Provision that executive compensation must be put to a nonbinding vote by shareholders.

Compensation Cap: Limits senior executives from receiving more than $500,000 in total compensation plus restricted stock, unless waived by full public disclosure and a "Say on Pay" shareholder resolution.

Clawbacks: Mandatory clawback of any bonus or incentive compensation paid to an SEO will be enforced if based on statements of earnings, gains, or other criteria that are later proven to be materially inaccurate.

Golden Parachutes: Prohibits any severance payment to the top five senior executives that is greater than one year's compensation.

Luxury Expenditures: TARP recipients' boards of directors must adopt company-wide policy on expenditures related to aviation, facility renovations, entertainment and parties, and conferences.

Before regulations imposing the Administration's executive compensation restrictions could be issued, however, Section 111 of EESA was amended by ARRA.[311]

EESA, as Amended

On February 17, 2009, EESA was amended with the passing of ARRA. Section 7001 of ARRA outlines the executive compensation guidelines that will replace those set forth in Section 111 of EESA. As of March 31, 2009, Treasury regulations implementing these guidelines had not been released. The amendments to EESA are more expansive as to whom the executive compensation restrictions apply, as well as include provisions for the creation of a Board Compensation Committee, certification of compliance, and review of prior payments to executives.[312] Treasury has indicated that it intends to issue new regulations that implement amended Section 111 of EESA, but it has not yet determined which restrictions set forth in the Administration's February 4, 2009, announcement, if any, will be included. As of March 31, 2009, the updated regulations had not been issued.[313]

Bonus and Incentive

There are three requirements in Section 7001 of ARRA by which all TARP recipients must abide, and a fourth bonus requirement that is applied to a varying number of executives depending upon the amount of TARP funding received by the institution. All requirements apply over the entire time that any obligation arising from TARP assistance is outstanding. The Chief Executive Officer and the Chief Financial Officer of each TARP recipient must provide a written certification of compliance for the following requirements to either the Securities and Exchange Commission ("SEC") (public companies) or the Treasury Secretary (private companies).[314] Requirements for TARP recipients are as follows:[315]

Excessive Risk: limits on compensation that are based upon unnecessary and excessive risks that threaten the value of the TARP recipient

Clawbacks: recovery (clawback) of any bonus, retention award, or incentive compensation paid to an **SEO** and any of the next 20 highest compensated employees resulting from materially inaccurate earnings, revenues, or gains

Golden Parachutes: prohibits any severance payment to any SEO or any of the next five highly compensated employees

Bonus: prohibits the payments or accruing of any bonus, retention award, or incentive compensation to the applicable employees shown in Table 2.35

Senior Executive Officer ("SEO") (definition under ARRA): An individual who is one of the top five most highly paid executives of a public company, whose compensation is required to be disclosed pursuant to the Securities Exchange Act of 1934, and any regulations issued thereunder, and non-public company counterparts.

Golden Parachute (definition under ARRA): Any payment to a senior executive Officer for departure from a company for any reason, except for payments for services performed or benefits accrued.

The following bonus payments are allowed under Section 7001 of ARRA: (i) any bonus payment required to be paid pursuant to an employment contract executed before February 11, 2009, and (ii) payment of long-term restricted stock that meets the following criteria:[316]

does not fully **vest** during the period of any obligation arising from TARP assistance
has a value of not greater than 1/3 of the total amount of the annual compensation of the employee receiving stock
is subject to other terms and conditions as the Treasury Secretary determines is in the public interest

Further, ARRA requires Treasury to review all bonuses, retention awards, and other compensation paid, before February 17, 2009, to SEOs and the next 20 highest compensated employees. This review is intended to determine if the payments made were "inconsistent with the purposes of this section or the TARP or were otherwise contrary to the public interest." Should the Treasury Secretary find the payments were inappropriate, he is required to seek to negotiate for reimbursement to the Federal Government.[317]

Board Compensation Committee

Under ARRA, each TARP recipient must establish a Board Compensation Committee. Board members must be independent directors, and the board will convene for the purpose of reviewing employee compensation plans. The committee is required to meet at least semiannually to review the compensation plans proposed and assess any risk that these compensation plans may create for the TARP recipient. The exception to this requirement is made for TARP recipients that are not registered under the Securities Exchange Act of 1934 and have received $25 million or less in TARP assistance. These institutions may have their board of directors carry out the duties of the Board Compensation Committee.[318]

> **Vest:** To become exercisable. Typically used in the context of an employee stock ownership or option program.

"Say on Pay"

Section 7001 of ARRA includes a provision for a non-binding vote by shareholders on executive compensation, otherwise known as "Say on Pay." This provision requires TARP recipients to permit an annual non-binding vote by shareholders on executive compensation. The shareholder vote shall be non-binding on the board of directors and will not override any board decisions. The executive compensation voted on by the shareholders must be disclosed in the annual report.[319]

Table 2.35. Bonus Limits, by Size of TARP Funding

Amount of TARP Funding	Applicable Employees
< $25,000,000	most highly compensated employee
≥ $25,000,000 < $250,000,000	5 most highly compensated employees
≥ $250,000,000 < $500,000,000	SEOs and at least 10 next highly compensated employees
≥ $ 500,000,000	SEOs and at least 20 next highly compensated employees

Note: The Treasury Secretary may determine a higher number based on the public's best interest.
Source: ARRA, P.L. 111-5, 2/17/2009.

Luxury Expenditures

Section 7001 of ARRA also addresses corporate luxury expenses; the legislation states that the board of directors of any institution receiving TARP funds must have a company-wide policy which includes excessive expenditures on entertainment or events, of ce and facility renovations, aviation or other transportation services, and other activities or events that are not reasonable expenditures for the following activities:[320]

staff development
reasonable performance incentives
other activities conducted in the normal course of business operations

The Treasury Secretary must promulgate regulations to implement these amendments to EESA. As of March 31, 2009, the Treasury Secretary has not done so.

End Notes

[1] Treasury, response to SIGTARP data call, 4/8/2009.
[2] Emergency Economic Stabilization Act of 2008, P.L. 110-343, 10/3/2008.

[3] Treasury, response to SIGTARP data call, 4/8/2009. This 2 gure represents Treasury's announced plans for TARP funding. GAO-09-539T reported the same 2 gure as the "projected use of funds."
[4] Treasury, *Transactions Report,* 4/2/2009, www.2 nancialstability.gov, accessed 4/3/2009.
[5] Treasury, *Transactions Report,* 4/2/2009, www.2 nancialstability.gov, accessed 4/3/2009.
[6] Treasury, "Fact Sheet: Financial Stability Plan," 2/10/2009, www.2 nancialstability.gov, accessed 3/18/2009.
[7] Treasury, "Capital Purchase Program," no date, www.treas.gov, accessed 3/18/2009.
[8] Treasury, *Transactions Report,* 4/2/2009, www.2 nancialstability.gov, accessed 4/3/2009.
[9] CPP, TALF, and PPIP: Treasury, Office of Financial Stability, Chief of Compliance and CFO, SIGTARP interview, 3/30/2009.
[10] Treasury Press Release, "Treasury Announces Participation in Citigroup's Exchange Offering," 2/27/2009, www.treas.gov, accessed 3/26/2009.
[11] Treasury, "Treasury White Paper: The Capital Assistance Program and Its Role in the Financial Stability Plan," no date, www.treas.gov, accessed 3/25/2009.
[12] Treasury, GAO, SIGTARP meeting on CAP, 3/12/2009.
[13] Treasury, "Guidelines for Systemically Signi2 cant Failing Institutions Program," no date, www.treas.gov, accessed 3/18/2009.
[14] Treasury, *Transactions Report,* 4/2/2009, www.2 nancialstability.gov, accessed 4/3/2009.
[15] Treasury Press Release, "U.S. Treasury and Federal Reserve Board Announce Participation in AIG Restructuring Plan," 3/2/2009, www.treas.gov, accessed 3/26/2009.
[16] Treasury, "Program Description: Targeted Investment Program," no date, www.treas.gov, accessed 3/18/2009.
[17] Treasury, *Transactions Report,* 4/2/2009, www.2 nancialstability.gov, accessed 4/3/2009.
[18] Treasury, *Report to Congress Pursuant to Section 102 of the Emergency Economic Stabilization Act,* 12/31/2008.
[19] Treasury Press Release, "U.S. Government Finalizes Terms of Citi Guarantee Announced in November," 1/16/2009, www.treas.gov, accessed 3/26/2009.
[20] Treasury, *Transactions Report,* 4/2/2009, www.2 nancialstability.gov, accessed 4/3/2009.
[21] Treasury Press Release, "Treasury, Federal Reserve and the FDIC Provide Assistance to Bank of America," 1/16/2009, www.treas.gov, accessed 3/31/2009.
[22] Treasury, "Automotive Industry Financing Program," no date, www.treas.gov, accessed 3/31/2009.
[23] Treasury, *Transactions Report,* 4/2/2009, www.2 nancialstability.gov, accessed 4/3/2009.
[24] Treasury, response to SIGTARP data call, 2/23/2009.
[25] Treasury, "General Motors Corporation 2009 – 2014 Restructuring Plan," 2/17/2009, www.treas.gov, accessed 2/17/2009.
[26] Treasury, SIGTARP brie2 ng on auto industry, 4/14/2009.
[27] Treasury, "Auto Supplier Support Program: Stabilizing the Auto Industry at a Time of Crisis," 3/19/2009, www.treas.gov, accessed 3/19/2009.
[28] Treasury, SIGTARP brie2 ng on auto industry, 4/14/2009.
[29] FRBNY, "Term Asset-Backed Securities Loan Facility: Terms and Conditions," 3/19/2009, www.newyorkfed.org, accessed 3/25/2009.
[30] FRBNY Press Release, "Joint Press Release," 3/3/2009, www.newyorkfed.org, accessed 3/25/2009.
[31] Treasury, Office of Financial Stability, Chief of Compliance and CFO, SIGTARP interview, 3/30/2009.
[32] Treasury Press Release, "Treasury Department Releases Details on Public Private Partnership Investment Program," 3/23/2009, www.treas.gov, accessed 3/26/2009.
[33] Treasury, "Unlocking Credit for Small Businesses Fact Sheet," 3/16/2009, www.treas.gov, accessed 3/26/2009.
[34] Treasury, "Making Home Affordable: Updated Detailed Program Description," 3/4/2009, www.treas.gov, accessed 3/4/2009.
[35] Treasury Press Release, "Relief for Responsible Homeowners One Step Closer Under New Treasury Guidelines, With Detailed Program Requirements, Servicers Can Now Begin 'Making Home Affordable' Loan Modi2 cations, Extensive Borrower Outreach Efforts Underway," 3/4/2009, www.treas.gov, accessed 3/26/2009.
[36] Treasury, "Making Home Affordable Updated Detailed Program Description," 3/4/2009, www.treas.gov, accessed 3/26/2009.
[37] Treasury, Office of Financial Stability, Chief of Compliance and CFO, SIGTARP interview, 3/30/2009.
[38] Treasury, "Program Descriptions: Capital Purchase Program," 3/24/2009, www.treas.gov, accessed 3/24/2009.
[39] Treasury, "Interim Assistant Secretary for Financial Stability Neel Kashkari Review of the Financial Market Crisis and the Troubled Assets Relief Program," 1/13/2009, www.treas.gov, accessed 3/16/2009.
[40] Treasury, "Treasury, Regulators Issue Additional Guidance on Capital Purchase Program," 10/20/2008, www.treas.gov, accessed 3/16/2009.
[41] Treasury, "Treasury Releases Capital Purchase Program Term Sheet for Privately Held Financial Institutions," 11/17/2008, www.treas.gov, accessed 3/16/2009.
[42] Treasury, "Treasury Releases Capital Purchase Program Term," 1/14/2009, www.treas.gov, accessed 3/16/2009.
[43] Treasury, "Process Related FAQs for the Capital Purchase Program, Mutual Holding Company FAQs," 4/7/2009, www.2 nancialstability.gov, accessed 4/7/2009.
[44] American Recovery and Reinvestment Act of 2009, P.L. 11-5, 2/13/2009.

[45] Treasury, *Transactions Report,* 4/2/2009, www.2 nancialstability.gov, accessed 4/3/2009. Two institutions, Bank of America Corporation and SunTrust Banks, Inc., each received investments in two separate installments.
[46] Congressional Oversight Panel, "February Oversight Report," 2/6/2009, cop.senate.gov, accessed 3/26/2009.
[47] Congressional Budget Office, "A Preliminary Analysis of the President's Budget and an Update of CBO's Budget and Economic Outlook," March 2009, www.cbo.gov, accessed 4/10/2009. "Oversight and Analysis Estimate of TARP's Cost to Taxpayers Increases," *Wall Street Journal,* 4/3/2009, www.wsj. com, accessed 4/4/2009.
[48] Warrants for private QFIs are generally exercised immediately. Certain Community Development Financial Institutions (CDFIs) are not required to issue warrants.
[49] Treasury, response to SIGTARP data call, 3/31/2009.
[50] American Recovery and Reinvestment Act of 2009, P.L. 11-5, 2/13/2009.
[51] Treasury, response to SIGTARP data call, 4/10/2009.
[52] Treasury, response to SIGTARP data call, 4/8/2009.
[53] Treasury, response to SIGTARP data call, 4/8/2009.
[54] Treasury, "Treasury Releases First Monthly Bank Lending Survey," 2/17/2009, www.treas.gov, accessed 3/19/2009.
[55] Treasury, "Interim Assistant Secretary for Financial Stability, Neel Kashkari Remarks at Brookings Institute," 1/8/2009, www.treas.gov, accessed 1/12/2009.
[56] Treasury, response to SIGTARP data call, 3/31/2009.
[57] Treasury, "Treasury Department Monthly Lending and Intermediation Snapshot," 2/17/2009, www.treas.gov, accessed 3/4/2009.
[58] Treasury, letter to Jeffrey B. Weeden, 1/16/2009, received 1/22/2009.
[59] Treasury, SIGTARP response to data call, 3/31/2009.
[60] Treasury, "Treasury Department Monthly Lending and Intermediation Snapshot," 2/17/2009, www.treas.gov, accessed 3/19/2009.
[61] Treasury, "Treasury Department Monthly Lending and Intermediation Snapshot," 2/17/2009, www.treas.gov, accessed 3/19/2009.
[62] Treasury, "Treasury Department Monthly Lending and Intermediation Snapshot," 2/17/2009, www.treas.gov, accessed 3/19/2009.
[63] Treasury, *Transactions Report,* 4/2/2009, www.2 nancialstability.gov, accessed 4/3/2009.
[64] Treasury, "Treasury Department Monthly Lending and Intermediation Snapshot," 3/16/2009, www.treas.gov, accessed 3/19/2009.
[65] Treasury, "Treasury Department Monthly Lending and Intermediation Snapshot," 3/16/2009, www.treas.gov, accessed 3/19/2009.
[66] Treasury, "Treasury Department Monthly Lending and Intermediation Snapshot," 3/16/2009, www.treas.gov, accessed 3/19/2009.
[67] Treasury, "Secretary Geithner Introduces Financial Stability Plan," 2/10/2009, www.treas.gov, accessed 3/25/2009.
[68] Treasury, "Treasury White Paper: The Capital Assistance Program and Its Role in the Financial Stability Plan," no date, www.treas.gov, accessed 3/25/2009.
[69] FDIC, "FAQs — Supervisory Capital Assessment Program," 2/25/2009, www.fdic.gov, accessed 3/25/2009.
[70] Federal Reserve, response to SIGTARP draft, 4/9/2009.
[71] Bureau of Labor and Statistics, "The Employment Situation: March 2009," 4/3/2009, www.bls.gov, accessed 4/5/2009.
[72] Treasury, "Treasury White Paper: The Capital Assistance Program and Its Role in the Financial Stability Plan," no date, www.treas.gov, accessed 3/25/2009.
[73] FDIC Press Release, "Agencies to Begin Forward-Looking Economic Assessments," 2/25/2009, www.fdic.gov, accessed 3/25/2009.
[74] FDIC, "FAQs — Supervisory Capital Assessment Program," 2/25/2009, www.fdic.gov, accessed 3/25/2009.
[75] FDIC, "FAQs — Supervisory Capital Assessment Program," 2/25/2009, www.fdic.gov, accessed 3/25/2009.
[76] Treasury, White Paper, "The Capital Assistance Program and Its Role in the Financial Stability Plan," no date, www.treas.gov, accessed 3/25/2009.
[77] Treasury, "Summary of Mandatorily Convertible Preferred Stock Terms," 3/25/2009, www.treas.gov, accessed 3/25/2009.
[78] Treasury, *Transactions Report,* 4/2/2009, www.2 nancialstability.gov, accessed 4/3/2009.
[79] Treasury, "Fact Sheet, Financial Stability Plan," 2/10/2009, www.2 nancialstability.gov, accessed 3/25/2009.
[80] Treasury, "Summary of Mandatorily Convertible Preferred Stock Terms," 3/25/2009, www.treas.gov, accessed 3/25/2009.
[81] Treasury, "Summary of Mandatorily Convertible Preferred Stock Terms," 3/25/2009, www.treas.gov, accessed 3/25/2009.
[82] Treasury, "Summary of Mandatorily Convertible Preferred Stock Terms," 3/25/2009, www.treas.gov, accessed 3/25/2009.

[83] Treasury, "Capital Assistance Program FAQs," no date, www.treas.gov, accessed 3/25/2009.
[84] Treasury, "Summary of Mandatorily Convertible Preferred Stock Terms," 3/25/2009, www.treas.gov, accessed 3/25/2009
[85] Treasury, "Application Guidelines for Capital Assistance Program," no date, www.treas.gov, accessed 3/25/2009.
[86] Treasury, "Summary of Mandatorily Convertible Preferred Stock Terms," no date, accessed 3/25/2009.
[87] Treasury, White Paper, "The Capital Assistance Program and Its Role in the Financial Stability Plan," no date, https://ustreas.gov/press/releases/reports/tg40_capwhitepaper.pdf, accessed 4/3/2009.
[88] Treasury, "Testimony By Interim Assistant Secretary for Financial Stability Neel Kashkari, before the Senate Appropriations Subcommittee on Financial Services and General Government," 12/4/2008, www.treas.gov, accessed 4/8/2009.
[89] FDIC, "A Brief History of Deposit Insurance in the United States," no date, http://www.fdic.gov /bank/historical/brief/brhist.pdf, accessed 4/3/2009.
[90] OCC, "Supervisory Guidance, Supervisory Review Process Related to the Implementation of the Basel II Advanced Capital Framework," no date, www.occ.gov\ftp\release\2008-81a.pdf, accessed 4/3/2009.
[91] Federal Reserve Board, "Basel II Capital Accord, Notice of Proposed Rulemaking," 3/30/2006, www.federalreserve.gov, accessed 4/9/2009.
[92] FDIC, "FAQs—Supervisory Capital Assessment Program," no date, www.fdic.gov/news/press/ 2009/pr09025a.pdf, accessed 4/15/2009.
[93] SIGTARP, "Initial Report to Congress," 2/6/2009, www.sigtarp.gov, accessed 3/25/2009.
[94] As of March 31, 2009, $122.5 billion has been allocated to institution-speci2 c participants, $85 billion has been expended, while $37.5 billion has been announced but not disbursed. This is a total increase of $30 billion since SIGTARP's Initial Report.
[95] AIG, "Securities Purchase Agreement," 11/25/2008.
[96] Treasury, Press Release, "U.S. Treasury and Federal Reserve Board Announce Participation in AIG Restructuring Plan," 3/2/2009, www.treas.gov, accessed 3/4/2009.
[97] Treasury, Press Release, "U.S. Treasury and Federal Reserve Board Announce Participation in AIG Restructuring Plan," 3/2/2009, www.treas.gov, accessed 3/4/2009.
[98] Treasury, Press Release, "U.S. Treasury and Federal Reserve Board Announce Participation in AIG Restructuring Plan," 3/2/2009, www.treas.gov, accessed 3/4/2009.
[99] Treasury, Press Release, response to SIGTARP draft report, 4/9/2009.
[100] Treasury, "U.S. Treasury and Federal Reserve Board Announce Participation in AIG Restructuring Plan," 3/2/2009, www.treas.gov, accessed 3/4/2009.
[101] Treasury, Press Release, "U.S. Treasury and Federal Reserve Board Announce Participation in AIG Restructuring Plan," 3/2/2009, www.treas.gov, accessed 3/4/2009.
[102] Treasury, Press Release, "U.S. Treasury and Federal Reserve Board Announce Participation in AIG Restructuring Plan," 3/2/2009, www.treas.gov, accessed 3/4/2009.
[103] Federal Reserve, response to SIGTARP draft report, 4/9/2009.
[104] AIG, 8-K, 2/14/2009, www.sec.gov, accessed 3/6/2009.
[105] Treasury, Press Release, "U.S. Treasury and Federal Reserve Board Announce Participation in AIG Restructuring Plan," 3/2/2009, www.treas.gov, accessed 3/4/2009.
[106] AIG, Restructuring Term Sheet, "Exchange of Series D Fixed Rate Cumulative Perpetual Preferred Stock for Series E Fixed Rate Non-Cumulative Perpetual Preferred Stock," 3/2/2009.
[107] Treasury, response to SIGTARP data call, 4/6/2009.
[108] AIG Restructuring Term Sheet, "Exchange of Series D Fixed Rate Cumulative Perpetual Preferred Stock for Series E Fixed Rate Non-Cumulative Perpetual Preferred Stock," 3/2/2009.
[109] AIG, Restructuring Term Sheet, "Exchange of Series D Fixed Rate Cumulative Perpetual Preferred Stock for Series E Fixed Rate Non-Cumulative Perpetual Preferred Stock," 3/2/2009.
[110] AIG, Restructuring Term Sheet, "Exchange of Series D Fixed Rate Cumulative Perpetual Preferred Stock for Series E Fixed Rate Non-Cumulative Perpetual Preferred Stock," 3/2/2009.
[111] AIG, Restructuring Term Sheet, "Issuance of Additional Preferred Stock," 3/2/2009.
[112] New York Stock Exchange, 3/31/2009, www.nyse.com, accessed 3/31/2009.
[113] AIG, Restructuring Term Sheet, "Issuance of Additional Preferred Stock," 3/2/2009.
[114] Treasury, "Treasury Department Releases Text of Letter From Secretary Geithner to Hill Leadership on AIG," 3/17/2009, www.treas.gov, accessed 3/19/2009.
[115] Treasury, "Treasury Department Releases Text of Letter From Secretary Geithner to Hill Leadership on AIG," 3/17/2009, www.treas.gov, accessed 3/19/2009.
[116] Treasury Press Release, "U.S. Treasury and Federal Reserve Board Announce Participation in AIG Restructuring Plan," 3/2/2009, www.treas.gov, accessed 3/4/2009.
[117] Treasury Press Release, "U.S. Treasury and Federal Reserve Board Announce Participation in AIG Restructuring Plan," 3/2/2009, www.treas.gov, accessed 3/4/2009.
[118] American Recovery and Reinvestment Act of 2009, P.L. 115-5, 2/17/2009.

[119] Treasury, "Treasury Department Releases Text of Letter From Secretary Geithner to Hill Leadership on AIG," 3/17/2009, www.treas.gov, accessed 3/19/2009.
[120] American Recovery and Reinvestment Act of 2009, P.L. 111-5, 2/17/2009.
[121] Treasury, *Fifth Tranche Report to Congress*, 2/6/2009, www.treas.gov, accessed 2/24/2009.
[122] Treasury, *Transactions Report*, 3/31/2009, www.2 nancialstability.gov, accessed 3/31/2009.
[123] Citigroup Inc., "Securities Purchase Agreement," 12/31/2008.
[124] Citigroup Inc., "What Citi is Doing to Expand the Flow of Credit, Support Homeowners and Help the U.S. Economy, TARP Progress Report for Fourth Quarter 2008," 2/6/2009, www.citigroup.com, accessed 2/24/2009.
[125] Citigroup Inc., "What Citi is Doing to Expand the Flow of Credit, Support Homeowners and Help the U.S. Economy, TARP Progress Report for Fourth Quarter 2008," 2/6/2009, www.citigroup.com, accessed 2/24/2009.
[126] Treasury, *Transactions Report*, 3/30/2009, www.2 nancialstability.gov, accessed 3/31/2009.
[127] Treasury Press Release, "U.S. Government Finalizes Terms of Citi Guarantee Announced in November," 1/16/2009, www.treas.gov, accessed 1/16/2009.
[128] Treasury Press Release, "Treasury Announces Participation in Citigroup's Exchange Offering," 2/27/2009. www.treas.gov, accessed 3/2/2009.
[129] Treasury Press Release, "Treasury Announces Participation in Citigroup's Exchange Offering," 2/27/2009, www.treas.gov, accessed 3/2/2009.
[130] Citigroup Inc., 8-K, "Citi to Exchange Preferred Securities for Common, Increasing Tangible Common Equity to as Much as $81 Billion," 2/27/2009, www.sec.gov, accessed 3/2/2009.
[131] Citigroup Inc., 8-K, "Citi Files Registration Statement for Exchange Offer," 3/19/2009, www.sec.gov, accessed 3/20/2009.
[132] Treasury, "Treasury Announces Participation in Citigroup's Exchange Offering," 2/27/2009, www.treas.gov, accessed 3/2/2009.
[133] Citigroup Inc., 8-K, "Citi to Exchange Preferred Securities for Common, Increasing Tangible Common Equity to as Much as $81 Billion," 2/27/2009, www.sec.gov, accessed 3/2/2009.
[134] Treasury Press Release, "Treasury Announces Participation in Citigroup's Exchange Offering," 2/27/2009, www.treas.gov, accessed 3/2/2009.
[135] The actual dollar value of these obligations would depend on the losses incurred as well as the deductibles, loss sharing provisions, and other terms of the agreements.
[136] Citigroup Inc., Master Agreement, 1/15/2009.
[137] Summary of Agreement between Citigroup, Treasury, FDIC, and the Federal Reserve Board.
[138] Citigroup Inc., Master Agreement, "Exhibit B," 1/15/2009.
[139] Citigroup Inc., Master Agreement, 1/15/2009.
[140] Citigroup Inc., Master Agreement, 1/15/2009.
[141] Treasury, "Treasury, FDIC, and Federal Reserve Announce Assistance to Citigroup," 11/23/2008, www.treas.gov, accessed 1/9/2009.
[142] Citigroup Inc., Master Agreement, 1/15/2009.
[143] Citigroup Inc., Master Agreement, 1/15/2009.
[144] Citigroup Inc., Master Agreement, 1/15/2009.
[145] Citigroup Inc., Master Agreement, "Schedule A," 1/15/2009.
[146] Citigroup Inc., Master Agreement, "Schedule A," 1/15/2009.
[147] Treasury, SIGTARP interview, 2/10/2009.
[148] Citigroup Inc., Master Agreement, "Exhibit B," 1/15/2009.
[149] Citigroup Inc., Master Agreement, "Exhibit B," 1/15/2009.
[150] Citigroup Inc., Master Agreement, "Exhibit B," 1/15/2009.
[151] Citigroup Inc., Master Agreement, "Exhibit B," 1/15/2009.
[152] Citigroup Inc., Master Agreement, "Exhibit B," 1/15/2009.
[153] Citigroup Inc., Master Agreement, "Exhibit B," 1/15/2009.
[154] Citigroup Inc., Master Agreement, 1/15/2009.
[155] Citigroup Inc., Master Agreement, 1/15/2009.
[156] Citigroup Inc., Master Agreement, "Exhibit B," 1/15/2009.
[157] Citigroup Inc., Master Agreement, 1/15/2009.
[158] Treasury, response to SIGTARP data call, 4/8/2009.
[159] Treasury, *Transactions Report,* 3/31/2009, www.2 nancialstability.gov, accessed 3/31/2009.
[160] Treasury Press Release, "Treasury, Federal Reserve, and the FDIC Provide Assistance to Bank of America," 1/16/2009, www.treas.gov, accessed 1/16/2009.
[161] Treasury, *Transactions Report,* 3/31/2009, www.2 nancialstability.gov, accessed 3/31/2009.
[162] FDIC, "FDIC Press Release," 1/16/2009, www.fdic.gov, accessed 1/23/2009.
[163] Treasury Press Release, "Treasury, Federal Reserve, and the FDIC Provide Assistance to Bank of America," 1/16/2009, www.treas.gov, accessed 1/16/2009.

[164] Treasury Press Release, "Treasury, Federal Reserve, and the FDIC Provide Assistance to Bank of America," 1/16/2009, www.treas.gov, accessed 1/16/2009.
[165] Bank of America Corp, "10-K," 2/27/2009, www.sec.gov, accessed 4/17/2009.
[166] Treasury, response to SIGTARP draft report, 4/9/2009.
[167] Treasury, "Program Descriptions Automotive Industry Financing Program," http://www.treas.gov, accessed 1/12/2009.
[168] White House Press Release, "Geithner, Summers Convene Official Designees to Presidential Task Force on the Auto Industry," 2/20/2009, www.whitehouse.gov, accessed 3/10/2009.
[169] Treasury, Office of Financial Stability, SIGTARP brie2 ng, 4/14/2009.
[170] Treasury, "Geithner, Summers Convene Official Designees to Presidential Task Force on the Auto Industry," 2/20/2009, www.treas.gov, accessed 3/16/2009.
[171] White House Press Release, "President Obama Announces Key Administration Posts," 2/23/2009, www.whitehouse.gov, accessed 3/16/2009.
[172] White House Press Release, "Obama Administration New Path to Viability for GM & Chrysler," 3/30/2009, www.whitehouse.gov, accessed 3/30/09.
[173] Treasury, "GM Viability Assessment," 3/30/2009, www.2 nancialstability.gov, accessed 4/3/2009.
[174] Treasury, "Tranche Report to Congress," 1/7/2009, www.2 nancialstability.gov, accessed 4/14/2009.
[175] Treasury, "General Motors Corporation 2009-2014 Restructuring Plan," p. 20, 2/17/2009, www.treas.gov, accessed 2/17/2009.
[176] Treasury, "General Motors Corporation 2009-2014 Restructuring Plan" pp. 35 – 36, 2/17/2009, www.treas.gov, accessed 2/17/2009.
[177] Treasury, brie2 ng on AIFP, 3/30/2009.
[178] General Motors Corporation, Form 10-K, Exhibit 23.a, 3/5/09, www.sec.gov, accessed 3/5/2009.
[179] Treasury Press Release, "Treasury Announces TARP Investment in GMAC," 12/29/2008, www.treas.gov, accessed 1/16/2009.
[180] GMAC, "GMAC Receives $5.0 Billion Investment from the U.S. Treasury," 12/29/2008, www.gmacfs.com, accessed 1/13/2009.
[181] Treasury, *Transactions Report,* 1/27/2009, www.2 nancialstability.gov, accessed 4/14/2009.
[182] SIGTARP Initial Report to Congress, Section 3: "TARP Implementation and Administration, Institution-speci2 c Assistance," 2/6/2009, www.sigtarp.gov, accessed 4/9/2009.
[183] Treasury, "Chrysler's Viability Assessment," 3/30/2009, www.2 nancialstability.gov, accessed 4/3/2009.
[184] White House Press Release, "Obama Administration New Path to Viability for GM & Chrysler," March 30, 2009, www.whitehouse.gov, accessed 3/30/2009.
[185] Treasury, brie2 ng on AIFP, 3/30/2009.
[186] Treasury, *Fifth Tranche Report to Congress,* 2/6/2009, www.2 nancialstability.gov, accessed 4/14/2009.
[187] Treasury, response to SIGTARP data call, 4/9/2009.
[188] Treasury, SIGTARP brie2 ng, 4/14/2009.
[189] Treasury Press Release, "Treasury Announces Auto Supplier Support Program; Program Will Aid Critical Sector of American Economy," 3/19/2009, www.treas.gov, accessed 3/19/2009.
[190] Treasury Press Release, "Treasury Announces Auto Supplier Support Program; Program Will Aid Critical Sector of American Economy," 3/19/2009, www.treas.gov, accessed 3/19/2009.
[191] Treasury, "Auto Supplier Support Program: Stabilizing the Auto Industry in a Time of Crisis," 3/19/2009, www.treas.gov, accessed 3/19/2009.
[192] Treasury, "Auto Supplier Support Program: Stabilizing the Auto Industry in a Time of Crisis," 3/19/2009, www.treas.gov, accessed 3/19/2009.
[193] Treasury, briefing on ASSP, 3/18/2009.
[194] Treasury, response to SIGTARP draft, 4/9/2009.
[195] Treasury, "Auto Supplier Support Program: Stabilizing the Auto Industry in a Time of Crisis," 3/19/2009, www.treas.gov, accessed 3/19/2009.
[196] Treasury, brie2 ng on ASSP, 3/18/2009.
[197] Treasury, "The U.S. Treasury Department Summary Response to February 6, 2009 Recommendations of SIGTARP," 4/7/2009, accessed 4/ 7/2009.
[198] Treasury, SIGTARP briefing, 4/14/2009.
[199] Treasury, briefing on ASSP, 3/18/2009.
[200] Treasury, briefing on ASSP, 3/18/2009.
[201] Program Description: Treasury, brie2 ng on ASSP, 3/18/2009; Discount Amounts: Treasury, response to SIGTARP draft, 4/9/2009.
[202] Treasury, response to SIGTARP draft, 4/9/2009.
[203] Treasury, response to SIGTARP draft, 4/9/2009.
[204] Treasury, response to SIGTARP draft, 4/9/2009.
[205] Treasury, briefing on ASSP, 3/18/2009.

[206] Treasury, "Obama Administration's New Warranty Commitment Program," 3/30/2009, www.treas.gov, accessed 3/30/2009.
[207] Treasury, SIGTARP brie2 ng, 4/14/2009.
[208] Treasury, "Obama Administration New Path to Viability for GM & Chrysler, GM and Chrysler Restructuring Fact Sheet," 3/30/09, www.2 nancialstability.gov, accessed 3/30/2009.
[209] Treasury, briefing with OFS Compliance, 4/6/2009.
[210] Treasury, "Obama Administration's New Warranty Commitment Program," 3/30/2009, www.treas.gov, accessed 3/30/2009.
[211] Treasury, "Obama Administration's New Warranty Commitment Program," 3/30/2009, www.treas.gov, accessed 3/30/2009.
[212] Treasury, "Obama Administration's New Warranty Commitment Program," 3/30/2009, www.treas.gov, accessed 3/30/2009.
[213] HUD, "Glossary," no date, www.hud.gov, accessed 3/31/2009.
[214] Standard & Poor's, "Guide to Credit Rating Essentials," no date, www.standardandpoors.com, accessed 3/3/2009.
[215] FRBNY, "Term Asset-Backed Securities Loan Facility: Terms and Conditions," 3/19/2009, www.newyorkfed.org, accessed 3/27/2009.
[216] Treasury, Office of Financial Stability, Chief of Compliance and CFO, SIGTARP interview, 3/30/2009.
[217] Treasury, White Paper, "The Consumer Business and Lending Initiative," 3/3/2009, www.treas.gov, accessed 3/10/2009.
[218] FRBNY, "Monetary Report to Congress," 2/24/2009, www.federalreserve.gov, accessed 3/10/2009.
[219] Treasury, White Paper, "The Consumer Business and Lending Initiative," 3/3/2009, www.treas.gov, accessed 3/27/2009.
[220] Treasury, White Paper, "Public Private Investment Program," 3/33/2009, www.treas.gov, accessed 3/27/2009.
[221] FRBNY, "Term Asset-Backed Securities Loan Facility: Terms and Conditions," 3/19/2009, www.newyorkfed.org, accessed 3/27/2009.
[222] FRBNY, "Term Asset-Backed Securities Loan Facility: Terms and Conditions," 3/19/2009, www.newyorkfed.org, accessed 3/27/2009.
[223] FRBNY, "Term Asset-Backed Securities Loan Facility: Terms and Conditions," 3/19/2009, www.newyorkfed.org, accessed 3/27/2009.
[224] FRBNY, "Term Asset-Backed Securities Loan Facility: Terms and Conditions," 3/19/2009, www.newyorkfed.org, accessed 3/27/2009.
[225] FRBNY, response to SIGTARP draft report, 4/9/2009.
[226] FRBNY, response to SIGTARP draft report, 4/9/2009.
[227] OFS, FRBNY, response to SIGTARP draft report, 4/9/2009
[228] Treasury, "TALF LLC Credit Agreement," 3/3/2009.
[229] FRBNY, response to SIGTARP draft report, 4/9/2009.
[230] Treasury, "TALF LLC Credit Agreement," 3/3/2009.
[231] FRBNY, response to SIGTARP draft report, 4/9/2009.
[232] FRBNY, "Term Asset-Backed Securities Loan Facility: Frequently Asked Questions," 3/19/2009, www.newyorkfed.org, accessed 3/27/2009.
[233] FRBNY, "Term Asset-Backed Securities Loan Facility: Frequently Asked Questions," 3/19/2009, www.newyorkfed.org, accessed 3/27/2009.
[234] FRBNY, "Master Loan and Security Agreement," 3/27/2009, www.newyorkfed.org, accessed 3/27/2009.
[235] FRBNY, "Term Asset-Backed Securities Loan Facility: Frequently Asked Questions," 3/19/2009, www.newyorkfed.org, accessed 3/27/2009.
[236] FRBNY, "Term Asset-Backed Securities Loan Facility: Terms and Conditions," 3/19/2009, www.newyorkfed.org, accessed 3/27/2009.
[237] FRBNY, "Term Asset-Backed Securities Loan Facility: Frequently Asked Questions," 3/19/2009, www.newyorkfed.org, accessed 3/27/2009.
[238] FRBNY, "Term Asset-Backed Securities Loan Facility: Frequently Asked Questions," 3/19/2009, www.newyorkfed.org, accessed 3/27/2009.
[239] FRBNY, response to SIGTARP draft report, 4/9/2009.
[240] FRBNY, "Term Asset-Backed Securities Loan Facility: Frequently Asked Questions," 3/19/2009, www.newyorkfed.org, accessed 3/27/2009.
[241] Treasury, response to SIGTARP letter dated 3/4/2009, received 3/9/2009.
[242] Treasury, White Paper, "Public-Private Investment Program," 3/23/2009, www.treas.gov, accessed 3/23/2009.
[243] FRBNY, Press Release, www.federalreserve.gov, 3/3/2009, accessed 3/27/2009.
[244] FRBNY, Press Release, www.federalreserve.gov, 3/3/2009, accessed 3/27/2009.
[245] Treasury Press Release, "Treasury Department Releases Details on Public Private Partnership Investment Program," 3/23/2009, www.treas.gov, accessed 3/23/2009.

[246] Treasury indicated projected funding of $75 billion to $100 billion for the new PPIP. As of March 31, 2009, PPIP funds have not officially been committed and thus this report uses a conservative estimate of $75 billion.
[247] Treasury, "Public-Private Investment Program: Fact Sheet," 3/23/2009, www.treas.gov, accessed 3/23/2009.
[248] Treasury, "Public-Private Investment Program: Fact Sheet," 3/23/2009, www.treas.gov, accessed 3/23/2009.
[249] Treasury, "Legacy Loans Program: Summary of Terms," 3/23/2009, www.treas.gov, accessed 3/23/2009.
[250] Treasury, "Public-Private Investment Program: Fact Sheet," 3/23/2009, www.treas.gov, accessed 3/23/2009.
[251] Treasury, response to SIGTARP draft, 4/9/2009.
[252] Treasury, "Legacy Loans Program: Summary of Terms," 3/23/2009, www.treas.gov, accessed 3/23/2009.
[253] Treasury, "Legacy Loans Program: Summary of Terms," 3/23/2009, www.treas.gov, accessed 3/23/2009.
[254] Treasury, "Legacy Loans Program: Summary of Terms," 3/23/2009, www.treas.gov, accessed 3/23/2009.
[255] Treasury, "Legacy Loans Program: Summary of Terms," 3/23/2009, www.treas.gov, accessed 3/23/2009.
[256] Treasury, response to SIGTARP draft, 4/9/2009. Treasury, "Legacy Securities Public-Private Investment Funds: Summary of Terms," 4/6/2009, www.treas.gov, accessed 4/6/2009.
[257] Treasury, "Legacy Securities Public-Private Investment Funds: Summary of Terms," 4/6/2009, www.treas.gov, accessed 4/6/2009.
[258] Treasury, "Legacy Securities Public-Private Investment Funds: Summary of Terms," 4/6/2009, www.treas.gov, accessed 4/6/2009.
[259] Treasury, "Legacy Securities Public-Private Investment Funds: Summary of Terms," 4/6/2009, www.treas.gov, accessed 4/6/2009.
[260] Treasury, "Legacy Securities Public-Private Investment Funds: Summary of Terms," 4/6/2009, www.treas.gov, accessed 4/6/2009.
[261] Treasury, "Legacy Securities Public-Private Investment Funds: Summary of Terms," 4/6/2009, www.treas.gov, accessed 4/6/2009.
[262] Treasury, "Public-Private Investment Program: White Paper," 3/23/2009, www.treas.gov, accessed 3/23/2009.
[263] Treasury Office of General Counsel, response to SIGTARP draft, 4/9/2009.
[264] Treasury, "Unlocking Credit for Small Businesses Fact Sheet," 3/16/2009, www.treas.gov, accessed 3/17/2009.
[265] SBA, "Recovery Act: Frequently Asked Questions," no date, www.treas.gov, accessed 3/18/2009.
[266] SBA, "Recovery Act: Frequently Asked Questions," no date, www.treas.gov, accessed 3/18/2009.
[267] Treasury, "Unlocking Credit for Small Businesses: FAQ on Implementation," 3/17/2009, www.treas.gov, accessed 3/18/2009.
[268] Treasury, "Unlocking Credit for Small Businesses Fact Sheet," 3/16/2009, www.treas.gov, accessed 3/17/2009.
[269] GAO, "Small Business Administration: Additional Guidance on Documenting Credit Elsewhere Decisions Could Improve 7(a) Program Oversight," 2/12/2009, www.gao.gov, accessed 3/17/2009.
[270] GAO, "Small Business Administration: Additional Guidance on Documenting Credit Elsewhere Decisions Could Improve 7(a) Program Oversight," 2/12/2009, www.gao.gov, accessed 3/17/2009.
[271] Treasury, "Unlocking Credit for Small Businesses Fact Sheet," 3/16/2009, www.treas.gov, accessed 3/17/2009.
[272] Treasury, "Unlocking Credit for Small Businesses Fact Sheet," 3/16/2009, www.treas.gov, accessed 3/17/2009.
[273] Treasury, "Unlocking Credit for Small Businesses: FAQ on Implementation," 3/17/2009, www.treas.gov, accessed 3/18/2009; Treasury, "Unlocking Credit for Small Businesses Fact Sheet," 3/16/2009, www.treas.gov, accessed 3/17/2009.
[274] Treasury, "Unlocking Credit for Small Businesses: FAQ on Implementation," 3/17/2009, www.treas.gov, accessed 3/18/2009.
[275] Treasury, "Unlocking Credit for Small Businesses Fact Sheet," 3/16/2009, www.treas.gov, accessed 3/17/2009.
[276] Treasury, "Unlocking Credit for Small Businesses Fact Sheet," 3/16/2009, www.treas.gov, accessed 3/17/2009.
[277] Treasury, "Unlocking Credit for Small Businesses Fact Sheet," 3/16/2009, www.treas.gov, accessed 3/17/2009.
[278] American Recovery and Reinvestment Act of 2009, P.L 111-5, 2/17/2009.
[279] Treasury, "Unlocking Credit for Small Businesses: FAQ on Implementation," 3/17/2009, www.treas.gov, accessed 3/18/2009.
[280] Treasury, "Unlocking Credit for Small Businesses: FAQ on Implementation," 3/17/2009, www.treas.gov, accessed 3/18/2009.
[281] Treasury, "Unlocking Credit for Small Businesses: FAQ on Implementation," 3/17/2009, www.treas.gov, accessed 3/18/2009.
[282] Treasury, "Unlocking Credit for Small Businesses Fact Sheet," 3/16/2009, www.treas.gov, accessed 3/17/2009.
[283] Treasury, "Unlocking Credit for Small Businesses: FAQ on Implementation," 3/17/2009, www.treas.gov, accessed 3/18/2009.
[284] Treasury, "Unlocking Credit for Small Businesses: FAQ on Implementation," 3/17/2009, www.treas.gov, accessed 3/18/2009.
[285] Treasury, response to SIGTARP draft, 4/9/2009.
[286] Emergency Economic Stabilization Act of 2008, P.L. 109, 10/3/2008.
[287] Emergency Economic Stabilization Act of 2008, P.L. 109, 10/3/2008.
[288] Treasury, "Making Home Affordable: Updated Detailed Program Description," 3/4/2009, www.treas.gov, accessed 3/4/2009.

[289] Treasury, "Making Home Affordable: Updated Detailed Program Description," 3/4/2009, www.treas.gov, accessed 3/4/2009.
[290] Treasury, "Making Home Affordable: Summary Guidelines," 3/4/2009, www.treas.gov, accessed 3/4/2009.
[291] Treasury, "Making Home Affordable: Updated Detailed Program Description," 3/4/2009, www.treas.gov, accessed 3/4/2009.
[292] Treasury, "Home Affordable Modification Guidelines: March 4, 2009," 3/4/2009, www.treas.gov, accessed 3/4/2009.
[293] Treasury, "Home Affordable Modification Guidelines: March 4, 2009," 3/4/2009, www.treas.gov, accessed 3/4/2009.
[294] Treasury, "Making Home Affordable: Updated Detailed Program Description," 3/4/2009, www.treas.gov, accessed 3/4/2009.
[295] Treasury, "Making Home Affordable: Updated Detailed Program Description," 3/4/2009, www.treas.gov, accessed 3/4/2009.
[296] Treasury, "Making Home Affordable: Updated Detailed Program Description," 3/4/2009, www.treas.gov, accessed 3/4/2009.
[297] Treasury, "Making Home Affordable: Updated Detailed Program Description," 3/4/2009, www.treas.gov, accessed 3/4/2009.
[298] Treasury, "Making Home Affordable: Updated Detailed Program Description," 3/4/2009, www.treas.gov, accessed 3/4/2009.
[299] American Recovery and Reinvestment Act of 2009, P.L 111-5, 2/17/2009.
[300] Office of the Special Inspector General, "Engagement Memo — Audit of the Use of TARP Funds and Audit of Controls Over Executive Compensation," 2/5/2009.
[301] Office of the Special Inspector General, "Engagement Memo — Review of Federal Oversight of Executive Compensation Requirements Including Bonus Payments to AIG and Other TARP Recipients," 3/20/2009.
[302] Emergency Economic Stabilization Act of 2008, P.L. 110-343, 10/3/2008.
[303] Emergency Economic Stabilization Act of 2008, P.L. 110-343, 10/3/2008.
[304] Treasury, "Treasury Regulation 31 CFR Part 30," 10/14/2008.
[305] Treasury, "Notice 2008-PSSFI," 1/16/2009, www.treas.gov, accessed 1/19/2009.
[306] Treasury, "Notice 2008-PSSFI," 1/16/2009, www.treas.gov, accessed 1/19/2009.
[307] Treasury, "U.S. Treasury and Federal Reserve Board Announce Participation in AIG Restructuring Plan," 3/12/2009, www.treas.gov, accessed 3/4/2009.
[308] Treasury, "Treasury Announces New Restrictions on Executive Compensation," 2/4/2009,www.treas.gov, accessed 3/20/2009.
[309] Treasury, "Treasury Announces New Restrictions on Executive Compensation," 2/4/2009,www.treas.gov, accessed 3/20/2009.
[310] Treasury, "Treasury Announces New Restrictions on Executive Compensation," 2/4/2009, www.treas.gov, accessed 3/20/2009.
[311] Treasury Office of General Counsel, response to SIGTARP draft report, 4/9/2009.
[312] American Recovery and Reinvestment Act of 2009, P.L 111-5, 2/17/2009.
[313] Treasury Office of General Counsel, response to SIGTARP draft report, 4/9/2009.
[314] American Recovery and Reinvestment Act of 2009, P.L 111-5, 2/17/2009.
[315] American Recovery and Reinvestment Act of 2009, P.L 111-5, 2/17/2009.
[316] American Recovery and Reinvestment Act of 2009, P.L 111-5, 2/17/2009.
[317] American Recovery and Reinvestment Act of 2009, P.L 111-5, 2/17/2009.
[318] American Recovery and Reinvestment Act of 2009, P.L 111-5, 2/17/2009.
[319] American Recovery and Reinvestment Act of 2009, P.L 111-5, 2/17/2009.
[320] American Recovery and Reinvestment Act of 2009, P.L 111-5, 2/17/2009.

In: Reassessing TARP
Editor: George T. Bernhardt

ISBN: 978-1-60741-965-5

Chapter 4

TARP OPERATIONS AND ADMINISTRATION

Under the Emergency Economic Stabilization Act of 2008 ("EESA"), Congress has authorized the Treasury Secretary to take such actions as necessary to build the operational and administrative infrastructure to support TARP activities. EESA authorized the establishment of an Office of Financial Stability ("OFS") within the Department of Treasury ("Treasury") to be responsible for the administration of the Troubled Asset Relief Program ("TARP").[1] Treasury has the authority to establish program vehicles, issue regulations, directly hire or appoint employees, enter into contracts, and designate financial institutions as financial agents of the Federal Government.[2] In addition to using permanent and interim staff, OFS relies on contractors and financial agents in legal, investment consulting, accounting, and other key service areas.[3]

TARP Administrative and Program Expenditures

Treasury stated that it had incurred $13.3 million in TARP-related administrative expenditures through March 31, 2009.[4] Table 3.1 summarizes these expenditures, as well as additional obligations through March 31, 2009. The majority of these costs are allocated to Personnel Services and Non-Personnel Other Services.

Table 3.2 indicates the allocation of administrative obligations for Non- Personnel Other Services for the period ending March 31, 2009.[5] Additionally, Treasury has released details of programmatic expenditures. These expenditures include costs to hire financial agents and legal firms associated with TARP operations. Table 3.3 shows the allocation of these programmatic costs as of March 31, 2009.

TARP operations are projected to cost approximately $175 million for fisical year 2009.[6] These costs are not re ected in determining any gains or losses on the TARP-related transactions and are not included in the $700 billion limit on asset purchases. Therefore, these expenditures will add to the Federal budget de cit regardless of whether the TARP transactions result in a gain or a loss for the Government.[7]

Table 3.1. TARP Administrative Expenditures and Obligations

Budget Object Class Title	Obligations for Period Ending 3/31/2009	Expenditures for Period Ending 3/31/2009
PERSONNEL SERVICES		
Personnel Compensation & Services	$3,830,093	$2,902,514
TOTAL PERSONNEL SERVICES	**$3,830,093**	**$2,902,514**
NON-PERSONNEL SERVICES		
Travel & Transportation of Persons	$28,714	$19,831
Transportation of Things	-	-
Rents, Communications, Utilities & Misc. Charges	598,902	534,152
Printing & Reproduction	395	395
Other Services	25,186,838	9,567,209
Supplies & Materials	209,446	87,790
Equipment	89,887	89,887
Land & Structures	103,878	97,522
TOTAL NON-PERSONNEL SERVICES	**$26,218,059**	**$10,396,785**
GRAND TOTAL	**$30,048,152**	**$13,299,298**

Note: Numbers affected by rounding.

Source: Treasury, response to SIGTARP data call, 4/8/2009.

Table 3.2. TARP Administrative Obligations – Other Services

Vendor Name	Obligations as of 3/31/2009
Alcohol and Tobacco Tax and Trade Bureau	$67,489
Congressional Oversight Panel	4,000,000
CSC Systems and Solutions, LLC	62,645
Cushman and Wake eld of VA, Inc.	8,750
Ernst & Young, LLP	1,968,012
Federal Tech SVC Nat IT Program	8,096
FI Consulting	–
Government Accountability Office	9,000,000
Lindholm & Associates, Inc.	212,717
Pat Taylor & Associates, Inc.	230,978
PricewaterhouseCoopers, LLP	6,914,303
Misc Oblig for Treasury (DO & BPD- ARC) Services	2,713,847
GRAND TOTAL	**$25,186,838**

Note: Numbers affected by rounding.

Source: Treasury, response to SIGTARP data call, 4/8/2009.

Table 3.3. TARP Programmatic Expenditures

Vendor Name	Expenditures as of 3/31/2009
The Bank of New York Mellon Corporation	$5,666,186
Cadwalader Wickersham & Taft, LLP	412,028
Ennis Knupp & Associates, Inc.	1,156,298
Hughes Hubbard & Reed, LLP	1,855,164
Locke Lord Bissell & Liddell, LLP	415,258
Pension Benet Guaranty Corporation	2,003,000
Simpson Thacher & Bartlett, LLP	1,376,543
Sonnenschein Nath & Rosenthal, LLP	2,699,151
Squire Sanders & Dempsey, LLP	1,804,672
Sonnenschein Nath & Rosenthal, LLP (formerly Thacher Proftt & Wood)	97,477
The Boston Consulting Group	925,000
Venable, LLP	663,578
Freddie Mac	-
Fannie Mae	-
EARNEST Partners	-
Haynes and Boone, LLP	-
McKee Nelson, LLP	-
GRAND TOTAL	**$19,074,355**

Note: Numbers affected by rounding.
Source: Treasury, response to SIGTARP data call, 4/8/2009.

Current Contractors and Financial Agents

As of March 31, 2009, Treasury had retained 36 outside contractors, including one asset manager to provide a range of services to assist in administering TARP.

As permitted in EESA, Treasury has used streamlined solicitation procedures and has structured several agreements and contracts to allow for fiexibility in obtaining the required services expeditiously. Table 3.4 lists outside vendors as of March 31, 2009.[8]

As required by EESA, SIGTARP must report the biographical information for each person or entity hired to manage the troubled assets associated with TARP.[9] On March 16, 2009, OFS announced the hiring of EARNEST Partners as the asset manager for the Small Business Initiative (Unlocking Credit for Small Businesses). EARNEST Partners is an employee-owned firm specializing in equity, fixed income, and alternative asset portfolio management. According to OFS, the firm has significant experience with issues guaranteed by the Small Business Administration. See Appendix C: "Reporting Requirements" for a biography on EARNEST Partners. As of March 31, 2009, OFS has not hired any asset managers for other TARP initiatives. In the absence of asset managers, Bank of New York Mellon, as Treasury's financial administrative agent, has subcontracted with Gifford Fong to perform initial valuations of CPP transactions.[10]

Table 3.4. Outside Vendors

Date	Vendor	Purpose	Type of Transaction*
10/10/2008	Simpson, Thacher & Bartlett, LLP	Legal Services	BPA
10/11/2008	Ennis Knupp & Associates, Inc.	Investment and Advisory Services	BPA
10/14/2008	The Bank of New York Mellon Corporation	Custodian and Cash Management	Financial Agent
10/16/2008	PricewaterhouseCoopers, LLP	Internal Control Services	BPA
10/18/2008	Ernst & Young, LLP	Accounting Services	BPA
10/23/2008	GSA – Turner Consulting**	Archiving Services	IAA
10/29/2008	Hughes Hubbard & Reed, LLP	Legal Services	BPA
10/29/2008	Squire Sanders & Dempsey, LLP	Legal Services	BPA
10/31/2008	Lindholm & Associates, Inc.**	Human Resources Services	Contract
11/7/2008	Thacher Prof tt & Wood***	Legal Services	BPA
11/14/2008	Securities and Exchange Commission	Detailees	IAA
11/14/2008	CSC Systems and Solutions, LLC	IT Services	Procurement
12/3/2008	Trade and Tax Bureau – Treasury	IT Services	IAA
12/5/2008	Department of Housing and Urban Development	Detailees	IAA
12/5/2008	Washington Post	Vacancy Announcement	Procurement
12/10/2008	Thacher Prof tt & Wood***	Legal Services	BPA
12/12/2008	Pension Benefit Guaranty Corporation	Legal Services	IAA
12/15/2008	Office of Thrift Supervision	Detailees	IAA
12/24/2008	Cushman and Wake eld of VA, Inc.	Painting	Procurement
1/6/2009	Office of the Controller of the Currency	Detailees	IAA
1/7/2009	Colonial Parking	Parking	Procurement
1/9/2009	Internal Revenue Service	Detailees	IAA
1/27/2009	Cadwalader Wickersham & Taft, LLP	Legal Services	BPA
1/27/2009	Whitaker Brothers Bus. Machines	Office Machines	Procurement
2/2/2009	Government Accountability Office	Oversight	IAA
2/9/2009	Pat Taylor and Associates, Inc.**	Temporary Employee Services	Contract
2/12/2009	Locke Lord Bissell & Lidell, LLP	Legal Services	Contract
2/18/2009	Freddie Mac	Homeownership Program	Financial Agent
2/18/2009	Fannie Mae	Homeownership Program	Financial Agent
2/20/2009	Congressional Oversight Panel	Oversight	IAA
2/20/2009	Simpson, Thacher & Bartlett, LLP	Legal Services	Contract
2/22/2009	Venable, LLP	Legal Services	Contract
3/6/2009	The Boston Consulting Group	Management Consulting Support	Contract
3/16/2009	EARNEST Partners	Asset Management Services	Financial Agent
3/23/2009	Heery International, Inc.	Architects	Procurement
3/30/2009	McKee Nelson, LLP	Legal Services	Contract
3/30/2009	Sonnenschein Nath & Rosenthal, LLP	Legal Services	Contract
3/30/2009	Cadwalader Wickersham & Taft, LLP	Legal Services	Contract
3/30/2009	Haynes and Boone, LLP	Legal Services	Contract
3/31/2009	FI Consulting**	Modeling and Analysis	BPA

* IAA = Interagency Agreement. BPA = Blanket Purchase Agreement.

** Small or Women-, or Minority-Owned Small Business.

*** Contract responsibilities assumed by Sonnenschein Nath & Rosenthal via novation.

Source: Treasury, response to SIGTARP data call, 4/8/2009.

Conflicts of Interest

Within the framework of TARP procurement and contracting, actual or potential con icts of interest ("COI") can exist at the organizational level or pertain to an individual employee. EESA provides the Treasury Secretary the authority to issue regulations or guidelines necessary to address and manage, or to prohibit, COI that can arise in connection with the administration and execution of TARP.[11]

TARP-related COI may occur due to a variety of situations, such as when retained entities perform similar work for Treasury and other clients. In these situations, contracted entities may find that their duty to certain clients may impair their objectivity when advising Treasury or may affect their judgment about the proper use of nonpublic information. Con icts may also arise from the personal inter-ests of individuals employed by retained entities. Accordingly, Treasury has issued interim guidelines to address potential COI.[12]

These interim COI rules require interested contractors to provide sufficient information to evaluate the potential for organizational COI and plans to mitigate them.[13] The mitigation plan then becomes a binding term of the contract arrangement. On potential personal COI, the provisions require that managers and employees of a hired entity disclose any financial holdings or personal and familial relationships that could impair their objectivity.[14]

Financial agents and contractors have identified potential COI, and these parties have proposed solutions to mitigate the identified con icts. In response to recommendations made to Treasury by the Comptroller General,[15] Treasury has taken steps to formalize its oversight and monitoring of potential COI.[16]

End Notes

[1] Emergency Economic Stabilization Act of 2008, P.L. 110-343, 10/3/2008.

[2] Emergency Economic Stabilization Act of 2008, P.L. 110-343, 10/3/2008.

[3] Treasury, response to SIGTARP data call, 4/08/2009.

[4] Treasury, response to SIGTARP data call, 4/08/2009.

[5] Treasury, response to SIGTARP data call, 4/08/2009.

[6] GAO-09-504, "Troubled Asset Relief Program: March 2009 Status of Efforts to Address Transparency and Accountability Issues," 3/31/2009.

[7] Congressional Budget Office, "Congressional Budget Office Press Release," 09/28/2008, www.cbo.gov, accessed 1/15/2009.

[8] Treasury, response to SIGTARP data call, 4/08/2009.

[9] Emergency Economic Stabilization Act of 2008, P.L. 110-343, 10/3/2008.

[10] Treasury, response to SIGTARP data call, 4/08/2009.

[11] Emergency Economic Stabilization Act of 2008, P.L. 110-343, 10/3/2008.

[12] Treasury, "U.S. Department of Treasury Press Release," 10/6/2008, www.treasury.gov, accessed 1/15/2009.

[13] TARP ConJ icts of Interest, Interim Rule, Billing Code 4810-25-P, 1/21/2009.

[14] GAO-09-161, "Troubled Asset Relief Program: Additional Actions Needed to Better Ensure Integrity, Accountability, and Transparency," 12/2/2008.

[15] GAO-09-161, "Troubled Asset Relief Program: Additional Actions Needed to Better Ensure Integrity, Accountability, and Transparency," 12/2/2008.

[16] Treasury, "Summary Response to Recommendations in December 2008 GAO Report," 1/22/2009.

Conflicts of Interest

[illegible]

In: Reassessing TARP
Editor: George T. Bernhardt
ISBN: 978-1-60741-965-5

Chapter 5

LOOKING FORWARD: SIGTARP'S RECOMMENDATIONS TO TREASURY

One of SIGTARP's responsibilities is to provide recommendations to the Department of Treasury ("Treasury") so that Troubled Asset Relief Program ("TARP") programs can be designed or modified to facilitate transparency and effective oversight and prevent fraud, waste, and abuse. SIGTARP's Initial Report to Congress, dated February 6, 2009 (the "Initial Report"), set forth a series of recommendations, some of which were adopted by Treasury and some of which were not. Appendix J: "Treasury Response to SIGTARP Recommendations" contains Treasury's detailed statement as to what it believes it has done to address those recommendations, and, for some of the recommendations that it has not implemented, why it has not done so. Set forth below are SIGTARP's recommendations, first with respect to implemented TARP programs and then for newly announced programs.

RECOMMENDATIONS FOR EXISTING PROGRAMS

Oversight Language in TARP Agreements and Requiring Recipients to Account for Use of TARP Funds

In its Initial Report, SIGTARP recommended that Treasury include language in each of its new TARP-related agreements to facilitate compliance and oversight. Although Treasury has not executed any agreements as part of a new program since the Initial Report, it has indicated that it will include some of the recommended oversight language in the finalized new agreement with American International Group, Inc. ("AIG") and in the Capital Assistance Program ("CAP") documents.

Treasury has indicated, however, that it will not adopt SIGTARP's recommendation that all TARP recipients be required to do the following:

account for the use of TARP funds
set up internal controls to comply with such accounting
report periodically to Treasury on the results, with appropriate sworn certifications

In light of the fact that the American taxpayer has been asked to fund this extraordinary effort to stabilize the financial system, it is not unreasonable that the public be told how those funds have been used by TARP recipients. Treasury is now conducting regular surveys of the banks' lending activities; however, with the exception of Citigroup and Bank of America, Treasury has refused to seek further details on TARP recipients' use of funds.

As a result, in late January, SIGTARP decided to undertake, itself, a use of funds project by conducting a survey of 364 TARP recipients that had received funds as of January 31, 2009. Included in that survey was a request for a description of what the recipients actually did or plan to do with the TARP funds.

Although the results of the survey still need to be analyzed, one thing is clear: Treasury's arguments that such an accounting was impractical, impossible, or a waste of time because of the inherent fungibility of money were unfounded. Banks generally provided a reasonable level of detail regarding their use of TARP funds, and, while the response quality was not uniform, some banks were able to provide detailed, at times even granular, descriptions of how they used taxpayer money.

Continuing Recommendation

SIGTARP continues to recommend that Treasury require all TARP recipients to report on the actual use of TARP funds in the manner previously suggested. This recommendation is particularly important with respect to the potential expansion of the Capital Purchase Program ("CPP") to include large insurance companies. The American people have a right to know how their tax dollars are being used, particularly as billions of dollars are going to institutions for which banking is certainly not part of the institution's core business and may be little more than a way to gain access to the low-cost capital provided under TARP. Similarly, in light of the controversy surrounding AIG's use of Government assistance, both through the paying of bonuses and in its dealings with counterparties, failure to impose this requirement with respect to the injection of yet another $30 billion into AIG would not only be a failure of oversight, but could call into further question the credibility of the Government's efforts with respect to the assistance provided to AIG. This recommendation applies not only to capital investment and lending programs involving banks and other financial institutions, but also to programs in which TARP funds are used to purchase troubled assets, including details of each transaction in the Public-Private Investment Program ("PPIP") as well as all transactions concerning the surrender of collateral (including the identity of the surrendering borrowers) in the Term Asset-Backed Securities Loan Facility ("TALF").

Asset Management and Valuation Issues

In its Initial Report, SIGTARP noted that "[t]o date, Treasury has not fully developed significant policies or controls with respect to asset management issues," and recommended that "Treasury needs, in the near term, to begin developing a more complete strategy on what to do with the substantial portfolio that it now manages on behalf of the American people."

As of the drafting of this report, however, no asset manager had been hired to manage the existing asset portfolio, and no investment strategy has been developed. Although Treasury did hire EARNEST Partners to manage the securities purchased under the Unlocking Credit for Small Businesses program, their role is limited to the program and, as of March 31, 2009, Treasury had not yet purchased securities under this particular program. Treasury has indicated that, while it has hired some individuals to develop internal models of valuation and believes that it "has developed a robust, defined valuation method for preferred stock and warrants received under the Capital Purchase Program," no such valuation, as of the drafting of this report, had occurred.[1] Even if Treasury intends to hold these assets for the foreseeable future, its delay in placing a value on these assets (and thus provide the American people with some indication of the performance of their investments), among other things, is detrimental to program transparency. Although other bodies have provided some valuation analysis (the Congressional Oversight Panel has estimated that Treasury overpaid by $68 billion in its acquisitions of assets and the Congressional Budget Office estimated that taxpayer loss in TARP will ultimately be as high as $356 billion), SIGTARP believes that Treasury should provide its own estimates on the value of the preferred shares, warrants of common stock, notes, and other instruments that it now holds as a result of TARP. Finally, as TARP recipients pay back their TARP funds, Treasury must liquidate the warrants, either by selling them back to the CPP recipient at a market price or by selling them in the open market. While Treasury, in discussing these recommendations with SIGTARP, has indicated that it has recently made asset management more of a priority and expects to retain asset managers soon, it must act quickly. The failure to have an asset manager, an investment plan, or an accurate valuation of the securities and warrants it holds will soon be a significant de ciency in the program if not promptly addressed.

Continuing Recommendations

As SIGTARP noted in the Initial Report, there are three particular aspects of asset management that Treasury needs to address:

Treasury should formalize its going-forward valuation methodology and begin providing values of the TARP investments to the public.

Treasury should develop an overall investment strategy to address the vast portfolio of securities that it holds.

Treasury should decide whether it has any intention of exercising warrants in order to hold the common stock. SIGTARP asked Treasury what its intentions are on this point in January 2009, and it has not yet indicated its strategy on this issue.

Potential Fraud Vulnerabilities Associated with TALF

In SIGTARP's Initial Report, SIGTARP made a series of recommendations with respect to the design and implementation of TALF. This section will discuss the status of the implementation of those recommendations and then describe new and ongoing recommendations for the design and operation of the program.

SIGTARP previously recommended in its Initial Report that:

Treasury should require that certain minimum underwriting standards and/ or other fraud prevention mechanisms are in place with respect to the assets underlying the asset-backed securities ("ABS") used for collateral.

Since the Initial Report, and after additional consultations with SIGTARP, the Federal Reserve Bank of New York ("FRBNY") and Treasury have taken some important steps with respect to adopting fraud prevention mechanisms far beyond what was initially contemplated for TALF. As set forth in greater detail in the TALF discussion in Section 2 of this report, FRBNY now requires, among other things, certifications from the sponsor, third-party attestations from accounting firms regarding the pledged collateral, and due diligence procedures at the primary dealer level. The TALF haircut methodology, which imposes different haircut percentages over different asset classes and maturities, has been designed, according to Treasury and FRBNY, to be risk-sensitive and therefore incentivizes TALF borrowers to conduct due diligence about the quality of the underlying securities. FRBNY has also imposed some oversight-enabling provisions for itself, including inspection rights and the ability to see through any special purpose vehicles ("SPVs") that borrowers may use to shield themselves from scrutiny. Although Treasury did not require minimum underwriting standards for the ABS acting as collateral for the TALF loans, it believes that the steps taken by FRBNY were sufficient, at least with respect to the originally announced consumer-lending-oriented asset classes. SIGTARP will continue to monitor this aspect of the program.

In its Initial Report, SIGTARP also recommended that:

Treasury should consider requiring that beneficiaries (*i.e.*, the TALF borrowers, the originators/sponsors, and the primary dealers) sign an agreement that includes oversight-enabling provisions.

Treasury should establish a compliance protocol with the Federal Reserve before TALF is put into effect.

In SIGTARP's view, Treasury did not receive sufficient oversight-enabling provisions in the agreements, nor has it established a sufficient compliance protocol with the Federal Reserve. Although Treasury did obtain certain inspection rights for the disposition SPV that it is funding, it has no oversight or access rights over any of the borrowers, including the borrowers who default on their loans and surrender the ABS collateral to the SPV. Indeed, Treasury does not even have the right to learn the identity of such borrowers. In other words, under its current agreement, Treasury does not have access to the identity, or any oversight authority over, the borrowers from whom, in effect, it will be buying surrendered ABS. Although FRBNY officials have assured SIGTARP that it will provide this information in the context of any audit or investigation that SIGTARP conducts, Treasury and Office of Financial Stability ("OFS")-Compliance did not obtain such access, for itself or for SIGTARP, in its agreements with FRBNY. This failure also calls into question SIGTARP's ability to fulfill its statutorily mandated reporting requirement of including in its quarterly reports a listing of all institutions from which TARP buys troubled assets, which arguably would include the identity of the party that surrenders TALF collateral. Furthermore, Treasury has only obtained limited access for itself and SIGTARP with respect to the issuers of the ABS, who only have to grant access if it is later determined that they pledged ineligible assets to the program. This, of course, presents a significant chicken-and-egg problem, as

Treasury (and SIGTARP) will be far less likely to detect any eligibility problems if they cannot inspect and test the assets in the first instance. Finally, as a result of its limited access, SIGTARP does not believe that Treasury has adopted SIGTARP's recommendation of establishing a sufficient compliance protocol concerning TALF.

In addressing the potential fraud vulnerabilities of TALF in the Initial Report, SIGTARP further recommended that:

Treasury should exercise extreme caution and give careful consideration before agreeing to the expansion of TALF to include mortgage-backed securities ("MBS") without further review and without considering certain minimum fraud protections.

Treasury should oppose any expansion of TALF to legacy MBS without significant modifications to the program to ensure a full assessment of risks associated with such an expansion.

Treasury and the Federal Reserve have signaled their intention to expand TALF to allow the posting of both new and legacy MBS — both commercial MBS ("CMBS") and residential MBS ("RMBS") — as collateral. As the terms of these expansions have neither been formalized nor given final approval by the Federal Reserve or Treasury, it remains to be seen if Treasury has exercised "extreme caution" in expanding TALF to newly issued MBS or whether it will require "signifi- cant modifications" before permitting legacy MBS to be included as well.

Accepting legacy MBS as collateral, in particular legacy RMBS, poses substantial issues from a credit loss and fraud loss perspective that are not readily addressed by the current TALF design. Credit ratings, cited as one of the primary credit protections in TALF as currently con gured, have been proven to be of questionable value in the general market for MBS, and for legacy RMBS they have proven to be unreliable and largely irrelevant to the actual value and performance of the security. Arguably, the wholesale failure of the credit rating agencies to rate adequately such securities is at the heart of the securitization market collapse, if not the primary cause of the current credit crisis. Furthermore, the underwriting standards (that is, the diligence the lender does before granting a loan, such as verifying a borrower's income or reported assets) for RMBS in particular, have proven to be woefully lax, potentially putting taxpayer money backing TALF in significant jeopardy. Finally, legacy MBS, particularly RMBS, pose substantial valuation challenges given how long the MBS market has been frozen, which gives rise to the same conflict of interest and collusion vulnerabilities discussed in the "Public- Private Investment Program ("PPIP")" discussion below.

As in the Initial Report, SIGTARP continues to recommend that Treasury not participate in a TALF program expanded to newly issued MBS without exercising an appropriate measure of caution, and, with respect to legacy assets, without significant modifications to the program. On that front, SIGTARP has had initial discussions with the Federal Reserve to discuss its plans for how the program will be modified to accommodate the use of MBS as posted collateral. SIGTARP has been informed by the Federal Reserve that it is considering, but has not yet adopted, the following modifications with respect to legacy RMBS, at least, in order to address the credit risks for such securities:

acceptance of legacy RMBS as collateral based upon an examination of the composition and performance of the loan portfolio underlying the RMBS, not rating agency determinations

a more granular determination of "haircut" percentages for RMBS, including a close examination of the underwriting standards associated with the loans that back the RMBS

significantly higher haircuts relative to the haircuts imposed on asset classes currently useable as collateral

As of the drafting of this report, FRBNY had not indicated what additional antifraud measures it will impose when TALF is expanded to MBS. This is of particular importance because some of the anti-fraud provisions that FRBNY and Treasury have cited as being significant (*e.g.*, third-party attestation of assets, credit ratings, *etc.*) for the original TALF program may not be relevant or useful for the expanded TALF. SIGTARP encourages the Federal Reserve to continue this process and will continue working with the Federal Reserve, FRBNY, and Treasury to recommend protections in the program to avoid as much fraud and abuse as possible.

Recommendations

In light of the previous discussion, SIGTARP thus recommends that:

Treasury and the Federal Reserve should provide to SIGTARP, for public disclosure in SIGTARP's quarterly reports, the identity of the borrowers who surrender collateral in TALF.

Treasury should dispense with rating agency determinations and require a security-by-security screening for each legacy RMBS. Treasury should refuse to participate if the program is not designed so that RMBS, whether new or legacy, will be rejected as collateral if the loans backing particular RMBS do not meet certain baseline underwriting criteria or are in categories that have been proven to be riddled with fraud, including certain undocumented subprime residential mortgages (*i.e.*, "liar loans").

Treasury should require significantly higher haircuts for all MBS, with particularly high haircuts for legacy RMBS, or other equally effective mitigation efforts.

Treasury should require additional anti-fraud and credit protection provisions, specific to all MBS, before participating in an expanded TALF, including minimum underwriting standards and other fraud prevention measures.

Treasury should design a robust compliance protocol, with complete access rights for itself, SIGTARP, and other relevant oversight bodies, to all TALF transaction participants.

Treasury officials, in discussing these recommendations with SIGTARP, stated that the potential expansion of the TALF program to include legacy MBS remains in the design phase and will include more stringent standards, including "CUSIP by CUSIP evaluation of underlying collateral, conducting due diligence with respect to the underlying collateral and applying appropriate haircuts."[2] They have also indicated that they will adopt SIGTARP's recommendation, at least with respect to newly issued RMBS, by reviewing certain minimum underwriting standards, including high credit scores and fully documented loans. These officials also stated they are in the process of hiring a fraud specialist to assist them in developing risk mitigation efforts for all TARP programs — an action that SIGTARP previously recommended and which could greatly assist in the design of TARP programs to account properly for the dangers of fraud.

Another new development with respect to TALF is that Treasury has announced, as part of PPIP, that Public-Private Investment Funds ("PPIFs") operated under the Legacy Securities Program will be able to use PPIF funds and Treasury leverage in TALF transactions. That issue, and SIGTARP's recommendation regarding the danger of such a practice, are discussed in the upcoming "Recommendations for Newly Announced Programs" portion of this section.

Executive Compensation

It has been more than two months since the American Recovery and Reinvestment Act imposed new executive compensation requirements on TARP recipients. As of the drafting of this report, Treasury has not issued regulations imposing these new requirements or the executive compensation restrictions that the Administration announced in early February. SIGTARP's initial review of responses to its survey of 364 TARP recipients demonstrates that the absence of clear guidance on this important issue has caused uncertainty among TARP recipients who have struggled to understand and implement the requirements. This lack of clarity in executive compensation limitations may also impede participation in other TARP programs.

Recommendation

Accordingly, SIGTARP recommends that:

Treasury should address the confusion and uncertainty on executive compensation by immediately issuing the required regulations.

Treasury officials, in discussing this recommendation with SIGTARP, stated that internal vetting on updated guidance is nearing completion and is expected to be provided to the Office of Management and Budget for final clearance shortly. They also indicated that the outcome of this effort is expected to be a "comprehensive rule" with applicability beyond CPP.

Lack of Resources within OFS-Compliance

The Compliance department within OFS has primary responsibility over a vast and complex array of compliance and risk management functions. This responsibility includes ensuring that appropriate internal controls are in place over OFS management of TARP programs, providing primary oversight of vendors that are providing services to OFS, and monitoring TARP recipients' compliance with their contractual and legal obligations. More than 500 financial institutions are already participating in various TARP programs; additional announced programs will expand OFS-Compliance's responsibilities to a mortgage modification program involving millions of mortgages and to public-private partnerships that will involve not only many new participants but also a whole new set of compliance challenges and types of risk.

To carry out all of these responsibilities, now six months into TARP operations, OFS-Compliance currently has a staff of approximately 10 employees. Although SIGTARP has plans for a future audit to assess the integration and effectiveness of OFS's risk assessment and compliance efforts, SIGTARP makes a preliminary observation that the current resource commitment for this vitally important function appears plainly inadequate. OFS has built substantially in the past six months, but its compliance Office has not grown in proportion to its historic task.

Recommendation

Accordingly, SIGTARP recommends as follows:

Treasury should significantly increase the staffing levels of OFS-Compliance and ensure the timely development and implementation of an integrated risk management and compliance program.

Treasury officials, in discussing this recommendation with SIGTARP, acknowledged that their compliance and risk management efforts have been understaffed but indicated they were in the process of making job offers to fill immediately five compliance positions dealing primarily with executive compensation. They also cited the use of Freddie Mac to facilitate compliance efforts in the area of home loan modifications and a vendor who is providing general fraud prevention advice. More broadly, they indicated that decisions are yet to be made concerning the ultimate size of their compliance efforts and the extent to which the functions would be performed in-house or under contract.

SIGTARP is encouraged by Treasury's efforts toward an increased emphasis on compliance, but believes additional near-term attention needs to be devoted to implement a comprehensive and integrated risk based compliance program.

Recommendations for Newly Announced Programs

Capital Assistance Program

The CAP, as described in Section 2, contemplates additional capital infusions into financial institutions and/or the conversion of the preferred shares that Treasury obtained under the CPP into convertible preferred shares. Treasury announced that it would require CAP applicants to set forth how they *intend* to use CAP funding. Notwithstanding this requirement, Treasury adamantly continues to refuse to adopt SIGTARP's recommendation that it require CAP recipients (and indeed all TARP recipients) to report on how they *actually used* TARP funds. Putting aside the value of this recommendation in other TARP programs, SIGTARP submits that it is largely meaningless to require an applicant to report on its intended use of funds without setting up a mechanism to monitor its actual use of funds.

Recommendations

SIGTARP therefore recommends that:

- Treasury should require CAP participants to (i) establish an internal control to monitor their actual use of TARP funds, (ii) provide periodic reporting on their actual use of TARP funds, and (iii) certify to OFS-Compliance, under the penalty of criminal sanction, that the report is accurate; the same criteria of internal controls and regular certified reports should be applied to all conditions imposed on CAP participants.
- Treasury should require CAP participants to acknowledge explicitly the jurisdiction and authority of SIGTARP and other oversight bodies, as appropriate, to oversee conditions contained in the agreement.

Operation of the Public-Private Investment Program

As discussed more fully in Section 2, PPIP is a program in which Government funds will be invested side-by-side with private investors to purchase legacy assets, including the "toxic" mortgages and legacy MBS widely believed to be one of the root causes of the current financial crisis. As announced, PPIP consists of separate subprograms.

- Under the Legacy Loans Program, newly formed PPIFs will bid on pools of legacy mortgages and other assets held on participating banks' balance sheets. The private equity in the PPIFs will be matched, dollar-for-dollar with TARP funds, and the PPIF will be able to obtain financing guaranteed by the Federal Deposit Insurance Corporation ("FDIC") up to a 6-to-1 debt-to-equity ratio. The pools of legacy loans will be assembled with the approval of FDIC, and the auction process will be managed by FDIC. By way of example, a group of pre-qualified private investors invests $50 million in a PPIF, which is then matched by $50 million in TARP funds. The PPIF obtains financing guaranteed by FDIC of up to $600 million (a 6-to-1 ratio of the total $ 100 million of equity) and uses the combined $700 million to purchase a pool of legacy mortgages. Any profits on these transactions are shared equally between the private investors and TARP; the private investors' total potential loss, however, is limited to their investment, $50 million, whereas Government interests could lose up to the remaining $650 million.
- Under the Legacy Securities Program, Treasury, through an application process, will pre-qualify fund managers to manage PPIFs. The fund managers will raise private capital for equity participation in the PPIF that will be matched, again, dollar-for-dollar, with TARP funds. The PPIF will then be able to obtain additional financing in TARP funds, depending upon the circumstances, of up to 100% of the amount of total equity. The fund manager, who earns a fee both from Treasury and from the private investors, will then use the money to purchase legacy MBS. For example, a fund manager selected by Treasury raises $500 million from private investors as equity in the PPIF. That $500 million is matched by $500 million in TARP funds, making the total equity in the PPIF $ 1 billion. The PPIF can then obtain up to an additional $ 1 billion loan (100% of the equity) in TARP funds and use the whole $2 billion to

purchase MBS. In this example, profits again are shared 50%/50% between the private equity investor and TARP. Losses are also suffered equally, but only up to the private investors' equity. If the PPIF failed completely, TARP would thus suffer 75% of the loss.

Finally, as a further extension of PPIP, TALF will be expanded to permit lending based on the posting of legacy MBS as collateral.

Areas of Vulnerability within PPIP

Many aspects of PPIP could make it inherently vulnerable to fraud, waste, and abuse. First, PPIP deals with assets that have recently been illiquid, making valuation difficult, therefore raising the danger that the Government will overpay for the assets. Second, many of the participants in these markets, such as hedge funds, are substantially unregulated and the internal oversight and compliance capability at those institutions vary widely. Next, the interrelationships between the market participants can be extremely complex and difficult to anticipate: the same entity might buy and sell toxic assets for its own benefit and manage portfolios of toxic assets for others, all while holding or managing equity or debt securities of the banks and other institutions that have large positions in the same toxic assets. Finally, the sheer size of the program — up to a trillion dollars for the PPIFs and up to another trillion dollars for the expansion of TALF — is so large and the leverage being provided to the private equity participants so beneficial, that the taxpayer risk is many times that of the private parties, thereby potentially skewing the economic incentives.

After receiving initial brie ngs from Treasury on PPIP and discussing the issue with law enforcement partners, SIGTARP has identified three of the most significant areas of potential vulnerability to fraud and abuse applicable across the program. Because SIGTARP has not been provided with many of the specific details of the mechanics of the various programs, SIGTARP's observations and recommendations are necessarily at a high level.

Conflicts of Interest

The first area of vulnerability is that the private parties managing the PPIFs might have a powerful incentive to make investment decisions that benefit themselves at the expense of the taxpayer. By their nature and design, including the availability of significant leverage, the PPIF transactions in these frozen markets will have a significant impact on how any particular asset is priced in the market. As a result, the increase in the price of such an asset will greatly benefit anyone who owns or manages the same asset, including the PPIF manager who is making the investment decisions.

As an extremely simplified example from the Legacy Securities Program, assume that the fund manager of the PPIF owns 1 million bonds of MBS X in its own account. MBS X is currently valued on the fund manager's books at 20% of its original value, or $20 per bond, for a total of $20 million. The fund manager does an estimate and believes that, in a fully functioning market, MBS X is actually worth 30% of face value, or $30 per bond. In the absence of a conflict of interest, the fund manager, using PPIF funds, might be willing to pay up to $30 per bond in the market. However, the fund manager realizes that it can make more money for itself if it drives the price even higher. It thus uses the funds it controls in the PPIF to buy 1 million MBS X bonds from someone else at $40 per bond, or $40 million. This transaction has the potential, in the current illiquid market, of setting the market price for that

MBS X at $40, even though that price is far above what the MBS is actually worth. As a result, the fund manager could sell the MBS on its own books and recognize a profit of $20 million. Over time, however, the price of MBS X declines to its actual value, $30 per bond, and results in a $10 million loss to the PPIF fund. This loss has no negative impact to the fund manager, however, because it did not have any of its own money invested in the fund. Indeed, the fund manager has made money on the PPIF, because it has received fees from both Treasury and the private investors based only on the total size of the PPIF. In other words, the conflict results in an enormous profit for the fund manager at the expense of the taxpayer.

The same incentives to overpay could exist in the Legacy Loans Program and in numerous other factual circumstances. The incentives exist, for example, even if the fund manager does not own MBS X but is merely managing other funds that hold MBS X, as the manager earns fees based on the value of that fund, a value that would, in this example, be significantly overstated (temporarily) as it can increase the value of that fund based on valuing, or "marking" the MBS X at the in ated "market" price that it set. The conflict can even exist if the manager holds or manages equity tied to the value of the banks from which the MBS are being purchased; here, using PPIF funds to overpay for bank assets may increase the bank's stock price, thus giving a greater profit to the fund manager.

Collusion

A closely related vulnerability is that PPIF managers might be persuaded, through kickbacks, *quid pro quo* transactions, or other collusive arrangements, to manage the PPIFs not for the benefit of the PPIF (and taxpayers), but rather for the benefit of themselves and their collusive partners. In both the Legacy Loans Program and the Legacy Securities Program, the significant Government- nanced leverage presents a great incentive for collusion between the buyer and seller of the asset, or the buyer and other buyers, whereby, once again, the taxpayer takes a significant loss while others profit.

This time, consider an example from the Legacy Loans Program. Imagine that a bank owns a pool of mortgage loans that both it and the private equity firm investing in a PPIF values at $600 million. The private equity firm invests $60 million into the PPIF, which is matched by $60 million of TARP funds, and which is leveraged by a loan of $720 million guaranteed by FDIC (the 6-to-1 debt-to-equity ratio). The PPIF private equity firm surreptitiously agrees with the bank to overpay for the pool of loans and causes the PPIF to bid $840 million at auction for that pool. After the auction, the bank secretly pays the PPIF private equity firm a kickback of $120 million, or half the difference between the auction price ($840 million) and the true value ($600 million). Although the PPIF will eventually perform poorly as a result of the overpayment, the private equity firm's loss is relatively small. Even if the PPIF was completely wiped out, the most the PPIF private equity firm could lose is $60 million, which would still give it a guaranteed profit of at least $60 million as a result of the kickback, a 100% return. Meanwhile, the bank would have gained an illegal benefit of $120 million, all at the expense of the taxpayer and FDIC. Of course, in practice, the collusive scheme would be far more complex and would likely involve a series of affiliates and offsetting transactions, but the principle would be the same.

The same collusion could occur in the Legacy Securities Program between buyer and seller. Similarly, collusion could occur among other buyers. For example, using the example described above involving MBS X, the fund manager could convince another PPIF fund manager to overpay for MBS X, yielding the same profits for the fund manager as if he himself directed the overpayment. In return, the original fund manager could overpay for a different MBS that is on the other PPIF fund manager's books. As a result, both fund managers could potentially reap significant illegal (and difficult to detect) profits, all at the expense of the taxpayer.

Money Laundering

National and international criminal organizations — from organized crime, to narcotics traffickers, to large-scale fraud operations — are continually looking for opportunities to make their illicit proceeds appear to be legitimate, thereby "laundering" those proceeds. It is estimated that the amount of funds laundered each year is in the hundreds of billions of dollars worldwide. Money-laundering organizations are highly sophisticated, utilizing the full arsenal of corporate, trust, and offshore financial structures, and vast sums of illicit proceeds can and do make it into the U.S. financial system each year.

Because of the significant leveraging available and the inherent imprimatur of legitimacy associated with PPIP and TALF, these programs present an ideal opportunity to money-laundering organizations. If a criminal organization can successfully invest $10 million of illicit proceeds into a PPIF, not only does the organization enjoy the possibility of profiting through the Government-backed leverage, but any eventual distributions from the PPIF are successfully laundered because they appear to be PPIF investment gains rather than drug, prostitution, or illegal gambling proceeds. It would of course be unacceptable if TARP funds, FRBNY loans, or FDIC guarantees were used to leverage the profits of drug cartels or organized crime groups. This vulnerability is particularly problematic in light of the contemplation of the use of SPVs — legal entities created for the purpose of holding PPIF assets — which can be, depending upon how they are designed, difficult to look behind to discern the true participants. Although the term sheets for PPIP place requirements on the individual PPIF managers to conduct some screening of the individual investors, it is not clear what ability Treasury will have to "look through" to each of the individual investors to identify them and assure their legitimacy, or have access to the individual investors' books and records.

Recommendations

To address these vulnerabilities, SIGTARP makes the following recommendations with respect to the design and implementation of PPIP.

Treasury should impose strict confliict-of-interest rules upon PPIF managers across all programs that specifically address whether and to what extent the managers can (i) invest PPIF funds in legacy assets that they hold or manage on behalf of themselves or their clients or (ii) conduct PPIF transactions with entities in which they have invested on behalf of themselves or others. SIGTARP recognizes that there is a trade-off between hiring managers with significant experience in the marketplace (who have the expertise to make them effective asset managers but who have complex conflict-of-interest issues as a result) and hiring managers who are not in the market at all (who have less expertise but also no conflicts); however, Treasury should at least consider whether its fund manager requirements address the serious conf ict issues. It may very well be that some of the conflicts cannot be mitigated under the current structure of the programs unless the fund managers have no interests (and have no clients who have interests) in the kinds of legacy assets that the PPIFs are purchasing. This may, in turn, significantly limit what entities should be making PPIF investment decisions.

Treasury should mandate transparency with respect to the participation and management of PPIFs. This should include disclosure of the beneficial owners of all of the private equity stakes in the PPIFs and of all transactions undertaken in them. In addition to the reporting requirements contained in the PPIP term sheets, Treasury should obtain and publicly disclose certified reports from all PPIFs across all programs that include all transactions and the current valuation of all assets. This transparency is necessary in light of the taxpayers' reasonable expectation of knowing how their money is being used, as a way to track and/or deter the types of conflicts of interest and collusion abuses previously described, and as a way to deter criminal organizations from trying to use PPIP to launder illicit proceeds. To the extent that PPIF managers are permitted to hold or engage in transactions in the same securities that they are buying and selling in the PPIFs, Treasury should require PPIF managers to report to Treasury on any and all holdings and transactions in the same types of legacy assets on their own behalf or on behalf of their clients. Such a disclosure would help identify conflicts of interest. Moreover, in addition to the requirement that SIGTARP will have access to all of the PPIF's books and records, as set forth in the term sheets, Treasury should impose a requirement that PPIF managers retain all books and records pertaining in any way to the PPIF (including all e-mails, instant messages, and all other documents), and permit SIGTARP and other oversight entities access to the fund manager's books and records and employees, upon request. In this manner, Treasury, SIGTARP, and other oversight bodies might be able to detect and address the potential conflicts and any indication of collusion. Treasury should also require access to the private investors' books and records, at least to the extent that they relate to the PPIF investment.

Treasury should require PPIF managers to provide PPIF equity stakeholders (including TARP) "most-favored nations clauses," requiring that the fund managers treat the PPIFs (and the taxpayers backing the PPIFs) on at least as favorable terms as given to all other parties with whom they deal. In that same vein, PPIF managers should be required to acknowledge that they owe the PPIF investors – both the private investors and TARP – a fiduciary duty with respect to the management of the PPIFs. Treasury should also require that each PPIF fund manager have a robust ethics policy in place and a compliance apparatus to ensure adherence to such code.

In order to prevent money laundering and the participation of actors prone to abusing the system, Treasury should require that all PPIF fund managers have stringent investor-screening procedures, including comprehensive "Know Your Customer" requirements at least as rigorous as that of a commercial bank or retail brokerage operation. Additionally, fund managers should be required to provide Treasury with the identities of all of the beneficial owners of the private interests in the fund so that Treasury can do appropriate diligence to ensure that investors in the funds are legitimate.

Interactions between PPIP and TALF

In announcing the details of PPIP, Treasury has indicated that PPIFs under the Legacy Securities Program could, in turn, use the leveraged PPIF funds (two-thirds of which will likely be taxpayer money) to purchase legacy MBS through TALF, greatly increasing taxpayer exposure to losses with no corresponding increase of potential profits. By way of example, a PPIF manager could raise $500 million of private equity, which would be matched with $500 million of TARP funds, and a loan of an additional $500 million from TARP funds (according to the term sheet, loans will only be given up to 50% of the total equity if investments will be made through TALF rather than 100% otherwise). The PPIF could then take the total $1.5 billion, bring it to the TALF window, and effectively use that money as the "haircut" amount in a TALF financing to purchase legacy RMBS. Assuming that the haircut will be 20% (larger than any existing haircut), the PPIF will be able to receive a non-recourse loan from FRBNY for an additional $6 billion, enabling the PPIF to purchase $7.5 billion in legacy RMBS. The private investors would thus enjoy 50% of the profits from this enhanced buying power, but only be exposed to less than 7% of the total losses if the fund were wiped out.

Aside from potential unfairness to the taxpayer, this leverage upon leverage on legacy RMBS raises other significant issues. First, it only magnifies the dangerous incentives discussed above (the conflicts of interest and collusion issues), because the fund manager now has up to five times the buying power than it would if it participated in the Legacy Securities PPIF alone. Moreover, it severely undermines the validity of the methodology that the Federal Reserve has used to build the haircut percentages in TALF thus far. The Federal Reserve has told SIGTARP that it has determined its haircut percentage based at least in part on the fact that the haircut represents a TALF borrower's "skin in the game" — someone's own capital at risk — that incentivizes appropriate due diligence on the borrower's part. If leveraged PPIFs are permitted to participate in TALF, that effectively lowers the private equity's skin in the game by at least the amount of money borrowed from TARP, materially diminishing the incentive to do due diligence. Put in simpler terms, an investor who is funding 100% of the haircut amount with his own money (as is typical in TALF) can logically be expected to be far more careful than one only put-ting up 33% (as would occur under this example).

Recommendations

Accordingly, SIGTARP recommends that:

Treasury should not allow Legacy Securities PPIFs to invest in TALF, unless significant mitigating measures are included to address these dangers. These might include prohibiting the use of TARP leverage if the PPIF invests through TALF, or proportionately increasing haircuts for PPIFs that do so.

Failure to adopt this recommendation may well protect the Federal Reserve's own balance sheet, but it would do so at the expense of putting at risk Treasury assets, hardly a victory from the taxpayers' perspective. SIGTARP thus further recommends:

All TALF modeling and decisions, whether on haircuts or any other credit or fraud loss mechanisms, should account for potential losses to Government interests broadly, including TARP funds, and not just potential losses to the Federal Reserve.

Treasury officials, in discussing these recommendations with SIGTARP, recognize the increased risks associated with this area of the program but suggested that flexibility would be needed to consider alternate ways of mitigating the risks to the extent possible.

SIGTARP will continue to monitor the development of the PPIP requirements and procedures and will make future recommendations concerning standards and mechanisms that will help protect against fraud, waste, and abuse in the program, as appropriate.

Design of the Mortgage Modification Program

Shortly after the February announcement of the Administration's intent to launch a mortgage modification plan, SIGTARP provided a series of high-level recommendations to address potential fraud in the program, first by providing OFS officials an outline of potential fraud issues and then in a series of discussions with OFS and other Treasury officials.

SIGTARP's recommendations were made in the context of the Special Inspector General's prior experience as the founder of the Mortgage Fraud Group in the United States Attorney's Office for the Southern District of New York and after consultation with and advice from mortgage fraud experts at the Federal Bureau of Investigation. The recommendations address some of the patterns of the rampant mortgage fraud that contributed to the current financial crisis, including corruption of many of the potential gatekeepers who were supposed to limit such fraud: attorneys, appraisers, notaries, mortgage brokers, title insurance agents, and insiders at banks and mortgage originators. Recognizing that many of the most prevalent frauds had common characteristics, SIGTARP's recommendations refl ected an attempt to shield the program from such schemes before they could be adapted to the mortgage modification plan.

In general, mortgage fraud schemes are viewed by law enforcement in two categories: (i) fraud for home, where a homeowner lies in order to get a mortgage for which he or she would otherwise not qualify; and (ii) fraud for profit, which involves rings of individuals whose goal is to defraud banks and individual homeowners for the purpose of profit. Recognizing that the greatest economic damage is done by those who commit mortgage fraud for profit, SIGTARP's recom-mendations primarily address this type of fraud.

In this section, SIGTARP's mortgage modification recommendations, followed by Treasury's response, are each discussed in detail.

Verification of Residence Recommendation

One of the most common characteristics of fraud-for-profit schemes is that the individual holding the mortgage, often a "straw purchaser," does not actually live in the home for which he or she is obtaining a mortgage. Recognizing this indicator, SIGTARP strongly recommended that Treasury include provisions to ensure that the individual applying for the mortgage modification actually lives in the home, including (i) a signed certification from the applicant, and (ii) third-party verification that the home is the applicant's primary residence.

Indeed, to guard against servicer failings (such as not doing the verification but then claiming that it had) or complicity (such as purposefully misrepresenting the residence of the applicant in furtherance of a fraud-for-profit scheme), SIGTARP recommended that Treasury require submission of third-party verification to Treasury or its agent prior to its funding a modification.

Status of Recommendation

Treasury has partially implemented this recommendation. It has taken some important steps, including requiring a signed certification from the applicant that he or she lives in the home and requiring the servicer to acquire from the applicant some proof of residence. Treasury has not required, however, that the servicer obtain third-party verification of the applicant's residence before submitting and implementing the mortgage modification. This is critical, as most fraud-for-profit schemes have ready access to forged documents (*e.g.,* false utility bills, pay stubs, bank account statements). As a result, the current system will not capture a fraud scheme that involves doctored documents or one involving the complicity or the negligence of the servicer, because the servicer is not required to submit proof of its verification of residence before receiving Government funding. Accordingly, SIGTARP continues to recommend that:

> Before funding a mortgage modification, Treasury should require the servicer to submit third-party verified evidence that the applicant is residing in the subject property.

Treasury, in discussions with SIGTARP about this recommendation, indi-cated that servicers will be able to obtain (i) the borrowers' tax return information from the IRS and (ii) credit reports. If Treasury requires servicers to provide such third-party verified information regarding residence to Treasury or its agent before funding a modification, it would represent a significant improvement in the program.

Closing Procedures Recommendation

Many fraud-for-profit schemes involved fraudulent closings, at which signatures were forged or where the homeowners and/or purchasers signed documents they did not understand and thus could be charged exorbitant fees without their knowledge. As a result, several states have tightened the requirements of the typical mortgage closing procedure with measures that increase deterrence and which greatly assist law enforcement in its investigation of mortgage fraud-for-profit schemes. Adopting some of the characteristics of these reforms, SIGTARP recommended that a closing-like procedure be conducted that would include:

- a closing warning sheet that would warn the applicant of the consequences of fraud
- the notarized signature and thumbprint of each participant
- mandatory collection, copying, and retention of copies of identification documents of all participants in the transaction
- verbal and written warnings regarding hidden fees and payments so that applicants are made fully aware of:

the benefits to which they are entitled under the program (to prevent a corrupt servicer from collecting payments from the Government and not passing the full amount of the subsidies to the homeowners)

the fact that no fee should be charged for the modification

Status of Recommendation

Treasury has decided against using a closing procedure, stating that mortgage modifications typically take place over the telephone and through the mail. Treasury has, however, attempted to address several of the concerns raised in this recommendation by: (i) including a fraud warning sheet with every mortgage modification solicitation that includes SIGTARP's hotline to report fraud; and (ii) beginning outreach efforts, along with other agencies, to warn homeowners that they should not pay fees as part of the program, as discussed more fully in the following paragraphs. SIGTARP remains concerned that Treasury has not taken sufficient action related to its previous recommendation. Accordingly, SIGTARP continues to recommend that:

Additional anti-fraud protections should be adopted to verify the identity of the participants in the transaction and to address the potential for servicers to steal from individuals by receiving Government subsidies without applying them for the benefit of the homeowner.

Treasury officials, in discussing this recommendation with SIGTARP, noted that they have a financial agent agreement with Freddie Mac to provide a range of compliance and anti-fraud efforts for the loan modification program and are consulting with an anti-fraud expert. They also indicated that these efforts would align with many of the issues and recommendations identified by SIGTARP pertaining to loan modifications and will include provisions that address potentially corrupt loan servicers.

Income Verification Recommendation

One of the most common features of traditional mortgage fraud is that applicants falsely in ate their income and support those lies with fraudulent documentation and employment verification. In the mortgage modification program, due to the increased subsidy for homeowners whose income is lower, there exists an incentive for applicants to understate their income intentionally. To address this potential fraud, SIGTARP recommended that Treasury require servicers to: (i) compare the income reported on their initial mortgage application with the income reported on the modification application, and, if they differ significantly, require an explanation and verifiable documentation of the change in income; and (ii) require third-party verification of employment.

Status of Recommendation

Treasury has not adopted this recommendation, but has taken some steps to verify income, including requiring the homeowner to sign a waiver so that the servicer can obtain tax return information for the applicant and requiring the applicant to provide documentation to verify income. Although this is helpful, SIGTARP believes that further action is still needed as it does not appear that Treasury is requiring the servicer actually to obtain and verify the income tax information before approving the modification. Tax return information, for example, even if obtained, may be of limited value given the time lag between the last income tax return and the date of the application. Further, as noted earlier in the discussion, relying on documentation provided by the borrower is unreliable given the prevalence and ease with which false pay stubs, W-2s, and 1099s can be generated. Accordingly, SIGTARP continues to recommend that:

Treasury require that verifiable, third-party information be obtained to con rm an applicant's income before any modification payments are made.

Timing of Incentive Payments Recommendation

Generally speaking, one of the fraud dangers to the mortgage modification program is the activity of "modification mills," corrupt servicers that will churn out unveri-fied or unlikely-to-perform mortgage modifications in order to collect the $1,000 up-front incentive payment. Because the servicer is not currently required to provide verified information prior to commencing a modification (and receiving the $1,000 up-front payment), there is a fraud incentive for servicers to push through modifications that do not necessarily meet the criteria and/or make modifications that they know will never be successful. Indeed, it is unfortunately foreseeable that a servicer could take a mortgage that is in default, submit fraudulent paper-work, and collect the $1,000 fee, without any intent on the part of the homeowner to make any further payments on the mortgage modification. SIGTARP thus recommended that Treasury delay the up-front payment by 90 days to ensure that the homeowner has made several payments as part of the mortgage modification program before awarding the servicer the $1,000 incentive payment.

Status of Recommendation

Treasury has implemented a procedure under which it will not pay the $1,000 incentive payment until after the homeowner has made three payments to the servicer; however, these payments occur prior to the Government's modification of the mortgage and require no independent verification. Although Treasury's insistence of a servicer-run trial period is certainly an improvement over a system of immediate incentive payments, it does not necessarily protect Treasury from a corrupt servicer who could fraudulently claim that an applicant has successfully completed a trial period even if not true. Accordingly, to protect against such fraud, SIGTARP continues to recommend that:

Treasury should defer payment of the $1,000 incentive to the servicer until after the homeowner has verifiably made a minimum number of payments under the mortgage modification program.

Treasury officials, in discussing this recommendation with SIGTARP, have indicated that they will work with their agents "to verify that the borrower makes the required number of payments under the trial modification."[3]

Education and Outreach Recommendation

One of the most insidious forms of mortgage fraud are "foreclosure rescue scams," in which fraudsters trick struggling homeowners into paying up-front fees by promising them assistance in navigating the foreclosure process. Sadly, most of the companies promising these services do nothing for the homeowner other than give them false hope while taking an exorbitant fee. SIGTARP therefore recommended that Treasury proactively educate homeowners about the nature of the program, warn them about these predators, and publicize that no fee is necessary to participate in the program.

Status of Recommendation

Treasury is doing an excellent job in implementing this recommendation. The Making Home Affordable website prominently features fraud warnings, and, in an April 6, 2009, press conference, the Treasury Secretary, along with the Attorney General, the Secretary of the Department of Housing and Urban Development, the head of the Federal Trade Commission, and the Attorney General for the State of Illinois, announced a coordinated and detailed outreach effort to educate homeowners about the dangers of such fraud, as well as efforts to detect and prosecute such scams. SIGTARP's Investigations Division will continue to work with its partners to bring the perpetrators of such fraud to justice.

Mandated Data Collection Recommendation

Mortgage fraud is often perpetrated by repeat offenders, and one of law enforcement's most powerful tools to detect this abuse is the capability to mine data to identify those individuals and entities (such as appraisers, mortgage brokers, straw purchasers, or attorneys) who repeatedly appear in connection with suspicious foreclosures. SIGTARP recommended that Treasury require its agents to keep track of the names and identifying information for each participant in each mortgage modification transaction and to maintain a database of such information. Not only would such a database assist law enforcement in the detection and apprehension of fraudsters, but it could also assist in fraud prevention. For example, a centralized database could identify if a potential homeowner applicant had already applied for or received a mortgage modification on a different property, a strong indicator of fraud (because an applicant can only live in one home, an application for an additional modification would strongly suggest that the homeowner had lied about his or her primary residence).

Status of Recommendation

Treasury officials, in discussing this recommendation with SIGTARP, recognized the importance of data mining to fraud prevention efforts and stated that they are working with Freddie Mac, their compliance agent, to determine the feasibility of this recommendation.

Auto Supplier Support Program

SIGTARP was briefed on the Auto Supplier Support Program shortly before it was announced. At the time of the brie ng, SIGTARP raised concerns regarding two potential fraud vulnerabilities. First, SIGTARP inquired as to what protections would be in place to prevent "phantom receivables" — auto parts that are subject to TARP funding but never make it to the automobile manufacturers. Second, SIGTARP warned of the dangers of commercial bribery, a vulnerability borne from the structure of the program, which empowered the automobile manufacturers with unfettered discretion to choose which suppliers and at what amounts the suppliers can participate in the program — effectively picking winners and losers with no clear restrictions.

In discussions concerning this recommendation, Treasury has indicated that certain financial aspects of the program would act as a disincentive to these vulnerabilities. SIGTARP awaits further brie ng on the program.

End Notes

[1] Treasury, "SIGTARP's Recommendations for the Operation of TARP, Comments by the Office of Financial Stability," 4/13/2009.

[2] Treasury, "SIGTARP's Recommendations for the Operation of TARP, Comments by the Office of Financial Stability," 4/13/2009.

[3] Treasury, "SIGTARP's Recommendations for the Operation of TARP, Comments by the Office of Financial Stability," 4/13/2009.

Sources for Figure 2.1. TARP Projected Funding: CPP, TALF, and PPIP: Treasury, Office of Financial Stability, Chief of Compliance and CFO, SIGTARP interview, 3/30/2009; AIFP: Treasury, *Fifth Tranche Report to Congress*, 3/6/2009, p. 2 states that Treasury will fund an additional $4 billion on 3/17/2009; ASSP: Treasury, "Auto Supplier Support Program: Stabilizing the Auto Industry in a Time of Crisis," 3/19/2009, www.treas. gov, accessed 3/19/2009; UCSB: Treasury, "Unlocking Credit for Small Businesses: FAQ on Implementation," 3/17/2009, www.treas.gov, accessed 3/18/2009; SSFI: Treasury, "U.S. Treasury and Federal Reserve Board Announce Participation in AIG Restructuring Plan," 3/2/2009, www.treas. gov, accessed 3/4/2009; TIP: Treasury, *Transactions Report*, 4/2/2009; AGP: Treasury, "Treasury, Federal Reserve, and FDIC Provide Assistance to Bank of America," 1/16/2009, www.treas.gov, accessed 1/16/2009; Treasury, "U.S. Government Finalizes Terms of Citi Guarantee Announced in November," 1/16/2009, www.treas.gov, accessed 3/30/2009; TALF: Treasury, "Financial Stability Plan Fact Sheet," 2/10/2009, www.treas.gov, accessed 3/17/2009; MHA: Treasury, "Making Home Affordable: Updated Detailed Program Description," 3/4/2009, www.treas.gov, accessed 3/4/2009; GAO, "Report to Congressional Committees: Troubled Asset Relief Program — March 2009 Status of Efforts to Address Transparency and Accountability Issues," 3/26/2009; PPIP: Treasury, "Public-Private Investment Program: Fact Sheet," 3/23/2009, www.treas.gov, accessed 3/23/2009; Treasury, SIGTARP brie2 ng, 4/14/2009.

APPENDICES

A. GLOSSARY

This appendix provides a glossary of terms that are used throughout the context of this report.

504 Community Development Loan Program: SBA loan program combining Government-guaranteed loans with private-sector mortgage loans to provide up to $10 million in financing for community development.

7(a) Program: SBA loan program guaranteeing a percentage of loans for small businesses that cannot otherwise obtain conventional loans at reasonable terms.

Accrual Assets: In the context of the Citigroup Master Agreement, accrual assets are those that are held on the bank's books at accrued value (*i.e.*, gains and accruals are earned but not necessarily received), as opposed to "markto-market" value.

Annual Coupon Rate: The annual amount of interest scheduled to be paid on a fixed income investment, such as a bond or a mortgage.

Asset-Backed Security ("ABS"): "A type of financial security that is very similar in structure to a mortgage-backed security (see Mortgage-Backed Security), but is backed by a pool of consumer loans and generally does not include mortgage loans. Most ABSs are backed by credit card receivables, auto loans, student loans, or other loan and lease obligations."

Asset Guarantee Program ("AGP"): "Established under section 102 of EESA, allows the Department of the Treasury to assume a loss position with specified attachment and detachment points on certain assets held by the qualifying financial institution; the set of insured assets would be selected by the Treasury and its agents in consultation with the financial institution receiving the guarantee."

Auction: "An asset sales strategy in which assets are sold either individually or in pools to the highest bidder."

Automotive Industry Financing Program ("AIFP"): The Automotive Industry Financing Program was created to provide strategic investments in U.S. automotive companies to prevent a significant disruption of the U.S. automotive industry or to financial markets.

Bad Bank: An entity (the "bad bank") that is legally separated from the bank that created it (the "good bank") and into which are placed problem loans (or other troubled assets). Usually created by banks seeking to clean up their balance sheets.

Balance Sheet: "The balance sheet is a snapshot of a company's financial standing at an instant in time. The balance sheet shows a company's financial position, what it owns (assets) and what it owes (liabilities). The 'bottom line' of a balance sheet must always balance (*i.e.*, assets = liabilities + net worth)."

Bank: "Means:

A. a banking institution organized under the laws of the United States, or a Federal savings association, as de ned in section 2(5) of the Home Owners' Loan Act [12 USCS 1462(5)],
B. a member bank of the Federal Reserve System,
C. any other banking institution, whether incorporated or not, doing business under the laws of any State or of the United States, a substantial portion of the business of which consists of receiving deposits or exercising fiduciary powers similar to those permitted to national banks under the authority of the Comptroller of the Currency pursuant to section 92a of Title 12, and which is supervised and examined by State or Federal authority having supervision over banks, and which is not operated for the purpose of evading the provisions of this title, and
D. a receiver, conservator, or other liquidating agent of any institution or firm included in clauses (A), (B), or (C) of this paragraph."

Bank Holding Company ("BHC"): "A company that owns and/or controls one or more U.S. banks or one that owns, or has controlling interest in, one or more banks. A bank holding company may also own another bank holding company, which in turn owns or controls a bank; the company at the top of the ownership chain is called the top holder."

Baseline Value: In reference to Citigroup Master Agreement, Baseline Value is the value of each covered asset on November 21, 2008. For mark-tomarket assets, it is the fair market value, and accrual assets, it is the unpaid principal balance.

Basic Exchange: In reference to Citigroup exchange offer, taking one type of stock (*i.e.*, preferred) and converting it at a specific rate to another type of stock (*i.e.*, common).

Basis Points: One-hundredth of a percentage point. (For example, the difference between interest rates of 5.5% and 5.0% is 50 basis points.)

Bonus Pool: A pool or fund of money accumulated during the year by a business to be paid out at the end of a specified time period, typically a year, as compensation to employees of the business as a reward for achieving certain de ned levels of company and/or employee performance.

Call Report: Quarterly report of financial condition commercial banks file with their Federal and state regulatory agencies.

Capital: "Tangible and intangible resources that can be used or invested to produce a stream of benefits over time."

Capital Purchase Program ("CPP"): The Capital Purchase Program is a program that is part of the Troubled Asset Relief Program ("TARP"). It is a program that will invest in Qualifying Financial Institutions by purchasing preferred stock and equity warrants.

Clawback: In reference to EESA, "Provision for the recovery of bonuses or incentive compensation paid to a senior executive based on statements of earnings, gains, or other criteria that are later proven to be materially inaccurate."

Closing Date: In reference to the Citigroup Master Agreement, "the time and date on which the closing occurs is the closing date."

Collateral: An asset pledged by a borrower to a lender until a loan is repaid.

Collateralized: Securing a loan with assets.

Collateralized Debt Obligation ("CDO"): "A collateralized debt obligation (CDO) is a security that entitles the purchaser to some portion of the cash flows from a portfolio of assets, which may include bonds, loans, mortgage- backed securities, or other CDOs. For a given pool, CDOs designated as senior debt, mezzanine debt, subordinated debt, and equity often are issued."

Commercial Mortgage-Backed Securities ("CMBS"): "A financial instrument that is backed by a mortgage or a group of mortgages that are packaged together. The security is bought and sold in financial markets. An MBS can be backed either by residential real estate loans ("RMBS") or commercial real estate loans ("CMBS")."

Commitment: "Any legally binding arrangements that obligate a bank to extend credit in the form of loans or lease financing receivables; to purchase loans, securities, or other assets; or to participate in loans and leases. Commitments also include overdraft facilities, revolving credit, home equity and mortgage lines of credit, eligible ABCP liquidity facilities, and similar transactions. Normally, commitments involve a written contract or agreement and a commitment fee, or some other form of consideration."

Common Stock: "A security that provides voting rights in a corporation and pays a dividend after preferred stock holders have been paid."

Convertible Preferred Stock: Traditionally, "convertible preferred stock" referred to preferred stock that could be converted into common stock at the option of the shareholder. In the context of TARP's CAP, however, the conversion is at the option of the QFI (qualifying financial institution), and the shareholder must mandatorily accept common stock upon notice of conversion.

Covered Asset: In reference to the Citigroup Master Agreement, Covered Asset is an asset owned by Citigroup or any of its subsidiaries that is included in the ring-fence.

Credit Enhancement: "Techniques whereby a company attempts to reduce the credit risk of its obligations. Credit enhancement may be provided by a third party (external credit enhancement) or by the originator (internal credit enhancement), and more than one type of enhancement may be associated with a given issuance." For example, an MBS issuer may purchase an insurance policy which will pay investors if MBS losses rise above a certain level.

Credit Protection: Security against losses on an investment. For TALF purposes, TARP funding is used as credit protection on the Federal Reserve loans (*i.e.,* losses on the loans are absorbed by TARP funds up to the commitment amount).

Credit Rating: An assessment of the willingness and ability to pay of a borrower for a fixed-income security. Ratings are issued primarily by national firms such as Moody's, Standard & Poor's, and Fitch.

CUSIP: CUSIP stands for Committee on Uniform Securities Identification Procedures. A CUSIP number identifies most securities, including stocks of all registered U.S. and Canadian companies, and U.S. Government and municipal bonds.

Custodian: "A bank, trust, or other financial institution that agrees to hold and manage assets on behalf of another person or entity."

Default: The failure to live up to the terms of a contract. Generally, default is used to indicate the inability of a borrower to pay the interest or principal on a debt when it is due.

Derivative Asset: An asset whose stated value or cash fiow is determined by reference to the value or cash fiow of another asset (the "underlying asset").

Derivative Instrument: See Derivative Asset.

Distributions: Payments of cash or other consideration from a trust fund or corporation to an investor.

Divestiture: Change of ownership and/or control of a business from a majority (non-disadvantaged) to disadvantaged persons.

Dividend: "Distributions to stockholders of cash or stock declared by the company's board of directors."

Emergency Economic Stabilization Act of 2008 ("EESA"): "An act to provide authority for the Federal Government to purchase and insure certain types of troubled assets for the purposes of providing stability to and preventing disruption in the economy and financial system and protecting taxpayers, to amend the Internal Revenue Code of 1986 to provide incentives for energy production and conservation, to extend certain expiring provisions, to provide individual income tax relief, and for other purposes."

Equity: The ownership interest of stockholders in a company.

Equity Capital Facility: An agreement between two parties under which Party A may require Party B to make an equity investment in Party A.

Equity Interest: See Equity.

Equity Security: "Any stock or similar security, certificate of interest or participation in any profit sharing agreement, preorganization certificate or subscription, transferable share, voting trust certificate or certificate of deposit for an equity security, limited partnership interest, interest in a joint venture, or certificate of interest in a business trust; any security future on any such security; or any security convertible, with or without consideration into such a security, or carrying any warrant or right to subscribe to or purchase such a security; or any such warrant or right; or any put, call, straddle, or other option or privilege of buying such a security from or selling such a security to another without being bound to do so."

Exceptional Assistance: In reference to TARP, institutions requiring assistance beyond the assistance of the widely available program *(i.e.*, CPP and CAP) are classified as requiring "Exceptional Assistance."

Executive Compensation: The terminology for how top executives of business corporations are paid for the services they provide. The forms of compensation typically include a base salary, bonuses, shares, options, and other company benefits.

Expenditure: The actual spending of money — an outlay.

Expense: "Outflow or other depletion of assets or incurrences of liabilities (or a combination of both) during some period as a result of providing goods, rendering services, or carrying out other activities related to an entity's programs and missions, the benefits from which do not extend beyond the present operating period."

Facility: In the context of finance, a "facility" is an agreement between two parties under which one may require the other to provide capital to the requestor. The provider of the facility provides funds in the form of either debt or equity.

Federal Banking Agency ("FBA"): "The term appropriate Federal banking agency means—

(1) the Comptroller of the Currency, in the case of any national banking association, or any Federal branch or agency of a foreign bank;
(2) the Board of Governors of the Federal Reserve System, in the case of—
   (A) any State member insured bank,
   (B) any branch or agency of a foreign bank with respect to any provision of the Federal Reserve Act which is made applicable under the International Banking Act of 1978,
   (C) any foreign bank which does not operate an insured branch,
   (D) any agency or commercial lending company other than a Federal agency,
   (E) supervisory or regulatory proceedings arising from the authority given to the Board of Governors under section 7(c)(1) of the International Banking Act of 1978, including such proceedings under the Financial Institutions Supervisory Act of 1966, and
   (F) any bank holding company and any subsidiary of a bank holding company (other than a bank);
(3) the Federal Deposit Insurance Corporation in the case of a State nonmember insured bank, or a foreign bank having an insured branch; and
(4) the Director of the Office of Thrift Supervision in the case of any savings association or any savings and loan holding company.
   Under the rule set forth in this subsection, more than one agency may be an appropriate Federal banking agency with respect to any given institution."

Federal Funds Rate: "The interest rate that financial institutions charge each other for overnight loans of their monetary reserves."

Financial Guarantor Counterparty Exposure: The maximum amount that may be lost by a financial institution if there is a failure to pay a financial guaranty claim by the fi nancial institution (the "counterparty") who had promised to guarantee against a loss.

Financial Stability Plan: Plan to stabilize and repair the financial system, and support the fiow of credit necessary for recovery.

Fiscal Year: "A yearly accounting period. The Federal Government's fiscal year begins October 1 and ends September 30. Fiscal years are designated by the calendar years in which they end — for example, fiscal year 2009 will begin on October 1, 2008, and end on September 30, 2009. The budget year is the fiscal year for which the budget is being considered; in relation to a session of Congress, it is the fiscal year that starts on October 1 of the calendar year in which that session of Congress began."

Floorplan: In reference to the TALF program, revolving lines of credit (similar to a credit card) to finance automobile dealer inventories (cars on the lot). A form of retail goods inventory financing in which each loan advance is made against a specific piece of collateral. As each piece of collateral is sold by the dealer, the loan advance against the piece of collateral is repaid.

Generally Available Programs: Programs having the same terms for all recipients, with limits on the amount each institution may receive and specified returns for taxpayers (*i.e.*, CPP or CAP).

Going Concern: Term used by auditors to refer to a company that is able to operate into the foreseeable future.

Golden Parachute (as defined in original Section 111 of EESA): Compensation to (or for the benefit of) a senior executive Officer made upon severance from employment that exceeds specified thresholds. Under EESA, such compensation is limited to three times the executive's annual base salary.

Golden Parachute (definition under ARRA): Any payment to a senior executive Officer for departure from a company for any reason, except for payments for services performed or benefits accrued.

Guarantee: A commitment from a third-party lending institution ensuring that liabilities of a borrower will be met. If the borrower fails to make payments, the guarantor will step in and make the payment on the borrower's behalf.

Guaranty: Can be used interchangeably with Guarantee. Historically, guarantee had been used as a verb and guaranty had been used as a noun. Guaranty is now primarily seen in financial and banking contexts.

Haircut: Difference in the value of the collateral and the value of the loan; that is, the collateral value of the loan minus the loan amount. For example: A borrower has $100 worth of collateral for a loan. The bank issues the borrower a $90 loan backed by the $100 of collateral. The bank has applied a 10% haircut to that collateral. Generally, the higher the haircut, the riskier the collateral is perceived to be.

Holding Company: A company whose primary business is holding a controlling interest in the securities of other companies. Technically, "A) any bank holding company (as defined in section 2 of the Bank Holding Company Act of 1956); B) any company described in section 4(f)(1) of the Bank Holding Company Act of 1956; and C) any savings and loan holding company (as defined in the Home Owners' Loan Act)."

HOPE for Homeowners Program: "A program under the Department of Housing and Urban Development ("HUD"), designed to help mortgage borrowers at risk of default and foreclosure to refinance into more affordable, sustainable loans which are in turn guaranteed by HUD."

Illiquid: Assets that cannot be quickly converted to cash.

Impaired Capital: "Capital position of a bank where the par value of all of its capital stock is less than the sum of paid in capital, surplus, and undivided profits."

Insolvent: A condition where a financial institution has liabilities that exceed its assets. By definition, shareholders' equity in such a situation would be negative.

Interest: "Interest means any payment to a consumer or to an account for the use of funds in an account, calculated by application of a periodic rate to the balance. The term does not include the payment of a bonus or other consideration worth $10 or less given during a year, the waiver or reduction of a fee, or the absorption of expenses."

In-the-Money: "A term used to describe an option contract that has a positive value if exercised. A call with a strike price of $390 on gold trading at $400 is in-the-money by $10."

Legacy Assets: Also known as troubled assets, real estate-related loans and securities that remain on banks' balance sheets and that have lost value, but are difficult to price due to the recent market disruption.

Legacy Loans: Underperforming real estate-related loans held by a bank that it wishes to sell, but recent market disruptions have made difficult to price.

Legacy Securities: Troubled real estate-related securities [Residential Mortgage-Backed Securities ("RMBS"), Commercial Mortgage-Backed Securities ("CMBS"), and Asset-Backed Securities ("ABS")] on institutions' balance sheets due to an inability to determine value.

Leverage: The ratio of a company's debt to its equity.

LIBOR: "The London Interbank Offered Rate. The rate of interest at which banks borrow funds from other banks, in marketable size, in the London interbank market. LIBOR rates are disseminated by the British Bankers Association. Some interest rate futures contracts, including Eurodollar futures, are cash settled based on LIBOR."

Liquidity: A measure of the ease with which assets can be bought and sold in the markets, often characterized by "bid" and "asked" prices that are close, and the presence of a willing pool of buyers and sellers. In the context of financial institution balance sheets, "liquidity" often refers to the availability of cash for lending.

Loan Portfolio: The total amount of dollars the bank has lent to customers and expects to be repaid.

Loan-to-value ratio: In real estate lending, the amount of the loan divided by the appraised value of the property underlying the loan.

Market Capitalization: The value of a corporation determined by multiplying the current market price of one share of the corporation by the number of total outstanding shares. This metric is often used to determine the aggregate value of a company.

Market Value: The price at which an asset can be sold in an orderly market, to a willing buyer by a willing seller, in a reasonable amount of time.

Mark-to-Market Assets: In the context of the Citigroup Master Agreement, the portion of the covered assets that are valued at current market value.

Mortgage Holder: Investor/lender who owns the right to the borrower's monthly payments.

Mortgage-Backed Securities ("MBS"): "Debt obligations that represent claims to the cash fiows from pools of mortgage loans, most commonly on residential property. Mortgage loans are purchased from banks, mortgage companies, and other originators and then assembled into pools by a Governmental, quasi-Governmental, or private entity. The entity then issues securities that represent claims on the principal and interest payments made by borrowers on the loans in the pool, a process known as securitization."

Mutual Organization: A company that is owned effectively by its customers, through shares of ownership related to the depositors

Net Loss: Net loss occurs when total expenses exceed total revenues.

Net Present Value: "The present value of the estimated future cash inflows minus the present value of the cash outflows."

Non-Agency Residential Mortgage-Backed Securities: Mortgage-backed securities in which the securities, and the loans underlying the securities, are serviced or originated by private investors and not by Fannie Mae or Freddie Mac.

Non-Cumulative Preferred Shares: Shares where unpaid dividends do not accrue when a company misses a dividend payment.

Non-Recourse Funding/Loan: "A debt for which the debtor's obligation to repay is limited to the collateral securing the debt and for which a deficiency judgment against the debtor is not permitted, and would limit the amount of a non-recourse debt to the net equity in the collateral, as defined."

Obligation: The legal responsibility to make a payment to another party, usually by contract.

Offering Documents: Documents which disclose and describe a securities offering to either public or private investors, containing information required under Federal and state securities laws as applicable.

Office of Financial Stability ("OFS"): "Office within the Department of the Treasury created by EESA to operate the TARP."

Overcollateralization: The pledge of more collateral than the face amount of a loan. See Haircut definition for an example.

Pool: A collection of assets, usually fixed-income assets such as loans or mortgages, placed into a legally separate account for the benefit Officertain investors.

Pool Assemblers: See Securities Issuer.

Preferred Stock: "A form of ownership in a company that generally entitles the owner of the shares (an investor) to collect dividend payments. Preferred shares are senior to common stock, but junior to debt."

Premium(s): As referenced in a financial guaranty discussion, the institution receiving the guarantee pays the guarantor an agreed-upon amount for the protection offered by the guarantee — the same way auto insurance premiums ensure protection for damage or loss.

President's Corporate Fraud Task Force: The President's Corporate Fraud Task Force was created by Executive Order of President George W. Bush to "provide direction for the investigation and prosecution of cases of securities fraud, accounting fraud, mail and wire fraud, money laundering, tax fraud based on such predicate offenses, and other related financial crimes committed by commercial entities and directors, Officers, professional advisers, and employees thereof." Created in 2002, it is an inter-agency group that coordinates enforcement efforts among several agencies including the Department of Justice, the Commodities Futures Trading Commission, the Federal Energy Regulatory Commission, Treasury, Labor, the Securities and Exchange Commission, and U.S. Postal Inspection Service.

President's Designee: One or more Officers from the Executive Branch designated by the President.

Primary Dealer: "S securities dealer or Government securities dealer that is designated as a primary dealer by the Federal Reserve Bank of New York from time to time."

Private Applicant: In reference to TARP, a private applicant is any Qualifying Financial Institution whose shares are not traded on a national securities exchange, excluding S corporations and mutual organizations.

Private-Label Mortgage: Loans that are not issued or guaranteed by Fannie Mae, Freddie Mac, Ginnie Mae, or other Federal agency.

Private-Label Residential Mortgage-Backed Securities: A mortgage- backed security that is backed by private-label mortgages.

Procurement: "In the Federal Government, the process of obtaining services, supplies, and equipment in conformance with applicable laws and regulations."

Professional Forecaster: Economic forecasters conduct analysis to predict economic growth, in ation, interest rates, and many other critical indicators of future business activity. Provides an expert opinion on the future performance of the economy. The three forecasters used for the purpose of the Stress Test were the Consensus Forecasts, the Blue Chip Survey, and the Survey of Professional Forecasters.

Profit: The difference between the selling price of a good and the cost of that good.

Prospectus: See Offering Documents.

Public Applicant: In reference to TARP, a public applicant is a Qualifying Financial Institution whose securities are traded on a national securities exchange and that is required to file, under national securities laws, periodic reports with either the Securities and Exchange Commission or its primary Federal banking regulator.

Purchasing Authority: The authority to purchase goods and services.

Qualifying Financial Institution ("QFI"): As it relates to TARP, "Qualifying Financial Institution (QFI) means (i) any U.S. bank or U.S. savings association not controlled by a Bank Holding Company ('BHC') or Savings and Loan Company ('SLHC'); (ii) any top-tier U.S. BHC, (iii) any top-tier U.S. SLHC which engages solely or predominately in activities that are permitted for financial holding companies under relevant law; and (iv) any U.S. bank or U.S. savings association controlled by a U.S. SLHC that does not engage solely or predominately in activities that are permitted for financial holding companies under relevant law. QFI shall not mean any BHC, SLHC, bank or savings association controlled by a foreign bank or company."

Realized Profit or Loss: The profit or loss realized by an investor on a security after it has been finally sold and all costs and benefits of the holding have been accounted for.

Receivables: Accounts receivable represent claims to cash or other assets that arise from the sale of goods or services, duties, certain license fees, recoveries, or other provisions of the law.

Redeem: To buy back a prior obligation. In the case of CAP, the QFI can buy back (redeem) its CPP shares with the funds received from the CAP investment.

Regulatory Capital: The net capital position of a financial institution as determined by the rules of the applicable Federal or state banking regulator.

Reorganization: A plan overseen by a bankruptcy court under which a debtor firm resolves its obligations to its creditors and recapitalizes for the future.

Restructuring Period: Begins the date the announcement to restructure was made and ends the date that restructuring is complete.

Restructuring Plan: A plan to achieve and sustain the long-term viability, international competitiveness, and energy efficiency of the Company and its subsidiaries.

Revenue: Money obtained for sale of goods and services during a specific period.

Rights Offering: "Means offers and sales for cash of equity securities where: 1) The issuer grants the existing security holders of a particular class of equity securities (including holders of depositary receipts evidencing those securities) the right to purchase or subscribe for additional securities of that class; and 2) The number of additional shares an existing security holder may purchase initially is in proportion to the number of securities he or she holds of record on the record date for the rights offering. If an existing security holder holds depositary receipts, the proportion must be calculated as if the underlying securities were held directly."

Ring-Fencing: Segregating assets from the rest of a financial institution, often so that the assets' problems can be addressed in isolation.

Risk-Based Premium: A premium is the price of insurance protection for a specified risk for a specified period of time. A risk-based premium is where the price paid escalates in line with the probability of default and loss upon default.

Risk-Weighted Assets: "The amount of a bank's total assets after adjusting based on the risk factor assigned to each individual asset."

S Corporation: "Any U.S. bank, U.S. savings association, bank holding company ("BHC"), or savings and loan holding company ("SLHC") organized such that it is exempt from most Federal income taxes as they are passed through to the shareholders."

Savings and Loan Association: "A financial institution that accepts deposits primarily from individuals and channels its funds primarily into residential mortgage loans."

Savings and Loan Holding Company ("SLHC"): Any company that directly or indirectly controls a savings association or that controls any other company that is a savings and loan holding company, excluding bank holding companies that are registered under, and subject to, the Bank Holding Company Act of 1956, or to any company directly or indirectly controlled by such company (other than a savings association).

Savings Association: "Any Federal savings association or Federal savings bank; any building and loan association, savings and loan association, homestead association, or cooperative bank if such association or cooperative bank is a member of the Deposit Insurance Fund; and any savings bank or cooperative bank which is deemed by the Director of the Office of Thrift Supervision to be a savings association under section 10(1) of the Home Owners' Loan Act."

Say on Pay: In reference to TARP, "say on pay" is a provision where executive compensation must be approved by shareholders.

Schedule A: In reference to the Citigroup Master Agreement, Schedule A lists covered assets.

Second Lien Debt: Debt that is ranked lower than senior debt in the event of a liquidation or bankruptcy restructuring.

Secondary Market: Created when banks sell a portion of their loans to a dealer who then pools the loans together and sells portions of the loan pools as securities to investors. The secondary market serves as a source of cash for banks, providing them money to make new loans.

Secure: A process where the borrower offers an asset to which the lender has access in the event of the borrower failing to make repayment. A mortgage backed by property is an example.

Securities: A security is "any note, stock, treasury stock, security future, bond, debenture, evidence of indebtedness, certificate of interest or participation in any profit-sharing agreement, collateral-trust certificate, preorganization certificate or subscription, transferable share, investment contract, voting-trust certificate, certificate of deposit for a security, fractional undivided interest in oil, gas, or other mineral rights, any put, call, straddle, option, or privilege on any security (including a certificate of deposit) or on any group or index of securities (including any interest therein or based on the value thereof), or any put, call, straddle, option, or privilege entered into on a national securities exchange relating to foreign currency, or, in general, any interest or instrument commonly known as a 'security,' or any certificate of interest or participation in, temporary or interim certificate for, receipt for, guarantee of, or warrant or right to subscribe to or purchase, any of the foregoing."

Securities Issuer: A separate legal entity that buys cash-flow-producing assets such as loans, pools them together, and sells portions of the pools of loans as securities.

Securitization: "The process by which financial assets are transformed into securities."

Senior Debt: Debt that is ranked higher than subordinated debt in the event of a liquidation or bankruptcy restructuring.

Senior Executive Officer ("SEO" as defined in ARRA): An individual who is one of the top five most highly paid executives of a public company, whose compensation is required to be disclosed pursuant to the Securities Exchange Act of 1934, and any regulations issued thereunder, and non-public company counterparts.

Senior Executive Officer ("SEO" as defined in EESA): The top five highly paid executives.

Senior Oversight Committee ("SOC"): In reference to Citigroup Master Agreement, SOC consists of Citigroup's Chief Financial Officer, Chief Risk Officer, General Counsel, Controller, Chief Accounting Officer, and the Treasurer.

Senior Preferred Stock: Shares that give the stockholder priority dividend and liquidation claims over junior preferred and common stockholders.

Senior Secured Interest: A senior proprietary right in a debtor's property that secures payment for performance of an obligation.

Servicing Advance Receivables: Receivables accrued by a loan servicing company when it advances its own funds for customary expenses involved in servicing a portfolio of loans. Examples of such expenses include collection expenses, property maintenance, *etc*.

Settlement: The physical act of exchanging cash for securities on the settlement date.

Settlement Date: The closing date for the sale of an investment, similar to the closing date for a home purchase. On the settlement date (three days after trade in the case of U.S. equities), funds and securities trade hands and any necessary legal documents are signed.

Skin in the Game: Equity stake in an investment; down payment; amount an investor can lose.

Special Inspector General for the Troubled Asset Relief Program Act of 2009: Would expand the authority of the TARP Special Inspector General to conduct, supervise, and coordinate audits and investigations regarding any action taken pursuant to EESA.

Special Purpose Company: See Special Purpose Vehicle.

Special Purpose Vehicle ("SPV"): "Any vehicle that places the transferred assets presumptively beyond the reach of the transferor (*e.g.*, legally isolated)."

Spread: The difference between the interest rate paid and the interest rate received.

Strike Price: "The price, specified in the option contract, at which the underlying futures contract, security, or commodity will move from seller to buyer." Also called exercise price.

Subordinated: A claim that is lower in rank than senior in the event of a liquidation or reorganization.

Subordinated Debt: Funding that has a lesser priority than other debt issued.

Subprime: "Refers to borrowers who do not qualify for prime interest rates because they exhibit one or more of the following characteristics: weakened credit histories typically characterized by payment delinquencies, previous charge-offs, judgments, or bankruptcies; low credit scores; high debt-burden ratios; or high loan-to-value ratios."

Subscription Date: Loan request date. For TALF loan requests, includes: ABS collateral expected to pledge, loan amount, and interest rate format (fixed or fioating).

Synthetic ABS: A security that derives its value and cash fiow from derivative and physical sources other than from a physical set of reference assets.

Systemically Significant: A financial institution whose failure would impose significant losses on creditors and counterparties, call into question the financial strength of other similarly situated financial institutions, disrupt financial markets, raise borrowing costs for households and businesses, and reduce household wealth.

Systemically Significant Failing Institution ("SSFI"): "Established to provide stability and prevent disruptions to financial markets from the failure of institutions that are critical to the functioning of the nation's financial system."

TALF: Term Asset-Backed Securities Loan Facility is a Federal Reserve loan program intended to increase the availability of loans to consumers and small businesses. TARP funds will be indirectly invested in this program through a special purpose vehicle.

Tangible Common Equity ("TCE"): Common equity minus intangibles assets. TCE is a more conservative measure of capital. Only capital that is 'real' and possessing the last claim on the assets of a company can be counted as TCE. It can be thought of as the amount that would be left over if the bank were dissolved and all creditors and higher levels of stock, such as preferred stock, were paid off. TCE is the highest "quality" of capital in the sense of providing a buffer against loss by claimants on the bank.

Tangible Common Equity Ratio ("TCE Ratio"): Is Tangible Common Equity (TCE) divided by Risk-Adjusted Assets. TCE Ratio determines what percentage of a bank's total assets is categorized as TCE (the higher the percentage, the better it is for the bank).

Targeted Investment Program ("TIP"): TARP program that was created "to stabilize the financial system by making investments in institutions that are critical to the functioning of the financial system. This program focuses on the complex relationships and reliance of institutions within the financial system. Investments made through the TIP seek to avoid significant market disruptions resulting from the deterioration of one financial institution that can threaten other financial institutions and impair broader financial markets and pose a threat to the overall economy."

TARP Investment Committee: Includes the Troubled Asset Relief Program's ("TARP's") Chief Investment Officer and senior of cials on financial markets, economic policy, financial institutions, and financial stability.

Tier One Capital ("T1"): Common Equity + Preferred Equity + Retained Earnings – Goodwill. Often called "core capital," it is the measure of bank capital traditionally used by regulators in the United States. It can be described as a measure of the bank's ability to sustain future losses and still meet depositor's demands. T1 is a concept coordinated internationally through an agreement known as the "Basel II Accord."

Tier One Capital Ratio ("T1 Ratio"): Is Tier One Capital divided by Risk- Adjusted Assets.

Trading Counterparty Exposure: The maximum amount that may be lost by a securities trader if there is a failure to make good on a trade arranged with another financial institution (the "counterparty").

Troubled Assets: The term "troubled assets" means—

(A) residential or commercial mortgages and any securities, obligations, or other instruments that are based on or related to such mortgages, that in each case was originated or issued on or before March 14, 2008, the purchase of which the Secretary determines promotes financial market stability; and
(B) any other financial instrument that the Secretary, after consultation with the Chairman of the Board of Governors of the Federal Reserve System, determines the purchase of which is necessary to promote financial market stability, but only upon transmittal of such determination, writing, to the appropriate committees of Congress.

Trust Preferred Security: A security that has both equity and debt characteristics. Trust Preferred Security is created by creation of a trust and issuing debt to the trust. A company would create a trust preferred security to realize tax benefits, since the trust is tax deductible.

Variable Rate of Interest: "Interest rate that changes periodically in relation to an index."

Vest: To become exercisable. Typically used in the context of an employee stock ownership or option program.

Volatility: "A statistical measurement of the rate of price change of a futures contract, security, or other instrument underlying an option."

Warrant: "A certificate issued by a company giving the holder the right to purchase securities at a stipulated price within specific time limits or with no expiration date (perpetual warrant). A warrant is sometimes offered by a company as an inducement to buy other securities."

Warranty: Usually written, it is a guarantee of the integrity of a product, and the manufacturer's responsibility for the repair or replacement of defective parts.

Write Down: The act of recognizing the loss on an asset as permanent on a bank's balance sheet

SOURCES

American Recovery and Reinvestment Act of 2009, P.L. 111-5, 2/13/2009.
California State Senate, "Senate Bill 668"
Citigroup Inc., Master Agreement, 1/15/2009
Commodities and Futures Trading Commission, "CFTC Glossary," no date
Comptroller of the Currency, "Floor Plan Loans: Comptroller's Handbook," May 1998
Congressional Budget Of= ce, "The Budget and Economic Outlook"
Department of Justice, Executive Order 13271—Establishment of the Corporate Fraud Task Force,7/9/2002
Emergency Economic Stabilization Act of 2008, P.L. 110-343, 10/3/2008,
FDIC, "Accounting for Loss Contingencies," no date, FDIC, "Credit Card Securitization Manual," no date,
FDIC, "FAQS-Supervisory Capital Assessment Program," 2/25/2009, accessed3/25/2009.
FDIC, "6500 – Consumer Protection, FDIC Laws, Regulations, Related Acts,"
FDIC, "Right to Financial Privacy Act, 6500 – Consumer Protection, FDIC Laws, Regulations, Related Acts,"
FDIC, 2000 – FDIC Rules and Regulations, Appendix D to Part 325 — Capital Adequacy Guidelines for
Banks: Internal- Ratings-Based and Advanced Measurement Approaches, accessed 1/28/2009.
FDIC, Federal Deposit Insurance Act, 2/29/2008, p. 1065, accessed 1/28/2009.
FDIC, "List of Abbreviations and Terms," accessed 1/28/2009.
Federal Housing Finance Agency, "Mortgage Markets and the Enterprises 2007," accessed 4/9/2009.
Federal Register, 69 Fed. Reg. 44,923, 7/28/2004, accessed 1/28/2009.
Federal Reserve Board, "Subprime mortgages," Sandra F. Braunstein, Director, Division of Consumer and Community Affairs, 3/27/2007, accessed 4/9/2009.
Federal Reserve Board, "Basel II Capital Accord," Notice of Proposed Rulemaking, March 30, 2006, accessed 4/15/2009.
Federal Reserve Board, comments on SIGTARP draft report, 1/29/2009.
Federal Reserve Board, Federal Reserve Banks Operating Circular No. 8: Collateral, accessed 1/28/2009.
Financial Industry Regulatory Authority, "Glossary," accessed 1/28/2009.
FRBNY, "Term Asset-Backed Securities Loan Facility: Terms and Conditions," 3/19/2009, accessed 3/27/2009.
GAO, "Small Business Administration: Additional Guidance on Documenting Credit Elsewhere Decisions Could Improve 7(a) Program Oversight," 2/12/2009, accessed 3/17/2009.
GAO-05-734SP, "A Glossary of Terms Used in the Federal Budget Process, September 2005," accessed 1/28/2009.

GOP.gov, "Legislative Digest," no date, accessed 4/10/2009.

GPO, "H. R. 1424," 1/3/2008, accessed 4/13/2009.

House of Representatives, "Governor Kevin Warsh, Hedge funds, Before the Committee on Financial Services," July 11, 2007, accessed 1/28/2009.

House of Representatives, Investment Company Act of 1940, 15 U.S.C. § 80-1, accessed 1/28/2009.

Housing and Urban Development, "Hope for Homeowners," accessed 1/28/2009.

Internal Revenue Service, "Glossary of Offshore Terms," no date, accessed 4/8/2009.

Internal Revenue Service, "S Corporations," 1/6/2009, accessed 4/8/2009.

National Archives and Records Administration, "Code of Federal Regulations - Title 12: Banks and Banking," 12/2005, accessed1/28/2009.

National Information Center, "Institution Types Defined," accessed 1/28/2009.

Seattle Government, "Glossary for Professionals and Advocates," no date, accessed 4/8/2009.

Securities and Exchange Commission, "Final Rule: Amendment to De= nition of Equity Security," 6/7/2002, accessed 4/8/2009.

Securities and Exchange Commission, "Market Capitalization," accessed 03/31/2009.

Securities and Exchange Commission, "Final Rule: Cross-Border Tender and Exchange Offers, Business Combinations and Rights Offerings," accessed1/28/2009.

Securities and Exchange Commission, "Memorandum of Understanding between the U.S. and the Boardof Governors of the Federal System," 7/8/2008, accessed 1/28/2009.

Securities and Exchange Commission, Securities Exchange Act of 1934, 15 U.S.C. § 78a, accessed 1/28/2009.

Securities and Exchange Commission, "CUSIP," accessed4/6/2009.

Small Business Administration (SBA), Financial Statements, accessed 1/28/2009.

Small Business Administration, "Glossary," no date, accessed 4/9/2009.

The Library of Congress, "House Report 104-863 Making Omnibus Consolidated Appropriations for FiscalYear 1997," no date, accessed 4/6/2009.

Treasury, "A Citizen's Guide to the 2008 Financial Report of the United States Government," 2008, accessed 3/30/2009.

Treasury, "Decoder," no date, accessed4/9/2009.

Treasury, "Indicative Summary of Terms for Secured Term Loan Facility," 12/19/2008, accessed on 4/8/2009.

Treasury, "Term Sheet - Capital Assistance Program," no date, accessed 4/8/2009.

Treasury, "Capital Assistance Program FAQs," no date, accessed 3/25/2009.

Treasury, "Making Home Affordable: Updated Detailed Program Description," 3/4/2009, accessed 3/4/2009.

Treasury, "Secretary Geithner Introduces Financial Stability Plan," Remarks by Treasury Secretary Timothy Geithner, 2/10/2009, accessed 4/10/2009.

Treasury, "TARP Capital Purchase Program (Non-Public QFIs, excluding S Corps and Mutual Organizations)

Preferred Securities, Summary of Preferred Terms," 11/17/2008, accessed 3/16/2009.

Treasury, "TARP Capital Purchase Program, Senior Preferred Stock and Warrants, Summary of Preferred

Terms," 10/14/2008, accessed 1/25/2009.

Treasury, "Treasury Announces New Restrictions on Executive Compensation," 2/4/2009, accessed 3/20/2009.

Treasury, "Unlocking Credit for Small Businesses Fact Sheet," 3/16/2009, accessed 3/17/2009.

U.S. Dept. of Housing and Urban Development, "Glossary," no date, accessed 4/8/2009.

USDA, "Glossary," no date, 4/8/2009.

B. ACRONYMS

ABS	Asset-Backed Securities
AGP	Asset Guarantee Program
AIFP	Automotive Industry Financing Program
AIG	American International Group, Inc.
AIGI	Assistant Inspector General for Investigations
ARRA	American Recovery and Reinvestment Act of 2009
ASSP	Auto Supplier Support Program
BHC	Bank Holding Company
BNYM	Bank of New York Mellon
bps	Basis Points
CAP	Capital Assistance Program
CBO	Congressional Budget Ofce
CDFI	Community Development Financial Institution
CDO	Collateralized Debt Obligation
CEO	Chief Executive Ofcer
CIO	Chief Information Ofcer
CMBS	Commercial Mortgage-Backed Securities
COI	Conicts of Interest
COP	Congressional Oversight Panel
CPP	Capital Purchase Program
DOJ	Department of Justice
DTI	Debt to Income
EESA	Emergency Economic Stabilization Act of 2008
FBA	Federal Banking Agency
FBI	Federal Bureau of Investigation
FDIC	Federal Deposit Insurance Corporation
FHA	Federal Housing Administration
FHFA	Federal Housing Finance Agency
FinCEN	Financial Crimes Enforcement Network
FRBNY	Federal Reserve Bank of New York
FSOB	Financial Stability Oversight Board
FSP	Financial Stability Plan
GAO	Government Accountability Ofce
GM	General Motors Corporation
GMAC	GMAC LLC
HAMP	Home Affordable Modication Program
HARP	Home Affordable Renancing Program

HERA	Housing and Economic Recovery Act
HUD	Department of Housing and Urban Development
ICE	U.S. Immigration and Customs Enforcement
IG	Inspector General
IRS-CI	Internal Revenue Service Criminal Investigation
LSA	Loan and Security Agreement
LIBOR	London Interbank Offered Rate
LLC	Limited Liability Company
MBS	Mortgage-Backed Securities
MHA	Making Home Affordable
NRSRO	Nationally Recognized Statistical Rating Organization
NPV	Net Present Value
NY HIFCA	New York High Intensity Financial Crime Area
OCC	Office of the Comptroller of the Currency
OFS	Office of Financial Stability
OGC	Office of General Counsel
P.L.	Public Law
PEO	Principal Executive Officer
PFO	Principal Finance Officer
PITIA	Principal, Interest, Taxes, Insurance, and Association Fees
PPIF	Public-Private Investment Fund
PPIP	Public-Private Investment Program
QFI	Qualifying Financial Institution
RMBS	Residential Mortgage-Backed Securities
SBA	Small Business Administration
SEC	Securities and Exchange Commission
SEO	Senior Executive Officer
SIGTARP	Special Inspector General for the Troubled Asset Relief Program
SIGTARP Act	Special Inspector General for the Troubled Asset Relief Program Act of 2009
SLHC	Savings and Loan Holding Company
SOC	Senior Oversight Committee
SPV	Special Purpose Vehicle
SSFI	Systemically Signicant Failing Institution
T1	Tier One Capital
TALF	Term Asset-Backed Securities Loan Facility
TARP	Troubled Asset Rclief Program
TARP-IGC	TARP Inspector General Council
TCE	Tangible Common Equity
TIP	Targeted Investment Program
UAW	United Auto Workers
UCSB	Unlocking Credit for Small Businesses
USDOT	U.S. Department of Transportation
USPIS	U.S. Postal Inspection Service
VEBA	Voluntary Employees Beneciary Association

C. Reporting Requirements

This appendix provides a compilation of the data necessary to meet the reporting requirements of the Special Inspector General for the Troubled Asset Relief Program outlined in EESA Section 121. Italics style indicates narrative taken as verbatim from source documents.

A. *a description of the categories of troubled assets purchased or otherwise procured by the Secretary.*
B. *a listing of the troubled assets purchased in each such category described under* [the first bullet].
C. *an explanation of the reasons the Secretary deemed it necessary to purchase each such troubled asset.*
D. *a listing of each financial institution that such troubled assets were purchased from.*
E. *a listing of and detailed biographical information on each person or entity hired to manage such troubled assets.*
F. *a current estimate of the total amount of troubled assets purchased pursuant to any program established under section 101, the amount of troubled assets on the books of the Treasury, the amount of troubled assets sold, and the profit and loss incurred on each sale or disposition of each such troubled asset.*
G. *a listing of the insurance contracts issued under section 102.*
H. *a detailed statement of all purchases, obligations, expenditures, and revenues associated with any program established by the Secretary of the Treasury under sections 101 and 102.*

A—Description of Categories[1]

In response to SIGTARP's data call, Treasury stated:

Treasury posts several documents on its public website that are responsive to this question. The tranche reports and reports under section 105(a) describe, at a high level, Treasury's programs and troubled asset purchases. The transaction reports describe these purchases in detail, including the type of asset purchased, the identity of the institution selling the asset, and the price Treasury paid for the asset.[2]

Set forth below are descriptions of the TARP programs provided by Treasury on its website. Sections 2 and 3 of this Report provide more detailed descriptions of each type of asset and each TARP program as of March 31, 2009.

A.1. Capital Purchase Program[3]

Treasury created the Capital Purchase Program (CPP) in October 2008 to stabilize the financial system by providing capital to viable financial institutions of all sizes throughout the nation. With a strengthened capital base, financial institutions have an increased capacity to lend to U.S. businesses and consumers and to support the U.S. economy.

Through the CPP, Treasury will invest up to $250 billion in U.S. banks that are healthy, but desire an extra layer of capital for stability or lending. Since its inception in October

2008, the CPP has strengthened regional, small and large financial institutions as well as Community Development Financial Institutions in over 48 states and Puerto Rico and the District of Columbia. Treasury and the nation's Federal banking agencies (FBA), which include the FDIC, the Federal Reserve, The Office of the Comptroller of the Currency (OCC), and the Office of Thrift Supervision (OTS), are currently in the process of analyzing and evaluating the applications that have been received for CPP.

A.2. Capital Assistance Program[4]

On February 25, 2009 the U.S. Department of the Treasury announced the terms and conditions for the Capital Assistance Program (CAP). The CAP is a core element of the Administration's Financial Stability Plan.

The purpose of the CAP is to restore con dence throughout the financial system that the nation's largest banking institutions have a sufficient capital cushion against larger than expected future losses, should they occur due to a more severe economic environment, and to support lending to creditworthy borrowers.

Under CAP, Federal banking supervisors will conduct forward- looking assessments to evaluate the capital needs of the major U.S. banking institutions under a more challenging economic environment. Should that assessment indicate that an additional capital buffer is warranted, banks will have an opportunity to turn first to private sources of capital. In light of the current challenging market environment, the Treasury is making Government capital available immediately through the CAP to eligible banking institutions to provide this buffer.

Eligible U.S. banking institutions with assets in excess of $ 100 billion on a consolidated basis are required to participate in the coordinated supervisory assessments, and may access the CAP immediately as a means to establish any necessary additional buffer. Eligible U.S. banking institutions with consolidated assets below $100 billion may also obtain capital from the CAP.

A.3. Systemically Significant Failing Institution Program[5]

This program was established to provide stability and prevent disruptions to financial markets from the failure of institutions that are critical to the functioning of the nation's financial system.

A.4. Targeted Investment Program[6]

Treasury created the Targeted Investment Program (TIP) to stabilize the financial system by making investments in institutions that are critical to the functioning of the financial system. This program focuses on the complex relationships and reliance of institutions within the financial system. Investments made through the TIP seek to avoid significant market disruptions resulting from the deterioration of one financial institution that can threaten other financial institutions and impair broader financial markets and pose a threat to the overall economy. Through the TIP, Treasury is working to stabilize the financial system by reducing the chance that one firm's distress will threaten otherwise financially-sound businesses, institutions, and municipalities, which could cause an adverse spillover effect on employment, output, and incomes.

Treasury will determine the form, terms, and conditions of any investment made pursuant to this program on a case-by-case basis in accordance with the considerations mandated in

The Emergency Economic Stabilization Act of 2008 (EESA). Treasury may invest in any financial instrument, including debt, equity, or warrants, that the Secretary of the Treasury determines to be a troubled asset, after consultation with the Chairman of the Board of Governors of the Federal Reserve System and notice to Congress. Treasury will require any institution participating in this program to provide Treasury with warrants or alternative consideration, as necessary, to minimize the long-term costs and maximize the benefits to the taxpayers in accordance with EESA.

A.5. Asset Guarantee Program[7]

Under the Asset Guarantee Program (AGP), Treasury will guarantee certain assets held by the qualifying financial institution. The set of insured assets is selected by the Treasury and its agents in consultation with the financial institution receiving the guarantee. In accordance with section 102(a), assets to be guaranteed must have been originated before March 14, 2008. Treasury determines the eligibility of participants and the allocation of resources on a case-by-case basis. The program is meant for systemically significant institutions, and could be used in coordination with other programs. Treasury may, on a case-by-case basis, use this program in coordination with a broader guarantee involving other agencies of the United States Government.

In implementing the AGP, Treasury collects a premium, deliverable in a form deemed appropriate by the Treasury Secretary. As required by the statute, an actuarial analysis would be used to ensure that the expected value of the premium is no less than the expected value of the losses to TARP from the guarantee. The United States Government would also provide a set of portfolio management guidelines to which the institution must adhere for the guaranteed portfolio.

A.6. Automotive Industry Financing Program[8]

The objective of the Automotive Industry Financing Program (AIFP) is to prevent a significant disruption of the American automotive industry, which would pose a systemic risk to financial market stability and have a negative effect on the economy of the United States. The program requires participating institutions to implement plans that will achieve long-term viability.

Participating institutions must also adhere to rigorous executive compensation standards and other measures to protect the taxpayer's interests, including limits on the institution's expenditures and other corporate governance requirements.

A.7. Automotive Supplier Support Program

On March 19, 2009, Treasury announced a new program aimed at supporting the suppliers to the U.S. auto manufacturing industry. The Auto Supplier Support Program ("ASSP") is a renewable one-year program that will provide up to $5 billion in financing that is intended to benefit both the suppliers and the auto manufacturers. The program provides Government-backed protection to the suppliers against any failure by the manufacturers to make payments on goods that they receive from their suppliers, even if the manufacturers file for bankruptcy.[9]

A.8. Auto Warranty Commitment Program

As another complementary program to AIFP, the Auto Warranty Commitment Program was devised by the Administration to bolster consumer con dence in automobile warranties on domestically produced vehicles. Currently, only GM and Chrysler have agreed to participate in this program. In order to reassure consumers that their auto warranties will be honored during this period of restructuring, the Administration will provide Government-back financing.[10]

A.9. Term Asset-Backed Securities Loan Facility

Under the initial terms and conditions announced for the TALF, the Federal Reserve will lend on a non-recourse basis to holders Officertain AAA-rated ABS fully secured by newly and recently originated consumer and small business loans. TALF loans will have a one-year term and will be secured by eligible collateral. Haircuts (a percentage reduction used for collateral valuation) will be determined based on the price volatility of the class of eligible collateral and will provide additional protection to the taxpayers by protecting the Government from loss. Treasury will purchase up to $20 billion of subordinated debt backed by the collateral received, which will be priced at the loan value plus accrued interest. The TARP CPP guidelines on executive compensation will be applied to the originators of the credit exposures underlying the ABS.[11]

On February 10, 2009, the Administration announced the expansion of TALF to up to $1 trillion as part of the Consumer and Business Lending Initiatives under the Financial Stability Plan.[12] According to Treasury, the expected expansion of TALF will increase TARP credit protection from $20 billion to up to $80 billion.[13]

A.10. Public-Private Investment Program[14]

To address the challenge of legacy assets, Treasury – in conjunction with the Federal Deposit Insurance Corporation and the Federal Reserve – has announced the Public-Private Investment Program as part of its efforts to repair balance sheets throughout our financial system and ensure that credit is available to the households and businesses, large and small, that will help drive us toward recovery.

Using $75 to $100 billion in TARP capital and capital from private investors, the Public-Private Investment Program will generate $500 billion in purchasing power to buy legacy assets – with the potential to expand to $1 trillion over time. The Public- Private Investment Program will be designed around three basic principles: maximizing the impact of each taxpayer dollar, shared risk and profits with private sector participants, and private sector price discovery.

A.11. Unlocking Credit for Small Businesses[15]

As another part of the Consumer and Business Lending Initiative, the Treasury Department will begin making direct purchases of securities backed by SBA loans to get the credit market moving again, and it will stand ready to purchase new securities to ensure that community banks and credit unions feel con dent in extending new loans to local businesses. These purchases, combined with higher loan guarantees and reduced fees, will help provide lenders with the con dence that they need to extend credit, knowing they both have a backstop against their risk and a source of liquidity. These measures will complement other steps the

Administration is taking to help small businesses recover and grow, including several tax cuts under the Recovery Act.

A.12. Making Home Affordable Program[16]

The Administration's Making Home Affordable program will offer assistance to as many as 7 to 9 million homeowners making a good- faith effort to make their mortgage payments, while attempting to prevent the destructive impact of the housing crisis on families and communities. It will not provide money to speculators, and it will target support to the working homeowners who have made every possible effort to stay current on their mortgage payments. Just as the American Recovery and Reinvestment Act works to save or create several million new jobs and the Financial Stability Plan works to get credit flowing, the Making Home Affordable program will support a recovery in the housing market and ensure that these workers can continue paying off their mortgages.

By supporting low mortgage rates by strengthening con dence in Fannie Mae and Freddie Mac, providing up to 4 to 5 million homeowners with new access to re nancing and creating a comprehensive stability initiative to offer reduced monthly payments for up to 3 to 4 million at-risk homeowners, this plan brings together the Government, lenders, loan servicers, investors and borrowers to share responsibility towards ensuring working Americans can afford to stay in their homes.

B. Listing of Troubled Assets Purchased, by Category and Financial Institution

In response to SIGTARP's data call question regarding this reporting requirement, Treasury stated:

> *Treasury posts transaction reports for all the troubled asset purchases on its public website within two business days after each transaction. Since the publication of the SIGTARP Report in February, Treasury continues to invest funds in financial institutions across the United States through the Capital Purchase Program (CPP), and has committed to lend $20 billion to support the Term Asset-Backed Securities Loan Facility. Additional responsive information about these programs and the purchases made under them is in [TARP] tranche reports and the section 105(a) reports, which are also posted on Treasury's website.*

Table C. 1 provides details on TARP transactions, as of March 31, 2009.

Table C.1. TARP Transaction Detail, Through March 31, 2009

			Seller			Purchase Details				Capital Re-payment Details	
Program	Note	Purchase Date	Name of Institution	City	State	Investment Description	Investment Price	Pricing Mechanism	Market Capitalization as of 3/31/2009	Capital Repayment Date	Capital Repayment Amount (f)
CPP		10/28/2008	Bank of America Corporation	Charlotte	NC	Preferred Stock w/Warrants	$15,000,000,000	Par	$43,657,466,160		
CPP		10/28/2008	Bank of New York Mellon Corporation	New York	NY	Preferred Stock w/Warrants	$3,000,000,000	Par	$32,470,578,250		
CPP		10/28/2008	Citigroup Inc.	New York	NY	Preferred Stock w/Warrants	$25,000,000,000	Par	$13,947,814,100		
CPP		10/28/2008	The Goldman Sachs Group, Inc.	New York	NY	Preferred Stock w/Warrants	$10,000,000,000	Par	$48,996,918,130		
CPP		10/28/2008	JPMorgan Chase & Co.	New York	NY	Preferred Stock w/Warrants	$25,000,000,000	Par	$99,885,593,340		
CPP		10/28/2008	Morgan Stanley	New York	NY	Preferred Stock w/Warrants	$10,000,000,000	Par	$24,641,694,000		
CPP		10/28/2008	State Street Corporation	Boston	MA	Preferred Stock w/Warrants	$2,000,000,000	Par	$13,347,223,740		
CPP		10/28/2008	Wells Fargo & Company	San Francisco	CA	Preferred Stock w/Warrants	$25,000,000,000	Par	$60,432,395,520		
CPP		11/14/2008	Bank of Commerce Holdings	Redding	CA	Preferred Stock w/Warrants	$17,000,000	Par	$43,903,440		
CPP		11/14/2008	1st FS Corporation	Hendersonville	NC	Preferred Stock w/Warrants	$16,369,000	Par	$23,735,750		

Table C.1. (Continued)

			Seller			Purchase Details				Capital Re-payment Details	
Program	Note	Purchase Date	Name of Institution	City	State	Investment Description	Investment Price	Pricing Mechanism	Market Capitalization as of 3/31/2009	Capital Repayment Date	Capital Repayment Amount (f)
CPP		11/14/2008	UCBH Holdings, Inc.	San Francisco	CA	Preferred Stock w/Warrants	$298,737,000	Par	$181,858,360		
CPP		11/14/2008	Northern Trust Corporation	Chicago	IL	Preferred Stock w/Warrants	$1,576,000,000	Par	$13,367,556,660		
CPP		11/14/2008	SunTrust Banks, Inc.	Atlanta	GA	Preferred Stock w/Warrants	$3,500,000,000	Par	$4,202,497,360		
CPP		11/14/2008	Broadway Financial Corporation	Los Angeles	CA	Preferred Stock w/Warrants	$9,000,000	Par	$9,133,320		
CPP		11/14/2008	Washington Federal Inc.	Seattle	WA	Preferred Stock w/Warrants	$200,000,000	Par	$1,170,144,630		
CPP		11/14/2008	BB&T Corp.	Winston-Salem	NC	Preferred Stock w/Warrants	$3,133,640,000	Par	$9,482,120,280		
CPP		11/14/2008	Provident Bancshares Corp.	Baltimore	MD	Preferred Stock w/Warrants	$151,500,000	Par	$236,259,600		
CPP		11/14/2008	Umpqua Holdings Corp.	Portland	OR	Preferred Stock w/Warrants	$214,181,000	Par	$545,230,800		
CPP		11/14/2008	Comerica Inc.	Dallas	TX	Preferred Stock w/Warrants	$2,250,000,000	Par	$2,767,794,530		
CPP		11/14/2008	Regions Financial Corp.	Birmingham	AL	Preferred Stock w/Warrants	$3,500,000,000	Par	$2,959,132,320		
CPP		11/14/2008	Capital One Financial Corporation	McLean	VA	Preferred Stock w/Warrants	$3,555,199,000	Par	$4,798,190,160		

Table C.1. (Continued)

			Seller			Purchase Details				Capital Repayment Details	
Program	Note	Purchase Date	Name of Institution	City	State	Investment Description	Investment Price	Pricing Mechanism	Market Capitalization as of 3/31/2009	Capital Repayment Date	Capital Repayment Amount (f)
CPP		11/14/2008	First Horizon National Corporation	Memphis	TN	Preferred Stock w/Warrants	$866,540,000	Par	$2,207,553,300		
CPP		11/14/2008	Huntington Bancshares	Columbus	OH	Preferred Stock w/Warrants	$1,398,071,000	Par	$607,815,640		
CPP		11/14/2008	KeyCorp	Cleveland	OH	Preferred Stock w/Warrants	$2,500,000,000	Par	$3,893,328,350		
CPP		11/14/2008	Valley National Bancorp	Wayne	NJ	Preferred Stock w/Warrants	$300,000,000	Par	$1,670,246,880		
CPP		11/14/2008	Zions Bancorporation	Salt Lake City	UT	Preferred Stock w/Warrants	$1,400,000,000	Par	$1,133,752,880		
CPP		11/14/2008	Marshall & Ilsley Corporation	Milwaukee	WI	Preferred Stock w/Warrants	$1,715,000,000	Par	$1,493,779,750		
CPP		11/14/2008	U.S. Bancorp	Minneapolis	MN	Preferred Stock w/Warrants	$6,599,000,000	Par	$25,690,779,180		
CPP		11/14/2008	TCF Financial Corporation	Wayzata	MN	Preferred Stock w/Warrants	$361,172,000	Par	$1,502,245,920		
CPP		11/21/2008	First Niagara Financial Group	Lockport	NY	Preferred Stock w/Warrants	$184,011,000	Par	$1,291,630,230		
CPP		11/21/2008	HF Financial Corp.	Sioux Falls	SD	Preferred Stock w/Warrants	$25,000,000	Par	$51,267,750		
CPP		11/21/2008	Centerstate Banks of Florida Inc.	Davenport	FL	Preferred Stock w/Warrants	$27,875,000	Par	$137,338,740		

Table C.1. (Continued)

			Seller			Purchase Details				Capital Re-payment Details	
Program	Note	Purchase Date	Name of Institution	City	State	Investment Description	Investment Price	Pricing Mechanism	Market Capitalization as of 3/31/2009	Capital Repayment Date	Capital Repayment Amount (f)
CPP		11/21/2008	City National Corporation	Beverly Hills	CA	Preferred Stock w/Warrants	$400,000,000	Par	$1,638,858,100		
CPP		11/21/2008	First Community Bankshares Inc.	Bluefield	VA	Preferred Stock w/Warrants	$41,500,000	Par	$134,986,890		
CPP		11/21/2008	Western Alliance Bancorpo-ration	Las Vegas	NV	Preferred Stock w/Warrants	$140,000,000	Par	$177,429,600		
CPP		11/21/2008	Webster Financial Corporation	Waterbury	CT	Preferred Stock w/Warrants	$400,000,000	Par	$224,595,500		
CPP		11/21/2008	Pacific Capital Bancorp	Santa Barbara	CA	Preferred Stock w/Warrants	$180,634,000	Par	$319,388,290		
CPP		11/21/2008	Heritage Commerce Corp.	San Jose	CA	Preferred Stock w/Warrants	$40,000,000	Par	$62,060,250		
CPP		11/21/2008	Ameris Bancorp	Moultrie	GA	Preferred Stock w/Warrants	$52,000,000	Par	$63,928,830		
CPP		11/21/2008	Porter Bancorp Inc.	Louisville	KY	Preferred Stock w/Warrants	$35,000,000	Par	$93,902,280		
CPP		11/21/2008	Banner Corporation	Walla Walla	WA	Preferred Stock w/Warrants	$124,000,000	Par	$50,846,430		
CPP		11/21/2008	Cascade Financial Corporation	Everett	WA	Preferred Stock w/Warrants	$38,970,000	Par	$30,275,000		

Table C.1. (Continued)

			Seller			Purchase Details				Capital Re-payment Details	
Program	Note	Purchase Date	Name of Institution	City	State	Investment Description	Investment Price	Pricing Mechanism	Market Capitalization as of 3/31/2009	Capital Repayment Date	Capital Repayment Amount (f)
CPP		11/21/2008	Cascade Financial Corporation	Everett	WA	Preferred Stock w/Warrants	$38,970,000	Par	$30,275,000		
CPP		11/21/2008	Columbia Banking System, Inc.	Tacoma	WA	Preferred Stock w/Warrants	$76,898,000	Par	$116,825,600		
CPP		11/21/2008	Heritage Financial Corporation	Olympia	WA	Preferred Stock w/Warrants	$24,000,000	Par	$70,422,550		
CPP		11/21/2008	First PacTrust Bancorp, Inc.	Chula Vista	CA	Preferred Stock w/Warrants	$19,300,000	Par	$28,701,000		
CPP		11/21/2008	Severn Bancorp, Inc.	Annapolis	MD	Preferred Stock w/Warrants	$23,393,000	Par	$31,711,050		
CPP		11/21/2008	Boston Private Financial Holdings, Inc.	Boston	MA	Preferred Stock w/Warrants	$154,000,000	Par	$224,945,370		
CPP		11/21/2008	Associated Banc-Corp	Green Bay	WI	Preferred Stock w/Warrants	$525,000,000	Par	$1,975,437,000		
CPP		11/21/2008	Trustmark Corporation	Jackson	MS	Preferred Stock w/Warrants	$215,000,000	Par	$1,053,633,500		
CPP		11/21/2008	First Community Corporation	Lexington	SC	Preferred Stock w/Warrants	$11,350,000	Par	$21,357,600		
CPP		11/21/2008	Taylor Capital Group	Rosemont	IL	Preferred Stock w/Warrants	$104,823,000	Par	$49,417,250		
CPP		11/21/2008	Nara Bancorp, Inc.	Los Angeles	CA	Preferred Stock w/Warrants	$67,000,000	Par	$77,166,180		

Table C.1. (Continued)

			Seller			Purchase Details				Capital Re-payment Details	
Program	Note	Purchase Date	Name of Institution	City	State	Investment Description	Investment Price	Pricing Mechanism	Market Capitalization as of 3/31/2009	Capital Repayment Date	Capital Repayment Amount (f)
CPP		12/5/2008	Midwest Banc Holdings, Inc.	Melrose Park	IL	Preferred Stock w/Warrants	$84,784,000	Par	$28,937,510		
CPP		12/5/2008	MB Financial Inc.	Chicago	IL	Preferred Stock w/Warrants	$196,000,000	Par	$475,102,400		
CPP		12/5/2008	First Midwest Bancorp, Inc.	Itasca	IL	Preferred Stock w/Warrants	$193,000,000	Par	$417,740,290		
CPP		12/5/2008	United Community Banks, Inc.	Blairsville	GA	Preferred Stock w/Warrants	$180,000,000	Par	$200,066,880		
CPP		12/5/2008	Wesbanco Bank Inc.	Wheeling	WV	Preferred Stock w/Warrants	$75,000,000	Par	$606,387,630		
CPP		12/5/2008	Encore Bancshares Inc.	Houston	TX	Preferred Stockw/ Warrants	$34,000,000	Par	$90,474,000		
CPP		12/5/2008	Manhattan Bancorp	El Segundo	CA	Preferred Stockw/ Warrants	$1,700,000	Par	$18,943,000		
CPP		12/5/2008	Iberiabank Corporation	Lafayette	LA	Preferred Stockw/ Warrants	$90,000,000	Par	$735,085,940	3/31/2009 (e)	$90,000,000
CPP		12/5/2008	Eagle Bancorp, Inc.	Bethesda	MD	Preferred Stock w/Warrants	$38,235,000	Par	$79,656,250		
CPP		12/5/2008	Sandy Spring Bancorp, Inc.	Olney	MD	Preferred Stock w/Warrants	$83,094,000	Par	$183,068,640		
CPP		12/5/2008	Coastal Banking Company, Inc.	Fernandina Beach	FL	Preferred Stock w/Warrants	$9,950,000	Par	$15,414,000		
CPP		12/5/2008	East West Bancorp	Pasadena	CA	Preferred Stock w/Warrants	$306,546,000	Par	$291,314,650		

Table C.1. (Continued)

			Seller			Purchase Details				Capital Re-payment Details	
Program	Note	Purchase Date	Name of Institution	City	State	Investment Description	Investment Price	Pricing Mechanism	Market Capitalization as of 3/31/2009	Capital Repayment Date	Capital Repayment Amount (f)
CPP		12/5/2008	South Financial Group, Inc.	Greenville	SC	Preferred Stock w/Warrants	$347,000,000	Par	$93,256,900		
CPP		12/5/2008	Great Southern Bancorp	Springfield	MO	Preferred Stock w/Warrants	$58,000,000	Par	$187,467,810		
CPP		12/5/2008	Cathay General Bancorp	Los Angeles	CA	Preferred Stock w/Warrants	$258,000,000	Par	$516,650,050		
CPP		12/5/2008	Southern Community Financial Corp.	Winston-Salem	NC	Preferred Stock w/Warrants	$42,750,000	Par	$59,701,200		
CPP		12/5/2008	CVB Financial Corp	Ontario	CA	Preferred Stock w/Warrants	$130,000,000	Par	$552,192,810		
CPP		12/5/2008	First Defiance Financial Corp.	Defiance	OH	Preferred Stock w/Warrants	$37,000,000	Par	$49,351,360		
CPP		12/5/2008	First Financial Holdings Inc.	Charleston	SC	Preferred Stock w/Warrants	$65,000,000	Par	$89,482,050		
CPP		12/5/2008	Superior Bancorp Inc.	Birmingham	AL	Preferred Stock w/Warrants	$69,000,000	Par	$40,198,000		
CPP		12/5/2008	Southwest Bancorp, Inc.	Stillwater	OK	Preferred Stock w/Warrants	$70,000,000	Par	$137,023,040		
CPP		12/5/2008	Popular, Inc.	San Juan	PR	Preferred Stock w/Warrants	$935,000,000	Par	$609,195,600		
CPP		12/5/2008	Blue Valley Ban Corp	Overland Park	KS	Preferred Stock w/Warrants	$21,750,000	Par	$33,120,000		

Table C.1. (Continued)

			Seller			Purchase Details				Capital Re-payment Details	
Program	Note	Purchase Date	Name of Institution	City	State	Investment Description	Investment Price	Pricing Mechanism	Market Capitalization as of 3/31/2009	Capital Repayment Date	Capital Repayment Amount (f)
CPP		12/5/2008	Central Federal Corporation	Fairlawn	OH	Preferred Stock w/Warrants	$7,225,000	Par	$11,895,800		
CPP		12/5/2008	Bank of Marin Bancorp	Novato	CA	Preferred Stock w/Warrants	$28,000,000	Par	$110,862,540	3/31/2009 (d)	$28,000,000
CPP		12/5/2008	Bank of North Carolina	Thomasville	NC	Preferred Stock w/Warrants	$31,260,000	Par	$44,497,750		
CPP		12/5/2008	Central Bancorp, Inc.	Somerville	MA	Preferred Stock w/Warrants	$10,000,000	Par	$7,773,440		
CPP		12/5/2008	Southern Missouri Bancorp, Inc.	Poplar Bluff	MO	Preferred Stock w/Warrants	$9,550,000	Par	$22,550,400		
CPP		12/5/2008	State Bancorp, Inc.	Jericho	NY	Preferred Stock w/Warrants	$36,842,000	Par	$111,873,300		
CPP		12/5/2008	TIB Financial Corp	Naples	FL	Preferred Stock w/Warrants	$37,000,000	Par	$42,055,890		
CPP		12/5/2008	Unity Bancorp, Inc.	Clinton	NJ	Preferred Stock w/Warrants	$20,649,000	Par	$22,695,370		
CPP		12/5/2008	Old Line Bancshares, Inc.	Bowie	MD	Preferred Stock w/Warrants	$7,000,000	Par	$22,785,800		
CPP		12/5/2008	FPB Bancorp, Inc.	Port St. Lucie	FL	Preferred Stock w/Warrants	$5,800,000	Par	$5,145,000		
CPP		12/5/2008	Sterling Financial Corporation	Spokane	WA	Preferred Stock w/Warrants	$303,000,000	Par	$108,457,650		

Table C.1. (Continued)

			Seller			Purchase Details				Capital Re-payment Details	
Program	Note	Purchase Date	Name of Institution	City	State	Investment Description	Investment Price	Pricing Mechanism	Market Capitalization as of 3/31/2009	Capital Repayment Date	Capital Repayment Amount (f)
CPP		12/5/2008	Oak Valley Bancorp	Oakdale	CA	Preferred Stock w/Warrants	$13,500,000	Par	$28,732,500		
CPP		12/12/2008	Old National Bancorp	Evansville	IN	Preferred Stock w/Warrants	$100,000,000	Par	$740,113,030	3/31/2009 (d)	$100,000,000
CPP		12/12/2008	Capital Bank Corporation	Raliegh	NC	Preferred Stock w/Warrants	$41,279,000	Par	$51,528,000		
CPP		12/12/2008	Pacific International Bancorp	Seattle	WA	Preferred Stock w/Warrants	$6,500,000	Par	N/A		
CPP		12/12/2008	SVB Financial Group	Santa Clara	CA	Preferred Stock w/Warrants	$235,000,000	Par	$658,989,330		
CPP		12/12/2008	LNB Bancorp Inc.	Lorain	OH	Preferred Stock w/Warrants	$25,223,000	Par	$36,480,000		
CPP		12/12/2008	Wilmington Trust Corporation	Wilmington	DE	Preferred Stock w/Warrants	$330,000,000	Par	$669,704,970		
CPP		12/12/2008	Susquehanna Bancshares, Inc	Lititz	PA	Preferred Stock w/Warrants	$300,000,000	Par	$804,115,380		
CPP		12/12/2008	Signature Bank	New York	NY	Preferred Stock w/Warrants	$120,000,000	Par	$993,131,400	3/31/2009 (d)	$120,000,000
CPP		12/12/2008	HopFed Bancorp	Hopkinsville	KY	Preferred Stock w/Warrants	$18,400,000	Par	$34,963,500		
CPP		12/12/2008	Citizens Republic Bancorp, Inc.	Flint	MI	Preferred Stock w/Warrants	$300,000,000	Par	$195,777,400		

Table C.1. (Continued)

			Seller			Purchase Details				Capital Re-payment Details	
Program	Note	Purchase Date	Name of Institution	City	State	Investment Description	Investment Price	Pricing Mechanism	Market Capitalization as of 3/31/2009	Capital Repayment Date	Capital Repayment Amount (f)
CPP		12/12/2008	Indiana Community Bancorp	Columbus	IN	Preferred Stock w/Warrants	$21,500,000	Par	$43,654,000		
CPP		12/12/2008	Bank of the Ozarks, Inc.	Little Rock	AR	Preferred Stock w/Warrants	$75,000,000	Par	$389,244,200		
CPP		12/12/2008	Center Financial Corporation	Los Angeles	CA	Preferred Stock w/Warrants	$55,000,000	Par	$47,342,160		
CPP		12/12/2008	NewBridge Bancorp	Greensboro	NC	Preferred Stock w/Warrants	$52,372,000	Par	$33,034,160		
CPP		12/12/2008	Sterling Bancshares, Inc.	Houston	TX	Preferred Stock w/Warrants	$125,198,000	Par	$479,709,000		
CPP		12/12/2008	The Bancorp, Inc.	Wilmington	DE	Preferred Stock w/Warrants	$45,220,000	Par	$61,751,360		
CPP		12/12/2008	TowneBank	Portsmouth	VA	Preferred Stock w/Warrants	$76,458,000	Par	$383,395,740		
CPP		12/12/2008	Wilshire Bancorp, Inc.	Los Angeles	CA	Preferred Stock w/Warrants	$62,158,000	Par	$151,776,240		
CPP		12/12/2008	Valley Financial Corporation	Roanoke	VA	Preferred Stock w/Warrants	$16,019,000	Par	$22,276,800		
CPP		12/12/2008	Independent Bank Corporation	Ionia	MI	Preferred Stock w/Warrants	$72,000,000	Par	$56,230,200		
CPP		12/12/2008	Pinnacle Financial Partners, Inc.	Nashville	TN	Preferred Stock w/Warrants	$95,000,000	Par	$569,040,000		

Table C.1. (Continued)

			Seller			Purchase Details				Capital Re-payment Details	
Program	Note	Purchase Date	Name of Institution	City	State	Investment Description	Investment Price	Pricing Mechanism	Market Capitalization as of 3/31/2009	Capital Repayment Date	Capital Repayment Amount (f)
CPP		12/12/2008	First Litchfield Financial Corporation	Litchfield	CT	Preferred Stock w/Warrants	$10,000,000	Par	$16,499,000		
CPP		12/12/2008	National Penn Bancshares, Inc.	Boyertown	PA	Preferred Stock w/Warrants	$150,000,000	Par	$681,513,000		
CPP		12/12/2008	Northeast Bancorp	Lewiston	ME	Preferred Stock w/Warrants	$4,227,000	Par	$17,430,710		
CPP		12/12/2008	Citizens South Banking Corporation	Gastonia	NC	Preferred Stock w/Warrants	$20,500,000	Par	$38,181,280		
CPP		12/12/2008	Virginia Commerce Bancorp	Arlington	VA	Preferred Stock w/Warrants	$71,000,000	Par	$101,147,520		
CPP		12/12/2008	Fidelity Bancorp, Inc.	Pittsburgh	PA	Preferred Stock w/Warrants	$7,000,000	Par	$30,612,800		
CPP		12/12/2008	LSB Corporation	North Andover	MA	Preferred Stock w/Warrants	$15,000,000	Par	$39,970,740		
CPP		12/19/2008	Intermountain Community Bancorp	Sandpoint	ID	Preferred Stock w/Warrants	$27,000,000	Par	$38,446,800		
CPP		12/19/2008	Community West Bancshares	Goleta	CA	Preferred Stock w/Warrants	$15,600,000	Par	$15,615,600		
CPP		12/19/2008	Synovus Financial Corp.	Columbus	GA	Preferred Stock w/Warrants	$967,870,000	Par	$1,073,699,250		
CPP		12/19/2008	Tennessee Commerce Bancorp, Inc.	Franklin	TN	Preferred Stock w/Warrants	$30,000,000	Par	$36,341,760		

Table C.1. (Continued)

			Seller			Purchase Details				Capital Re-payment Details	
Program	Note	Purchase Date	Name of Institution	City	State	Investment Description	Investment Price	Pricing Mechanism	Market Capitalization as of 3/31/2009	Capital Repayment Date	Capital Repayment Amount (f)
CPP		12/19/2008	Community Bankers Trust Corporation	Glen Allen	VA	Preferred Stock w/Warrants	$17,680,000	Par	$72,991,200		
CPP		12/19/2008	BancTrust Financial Group, Inc.	Mobile	AL	Preferred Stock w/Warrants	$50,000,000	Par	$111,838,440		
CPP		12/19/2008	Enterprise Financial Services Corp.	St. Louis	MO	Preferred Stock w/Warrants	$35,000,000	Par	$125,230,560		
CPP		12/19/2008	Mid Penn Bancorp, Inc.	Millersburg	PA	Preferred Stock w/Warrants	$10,000,000	Par	$66,120,000		
CPP		12/19/2008	Summit State Bank	Santa Rosa	CA	Preferred Stock w/Warrants	$8,500,000	Par	$21,827,000		
CPP		12/19/2008	VIST Financial Corp.	Wyomissing	PA	Preferred Stock w/Warrants	$25,000,000	Par	$40,096,000		
CPP		12/19/2008	Wainwright Bank & Trust Company	Boston	MA	Preferred Stock w/Warrants	$22,000,000	Par	$47,232,720		
CPP		12/19/2008	Whitney Holding Corporation	New Orleans	LA	Preferred Stock w/Warrants	$300,000,000	Par	$771,523,900		
CPP		12/19/2008	The Connecticut Bank and Trust Company	Hartford	CT	Preferred Stock w/Warrants	$5,448,000	Par	$11,592,750		
CPP		12/19/2008	CoBiz Financial Inc.	Denver	CO	Preferred Stock w/Warrants	$64,450,000	Par	$122,871,000		

Table C.1. (Continued)

			Seller			Purchase Details				Capital Re-payment Details	
Program	Note	Purchase Date	Name of Institution	City	State	Investment Description	Investment Price	Pricing Mechanism	Market Capitalization as of 3/31/2009	Capital Repayment Date	Capital Repayment Amount (f)
CPP		12/19/2008	Santa Lucia Bancorp	Atascadero	CA	Preferred Stock w/Warrants	$4,000,000	Par	$22,114,500		
CPP		12/19/2008	Seacoast Banking Corporation of Florida	Stuart	FL	Preferred Stock w/Warrants	$50,000,000	Par	$58,090,490		
CPP		12/19/2008	Horizon Bancorp	Michigan City	IN	Preferred Stock w/Warrants	$25,000,000	Par	$36,119,400		
CPP		12/19/2008	Fidelity Southern Corporation	Atlanta	GA	Preferred Stock w/Warrants	$48,200,000	Par	$23,352,000		
CPP		12/19/2008	Community Financial Corporation	Staunton	VA	Preferred Stock w/Warrants	$12,643,000	Par	$17,448,000		
CPP		12/19/2008	Berkshire Hills Bancorp, Inc.	Pittsfield	MA	Preferred Stock w/Warrants	$40,000,000	Par	$280,999,200		
CPP		12/19/2008	First California Financial Group, Inc	Westlake Village	CA	Preferred Stock w/Warrants	$25,000,000	Par	$48,741,000		
CPP		12/19/2008	AmeriServ Financial, Inc.	Johnstown	PA	Preferred Stock w/Warrants	$21,000,000	Par	$35,295,450		
CPP		12/19/2008	Security Federal Corporation	Aiken	SC	Preferred Stock w/Warrants	$18,000,000	Par	$38,099,000		
CPP		12/19/2008	Wintrust Financial Corporation	Lake Forest	IL	Preferred Stock w/Warrants	$250,000,000	Par	$293,687,100		

Table C.1. (Continued)

			Seller			Purchase Details				Capital Re-payment Details	
Program	Note	Purchase Date	Name of Institution	City	State	Investment Description	Investment Price	Pricing Mechanism	Market Capitalization as of 3/31/2009	Capital Repayment Date	Capital Repayment Amount (f)
CPP		12/19/2008	Flushing Financial Corporation	Lake Success	NY	Preferred Stock w/Warrants	$70,000,000	Par	$130,730,320		
CPP		12/19/2008	Monarch Financial Holdings, Inc.	Chesapeake	VA	Preferred Stock w/Warrants	$14,700,000	Par	$29,299,500		
CPP		12/19/2008	StellarOne Corporation	Charlottesville	VA	Preferred Stock w/Warrants	$30,000,000	Par	$270,142,620		
CPP		12/19/2008	Union Bankshares Corporation	Bowling Green	VA	Preferred Stock w/Warrants	$59,000,000	Par	$188,276,900		
CPP		12/19/2008	Tidelands Bancshares, Inc	Mt. Pleasant	SC	Preferred Stock w/Warrants	$14,448,000	Par	$13,044,850		
CPP		12/19/2008	Bancorp Rhode Island, Inc.	Providence	RI	Preferred Stock w/Warrants	$30,000,000	Par	$82,995,510		
CPP		12/19/2008	Hawthorn Bancshares, Inc.	Lee's Summit	MO	Preferred Stock w/Warrants	$30,255,000	Par	$48,597,590		
CPP		12/19/2008	The Elmira Savings Bank, FSB	Elmira	NY	Preferred Stock w/Warrants	$9,090,000	Par	$20,528,200		
CPP		12/19/2008	Alliance Financial Corporation	Syracuse	NY	Preferred Stock w/Warrants	$26,918,000	Par	$82,147,260		
CPP		12/19/2008	Heartland Financial USA, Inc.	Dubuque	IA	Preferred Stock w/Warrants	$81,698,000	Par	$220,349,960		

Table C.1. (Continued)

			Seller			Purchase Details				Capital Re-payment Details	
Program	Note	Purchase Date	Name of Institution	City	State	Investment Description	Investment Price	Pricing Mechanism	Market Capitalization as of 3/31/2009	Capital Repayment Date	Capital Repayment Amount (f)
CPP		12/19/2008	Citizens First Corporation	Bowling Green	KY	Preferred Stock w/Warrants	$8,779,000	Par	$7,876,000		
CPP	(b)	12/19/2008	FFW Corporation	Wabash	IN	Preferred Stock w/ Exercised Warrants	$7,289,000	Par	N/A		
CPP	(b)	12/19/2008	Plains Capital Corporation	Dallas	TX	Preferred Stock w/ Exercised Warrants	$87,631,000	Par	N/A		
CPP	(b)	12/19/2008	Tri-County Financial Corporation	Waldorf	MD	Preferred Stock w/ Exercised Warrants	$15,540,000	Par	N/A		
CPP	(c)	12/19/2008	OneUnited Bank	Boston	MA	Preferred Stock	$12,063,000	Par	N/A		
CPP	(b)	12/19/2008	Patriot Bancshares, Inc.	Houston	TX	Preferred Stock w/ Exercised Warrants	$26,038,000	Par	N/A		
CPP	(b)	12/19/2008	Pacific City Finacial Corporation	Los Angeles	CA	Preferred Stock w/ Exercised Warrants	$16,200,000	Par	N/A		
CPP	(b)	12/19/2008	Marquette National Corporation	Chicago	IL	Preferred Stock w/ Exercised Warrants	$35,500,000	Par	N/A		
CPP	(b)	12/19/2008	Exchange Bank	Santa Rosa	CA	Preferred Stock w/ Exercised Warrants	$43,000,000	Par	N/A		
CPP	(b)	12/19/2008	Monadnock Bancorp, Inc.	Peterbo-rough	NH	Preferred Stock w/ Exercised Warrants	$1,834,000	Par	N/A		

Table C.1. (Continued)

			Seller			Purchase Details				Capital Re-payment Details	
Program	Note	Purchase Date	Name of Institution	City	State	Investment Description	Investment Price	Pricing Mechanism	Market Capitalization as of 3/31/2009	Capital Repayment Date	Capital Repayment Amount (f)
CPP	(b)	12/19/2008	Bridgeview Bancorp, Inc.	Bridgeview	IL	Preferred Stock w/ Exercised Warrants	$38,000,000	Par	N/A		
CPP	(b)	12/19/2008	Fidelity Financial Corporation	Wichita	KS	Preferred Stock w/ Exercised Warrants	$36,282,000	Par	N/A		
CPP	(b)	12/19/2008	Patapsco Bancorp, Inc.	Dundalk	MD	Preferred Stock w/ Exercised Warrants	$6,000,000	Par	N/A		
CPP	(b)	12/19/2008	NCAL Bancorp	Los Angeles	CA	Preferred Stock w/ Exercised Warrants	$10,000,000	Par	N/A		
CPP	(b)	12/19/2008	FCB Bancorp, Inc.	Louisville	KY	Preferred Stock w/ Exercised Warrants	$9,294,000	Par	N/A		
CPP		12/23/2008	First Financial Bancorp	Cincinnati	OH	Preferred Stock w/ Warrants	$80,000,000	Par	$357,193,930		
CPP		12/23/2008	Bridge Capital Holdings	San Jose	CA	Preferred Stock w/ Warrants	$23,864,000	Par	$30,996,000		
CPP		12/23/2008	International Bancshares Corporation	Laredo	TX	Preferred Stock w/ Warrants	$216,000,000	Par	$535,103,400		
CPP		12/23/2008	First Sound Bank	Seattle	WA	Preferred Stock w/ Warrants	$7,400,000	Par	N/A		
CPP		12/23/2008	M&T Bank Corporation	Buffalo	NY	Preferred Stock w/ Warrants	$600,000,000	Par	$5,024,309,160		

Table C.1. (Continued)

			Seller			Purchase Details				Capital Re-payment Details	
Program	Note	Purchase Date	Name of Institution	City	State	Investment Description	Investment Price	Pricing Mechanism	Market Capitalization as of 3/31/2009	Capital Repayment Date	Capital Repayment Amount (f)
CPP		12/23/2008	Emclaire Financial Corp.	Emlenton	PA	Preferred Stock w/ Warrants	$7,500,000	Par	$30,766,500		
CPP		12/23/2008	Park National Corporation	Newark	OH	Preferred Stock w/ Warrants	$100,000,000	Par	$778,939,000		
CPP		12/23/2008	Green Bankshares, Inc.	Greeneville	TN	Preferred Stock w/ Warrants	$72,278,000	Par	$115,957,600		
CPP		12/23/2008	Cecil Bancorp, Inc.	Elkton	MD	Preferred Stock w/ Warrants	$11,560,000	Par	$18,813,900		
CPP		12/23/2008	Financial Institutions, Inc.	Warsaw	NY	Preferred Stock w/ Warrants	$37,515,000	Par	$82,334,100		
CPP		12/23/2008	Fulton Financial Corporation	Lancaster	PA	Preferred Stock w/ Warrants	$376,500,000	Par	$1,163,114,160		
CPP		12/23/2008	United Bancorporation of Alabama, Inc.	Atmore	AL	Preferred Stock w/ Warrants	$10,300,000	Par	N/A		
CPP		12/23/2008	MutualFirst Financial, Inc.	Muncie	IN	Preferred Stock w/ Warrants	$32,382,000	Par	$33,528,000		
CPP		12/23/2008	BCSB Bancorp, Inc.	Baltimore	MD	Preferred Stock w/ Warrants	$10,800,000	Par	$27,308,750		
CPP		12/23/2008	HMN Financial, Inc.	Rochester	MN	Preferred Stock w/ Warrants	$26,000,000	Par	$12,905,300		
CPP		12/23/2008	First Community Bank Corporation of America	Pinellas Park	FL	Preferred Stock w/ Warrants	$10,685,000	Par	$17,019,100		

Table C.1. (Continued)

			Seller			Purchase Details				Capital Re-payment Details	
Program	Note	Purchase Date	Name of Institution	City	State	Investment Description	Investment Price	Pricing Mechanism	Market Capitalization as of 3/31/2009	Capital Repayment Date	Capital Repayment Amount (f)
CPP		12/23/2008	Sterling Bancorp	New York	NY	Preferred Stock w/ Warrants	$42,000,000	Par	$179,249,400		
CPP		12/23/2008	Intervest Bancshares Corporation	New York	NY	Preferred Stock w/ Warrants	$25,000,000	Par	$17,782,250		
CPP		12/23/2008	Peoples Bancorp of North Carolina, Inc.	Newton	NC	Preferred Stock w/ Warrants	$25,054,000	Par	$31,849,250		
CPP		12/23/2008	Parkvale Financial Corporation	Monr-oeville	PA	Preferred Stock w/ Warrants	$31,762,000	Par	$59,599,440		
CPP		12/23/2008	Timberland Bancorp, Inc.	Hoquiam	WA	Preferred Stock w/ Warrants	$16,641,000	Par	$36,352,200		
CPP		12/23/2008	1st Constitution Bancorp	Cranbury	NJ	Preferred Stock w/ Warrants	$12,000,000	Par	$26,350,000		
CPP		12/23/2008	Central Jersey Bancorp	Oakhurst	NJ	Preferred Stock w/ Warrants	$11,300,000	Par	$58,623,500		
CPP	(b)	12/23/2008	Western Illinois Bancshares Inc.	Monmouth	IL	Preferred Stock w/ Exercised Warrants	$6,855,000	Par	N/A		
CPP	(b)	12/23/2008	Saigon National Bank	Westmi-nster	CA	Preferred Stock w/ Exercised Warrants	$1,549,000	Par	N/A		
CPP	(b)	12/23/2008	Capital Pacific Bancorp	Portland	OR	Preferred Stock w/ Exercised Warrants	$4,000,000	Par	N/A		

Table C.1. (Continued)

			Seller			Purchase Details				Capital Re-payment Details	
Program	Note	Purchase Date	Name of Institution	City	State	Investment Description	Investment Price	Pricing Mechanism	Market Capitalization as of 3/31/2009	Capital Repayment Date	Capital Repayment Amount (f)
CPP	(b)	12/23/2008	Uwharrie Capital Corp	Albemarle	NC	Preferred Stock w/ Exercised Warrants	$10,000,000	Par	N/A		
CPP	(c)	12/23/2008	Mission Valley Bancorp	Sun Valley	CA	Preferred Stock	$5,500,000	Par	$14,202,750		
CPP	(b)	12/23/2008	The Little Bank, Incorporated	Kinston	NC	Preferred Stock w/ Exercised Warrants	$7,500,000	Par	N/A		
CPP	(b)	12/23/2008	Pacific Commerce Bank	Los Angeles	CA	Preferred Stock w/ Exercised Warrants	$4,060,000	Par	N/A		
CPP	(b)	12/23/2008	Citizens Community Bank	South Hill	VA	Preferred Stock w/ Exercised Warrants	$3,000,000	Par	N/A		
CPP	(b)	12/23/2008	Seacoast Commerce Bank	Chula Vista	CA	Preferred Stock w/ Exercised Warrants	$1,800,000	Par	N/A		
CPP	(b)	12/23/2008	TCNB Financial Corp.	Dayton	OH	Preferred Stock w/ Exercised Warrants	$2,000,000	Par	N/A		
CPP	(b)	12/23/2008	Leader Bancorp, Inc.	Arlington	MA	Preferred Stock w/ Exercised Warrants	$5,830,000	Par	N/A		
CPP	(b)	12/23/2008	Nicolet Bankshares, Inc.	Green Bay	WI	Preferred Sto-ck w/ Exer-cised Warrants	$14,964,000	Par	N/A		

Table C.1. (Continued)

			Seller			Purchase Details				Capital Re-payment Details	
Program	Note	Purchase Date	Name of Institution	City	State	Investment Description	Investment Price	Pricing Mechanism	Market Capitalization as of 3/31/2009	Capital Repayment Date	Capital Repayment Amount (f)
CPP	(b)	12/23/2008	Magna Bank	Memphis	TN	Preferred Sto-ck w/ Exer-cised Warrants	$13,795,000	Par	N/A		
CPP	(b)	12/23/2008	Western Community Bancshares, Inc.	Palm Desert	CA	Preferred Stock w/ Exercised Warrants	$7,290,000	Par	N/A		
CPP	(b)	12/23/2008	Community Investors Bancorp, Inc.	Bucyrus	OH	Preferred Stock w/ Exercised Warrants	$2,600,000	Par	N/A		
CPP	(b)	12/23/2008	Capital Bancorp, Inc.	Rockville	MD	Preferred Stock w/ Exercised Warrants	$4,700,000	Par	N/A		
CPP	(b)	12/23/2008	Cache Valley Banking Company	Logan	UT	Preferred Stock w/ Exercised Warrants	$4,767,000	Par	N/A		
CPP	(b)	12/23/2008	Citizens Bancorp	Nevada City	CA	Preferred Stock w/ Exercised Warrants	$10,400,000	Par	N/A		
CPP	(b)	12/23/2008	Tennessee Valley Financial Holdings, Inc.	Oak Ridge	TN	Preferred Stock w/ Exercised Warrants	$3,000,000	Par	N/A		
CPP	(b)	12/23/2008	Pacific Coast Bankers' Bancshares	San Francisco	CA	Preferred Stock w/ Exercised Warrants	$11,600,000	Par	N/A		
CPP		12/31/2008	SunTrust Banks, Inc.	Atlanta	GA	Preferred Stock w/ Warrants	$1,350,000,000	Par	$4,202,497,360		

Table C.1. (Continued)

			Seller			Purchase Details				Capital Re-payment Details	
Program	Note	Purchase Date	Name of Institution	City	State	Investment Description	Investment Price	Pricing Mechanism	Market Capitalization as of 3/31/2009	Capital Repayment Date	Capital Repayment Amount (f)
CPP		12/31/2008	The PNC Financial Services Group Inc.	Pittsburgh	PA	Preferred Stock w/ Warrants	$7,579,200,000	Par	$13,021,631,040		
CPP		12/31/2008	Fifth Third Bancorp	Cincinnati	OH	Preferred Stock w/ Warrants	$3,408,000,000	Par	$1,688,165,880		
CPP		12/31/2008	Hampton Roads Bankshares, Inc.	Norfolk	VA	Preferred Stock w/ Warrants	$80,347,000	Par	$169,790,840		
CPP		12/31/2008	CIT Group Inc.	New York	NY	Preferred Stock w/ Warrants	$2,330,000,000	Par	$1,108,591,330		
CPP		12/31/2008	West Bancorp-oration, Inc.	West Des Moines	IA	Preferred Stock w/ Warrants	$36,000,000	Par	$129,659,800		
CPP	(b)	12/31/2008	First Banks, Inc.	Clayton	MO	Preferred Stock w/ Exercised Warrants	$295,400,000	Par	N/A		
CPP	(a)	1/9/2009	Bank of America Corporation	Charlotte	NC	Preferred Stock w/ Warrants	$10,000,000,000	Par	$43,657,466,160		
CPP		1/9/2009	FirstMerit Corporation	Akron	OH	Preferred Stock w/ Warrants	$125,000,000	Par	$1,482,499,200		
CPP		1/9/2009	Farmers Capital Bank Corporation	Frankfort	KY	Preferred Stock w/ Warrants	$30,000,000	Par	$115,284,190		
CPP		1/9/2009	Peapack-Gladstone Financial Corporation	Gladstone	NJ	Preferred Stock w/ Warrants	$28,685,000	Par	$149,630,970		

Table C.1. (Continued)

			Seller			Purchase Details				Capital Re-payment Details	
Program	Note	Purchase Date	Name of Institution	City	State	Investment Description	Investment Price	Pricing Mechanism	Market Capitalization as of 3/31/2009	Capital Repayment Date	Capital Repayment Amount (f)
CPP		1/9/2009	Commerce National Bank	Newport Beach	CA	Preferred Stock w/ Warrants	$5,000,000	Par	$15,982,000		
CPP		1/9/2009	The First Bancorp, Inc.	Damar-iscotta	ME	Preferred Stock w/ Warrants	$25,000,000	Par	$154,000,600		
CPP		1/9/2009	Sun Bancorp, Inc.	Vineland	NJ	Preferred Stock w/ Warrants	$89,310,000	Par	$113,951,640		
CPP		1/9/2009	Crescent Financial Corporation	Cary	NC	Preferred Stock w/ Warrants	$24,900,000	Par	$34,657,200		
CPP		1/9/2009	American Express Company	New York	NY	Preferred Stock w/ Warrants	$3,388,890,000	Par	$15,805,838,680		
CPP		1/9/2009	Central Pacific Financial Corp.	Honolulu	HI	Preferred Stock w/ Warrants	$135,000,000	Par	$160,944,000		
CPP		1/9/2009	Centrue Financial Corporation	St. Louis	MO	Preferred Stock w/ Warrants	$32,668,000	Par	N/A		
CPP		1/9/2009	Eastern Virginia Bankshares, Inc.	Tappahannock	VA	Preferred Stock w/ Warrants	$24,000,000	Par	$49,593,290		
CPP		1/9/2009	Colony Bankcorp, Inc.	Fitzgerald	GA	Preferred Stock w/ Warrants	$28,000,000	Par	$46,206,090		
CPP		1/9/2009	Independent Bank Corp.	Rockland	MA	Preferred Stock w/ Warrants	$78,158,000	Par	$240,203,750		
CPP		1/9/2009	Cadence Financial Corporation	Starkville	MS	Preferred Stock w/ Warrants	$44,000,000	Par	$52,664,300		

Table C.1. (Continued)

			Seller			Purchase Details				Capital Re-payment Details	
Program	Note	Purchase Date	Name of Institution	City	State	Investment Description	Investment Price	Pricing Mechanism	Market Capitalization as of 3/31/2009	Capital Repayment Date	Capital Repayment Amount (f)
CPP		1/9/2009	LCNB Corp.	Lebanon	OH	Preferred Stock w/ Warrants	$13,400,000	Par	$63,526,500		
CPP		1/9/2009	Center Bancorp, Inc.	Union	NJ	Preferred Stock w/ Warrants	$10,000,000	Par	$93,795,020		
CPP		1/9/2009	F.N.B. Corporation	Hermitage	PA	Preferred Stock w/ Warrants	$100,000,000	Par	$687,968,320		
CPP		1/9/2009	C&F Financial Corporation	West Point	VA	Preferred Stock w/ Warrants	$20,000,000	Par	$43,928,000		
CPP		1/9/2009	North Central Bancshares, Inc.	Fort Dodge	IA	Preferred Stock w/ Warrants	$10,200,000	Par	$16,451,750		
CPP		1/9/2009	Carolina Bank Holdings, Inc.	Greensboro	NC	Preferred Stock w/ Warrants	$16,000,000	Par	$14,225,400		
CPP		1/9/2009	First Bancorp	Troy	NC	Preferred Stock w/ Warrants	$65,000,000	Par	$198,917,460		
CPP		1/9/2009	First Financial Service Corporation	Elizabethtown	KY	Preferred Stock w/ Warrants	$20,000,000	Par	$51,936,900		
CPP		1/9/2009	Codorus Valley Bancorp, Inc.	York	PA	Preferred Stock w/ Warrants	$16,500,000	Par	$32,466,080		
CPP		1/9/2009	MidSouth Bancorp, Inc.	Lafayette	LA	Preferred Stock w/ Warrants	$20,000,000	Par	$67,768,320		
CPP		1/9/2009	First Security Group, Inc.	Chattanooga	TN	Preferred Stock w/ Warrants	$33,000,000	Par	$55,335,400		
CPP		1/9/2009	Shore Bancshares, Inc.	Easton	MD	Preferred Stock w/ Warrants	$25,000,000	Par	$140,783,750		

Table C.1. (Continued)

			Seller			Purchase Details				Capital Re-payment Details	
Program	Note	Purchase Date	Name of Institution	City	State	Investment Description	Investment Price	Pricing Mechanism	Market Capitalization as of 3/31/2009	Capital Repayment Date	Capital Repayment Amount (f)
CPP	(b)	1/9/2009	The Queensborough Company	Louisville	GA	Preferred Stock w/ Exercised Warrants	$12,000,000	Par	N/A		
CPP	(b)	1/9/2009	American State Banc-shares, Inc.	Great Bend	KS	Preferred Stock w/ Exercised Warrants	$6,000,000	Par	N/A		
CPP	(b)	1/9/2009	Security California Bancorp	Riverside	CA	Preferred Stock w/ Exercised Warrants	$6,815,000	Par	N/A		
CPP	(b)	1/9/2009	Security Business Bancorp	San Diego	CA	Preferred Stock w/ Exercised Warrants	$5,803,000	Par	N/A		
CPP	(b)	1/9/2009	Sound Banking Company	Morehead City	NC	Preferred Stock w/ Exercised Warrants	$3,070,000	Par	N/A		
CPP	(c)	1/9/2009	Mission Community Bancorp	San Luis Obispo	CA	Preferred Stock	$5,116,000	Par	N/A		
CPP	(b)	1/9/2009	Redwood Financial Inc.	Redwood Falls	MN	Preferred Stock w/ Exercised Warrants	$2,995,000	Par	N/A		
CPP	(b)	1/9/2009	Surrey Bancorp	Mount Airy	NC	Preferred Stock w/ Exercised Warrants	$2,000,000	Par	N/A		
CPP	(b)	1/9/2009	Independence Bank	East Greenwich	RI	Preferred Stock w/ Exercised Warrants	$1,065,000	Par	N/A		

Table C.1. (Continued)

			Seller			Purchase Details				Capital Re-payment Details	
Program	Note	Purchase Date	Name of Institution	City	State	Investment Description	Investment Price	Pricing Mechanism	Market Capitalization as of 3/31/2009	Capital Repayment Date	Capital Repayment Amount (f)
CPP	(b)	1/9/2009	Valley Community Bank	Pleasanton	CA	Preferred Stock w/ Exercised Warrants	$5,500,000	Par	N/A		
CPP	(b)	1/9/2009	Rising Sun Bancorp	Rising Sun	MD	Preferred Stock w/ Exercised Warrants	$5,983,000	Par	N/A		
CPP	(b)	1/9/2009	Community Trust Financial Corporation	Ruston	LA	Preferred Stock w/ Exercised Warrants	$24,000,000	Par	N/A		
CPP	(b)	1/9/2009	GrandSouth Bancorpo-ration	Greenville	SC	Preferred Stock w/ Exercised Warrants	$9,000,000	Par	N/A		
CPP	(b)	1/9/2009	Texas National Bancorp-oration	Jackso-nville	TX	Preferred Stock w/ Exercised Warrants	$3,981,000	Par	N/A		
CPP	(b)	1/9/2009	Congaree Bancshares, Inc.	Cayce	SC	Preferred Stock w/ Exercised Warrants	$3,285,000	Par	N/A		
CPP	(b)	1/9/2009	New York Private Bank & Trust Corporation	New York	NY	Preferred Stock w/ Exercised Warrants	$267,274,000	Par	N/A		
CPP		1/16/2009	Home Bancshares, Inc.	Conway	AR	Preferred Stock w/ Warrants	$50,000,000	Par	$396,704,050		

Table C.1. (Continued)

			Seller			Purchase Details				Capital Re-payment Details	
Program	Note	Purchase Date	Name of Institution	City	State	Investment Description	Investment Price	Pricing Mechanism	Market Capitalization as of 3/31/2009	Capital Repayment Date	Capital Repayment Amount (f)
CPP		1/16/2009	Washington Banking Company/ Whidbey Island Bank	Oak Harbor	WA	Preferred Stock w/ Warrants	$26,380,000	Par	$64,797,200		
CPP		1/16/2009	New Hampshire Thrift Bancshares, Inc.	Newport	NH	Preferred Stock w/ Warrants	$10,000,000	Par	$41,673,000		
CPP		1/16/2009	Bar Harbor Bankshares/ Bar Harbor Bank & Trust	Bar Harbor	ME	Preferred Stock w/ Warrants	$18,751,000	Par	$66,871,000		
CPP		1/16/2009	Somerset Hills Bancorp	Berna-rdsville	NJ	Preferred Stock w/ Warrants	$7,414,000	Par	$31,909,320		
CPP		1/16/2009	SCBT Financial Corporation	Columbia	SC	Preferred Stock w/ Warrants	$64,779,000	Par	$236,629,800		
CPP		1/16/2009	S&T Bancorp	Indiana	PA	Preferred Stock w/ Warrants	$108,676,000	Par	$586,180,770		
CPP		1/16/2009	ECB Bancorp, Inc./East Carolina Bank	Engelhard	NC	Preferred Stock w/ Warrants	$17,949,000	Par	$43,513,200		
CPP		1/16/2009	First BanCorp	San Juan	PR	Preferred Stock w/ Warrants	$400,000,000	Par	$394,250,220		
CPP		1/16/2009	Texas Capital Bancshares, Inc.	Dallas	TX	Preferred Stock w/ Warrants	$75,000,000	Par	$348,852,840		
CPP		1/16/2009	Yadkin Valley Financial Corporation	Elkin	NC	Preferred Stock w/ Warrants	$36,000,000	Par	$85,920,850		

Table C.1. (Continued)

			Seller			Purchase Details				Capital Re-payment Details	
Program	Note	Purchase Date	Name of Institution	City	State	Investment Description	Investment Price	Pricing Mechanism	Market Capitalization as of 3/31/2009	Capital Repayment Date	Capital Repayment Amount (f)
CPP	(c)	1/16/2009	Carver Bancorp, Inc	New York	NY	Preferred Stock	$18,980,000	Par	$8,422,700		
CPP		1/16/2009	Citizens & Northern Corporation	Wellsboro	PA	Preferred Stock w/ Warrants	$26,440,000	Par	$165,688,890		
CPP		1/16/2009	MainSource Financial Group, Inc.	Greensburg	IN	Preferred Stock w/ Warrants	$57,000,000	Par	$161,901,480		
CPP		1/16/2009	MetroCorp Bancshares, Inc.	Houston	TX	Preferred Stock w/ Warrants	$45,000,000	Par	$30,405,420		
CPP		1/16/2009	United Bancorp, Inc.	Tecumseh	MI	Preferred Stock w/ Warrants	$20,600,000	Par	$47,495,700		
CPP		1/16/2009	Old Second Bancorp, Inc.	Aurora	IL	Preferred Stock w/ Warrants	$73,000,000	Par	$87,801,450		
CPP		1/16/2009	Pulaski Financial Corp	Creve Coeur	MO	Preferred Stock w/ Warrants	$32,538,000	Par	$51,210,000		
CPP		1/16/2009	OceanFirst Financial Corp.	Toms River	NJ	Preferred Stock w/ Warrants	$38,263,000	Par	$126,370,300		
CPP	(b)	1/16/2009	Community 1st Bank	Roseville	CA	Preferred Stock w/ Exercised Warrants	$2,550,000	Par	N/A		
CPP	(b)	1/16/2009	TCB Holding Company, Texas Community Bank	The Woodlands	TX	Preferred Stock w/ Exercised Warrants	$11,730,000	Par	N/A		

Table C.1. (Continued)

			Seller			Purchase Details				Capital Re-payment Details	
Program	Note	Purchase Date	Name of Institution	City	State	Investment Description	Investment Price	Pricing Mechanism	Market Capitalization as of 3/31/2009	Capital Repayment Date	Capital Repayment Amount (f)
CPP	(b)	1/16/2009	Centra Financial Holdings, Inc./Centra Bank, Inc.	Morga-ntown	WV	Preferred Stock w/ Exercised Warrants	$15,000,000	Par	N/A	3/31/2009 (d)	$15,000,000
CPP	(b)	1/16/2009	First Bankers Trustshares, Inc.	Quincy	IL	Preferred Stock w/ Exercised Warrants	$10,000,000	Par	N/A		
CPP	(b)	1/16/2009	Pacific Coast National Bancorp	San Clemente	CA	Preferred Stock w/ Exercised Warrants	$4,120,000	Par	N/A		
CPP	(c)	1/16/2009	Community Bank of the Bay	Oakland	CA	Preferred Stock	$1,747,000	Par	N/A		
CPP	(b)	1/16/2009	Redwood Capital Bancorp	Eureka	CA	Preferred Stock w/ Exercised Warrants	$3,800,000	Par	N/A		
CPP	(b)	1/16/2009	Syringa Bancorp	Boise	ID	Preferred Stock w/ Exercised Warrants	$8,000,000	Par	N/A		
CPP	(b)	1/16/2009	Idaho Bancorp	Boise	ID	Preferred Stock w/ Exercised Warrants	$6,900,000	Par	N/A		
CPP	(b)	1/16/2009	Puget Sound Bank	Bellevue	WA	Preferred Stock w/ Exercised Warrants	$4,500,000	Par	N/A		
CPP	(b)	1/16/2009	United Financial Banking Companies, Inc.	Vienna	VA	Preferred Stock w/ Exercised Warrants	$5,658,000	Par	N/A		

Table C.1. (Continued)

			Seller			Purchase Details				Capital Re-payment Details	
Program	Note	Purchase Date	Name of Institution	City	State	Investment Description	Investment Price	Pricing Mechanism	Market Capitalization as of 3/31/2009	Capital Repayment Date	Capital Repayment Amount (f)
CPP	(b)	1/16/2009	Dickinson Financial Corporation II	Kansas City	MO	Preferred Stock w/ Exercised Warrants	$146,053,000	Par	N/A		
CPP	(b)	1/16/2009	The Baraboo Bancorporation	Baraboo	WI	Preferred Stock w/ Exercised Warrants	$20,749,000	Par	N/A		
CPP	(b)	1/16/2009	Bank of Commerce	Charlotte	NC	Preferred Stock w/ Exercised Warrants	$3,000,000	Par	N/A		
CPP	(b)	1/16/2009	State Bankshares, Inc.	Fargo	ND	Preferred Stock w/ Exercised Warrants	$50,000,000	Par	N/A		
CPP	(b)	1/16/2009	BNCCORP, Inc.	Bismarck	ND	Preferred Stock w/ Exercised Warrants	$20,093,000	Par	N/A		
CPP	(b)	1/16/2009	First Manitowoc Bancorp, Inc.	Manitowoc	WI	Preferred Stock w/ Exercised Warrants	$12,000,000	Par	N/A		
CPP	(c)	1/16/2009	Southern Bancorp, Inc.	Arkadelphia	AR	Preferred Stock	$11,000,000	Par	N/A		
CPP	(b)	1/16/2009	Morrill Bancshares, Inc.	Merriam	KS	Preferred Stock w/ Exercised Warrants	$13,000,000	Par	N/A		
CPP	(b)	1/16/2009	Treaty Oak Bancorp, Inc.	Austin	TX	Preferred Stock w/ Exercised Warrants	$3,268,000	Par	N/A		

Table C.1. (Continued)

			Seller			Purchase Details				Capital Re-payment Details	
Program	Note	Purchase Date	Name of Institution	City	State	Investment Description	Investment Price	Pricing Mechanism	Market Capitalization as of 3/31/2009	Capital Repayment Date	Capital Repayment Amount (f)
CPP		1/23/2009	1st Source Corporation	South Bend	IN	Preferred Stock w/ Warrants	$111,000,000	Par	$450,275,300		
CPP		1/23/2009	Princeton National Bancorp, Inc.	Princeton	IL	Preferred Stock w/ Warrants	$25,083,000	Par	$46,172,000		
CPP		1/23/2009	AB&T Financial Corporation	Gastonia	NC	Preferred Stock w/ Warrants	$3,500,000	Par	$16,008,000		
CPP		1/23/2009	First Citizens Banc Corp	Sandusky	OH	Preferred Stock w/ Warrants	$23,184,000	Par	$57,892,480		
CPP		1/23/2009	WSFS Financial Corporation	Wilmington	DE	Preferred Stock w/ Warrants	$52,625,000	Par	$137,849,400		
CPP	(b)	1/23/2009	Commonwealth Business Bank	Los Angeles	CA	Preferred Stock w/ Exercised Warrants	$7,701,000	Par	N/A		
CPP	(b)	1/23/2009	Seaside National Bank & Trust	Orlando	FL	Preferred Stock w/ Exercised Warrants	$5,677,000	Par	N/A		
CPP	(b)	1/23/2009	CalWest Bancorp	Rancho Santa Margarita	CA	Preferred Stock w/ Exercised Warrants	$4,656,000	Par	N/A		
CPP	(b)	1/23/2009	Fresno First Bank	Fresno	CA	Preferred Stock w/ Exercised Warrants	$1,968,000	Par	N/A		
CPP	(b)	1/23/2009	First ULB Corp.	Oakland	CA	Preferred Stock w/ Exercised Warrants	$4,900,000	Par	N/A		

Table C.1. (Continued)

			Seller			Purchase Details				Capital Re-payment Details	
Program	Note	Purchase Date	Name of Institution	City	State	Investment Description	Investment Price	Pricing Mechanism	Market Capitalization as of 3/31/2009	Capital Repayment Date	Capital Repayment Amount (f)
CPP	(b)	1/23/2009	Alarion Financial Services, Inc.	Ocala	FL	Preferred Stock w/ Exercised Warrants	$6,514,000	Par	N/A		
CPP	(b)	1/23/2009	Midland States Bancorp, Inc.	Effingham	IL	Preferred Stock w/ Exercised Warrants	$10,189,000	Par	N/A		
CPP	(b)	1/23/2009	Moscow Bancshares, Inc.	Moscow	TN	Preferred Stock w/ Exercised Warrants	$6,216,000	Par	N/A		
CPP	(b)	1/23/2009	Farmers Bank	Windsor	VA	Preferred Stock w/ Exercised Warrants	$8,752,000	Par	N/A		
CPP	(b)	1/23/2009	California Oaks State Bank	Thousand Oaks	CA	Preferred Stock w/ Exercised Warrants	$3,300,000	Par	N/A		
CPP	(b)	1/23/2009	Pierce County Bancorp	Tacoma	WA	Preferred Stock w/ Exercised Warrants	$6,800,000	Par	N/A		
CPP	(b)	1/23/2009	Calvert Financial Corporation	Ashland	MO	Preferred Stock w/ Exercised Warrants	$1,037,000	Par	N/A		
CPP	(b)	1/23/2009	Liberty Bancshares, Inc.	Jonesboro	AR	Preferred Stock w/ Exercised Warrants	$57,500,000	Par	N/A		
CPP	(b)	1/23/2009	Crosstown Holding Company	Blaine	MN	Preferred Stock w/ Exercised Warrants	$10,650,000	Par	N/A		

Table C.1. (Continued)

			Seller			Purchase Details				Capital Re-payment Details	
Program	Note	Purchase Date	Name of Institution	City	State	Investment Description	Investment Price	Pricing Mechanism	Market Capitalization as of 3/31/2009	Capital Repayment Date	Capital Repayment Amount (f)
CPP	(b)	1/23/2009	BankFirst Capital Corporation	Macon	MS	Preferred Stock w/ Exercised Warrants	$15,500,000	Par	N/A		
CPP	(b)	1/23/2009	Southern Illinois Bancorp, Inc.	Carmi	IL	Preferred Stock w/ Exercised Warrants	$5,000,000	Par	N/A		
CPP	(b)	1/23/2009	FPB Financial Corp.	Hammond	LA	Preferred Stock w/ Exercised Warrants	$3,240,000	Par	N/A		
CPP	(b)	1/23/2009	Stonebridge Financial Corp.	West Chester	PA	Preferred Stock w/ Exercised Warrants	$10,973,000	Par	N/A		
CPP		1/30/2009	Peoples Bancorp Inc.	Marietta	OH	Preferred Stock w/Warrants	$39,000,000	Par	$135,498,220		
CPP		1/30/2009	Anchor BanCorp Wisconsin Inc.	Madison	WI	Preferred Stock w/Warrants	$110,000,000	Par	$29,101,950		
CPP		1/30/2009	Parke Bancorp, Inc.	Sewell	NJ	Preferred Stock w/Warrants	$16,288,000	Par	$28,231,000		
CPP		1/30/2009	Central Virginia Bankshares, Inc.	Powhatan	VA	Preferred Stock w/Warrants	$11,385,000	Par	$10,254,200		
CPP		1/30/2009	Flagstar Bancorp, Inc.	Troy	MI	Preferred Stock w/Warrants	$266,657,000	Par	$67,784,250		
CPP		1/30/2009	Middleburg Financial Corporation	Middleburg	VA	Preferred Stock w/Warrants	$22,000,000	Par	$52,004,980		

Table C.1. (Continued)

			Seller			Purchase Details				Capital Re-payment Details	
Program	Note	Purchase Date	Name of Institution	City	State	Investment Description	Investment Price	Pricing Mechanism	Market Capitalization as of 3/31/2009	Capital Repayment Date	Capital Repayment Amount (f)
CPP		1/30/2009	Peninsula Bank Holding Co.	Palo Alto	CA	Preferred Stock w/Warrants	$6,000,000	Par	$18,530,000		
CPP		1/30/2009	PrivateBancorp, Inc.	Chicago	IL	Preferred Stock w/Warrants	$243,815,000	Par	$485,928,300		
CPP		1/30/2009	Central Valley Community Bancorp	Fresno	CA	Preferred Stock w/Warrants	$7,000,000	Par	$35,688,140		
CPP		1/30/2009	Plumas Bancorp	Quincy	CA	Preferred Stock w/Warrants	$11,949,000	Par	$28,608,240		
CPP		1/30/2009	Stewardship Financial Corporation	Midland Park	NJ	Preferred Stock w/Warrants	$10,000,000	Par	$45,461,900		
CPP		1/30/2009	Oak Ridge Financial Services, Inc.	Oak Ridge	NC	Preferred Stock w/Warrants	$7,700,000	Par	$6,984,900		
CPP		1/30/2009	First United Corporation	Oakland	MD	Preferred Stock w/Warrants	$30,000,000	Par	$51,302,360		
CPP		1/30/2009	Community Partners Bancorp	Middletown	NJ	Preferred Stock w/Warrants	$9,000,000	Par	$23,316,000		
CPP		1/30/2009	Guaranty Federal Bancshares, Inc.	Springfield	MO	Preferred Stock w/Warrants	$17,000,000	Par	$13,848,900		

Table C.1. (Continued)

			Seller			Purchase Details				Capital Re-payment Details	
Program	Note	Purchase Date	Name of Institution	City	State	Investment Description	Investment Price	Pricing Mechanism	Market Capitalization as of 3/31/2009	Capital Repayment Date	Capital Repayment Amount (f)
CPP		1/30/2009	Annapolis Bancorp, Inc.	Annapolis	MD	Preferred Stock w/Warrants	$8,152,000	Par	$10,474,720		
CPP		1/30/2009	DNB Financial Corporation	Downingtown	PA	Preferred Stock w/Warrants	$11,750,000	Par	$19,574,560		
CPP		1/30/2009	Firstbank Corporation	Alma	MI	Preferred Stock w/Warrants	$33,000,000	Par	$38,076,000		
CPP	(b)	1/30/2009	Valley Commerce Bancorp	Visalia	CA	Preferred Stock w/ Exercised Warrants	$7,700,000	Par	N/A		
CPP	(b)	1/30/2009	Greer Bancshares Incorporated	Greer	SC	Preferred Stock w/ Exercised Warrants	$9,993,000	Par	N/A		
CPP	(b)	1/30/2009	Ojai Community Bank	Ojai	CA	Preferred Stock w/ Exercised Warrants	$2,080,000	Par	N/A		
CPP	(b)	1/30/2009	Adbanc, Inc	Ogallala	NE	Preferred Stock w/ Exercised Warrants	$12,720,000	Par	N/A		
CPP	(b)	1/30/2009	Beach Business Bank	Manhattan Beach	CA	Preferred Stock w/ Exercised Warrants	$6,000,000	Par	N/A		
CPP	(c)	1/30/2009	Legacy Bancorp, Inc.	Milwaukee	WI	Preferred Stock	$5,498,000	Par	N/A		
CPP	(b)	1/30/2009	First Southern Bancorp, Inc.	Boca Raton	FL	Preferred Stock w/ Exercised Warrants	$10,900,000	Par	N/A		

Table C.1. (Continued)

			Seller			Purchase Details				Capital Re-payment Details	
Program	Note	Purchase Date	Name of Institution	City	State	Investment Description	Investment Price	Pricing Mechanism	Market Capitalization as of 3/31/2009	Capital Repayment Date	Capital Repayment Amount (f)
CPP	(b)	1/30/2009	Country Bank Shares, Inc.	Milford	NE	Preferred Stock w/ Exercised Warrants	$7,525,000	Par	N/A		
CPP	(b)	1/30/2009	Katahdin Bankshares Corp.	Houlton	ME	Preferred Stock w/ Exercised Warrants	$10,449,000	Par	N/A		
CPP	(b)	1/30/2009	Rogers Bancshares, Inc.	Little Rock	AR	Preferred Stock w/ Exercised Warrants	$25,000,000	Par	N/A		
CPP	(b)	1/30/2009	UBT Bancshares, Inc.	Marysville	KS	Preferred Stock w/ Exercised Warrants	$8,950,000	Par	N/A		
CPP	(b)	1/30/2009	Bankers' Bank of the West Bancorp, Inc.	Denver	CO	Preferred Stock w/ Exercised Warrants	$12,639,000	Par	N/A		
CPP	(b)	1/30/2009	W.T.B. Financial Corporation	Spokane	WA	Preferred Stock w/ Exercised Warrants	$110,000,000	Par	N/A		
CPP	(b)	1/30/2009	AMB Financial Corp.	Munster	IN	Preferred Stock w/ Exercised Warrants	$3,674,000	Par	N/A		
CPP	(b)	1/30/2009	Goldwater Bank, N.A.	Scottsdale	AZ	Preferred Stock w/ Exercised Warrants	$2,568,000	Par	N/A		

Table C.1. (Continued)

			Seller			Purchase Details				Capital Re-payment Details	
Program	Note	Purchase Date	Name of Institution	City	State	Investment Description	Investment Price	Pricing Mechanism	Market Capitalization as of 3/31/2009	Capital Repayment Date	Capital Repayment Amount (f)
CPP	(b)	1/30/2009	Equity Bancshares, Inc.	Wichita	KS	Preferred Stock w/ Exercised Warrants	$8,750,000	Par	N/A		
CPP	(b)	1/30/2009	WashingtonFirst Bank	Reston	VA	Preferred Stock w/ Exercised Warrants	$6,633,000	Par	N/A		
CPP	(b)	1/30/2009	Central Bancshares, Inc.	Houston	TX	Preferred Stock w/ Exercised Warrants	$5,800,000	Par	N/A		
CPP	(b)	1/30/2009	Hilltop Community Bancorp, Inc.	Summit	NJ	Preferred Stock w/ Exercised Warrants	$4,000,000	Par	N/A		
CPP	(b)	1/30/2009	Northway Financial, Inc.	Berlin	NH	Preferred Stock w/ Exercised Warrants	$10,000,000	Par	N/A		
CPP	(b)	1/30/2009	Monument Bank	Bethesda	MD	Preferred Stock w/ Exercised Warrants	$4,734,000	Par	N/A		
CPP	(b)	1/30/2009	Metro City Bank	Doraville	GA	Preferred Stock w/ Exercised Warrants	$7,700,000	Par	N/A		
CPP	(b)	1/30/2009	F & M Bancshares, Inc.	Trezevant	TN	Preferred Sto-ck w/ Exerc-ised Warrants	$4,609,000	Par	N/A		
CPP	(b)	1/30/2009	First Resource Bank	Exton	PA	Preferred Stock w/ Exercised Warrants	$2,600,000	Par	N/A		

Table C.1. (Continued)

			Seller			Purchase Details				Capital Re-payment Details	
Program	Note	Purchase Date	Name of Institution	City	State	Investment Description	Investment Price	Pricing Mechanism	Market Capitalization as of 3/31/2009	Capital Repayment Date	Capital Repayment Amount (f)
CPP		2/6/2009	MidWest One Financial Group, Inc.	Iowa City	IA	Preferred Stock w/Warrants	$16,000,000	Par	$80,438,050		
CPP		2/6/2009	Lakeland Bancorp, Inc.	Oak Ridge	NJ	Preferred Stock w/Warrants	$59,000,000	Par	$189,508,000		
CPP		2/6/2009	Monarch Community Bancorp, Inc.	Coldwater	MI	Preferred Stock w/Warrants	$6,785,000	Par	$7,075,890		
CPP		2/6/2009	The First Bancshares, Inc.	Hattiesburg	MS	Preferred Stock w/Warrants	$5,000,000	Par	$29,361,800		
CPP		2/6/2009	Carolina Trust Bank	Lincolnton	NC	Preferred Stock w/Warrants	$4,000,000	Par	$7,516,800		
CPP		2/6/2009	Alaska Pacific Bancshares, Inc.	Juneau	AK	Preferred Stock w/Warrants	$4,781,000	Par	$2,354,400		
CPP	(c)	2/6/2009	PGB Holdings, Inc.	Chicago	IL	Preferred Stock	$3,000,000	Par	N/A		
CPP	(b)	2/6/2009	The Freeport State Bank	Harper	KS	Preferred Stock w/ Exercised Warrants	$301,000	Par	N/A		
CPP	(b)	2/6/2009	Stockmens Financial Corporation	Rapid City	SD	Preferred Stock w/ Exercised Warrants	$15,568,000	Par	N/A		
CPP	(b)	2/6/2009	US Metro Bank	Garden Grove	CA	Preferred Stock w/ Exercised Warrants	$2,861,000	Par	N/A		
CPP	(b)	2/6/2009	First Express of Nebraska, Inc.	Gering	NE	Preferred Stock w/ Exercised Warrants	$5,000,000	Par	N/A		

Table C.1. (Continued)

			Seller			Purchase Details				Capital Re-payment Details	
Program	Note	Purchase Date	Name of Institution	City	State	Investment Description	Investment Price	Pricing Mechanism	Market Capitalization as of 3/31/2009	Capital Repayment Date	Capital Repayment Amount (f)
CPP	(b)	2/6/2009	Mercantile Capital Corp.	Boston	MA	Preferred Stock w/ Exercised Warrants	$3,500,000	Par	N/A		
CPP	(b)	2/6/2009	Citizens Commerce Bancshares, Inc.	Versailles	KY	Preferred Stock w/ Exercised Warrants	$6,300,000	Par	N/A		
CPP	(c)	2/6/2009	Liberty Financial Services, Inc.	New Orleans	LA	Preferred Stock	$5,645,000	Par	N/A		
CPP	(b)	2/6/2009	Lone Star Bank	Houston	TX	Preferred Stock w/ Exercised Warrants	$3,072,000	Par	N/A		
CPP	(b)	2/6/2009	First Market Bank, FSB	Richmond	VA	Preferred Stock w/ Exercised Warrants	$33,900,000	Par	N/A		
CPP	(b)	2/6/2009	Banner County Ban Corporation	Harrisburg	NE	Preferred Stock w/ Exercised Warrants	$795,000	Par	N/A		
CPP	(b)	2/6/2009	Centrix Bank & Trust	Bedford	NH	Preferred Stock w/ Exercised Warrants	$7,500,000	Par	N/A		
CPP	(b)	2/6/2009	Todd Bancshares, Inc.	Hopkins-ville	KY	Preferred Stock w/ Exercised Warrants	$4,000,000	Par	N/A		
CPP	(b)	2/6/2009	Georgia Commerce Bancshares, Inc.	Atlanta	GA	Preferred Stock w/ Exercised Warrants	$8,700,000	Par	N/A		

Table C.1. (Continued)

			Seller			Purchase Details				Capital Re-payment Details	
Program	Note	Purchase Date	Name of Institution	City	State	Investment Description	Investment Price	Pricing Mechanism	Market Capitalization as of 3/31/2009	Capital Repayment Date	Capital Repayment Amount (f)
CPP	(b)	2/6/2009	First Bank of Charleston, Inc.	Charleston	WV	Preferred Stock w/ Exercised Warrants	$3,345,000	Par	N/A		
CPP	(b)	2/6/2009	F & M Financial Corporation	Salisbury	NC	Preferred Stock w/ Exercised Warrants	$17,000,000	Par	N/A		
CPP	(b)	2/6/2009	The Bank of Currituck	Moyock	NC	Preferred Stock w/ Exercised Warrants	$4,021,000	Par	N/A		
CPP	(b)	2/6/2009	CedarStone Bank	Lebanon	TN	Preferred Stock w/ Exercised Warrants	$3,564,000	Par	N/A		
CPP	(b)	2/6/2009	Community Holding Company of Florida, Inc.	Miramar Beach	FL	Preferred Stock w/ Exercised Warrants	$1,050,000	Par	N/A		
CPP	(b)	2/6/2009	Hyperion Bank	Philad-elphia	PA	Preferred Stock w/ Exercised Warrants	$1,552,000	Par	N/A		
CPP	(b)	2/6/2009	Pascack Community Bank	Westwood	NJ	Preferred Stock w/ Exercised Warrants	$3,756,000	Par	N/A		
CPP	(b)	2/6/2009	First Western Financial, Inc.	Denver	CO	Preferred Stock w/ Exercised Warrants	$8,559,000	Par	N/A		

Table C.1. (Continued)

			Seller			Purchase Details				Capital Re-payment Details	
Program	Note	Purchase Date	Name of Institution	City	State	Investment Description	Investment Price	Pricing Mechanism	Market Capitalization as of 3/31/2009	Capital Repayment Date	Capital Repayment Amount (f)
CPP		2/13/2009	QCR Holdings, Inc.	Moline	IL	Preferred Stock w/Warrants	$38,237,000	Par	$36,429,240		
CPP		2/13/2009	Westamerica Bancorpor-ation	San Rafael	CA	Preferred Stock w/Warrants	$83,726,000	Par	$1,315,545,000		
CPP		2/13/2009	The Bank of Kentucky Financial Corporation	Crestview Hills	KY	Preferred Stock w/Warrants	$34,000,000	Par	$106,647,000		
CPP		2/13/2009	PremierWest Bancorp	Medford	OR	Preferred Stock w/Warrants	$41,400,000	Par	$99,564,950		
CPP		2/13/2009	Carrollton Bancorp	Baltimore	MD	Preferred Stock w/Warrants	$9,201,000	Par	$13,127,670		
CPP		2/13/2009	FNB United Corp.	Asheboro	NC	Preferred Stock w/Warrants	$51,500,000	Par	$29,712,800		
CPP	(b)	2/13/2009	First Menasha Bancshares, Inc.	Neenah	WI	Preferred Stock w/ Exercised Warrants	$4,797,000	Par	N/A		
CPP	(b)	2/13/2009	1st Enterprise Bank	Los Angeles	CA	Preferred Stock w/ Exercised Warrants	$4,400,000	Par	N/A		
CPP	(b)	2/13/2009	DeSoto County Bank	Horn Lake	MS	Preferred Stock w/ Exercised Warrants	$1,173,000	Par	N/A		
CPP	(b)	2/13/2009	Security Bancshares of Pulaski County, Inc.	Wayne-sville	MO	Preferred Stock w/ Exercised Warrants	$2,152,000	Par	N/A		

Table C.1. (Continued)

			Seller			Purchase Details				Capital Re-payment Details	
Program	Note	Purchase Date	Name of Institution	City	State	Investment Description	Investment Price	Pricing Mechanism	Market Capitalization as of 3/31/2009	Capital Repayment Date	Capital Repayment Amount (f)
CPP	(b)	2/13/2009	State Capital Corporation	Greenwood	MS	Preferred Stock w/ Exercised Warrants	$15,000,000	Par	N/A		
CPP	(b)	2/13/2009	BankGreen-ville	Greenville	SC	Preferred Stock w/ Exercised Warrants	$1,000,000	Par	N/A		
CPP	(b)	2/13/2009	Corning Savi-ngs and Loan Association	Corning	AR	Preferred Sto-ck w/ Exer-cised Warrants	$638,000	Par	N/A		
CPP	(b)	2/13/2009	Financial Security Corporation	Basin	WY	Preferred Stock w/ Exercised Warrants	$5,000,000	Par	N/A		
CPP	(b)	2/13/2009	ColoEast Bankshares, Inc.	Lamar	CO	Preferred Stock w/ Exercised Warrants	$10,000,000	Par	N/A		
CPP	(b)	2/13/2009	Santa Clara Valley Bank, N.A.	Santa Paula	CA	Preferred Stock w/ Exercised Warrants	$2,900,000	Par	N/A		
CPP	(b)	2/13/2009	Reliance Bancshares, Inc.	Frontenac	MO	Preferred Stock w/ Exercised Warrants	$40,000,000	Par	N/A	CPP	
CPP	(b)	2/13/2009	Regional Bankshares, Inc.	Hartsville	SC	Preferred Stock w/ Exercised Warrants	$1,500,000	Par	N/A		
CPP	(b)	2/13/2009	Peoples Bancorp	Lynden	WA	Preferred Stock w/ Exercised Warrants	$18,000,000	Par	N/A		

Table C.1. (Continued)

			Seller			Purchase Details				Capital Re-payment Details	
Program	Note	Purchase Date	Name of Institution	City	State	Investment Description	Investment Price	Pricing Mechanism	Market Capitalization as of 3/31/2009	Capital Repayment Date	Capital Repayment Amount (f)
CPP	(b)	2/13/2009	First Choice Bank	Cerritos	CA	Preferred Sto-ck w/ Exer-cised Warrants	$2,200,000	Par	N/A		
CPP	(b)	2/13/2009	Gregg Bancshares, Inc.	Ozark	MO	Preferred Stock w/ Exercised Warrants	$825,000	Par	N/A		
CPP	(b)	2/13/2009	Hometown Bancshares, Inc.	Corbin	KY	Preferred Stock w/ Exercised Warrants	$1,900,000	Par	N/A		
CPP	(b)	2/13/2009	Midwest Regional Bancorp, Inc.	Festus	MO	Preferred Stock w/ Exercised Warrants	$700,000	Par	N/A		
CPP	(b)	2/13/2009	Bern Bancshares, Inc.	Bern	KS	Preferred Stock w/ Exercised Warrants	$985,000	Par	N/A		
CPP	(b)	2/13/2009	Northwest Bancorporation, Inc.	Spokane	WA	Preferred Stock w/ Exercised Warrants	$10,500,000	Par	N/A		
CPP	(b)	2/13/2009	Liberty Bancshares, Inc.	Springfield	MO	Preferred Stock w/ Exercised Warrants	$21,900,000	Par	N/A		
CPP	(b)	2/13/2009	F&M Financial Corporation	Clarksville	TN	Preferred Stock w/ Exercised Warrants	$17,243,000	Par	N/A		

Table C.1. (Continued)

			Seller			Purchase Details				Capital Re-payment Details	
Program	Note	Purchase Date	Name of Institution	City	State	Investment Description	Investment Price	Pricing Mechanism	Market Capitalization as of 3/31/2009	Capital Repayment Date	Capital Repayment Amount (f)
CPP	(b)	2/13/2009	Meridian Bank	Devon	PA	Preferred Stock w/ Exercised Warrants	$6,200,000	Par	N/A		
CPP	(b)	2/13/2009	Northwest Commercial Bank	Lakewood	WA	Preferred Stock w/ Exercised Warrants	$1,992,000	Par	N/A		
CPP		2/20/2009	Royal Bancshares of Pennsylvania, Inc.	Narberth	PA	Preferred Stock w/Warrants	$30,407,000	Par	$27,839,010		
CPP		2/20/2009	First Merchants Corporation	Muncie	IN	Preferred Stock w/Warrants	$116,000,000	Par	$228,510,620		
CPP		2/20/2009	Northern States Financial Corporation	Waukegan	IL	Preferred Stock w/Warrants	$17,211,000	Par	$30,336,400		
CPP	(b)	2/20/2009	Sonoma Valley Bancorp	Sonoma	CA	Preferred Stock w/ Exercised Warrants	$8,653,000	Par	N/A		
CPP	(b)	2/20/2009	Guaranty Bancorp, Inc.	Woodsville	NH	Preferred Stock w/ Exercised Warrants	$6,920,000	Par	N/A		
CPP	(b)	2/20/2009	The Private Bank of California	Los Angeles	CA	Preferred Stock w/ Exercised Warrants	$5,450,000	Par	N/A		

Table C.1. (Continued)

			Seller			Purchase Details				Capital Re-payment Details	
Program	Note	Purchase Date	Name of Institution	City	State	Investment Description	Investment Price	Pricing Mechanism	Market Capitalization as of 3/31/2009	Capital Repayment Date	Capital Repayment Amount (f)
CPP	(b)	2/20/2009	Lafayette Bancorp, Inc.	Oxford	MS	Preferred Stock w/ Exercised Warrants	$1,998,000	Par	N/A		
CPP	(b)	2/20/2009	Liberty Shares, Inc.	Hinesville	GA	Preferred Stock w/ Exercised Warrants	$17,280,000	Par	N/A		
CPP	(b)	2/20/2009	White River Bancshares Company	Fayetteville	AR	Preferred Stock w/ Exercised Warrants	$16,800,000	Par	N/A		
CPP	(b)	2/20/2009	United American Bank	San Mateo	CA	Preferred Stock w/ Exercised Warrants	$8,700,000	Par	N/A		
CPP	(b)	2/20/2009	Crazy Woman Creek Bancorp, Inc.	Buffalo	WY	Preferred Stock w/ Exercised Warrants	$3,100,000	Par	N/A		
CPP	(b)	2/20/2009	First Priority Financial Corp.	Malvern	PA	Preferred Stock w/ Exercised Warrants	$4,579,000	Par	N/A		
CPP	(b)	2/20/2009	Mid-Wisconsin Financial Services, Inc.	Medford	WI	Preferred Stock w/ Exercised Warrants	$10,000,000	Par	N/A		
CPP	(b)	2/20/2009	Market Bancorporation, Inc.	New Market	MN	Preferred Stock w/ Exercised Warrants	$2,060,000	Par	N/A		
CPP	(b)	2/20/2009	Hometown Bancorp of Alabama, Inc.	Oneonta	AL	Preferred Stock w/ Exercised Warrants	$3,250,000	Par	N/A		

Table C.1. (Continued)

			Seller			Purchase Details				Capital Re-payment Details	
Program	Note	Purchase Date	Name of Institution	City	State	Investment Description	Investment Price	Pricing Mechanism	Market Capitalization as of 3/31/2009	Capital Repayment Date	Capital Repayment Amount (f)
CPP	(b)	2/20/2009	Security State Bancshares, Inc.	Charleston	MO	Preferred Stock w/ Exercised Warrants	$12,500,000	Par	N/A		
CPP	(b)	2/20/2009	CBB Bancorp	Cartersville	GA	Preferred Stock w/ Exercised Warrants	$2,644,000	Par	N/A		
CPP	(b)	2/20/2009	BancPlus Corporation	Ridgeland	MS	Preferred Stock w/ Exercised Warrants	$48,000,000	Par	N/A		
CPP	(b)	2/20/2009	Central Community Corporation	Temple	TX	Preferred Stock w/ Exercised Warrants	$22,000,000	Par	N/A		
CPP	(b)	2/20/2009	First BancTrust Corporation	Paris	IL	Preferred Stock w/ Exercised Warrants	$7,350,000	Par	N/A		
CPP	(b)	2/20/2009	Premier Service Bank	Riverside	CA	Preferred Sto-ck w/ Exerc-ised Warrants	$4,000,000	Par	N/A		
CPP	(b)	2/20/2009	Florida Business BancGroup, Inc.	Tampa	FL	Preferred Stock w/ Exercised Warrants	$9,495,000	Par	N/A		
CPP	(b)	2/20/2009	Hamilton State Bancshares	Hoschton	GA	Preferred Stock w/ Exercised Warrants	$7,000,000	Par	N/A		

Table C.1. (Continued)

			Seller			Purchase Details				Capital Re-payment Details	
Program	Note	Purchase Date	Name of Institution	City	State	Investment Description	Investment Price	Pricing Mechanism	Market Capitalization as of 3/31/2009	Capital Repayment Date	Capital Repayment Amount (f)
CPP		2/27/2009	Lakeland Financial Corporation	Warsaw	IN	Preferred Stock w/Warrants	$56,044,000	Par	$238,224,660		
CPP		2/27/2009	First M&F Corporation	Kosciusko	MS	Preferred Stock w/Warrants	$30,000,000	Par	$56,120,400		
CPP		2/27/2009	Southern First Bancshares, Inc.	Greenville	SC	Preferred Stock w/Warrants	$17,299,000	Par	$17,082,450		
CPP		2/27/2009	Integra Bank Corporation	Evansville	IN	Preferred Stock w/Warrants	$83,586,000	Par	$39,208,050		
CPP	(b)	2/27/2009	Community First Inc.	Columbia	TN	Preferred Stock w/ Exercised Warrants	$17,806,000	Par	N/A		
CPP	(b)	2/27/2009	BNC Financial Group, Inc.	New Canaan	CT	Preferred Stock w/ Exercised Warrants	$4,797,000	Par	N/A		
CPP	(b)	2/27/2009	California Bank of Commerce	Lafayette	CA	Preferred Stock w/ Exercised Warrants	$4,000,000	Par	N/A		
CPP	(b)	2/27/2009	Columbine Capital Corp.	Buena Vista	CO	Preferred Stock w/ Exercised Warrants	$2,260,000	Par	N/A		
CPP	(b)	2/27/2009	National Bancshares, Inc.	Bettendorf	IA	Preferred Stock w/ Exercised Warrants	$24,664,000	Par	N/A		
CPP	(b)	2/27/2009	First State Bank of Mobeetie	Mobeetie	TX	Preferred Stock w/ Exercised Warrants	$731,000	Par	N/A		

Table C.1. (Continued)

			Seller			Purchase Details				Capital Re-payment Details	
Program	Note	Purchase Date	Name of Institution	City	State	Investment Description	Investment Price	Pricing Mechanism	Market Capitalization as of 3/31/2009	Capital Repayment Date	Capital Repayment Amount (f)
CPP	(b)	2/27/2009	Ridgestone Financial Services, Inc.	Brookfield	WI	Preferred Stock w/ Exercised Warrants	$10,900,000	Par	N/A		
CPP	(b)	2/27/2009	Community Business Bank	West Sacramento	CA	Preferred Stock w/ Exercised Warrants	$3,976,000	Par	N/A		
CPP	(b)	2/27/2009	D.L. Evans Bancorp	Burley	ID	Preferred Stock w/ Exercised Warrants	$19,891,000	Par	N/A		
CPP	(b)	2/27/2009	TriState Capital Holdings, Inc.	Pittsburgh	PA	Preferred Stock w/ Exercised Warrants	$23,000,000	Par	N/A		
CPP	(b)	2/27/2009	Green City Bancshares, Inc.	Green City	MO	Preferred Stock w/ Exercised Warrants	$651,000	Par	N/A		
CPP	(b)	2/27/2009	First Gothenburg Bancshares, Inc.	Gothenburg	NE	Preferred Stock w/ Exercised Warrants	$7,570,000	Par	N/A		
CPP	(b)	2/27/2009	Green Circle Investments, Inc.	Clive	IA	Preferred Stock w/ Exercised Warrants	$2,400,000	Par	N/A		
CPP	(b)	2/27/2009	Private Bancorporation, Inc.	Minnea-polis	MN	Preferred Stock w/ Exercised Warrants	$4,960,000	Par	N/A		
CPP	(b)	2/27/2009	Regent Capital Corporation	Nowata	OK	Preferred Stock w/ Exercised Warrants	$2,655,000	Par	N/A		

Table C.1. (Continued)

			Seller			Purchase Details				Capital Re-payment Details	
Program	Note	Purchase Date	Name of Institution	City	State	Investment Description	Investment Price	Pricing Mechanism	Market Capitalization as of 3/31/2009	Capital Repayment Date	Capital Repayment Amount (f)
CPP	(b)	2/27/2009	Central Bancorp, Inc.	Garland	TX	Preferred Sto-ck w/ Exerc-ised Warrants	$22,500,000	Par	N/A		
CPP	(b)	2/27/2009	Medallion Bank	Salt Lake City	UT	Preferred Stock w/ Exercised Warrants	$11,800,000	Par	N/A		
CPP	(b)	2/27/2009	PSB Financial Corporation	Many	LA	Preferred Stock w/ Exercised Warrants	$9,270,000	Par	N/A		
CPP	(b)	2/27/2009	Avenue Financial Holdings, Inc.	Nashville	TN	Preferred Stock w/ Exercised Warrants	$7,400,000	Par	N/A		
CPP	(b)	2/27/2009	Howard Bancorp, Inc.	Ellicott City	MD	Preferred Stock w/ Exercised Warrants	$5,983,000	Par	N/A		
CPP	(b)	2/27/2009	FNB Bancorp	South San Francisco	CA	Preferred Stock w/ Exercised Warrants	$12,000,000	Par	N/A		
CPP	(b)	2/27/2009	The Victory Bank	Limerick	PA	Preferred Stock w/ Exercised Warrants	$541,000	Par	N/A		
CPP	(b)	2/27/2009	Catskill Hudson Bancorp, Inc	Rock Hill	NY	Preferred Stock w/ Exercised Warrants	$3,000,000	Par	N/A		

Table C.1. (Continued)

			Seller			Purchase Details				Capital Re-payment Details	
Program	Note	Purchase Date	Name of Institution	City	State	Investment Description	Investment Price	Pricing Mechanism	Market Capitalization as of 3/31/2009	Capital Repayment Date	Capital Repayment Amount (f)
CPP	(b)	2/27/2009	Midtown Bank & Trust Company	Atlanta	GA	Preferred Stock w/ Exercised Warrants	$5,222,000	Par	N/A		
CPP		3/6/2009	HCSB Financial Corporation	Loris	SC	Preferred Stock w/Warrants	$12,895,000	Par	$41,694,870		
CPP		3/6/2009	First Busey Corporation	Urbana	IL	Preferred Stock w/Warrants	$100,000,000	Par	$277,931,320		
CPP		3/6/2009	First Federal Bancshares of Arkansas, Inc.	Harrison	AR	Preferred Stock w/Warrants	$16,500,000	Par	$22,780,900		
CPP	(c)	3/6/2009	Citizens Bancshares Corporation	Atlanta	GA	Preferred Stock	$7,462,000	Par	$6,521,820		
CPP	(b)	3/6/2009	ICB Financial	Ontario	CA	Preferred Stock w/ Exercised Warrants	$6,000,000	Par	N/A		
CPP	(b)	3/6/2009	First Texas BHC, Inc.	Fort Worth	TX	Preferred Stock w/ Exercised Warrants	$13,533,000	Par	N/A		
CPP	(b)	3/6/2009	Farmers & Merchants Bancshares, Inc.	Houston	TX	Preferred Stock w/ Exercised Warrants	$11,000,000	Par	N/A		
CPP	(b)	3/6/2009	Blue Ridge Bancshares, Inc.	Indepen-dence	MO	Preferred Sto-ck w/ Exer-cised Warrants	$12,000,000	Par	N/A		

Table C.1. (Continued)

			Seller			Purchase Details				Capital Re-payment Details	
Program	**Note**	**Purchase Date**	**Name of Institution**	**City**	**State**	**Investment Description**	**Investment Price**	**Pricing Mechanism**	**Market Capitalization as of 3/31/2009**	**Capital Repayment Date**	**Capital Repayment Amount (f)**
CPP	(b)	3/6/2009	First Reliance Bancshares, Inc.	Florence	SC	Preferred Stock w/ Exercised Warrants	$15,349,000	Par	N/A		
CPP	(b)	3/6/2009	First Southwest Bancorporation, Inc.	Alamosa	CO	Preferred Stock w/ Exercised Warrants	$5,500,000	Par	N/A		
CPP	(b)	3/6/2009	Germantown Capital Corporation, Inc.	German-town	TN	Preferred Stock w/ Exercised Warrants	$4,967,000	Par	N/A		
CPP	(b)	3/6/2009	BOH Holdings, Inc.	Houston	TX	Preferred Stock w/ Exercised Warrants	$10,000,000	Par	N/A		
CPP	(b)	3/6/2009	AmeriBank Holding Company	Collinsville	OK	Preferred Stock w/ Exercised Warrants	$2,492,000	Par	N/A		
CPP	(b)	3/6/2009	Highlands Independent Bancshares, Inc.	Sebring	FL	Preferred Stock w/ Exercised Warrants	$6,700,000	Par	N/A		
CPP	(b)	3/6/2009	Pinnacle Bank Holding Company, Inc.	Orange City	FL	Preferred Stock w/ Exercised Warrants	$4,389,000	Par	N/A		
CPP	(b)	3/6/2009	Blue River Bancshares, Inc.	Shelbyville	IN	Preferred Stock w/ Exercised Warrants	$5,000,000	Par	N/A		
CPP	(b)	3/6/2009	Marine Bank & Trust Company	Vero Beach	FL	Preferred Stock w/ Exercised Warrants	$3,000,000	Par	N/A		

Table C.1. (Continued)

			Seller			Purchase Details				Capital Re-payment Details	
Program	Note	Purchase Date	Name of Institution	City	State	Investment Description	Investment Price	Pricing Mechanism	Market Capitalization as of 3/31/2009	Capital Repayment Date	Capital Repayment Amount (f)
CPP	(b)	3/6/2009	Community Bancshares of Kansas, Inc.	Goff	KS	Preferred Stock w/ Exercised Warrants	$500,000	Par	N/A		
CPP	(b)	3/6/2009	Regent Bancorp, Inc.	Davie	FL	Preferred Stock w/ Exercised Warrants	$9,982,000	Par	N/A		
CPP	(b)	3/6/2009	Park Bancorporation, Inc.	Madison	WI	Preferred Stock w/ Exercised Warrants	$23,200,000	Par	N/A		
CPP	(b)	3/6/2009	PeoplesSouth Bancshares, Inc.	Colquitt	GA	Preferred Stock w/ Exercised Warrants	$12,325,000	Par	N/A		
CPP		3/13/2009	First Place Financial Corp.	Warren	OH	Preferred Stock w/Warrants	$72,927,000	Par	$57,029,280		
CPP		3/13/2009	Salisbury Bancorp, Inc.	Lakeville	CT	Preferred Stock w/Warrants	$8,816,000	Par	$41,391,300		
CPP		3/13/2009	First Northern Community Bancorp	Dixon	CA	Preferred Stock w/Warrants	$17,390,000	Par	$43,183,460		
CPP		3/13/2009	Discover Financial Services	Riverwoods	IL	Preferred Stock w/Warrants	$1,224,558,000	Par	$3,038,006,290		
CPP		3/13/2009	Provident Community Bancshares, Inc.	Rock Hill	SC	Preferred Stock w/Warrants	$9,266,000	Par	$4,738,200		
CPP	(c)	3/13/2009	First American International Corp.	Brooklyn	NY	Preferred Stock	$17,000,000	Par	N/A		

Table C.1. (Continued)

			Seller			Purchase Details				Capital Re-payment Details	
Program	Note	Purchase Date	Name of Institution	City	State	Investment Description	Investment Price	Pricing Mechanism	Market Capitalization as of 3/31/2009	Capital Repayment Date	Capital Repayment Amount (f)
CPP	(b)	3/13/2009	BancIndependent, Inc.	Sheffield	AL	Preferred Stock w/ Exercised Warrants	$21,100,000	Par	N/A		
CPP	(b)	3/13/2009	Haviland Bancshares, Inc.	Haviland	KS	Preferred Stock w/ Exercised Warrants	$425,000	Par	N/A		
CPP	(b)	3/13/2009	1st United Bancorp, Inc.	Boca Raton	FL	Preferred Stock w/ Exercised Warrants	$10,000,000	Par	N/A		
CPP	(b)	3/13/2009	Madison Financial Corporation	Richmond	KY	Preferred Stock w/ Exercised Warrants	$3,370,000	Par	N/A		
CPP	(b)	3/13/2009	First National Corporation	Strasburg	VA	Preferred Stock w/ Exercised Warrants	$13,900,000	Par	N/A		
CPP	(b)	3/13/2009	St. Johns Bancshares, Inc.	St. Louis	MO	Preferred Stock w/ Exercised Warrants	$3,000,000	Par	N/A		
CPP	(b)	3/13/2009	Blackhawk Bancorp, Inc.	Beloit	WI	Preferred Stock w/ Exercised Warrants	$10,000,000	Par	N/A		
CPP	(b)	3/13/2009	IBW Financial Corporation	Washington	DC	Preferred Stock w/ Exercised Warrants	$6,000,000	Par	N/A		
CPP	(b)	3/13/2009	Butler Point, Inc.	Catlin	IL	Preferred Stock w/ Exercised Warrants	$607,000	Par	N/A		

Table C.1. (Continued)

			Seller			Purchase Details				Capital Re-payment Details	
Program	Note	Purchase Date	Name of Institution	City	State	Investment Description	Investment Price	Pricing Mechanism	Market Capitalization as of 3/31/2009	Capital Repayment Date	Capital Repayment Amount (f)
CPP	(b)	3/13/2009	Bank of George	Las Vegas	NV	Preferred Stock w/ Exercised Warrants	$2,672,000	Par	N/A		
CPP	(b)	3/13/2009	Moneytree Corporation	Lenoir City	TN	Preferred Sto-ck w/ Exerc-ised Warrants	$9,516,000	Par	N/A		
CPP	(b)	3/13/2009	Sovereign Bancshares, Inc.	Dallas	TX	Preferred Stock w/ Exercised Warrants	$18,215,000	Par	N/A		
CPP	(b)	3/13/2009	First Intercontinental Bank	Doraville	GA	Preferred Stock w/ Exercised Warrants	$6,398,000	Par	N/A		
CPP		3/20/2009	Heritage Oaks Bancorp	Paso Robles	CA	Preferred Stock w/Warrants	$21,000,000	Par	$32,174,950		
CPP	(b)	3/20/2009	Community First Bancshares Inc.	Union City	TN	Preferred Stock w/ Exercised Warrants	$20,000,000	Par	N/A		
CPP	(b)	3/20/2009	First NBC Bank Holding Company	New Orleans	LA	Preferred Stock w/ Exercised Warrants	$17,836,000	Par	N/A		
CPP	(b)	3/20/2009	First Colebrook Bancorp, Inc.	Colebrook	NH	Preferred Stock w/ Exercised Warrants	$4,500,000	Par	N/A		
CPP	(b)	3/20/2009	Kirksville Bancorp, Inc.	Kirksville	MO	Preferred Stock w/ Exercised Warrants	$470,000	Par	N/A		

Table C.1. (Continued)

			Seller			Purchase Details				Capital Re-payment Details	
Program	Note	Purchase Date	Name of Institution	City	State	Investment Description	Investment Price	Pricing Mechanism	Market Capitalization as of 3/31/2009	Capital Repayment Date	Capital Repayment Amount (f)
CPP	(b)	3/20/2009	Peoples Bancshares of TN, Inc	Madiso-nville	TN	Preferred Stock w/ Exercised Warrants	$3,900,000	Par	N/A		
CPP	(b)	3/20/2009	Premier Bank Holding Company	Tallahassee	FL	Preferred Stock w/ Exercised Warrants	$9,500,000	Par	N/A		
CPP	(b)	3/20/2009	Citizens Bank & Trust Company	Covington	LA	Preferred Stock w/ Exercised Warrants	$2,400,000	Par	N/A		
CPP	(b)	3/20/2009	Farmers & Merchants Financial Corporation	Argonia	KS	Preferred Stock w/ Exercised Warrants	$442,000	Par	N/A		
CPP	(b)	3/20/2009	Farmers State Bankshares, Inc.	Holton	KS	Preferred Stock w/ Exercised Warrants	$700,000	Par	N/A		
CPP	(b)	3/27/2009	SBT Bancorp, Inc.	Simsbury	CT	Preferred Stock w/ Exercised Warrants	$4,000,000	Par	N/A		
CPP	(b)	3/27/2009	CSRA Bank Corp.	Wrens	GA	Preferred Stock w/ Exercised Warrants	$2,400,000	Par	N/A		
CPP	(b)	3/27/2009	Trinity Capital Corporation	Los Alamos	NM	Preferred Sto-ck w/ Exer-cised Warrants	$35,539,000	Par	N/A		

Table C.1. (Continued)

			Seller			Purchase Details				Capital Re-payment Details	
Program	Note	Purchase Date	Name of Institution	City	State	Investment Description	Investment Price	Pricing Mechanism	Market Capitalization as of 3/31/2009	Capital Repayment Date	Capital Repayment Amount (f)
CPP	(b)	3/27/2009	Clover Community Bankshares, Inc.	Clover	SC	Preferred Stock w/ Exercised Warrants	$3,000,000	Par	N/A		
CPP	(b)	3/27/2009	Pathway Bancorp	Cairo	NE	Preferred Stock w/ Exercised Warrants	$3,727,000	Par	N/A		
CPP	(b)	3/27/2009	Colonial American Bank	West Conshohocken	PA	Preferred Stock w/ Exercised Warrants	$574,000	Par	N/A		
CPP	(b)	3/27/2009	MS Financial, Inc.	Kingwood	TX	Preferred Stock w/ Exercised Warrants	$7,723,000	Par	N/A		
CPP	(b)	3/27/2009	Triad Bancorp, Inc.	Frontenac	MO	Preferred Stock w/ Exercised Warrants	$3,700,000	Par	N/A		
CPP	(b)	3/27/2009	Alpine Banks of Colorado	Glenwood Springs	CO	Preferred Stock w/ Exercised Warrants	$70,000,000	Par	N/A		
CPP	(b)	3/27/2009	Naples Bancorp, Inc.	Naples	FL	Preferred Stock w/ Exercised Warrants	$4,000,000	Par	N/A		
CPP	(b)	3/27/2009	CBS Banc-Corp.	Russellville	AL	Preferred Stock w/ Exercised Warrants	$24,300,000	Par	N/A		
CPP	(b)	3/27/2009	IBT Bancorp, Inc.	Irving	TX	Preferred Stock w/ Exercised Warrants	$2,295,000	Par	N/A		

Table C.1. (Continued)

			Seller			Purchase Details				Capital Re-payment Details	
Program	Note	Purchase Date	Name of Institution	City	State	Investment Description	Investment Price	Pricing Mechanism	Market Capitalization as of 3/31/2009	Capital Repayment Date	Capital Repayment Amount (f)
CPP	(b)	3/27/2009	Spirit BankCorp, Inc.	Bristow	OK	Preferred Stock w/ Exercised Warrants	$30,000,000	Par	N/A		
CPP	(b)	3/27/2009	Maryland Financial Bank	Towson	MD	Preferred Stock w/ Exercised Warrants	$1,700,000	Par	N/A		
SSFI		11/25/2008	AIG	New York	NY	Preferred Stock w/ Warrants	$40,000,000,000	Par	$2,690,747,000		
AIFP		12/29/2008	GMAC LLC	Detroit	MI	Preferred Stock w/ Exercised Warrants	$5,000,000,000	Liquidation Preference	N/A		
AIFP	(g)	12/29/2008	General Motors Corporation	Detroit	MI	Debt Obligation	$884,024,131	N/A	$1,184,373,880		
AIFP		12/31/2008	General Motors Corporation	Detroit	MI	Debt Obligation w/ Warrants and Additional Note	$13,400,000,000	N/A	$1,184,373,880		
AIFP		1/2/2009	Chrysler Holding LLC	Auburn Hills	MI	Debt Oblig-ation w/ Add-itional Note	$4,000,000,000	N/A	NA		
AIFP	(h)	1/16/2009	Chrysler Financial Services Americas LLC	Farmington Hills	MI	Debt Obligation w/ Additional Note	$1,500,000,000	N/A	NA		
TIP		12/31/2008	Citigroup Inc.	New York	NY	Preferred Stock w/ Warrants	$20,000,000,000	Par	$13,947,814,100		

Table C.1. (Continued)

			Seller			Purchase Details				Capital Re-payment Details	
Program	**Note**	**Purchase Date**	**Name of Institution**	**City**	**State**	**Investment Description**	**Investment Price**	**Pricing Mechanism**	**Market Capitalization as of 3/31/2009**	**Capital Repayment Date**	**Capital Repayment Amount (f)**
TIP		1/16/2009	Bank of America Corporation	Charlotte	NC	Preferred Stock w/ Warrants	$20,000,000,000	Par	$43,657,466,160		
AGP	(j)	1/16/2009	Citigroup Inc.	New York	NY	Preferred Stock and Warrants	$5,000,000,000	N/A	$13,947,814,100		
CBLI	(i)	3/3/2009	TALF LLC	Wilmington	DE	Debt Obligation w/Additional Note	$20,000,000,000	N/A	N/A		
TOTA L							**$328,553,711,131**			**$353,000, 000**	

Notes:

(a) This transaction was included in previous Transactions Reports with Merrill Lynch & Co., Inc. listed as the qualifying institution and a 10/28/2008 transaction date, footnoted to indicate that settlement was deferred pending merger. The purchase of Merrill Lynch by Bank of America was completed on 1/1/2009, and this transaction under the CPP was funded on 1/9/2009.

(b) Privately-held quali= ed = nancial institution; Treasury received a warrant to purchase additional shares of preferred stock, which it exercised immediately.

(c) To promote community development = nancial institutions (CDFIs), Treasury does not require warrants as part of its investment in certi= ed CDFIs when the size of the investment is $50 million or less.

(d) Repayment pursuant to Title VII, Section 7001(g) of the American Recovery and Reinvestment Act of 2009.

(e) Redemption pursuant to a quali= ed equity offering.

(f) This amount does not include accrued and unpaid dividends, which must be paid at the time of capital repayment.

(g) Treasury committed to lend General Motors Corporation up to $1,000,000,000. The ultimate level of funding was dependent upon the level of investor participation in GMAC LLC's rights offering. The amount has been updated to rel ect the = nal level of funding.

(h) The loan was funded through Chrysler LB Receivables Trust, a special purpose vehicle created by Chrysler Financial. The Amount of $1,500,000,000 represents the maximum loan amount. The loan will be incrementally funded.

(i) The loan was funded through TALF LLC, a special purpose vehicle created by The Federal Reserve Bank of New York. The amount of $20,000,000,000 represents the maximum loan amount. The loan will be incrementally funded.

(j) Transaction type is a guarantee instead of a purchase.

Source: Transactions: Treasury, Transactions Report, 3/31/2009, www.= nancialstability.gov, accessed 4/9/2009; Market Capitalization: Capital IQ, Inc. (a division of Standard & Poor's), www.capitaliq.com, accessed 4/2/2009 at 2:00 pm EST.

Key:
CPP Capital Purchase Program
SSFI Systemically Signi= cant Failing Institution Program
AIFP Automotive Industry Financing Program
TIP Targeted Investment Program
AGP Asset Guarantee Program
CBLI Consumer and Business Lending Initiative Investment Program

C. Explanation of the Secretary

In its data call response, Treasury provided SIGTARP with determinations signed by the Treasury Secretary since SIGTARP's Initial Report. These determinations relate to the following programs:[17]

TALF
Auto Supplier Support Program
Home Affordable Modification Program ("HAMP")

Please refer to part A of this appendix for details provided on Treasury's website regarding the purpose of each program and part B for a listing of troubled asset purchases.

D. Financial Institutions

See part B of this appendix.

E. Listing and Detailed Biographical Information of Asset Manager[18]

In response to SIGTARP's data call question regarding this reporting requirement, Treasury stated:

The *Office of Financial Stability recently hired an asset manager* [EARNEST Partners] *for the Small Business Initiative* [Unlocking Credit for Small Businesses] *on March 16, 2009. As of March 31, 2009, OFS has not yet hired asset managers for any other TARP programs.*

EARNEST Partners is an employee-owned firm that has been managing institutional portfolios for almost 20 years. EARNEST Partners manage a broad range of equity, fixed income, and alternative asset portfolios for over 350 institutional clients. The firm's investment professionals possess considerable expertise and experience in analyzing not only the broad fixed income market but also several niche areas, including a long-standing and significant portfolio involvement with issues guaranteed by the Small Business Administration (SBA).

F. Summary of TARP Transactions by Program[19]

In response to SIGTARP's data call question regarding this reporting requirement, Treasury stated:

The Transactions Report that provides this information as of March 31, 2009 was posted on April 2, 2009.

As of March 31, 2009, no troubled assets have been sold, except for preferred stock repurchased by certain recipients of investments under the CPP. Treasury has received $353 million in principal and $2.3 million in accrued and unpaid dividends from the repurchase of *senior preferred shares by five financial institutions that participated in the CPP. Participants that are interested in repurchasing their senior preferred shares are required to repurchase these assets at par (i.e., the purchase price paid by Treasury). Therefore, Treasury has not taken a loss on the repurchase of senior preferred shares.*

As of March 31, 2009, Treasury continues to hold the warrants received from the four publicly traded financial institutions that repurchased preferred shares. Treasury also continues to hold the warrant preferred shares received upon exercise of the warrant from the one private financial institution that completed a repurchase transaction. Treasury is waiting to hear from the issuers whether they will invoke their right to purchase the warrants before they are offered for sale to a third-party. If the issuers choose not to exercise this right within 15 calendar days, Treasury will liquidate the warrants. The private institution has notified Treasury that it will repurchase its warrant preferred shares at their aggregate liquidation preference. Treasury will receive a profit from the sale of these assets, regardless of the final purchaser, since the Treasury did not incur any additional cost to acquire them.

SIGTARP will provide more information on this in its next quarterly report.

Table C.2 provides a summary of the total amount of troubled assets purchased and held on Treasury's books as of March 31, 2009.

G. Insurance Contracts[20]

In response to SIGTARP's data call question regarding this reporting requirement, Treasury stated:

On January 16, 2009, TARP closed on the guarantee transaction with Citigroup, as announced in a joint statement by the Treasury, Federal Reserve and FDIC on November 23, 2008. No other insurance contracts have been issued as of March 31, 2009.

Details of the terms and conditions of the Citigroup transaction are included in the Institution-Specific Assistance part of Section 2: "TARP Implementation."

H. Detailed Statement of Expenditures and Revenues

See part B of this appendix for Purchases and see part F of this appendix for TARP Transactions.

In response to SIGTARP's data call question regarding this reporting requirement, Treasury stated:

Treasury provides information about TARP purchases, obligations, expenditures, and revenues on Treasury's public website. Treasury posts a transaction report for each purchase of troubled assets two business days after the transaction. Treasury also posts a detailed financial statement as part of its report under section 105(a) of EESA.

Table C.2. Total Amount of Troubled Assets Purchased and Held on Treasury's Books, as of March 31, 2009 ($ Billions)

	Obligations[a]	Expended[b]	On Treasury's Books[c]
Capital Purchase Program ("CPP")	$198.8	$198.8	$198.8
Systemically Significant Failing Institutions ("SSFI")	40.0	40.0	40.0
Targeted Investment Program ("TIP")	40.0	40.0	40.0
Automotive Industry Financing Program ("AIFP")[d]	24.8	24.5	24.5
Asset Guarantee Program ("AGP")	5.0	-	-
Term Asset-Backed Securities Loan Facility ("TALF")[e]	20.0	0.1	0.1
TOTAL	**$328.6**	**$303.4**	**$303.4**

Note: Numbers affected by rounding.

a From a budgetary perspective, what Treasury has committed to spend (*e.g.* signed agreements with TARP recipients).

b Represents TARP cash that has left the Treasury.

c All assets are currently carried at par value.

d Treasury's $1.5 billion loan to Chrysler Financial represents the maximum loan amount. This $1.5 billion has not been fully expended because the loan will be funded incrementally at $100 million per week. As of 3/31/2009, $1,175 million out of the $1.5 billion has been funded.

e TALF falls under the Consumer and Business Lending Initiative. Treasury's $20 billion obligation to TALF represents the maximum obligated amount. This $20 billion has not been fully expended because the loan will be funded as needed by TALF. As of 3/31/2009, $100 million out of the $20 billion has been funded.

Sources: Treasury, *Transactions Report*, 4/02/2009, accessed 4/2/2009; Treasury, response to SIGTARP data call, 4/9/2009.

Table C.3. TARP Administrative Expenditures and Obligations

Budget Object Class Title	Obligations for Period Ending 3/31/2009	Expenditures for Period Ending 3/31/2009
PERSONNEL SERVICES		
Personnel Compensation & Benefits	$3,830,093	$2,902,514
TOTAL PERSONNEL SERVICES	**$3,830,093**	**$2,902,514**
NON-PERSONNEL SERVICES		
Travel & Transportation of Persons	$28,714	$19,831
Transportation of Things	–	–
Rents, Communications, Utilities & Misc. Charges	598,902	534,152
Printing & Reproduction	395	$395
Other Services	25,186,838	9,567,209

Table C.3. (Continued)

Budget Object Class Title	Obligations for Period Ending 3/31/2009	Expenditures for Period Ending 3/31/2009
Supplies & Materials	209,446	87,790
Equipment	89,887	89,887
Land & Structures	103,878	97,522
TOTAL NON-PERSONNEL SERVICES	**$26,218,059**	**$10,396,785**
TOTAL	**$30,048,152**	**$13,299,298**

Note: Numbers affected by rounding.

Source: Treasury, response to SIGTARP data call, 4/8/2009.

Table C.4. TARP Programmatic Expenditures ($ Millions)

Vendor Name	Expenditures as of 3/31/2009
The Bank of New York Mellon Corporation	$5.7
Cadwalader Wickersham & Taft, LLP	0.4
Ennis Knupp & Associates, Inc.	1.2
Hughes Hubbard & Reed, LLP	1.9
Locke Lord Bissell & Liddell, LLP	0.4
Pension Benefit Guaranty Corporation	2.0
Simpson Thacher & Bartlett MNP, LLP	1.4
Sonnenschein Nath & Rosenthal, LLP	2.7
Squire Sanders & Dempsey, LLP	1.8
Sonnenschein Nath & Rosenthal, LLP (formerly Thacher Profitt & Wood)	0.1
The Boston Consulting Group	0.9
Venable, LLP	0.7
Freddie Mac	–
Fannie Mae	–
EARNEST Partners	–
Haynes and Boone, LLP	–
McKee Nelson, LLP	–
TOTAL	**$19.1**

Note: Numbers affected by rounding. Data as of 3/31/2009.

Source: Treasury, response to SIGTARP data call, 4/8/2009.

Table C.5.Dividend and Interest Payments, by Program ($ Millions)

Program	**Amount**
CPP	$2,517.9
SSFI	–
TIP	328.9
AGP	26.9
AIFP	250.6
TOTAL	$3,124.3

Note: Numbers affected by rounding. Data as of 3/31/2009.

Source: Treasury, response to SIGTARP data call, 4/8/2009.

Treasury stated that it has incurred $13.3 million in TARP- related administrative expenditures through March 31, 2009. Table C.3 summarizes actual administrative TARP expenditures as of March 31, 2009.

In addition to administrative expenditures, Treasury has released the details of programmatic expenditures. These expenditures include costs to hire financial agents and legal firms associated with TARP operations. Table C.4 indicates the allocation of these programmatic costs as of March 31, 2009.

As of March 31, 2009, revenue to date has been received from various programs; the breakdown of such revenue is provided in Table C.5.

D. Principal/Income Transaction Report

This appendix provides a copy of the TARP Principal/Income Transaction Report, as of March 31, 2009. Treasury provided this document in its April 8, 2009, response to the SIGTARP data call.

Troubled Asset Relief Program Principal/Income Transaction Report

Payment Date	CUSIP	QFI Name	Program ID	Payment Type	Amount
AGP					
17-Feb-2009	17296C985	CITIGROUP INC	24	DIVIDEND PAYMENT	26,893,333.33
					26,893,333.33
AIFP					
17-Feb-2009	361859960	GMAC LLC	AIF0002	DIVIDEND PAYMENT	2,875,000.00
17-Feb-2009	361859986	GMAC LLC	AIF0002	DIVIDEND PAYMENT	51,111,111.11
17-Mar-2009	1712J19A6	CHRYSLER FINANCIAL SERVICES AMERICAS LLC	AIF0004	INTEREST PAYMENT	898,751.74
17-Mar-2009	1712J19A6	CHRYSLER FINANCIAL SERVICES AMERICAS LLC	AIF0004	PRINCIPAL PAYMENT	3,499,054.95
17-Mar-2009	1712J19B4	CHRYSLER FINANCIAL SERVICES AMERICAS LLC	AIF0004	INTEREST PAYMENT	33,218.75
31-Mar-2009	1712J89A1	CHRYSLER HOLDINGS LLC	AIF0003	INTEREST PAYMENT	48,888,888.89
31-Mar-2009	1712J89B9	CHRYSLER HOLDINGS LLC	AIF0003	INTEREST PAYMENT	3,263,333.33
31-Mar-2009	3704269M2	GENERAL MOTORS CORPORATION	AIF0001	INTEREST PAYMENT	9,085,803.57
31-Mar-2009	3704429B3	GENERAL MOTORS CORPORATION	AIF0001	INTEREST PAYMENT	125,083,333.93
31-Mar-2009	3704429E7	GENERAL MOTORS CORPORATION	AIF0001	INTEREST PAYMENT	9,356,970.50
					254,095,466.77
CPP					
01-Dec-2008	46625H894	JPMORGAN CHASE AND CO	29	DIVIDEND PAYMENT	114,583,333.33

Payment Date	CUSIP	QFI Name	Program ID	Payment Type	Amount
15-Dec-2008	857477897	STATE STREET CORPORATION	20	DIVIDEND PAYMENT	13,055,555.56
15-Dec-2008	867914608	SUNTRUST BANKS, INC.	5	DIVIDEND PAYMENT	15,069,444.44
22-Dec-2008	06426P982	BANK OF NEW YORK MELLON	15	DIVIDEND PAYMENT	21,666,666.67
15-Jan-2009	617446943	MORGAN STANLEY	18	DIVIDEND PAYMENT	106,944,444.00
12-Feb-2009	096065982	BLUE VALLEY BAN CORP	118	DIVIDEND PAYMENT	211,458.33
12-Feb-2009	702898966	PATAPSCO BANCORP, INC.	289	DIVIDEND PAYMENT	4,200.00
12-Feb-2009	702898982	PATAPSCO BANCORP, INC.	289	DIVIDEND PAYMENT	46,666.67
12-Feb-2009	882559966	TEXAS NATIONAL BANCORPORATION INC.	376	DIVIDEND PAYMENT	1,791.00
12-Feb-2009	882559982	TEXAS NATIONAL BANCORPORATION INC.	376	DIVIDEND PAYMENT	19,905.00
13-Feb-2009	029851961	AMERICAN STATE BANCSHARES, INC.	74	DIVIDEND PAYMENT	2,700.00
13-Feb-2009	029851987	AMERICAN STATE BANCSHARES, INC.	74	DIVIDEND PAYMENT	30,000.00
13-Feb-2009	03074A987	AMERISERV FINANCIAL, INC.	207	DIVIDEND PAYMENT	163,333.33
13-Feb-2009	063425201	BANK OF MARIN BANCORP	127	DIVIDEND PAYMENT	272,222.22
13-Feb-2009	101119972	BOSTON PRIVATE FINANCIAL	72	DIVIDEND PAYMENT	1,796,666.67
13-Feb-2009	108030982	BRIDGE CAPITAL HOLDINGS	115	DIVIDEND PAYMENT	172,351.11
13-Feb-2009	126600980	CVB FINANCIAL CORP.	106	DIVIDEND PAYMENT	1,263,888.89
13-Feb-2009	15201P984	CENTERSTATE BANKS OF FLORIDA INC.	23	DIVIDEND PAYMENT	325,208.33
13-Feb-2009	152418984	CENTRAL BANCORP, INC	133	DIVIDEND PAYMENT	97,222.22
13-Feb-2009	15346Q988	CENTRAL FEDERAL CORPORATION	123	DIVIDEND PAYMENT	70,243.06
13-Feb-2009	15643B981	CENTRUE FINANCIAL CORPORATION	248	DIVIDEND PAYMENT	163,340.00
13-Feb-2009	268253986	ECB BANCORP, INC.	349	DIVIDEND PAYMENT	72,294.58
13-Feb-2009	277196200	EASTERN VIRGINIA BANKSHARES, INC.	250	DIVIDEND PAYMENT	120,000.00
13-Feb-2009	289660987	THE ELMIRA SAVINGS BANK, FSB	293	DIVIDEND PAYMENT	70,700.00
13-Feb-2009	290828201	EMCLAIRE FINANCIAL CORP.	173	DIVIDEND PAYMENT	54,166.67
13-Feb-2009	302549969	FPB FINANCIAL CORP.	506	DIVIDEND PAYMENT	891.00
13-Feb-2009	302549985	FPB FINANCIAL CORP.	506	DIVIDEND PAYMENT	9,900.00
13-Feb-2009	309562981	FARMERS CAPITAL BANK CORPORATION	85	DIVIDEND PAYMENT	150,000.00

(Continued)

Payment Date	CUSIP	QFI Name	Program ID	Payment Type	Amount
13-Feb-2009	32022D983	FIRST FINANCIAL SERVICE CORPORATION	342	DIVIDEND PAYMENT	100,000.00
13-Feb-2009	320724982	FIRST LITCHFIELD FINANCIAL CORPORATION	185	DIVIDEND PAYMENT	87,500.00
13-Feb-2009	404172983	HF FINANCIAL CORP.	10	DIVIDEND PAYMENT	291,666.67
13-Feb-2009	426927984	HERITAGE COMMERCE CORP	55	DIVIDEND PAYMENT	466,666.67
13-Feb-2009	453397960	INDEPENDENCE BANK	203	DIVIDEND PAYMENT	477.00
13-Feb-2009	453397986	INDEPENDENCE BANK	203	DIVIDEND PAYMENT	5,325.00
13-Feb-2009	591650981	METROCORP BANCSHARES, INC.	440	DIVIDEND PAYMENT	181,250.00
13-Feb-2009	60520E989	MISSION VALLEY BANCORP	139	DIVIDEND PAYMENT	39,722.22
13-Feb-2009	60907Q985	MONARCH FINANCIAL HOLDINGS, INC.	233	DIVIDEND PAYMENT	114,333.33
13-Feb-2009	63080P980	NARA BANCORP, INC.	88	DIVIDEND PAYMENT	781,666.67
13-Feb-2009	65080T987	NEWBRIDGE BANCORP	141	DIVIDEND PAYMENT	458,255.00
13-Feb-2009	671807980	OAK VALLEY BANCORP	205	DIVIDEND PAYMENT	131,250.00
13-Feb-2009	67984M985	OLD LINE BANCSHARES, INC.	159	DIVIDEND PAYMENT	68,055.56
13-Feb-2009	69444Q986	PACIFIC INTERNATIONAL BANCORP	67	DIVIDEND PAYMENT	56,875.00
13-Feb-2009	72650P965	PLAINS CAPITAL CORPORATION	41	DIVIDEND PAYMENT	61,348.00
13-Feb-2009	72650P981	PLAINS CAPITAL CORPORATION	41	DIVIDEND PAYMENT	681,574.44
13-Feb-2009	742282981	PRINCETON NATIONAL BANCORP, INC.	372	DIVIDEND PAYMENT	76,642.50
13-Feb-2009	75777X969	REDWOOD CAPITAL BANCORP	389	DIVIDEND PAYMENT	1,377.50
13-Feb-2009	75777X985	REDWOOD CAPITAL BANCORP	389	DIVIDEND PAYMENT	15,305.56
13-Feb-2009	811707405	SEACOAST BANKING CORPORATION OF FLORIDA	175	DIVIDEND PAYMENT	388,888.89
13-Feb-2009	834728982	SOMERSET HILLS BANCORP	269	DIVIDEND PAYMENT	29,861.94
13-Feb-2009	84223P984	SOUTHERN BANCORP, INC.	490	DIVIDEND PAYMENT	44,305.56
13-Feb-2009	85856G209	STELLARONE CORPORATION	237	DIVIDEND PAYMENT	233,333.33
13-Feb-2009	887098986	TIMBERLAND BANCORP, INC.	365	DIVIDEND PAYMENT	120,185.00
13-Feb-2009	904214988	UMPQUA HOLDINGS CORP	14	DIVIDEND PAYMENT	2,707,009.86
13-Feb-2009	937303980	WASHINGTON BANKING COMPANY	157	DIVIDEND PAYMENT	106,252.78
13-Feb-2009	958372963	WESTERN ILLINOIS BANCSHARES, INC.	6	DIVIDEND PAYMENT	4,459.00

Payment Date	CUSIP	QFI Name	Program ID	Payment Type	Amount
13-Feb-2009	958372989	WESTERN ILLINOIS BANCSHARES, INC.	6	DIVIDEND PAYMENT	49,508.33
13-Feb-2009	97186T983	WILSHIRE BANCORP, INC.	158	DIVIDEND PAYMENT	543,882.50
17-Feb-2009	00037W981	AB&T FINANCIAL CORPORATION	379	DIVIDEND PAYMENT	10,694.44
17-Feb-2009	011634961	ALARION FINANCIAL SERVICES, INC.	378	DIVIDEND PAYMENT	1,793.00
17-Feb-2009	011634987	ALARION FINANCIAL SERVICES, INC.	378	DIVIDEND PAYMENT	19,903.89
17-Feb-2009	019205988	ALLIANCE FINANCIAL CORPORATION	311	DIVIDEND PAYMENT	209,362.22
17-Feb-2009	025816950	AMERICAN EXPRESS COMPANY	232	DIVIDEND PAYMENT	16,944,450.00
17-Feb-2009	03076K983	AMERIS BANCORP	58	DIVIDEND PAYMENT	606,666.67
17-Feb-2009	045487980	ASSOCIATED BANC-CORP	76	DIVIDEND PAYMENT	6,125,000.00
17-Feb-2009	054937958	BB AND T CORP	12	DIVIDEND PAYMENT	39,605,727.78
17-Feb-2009	055367981	BCSB BANCORP, INC.	294	DIVIDEND PAYMENT	78,000.00
17-Feb-2009	05566T986	BNC BANCORP	128	DIVIDEND PAYMENT	303,916.67
17-Feb-2009	055936967	BNCCORP, INC.	483	DIVIDEND PAYMENT	7,286.25
17-Feb-2009	055936983	BNCCORP, INC.	483	DIVIDEND PAYMENT	80,930.14
17-Feb-2009	059690982	BANCORP RHODE ISLAND, INC.	255	DIVIDEND PAYMENT	233,333.33
17-Feb-2009	05969A980	THE BANCORP, INC.	149	DIVIDEND PAYMENT	395,675.00
17-Feb-2009	05978R974	BANCTRUST FINANCIAL GROUP, INC.	131	DIVIDEND PAYMENT	388,888.89
17-Feb-2009	060505450	BANK OF AMERICA CORPORATION	38	DIVIDEND PAYMENT	50,000,000.00
17-Feb-2009	060505963	BANK OF AMERICA	21	DIVIDEND PAYMENT	222,916,666.67
17-Feb-2009	061590964	BANK OF COMMERCE	458	DIVIDEND PAYMENT	1,087.50
17-Feb-2009	061590980	BANK OF COMMERCE	458	DIVIDEND PAYMENT	12,083.33
17-Feb-2009	063904981	BANK OF THE OZARKS, INC.	130	DIVIDEND PAYMENT	656,250.00
17-Feb-2009	06424J988	BANK OF COMMERCE HOLDINGS	1	DIVIDEND PAYMENT	214,861.11
17-Feb-2009	066440967	BANKFIRST CAPITAL CORPORATION	461	DIVIDEND PAYMENT	4,262.50
17-Feb-2009	066440983	BANKFIRST CAPITAL CORPORATION	461	DIVIDEND PAYMENT	47,361.11
17-Feb-2009	06652V984	BANNER CORPORATION/BANNER BANK	63	DIVIDEND PAYMENT	1,446,666.67
17-Feb-2009	066849985	BAR HARBOR BANKSHARES	256	DIVIDEND PAYMENT	75,524.86

(Continued)

Payment Date	CUSIP	QFI Name	Program ID	Payment Type	Amount
17-Feb-2009	067021964	THE BARABOO BANCORPORATION, INC.	443	DIVIDEND PAYMENT	7,518.25
17-Feb-2009	067021980	THE BARABOO BANCORPORATION, INC.	443	DIVIDEND PAYMENT	83,572.36
17-Feb-2009	10855P968	BRIDGEVIEW BANCORP, INC.	253	DIVIDEND PAYMENT	26,600.00
17-Feb-2009	10855P984	BRIDGEVIEW BANCORP, INC.	253	DIVIDEND PAYMENT	295,555.56
17-Feb-2009	11144L982	BROADWAY FEDERAL BANK	7	DIVIDEND PAYMENT	113,750.00
17-Feb-2009	12466Q989	C&F FINANCIAL CORPORATION	324	DIVIDEND PAYMENT	100,000.00
17-Feb-2009	125581983	CIT GROUP INC.	247	DIVIDEND PAYMENT	14,562,500.00
17-Feb-2009	127171965	CACHE VALLEY BANKING COMPANY	314	DIVIDEND PAYMENT	3,094.00
17-Feb-2009	127171981	CACHE VALLEY BANKING COMPANY	314	DIVIDEND PAYMENT	34,428.33
17-Feb-2009	12738A986	CADENCE FINANCIAL CORPORATION	300	DIVIDEND PAYMENT	220,000.00
17-Feb-2009	130496961	CALIFORNIA OAKS STATE BANK	418	DIVIDEND PAYMENT	907.50
17-Feb-2009	130496987	CALIFORNIA OAKS STATE BANK	418	DIVIDEND PAYMENT	10,083.33
17-Feb-2009	131601965	CALVERT FINANCIAL CORPORATION	432	DIVIDEND PAYMENT	286.00
17-Feb-2009	131601981	CALVERT FINANCIAL CORPORATION	432	DIVIDEND PAYMENT	3,168.61
17-Feb-2009	13169Q961	CALWEST BANCORP	219	DIVIDEND PAYMENT	1,281.50
17-Feb-2009	13169Q987	CALWEST BANCORP	219	DIVIDEND PAYMENT	14,226.67
17-Feb-2009	139741961	CAPITAL BANCORP, INC.	307	DIVIDEND PAYMENT	3,055.00
17-Feb-2009	139741987	CAPITAL BANCORP, INC.	307	DIVIDEND PAYMENT	33,944.44
17-Feb-2009	139793988	CAPITAL BANK CORPORATION	61	DIVIDEND PAYMENT	361,191.25
17-Feb-2009	14040N979	CAPITAL ONE FINANCIAL CORP	22	DIVIDEND PAYMENT	44,933,765.14
17-Feb-2009	14042V961	CAPITAL PACIFIC BANCORP	64	DIVIDEND PAYMENT	2,600.00
17-Feb-2009	14042V987	CAPITAL PACIFIC BANCORP	64	DIVIDEND PAYMENT	28,888.89
17-Feb-2009	143785988	CAROLINA BANK HOLDINGS, INC.	338	DIVIDEND PAYMENT	80,000.00
17-Feb-2009	146875208	CARVER BANCORP, INC.	413	DIVIDEND PAYMENT	76,447.22
17-Feb-2009	147272983	CASCADE FINANCIAL CORPORATION	65	DIVIDEND PAYMENT	454,650.00
17-Feb-2009	149150989	CATHAY GENERAL BANCORP	103	DIVIDEND PAYMENT	2,508,333.33
17-Feb-2009	149841983	CECIL BANCORP, INC.	192	DIVIDEND PAYMENT	83,488.89

Payment Date	CUSIP	QFI Name	Program ID	Payment Type	Amount
17-Feb-2009	151408978	CENTER BANCORP, INC.	304	DIVIDEND PAYMENT	50,000.00
17-Feb-2009	15146R988	CENTER FINANCIAL CORPORATION	132	DIVIDEND PAYMENT	481,250.00
17-Feb-2009	15234K960	CENTRA FINANCIAL HOLDINGS, INC.	257	DIVIDEND PAYMENT	5,437.50
17-Feb-2009	15234K986	CENTRA FINANCIAL HOLDINGS, INC.	257	DIVIDEND PAYMENT	60,416.67
17-Feb-2009	153770987	CENTRAL JERSEY BANCORP	371	DIVIDEND PAYMENT	81,611.11
17-Feb-2009	154760987	CENTRAL PACIFIC FINANCIAL CORP.	241	DIVIDEND PAYMENT	675,000.00
17-Feb-2009	172922981	CITIZENS & NORTHERN CORPORATION	419	DIVIDEND PAYMENT	106,494.44
17-Feb-2009	172967499	CITIGROUP INC	24	DIVIDEND PAYMENT	371,527,777.78
17-Feb-2009	17315R963	CITIZENS BANCORP	325	DIVIDEND PAYMENT	6,760.00
17-Feb-2009	17315R989	CITIZENS BANCORP	325	DIVIDEND PAYMENT	75,111.11
17-Feb-2009	174420984	CITIZENS REPUBLIC BANCORP, INC.	116	DIVIDEND PAYMENT	2,625,000.00
17-Feb-2009	174532960	CITIZENS COMMUNITY BANK	164	DIVIDEND PAYMENT	1,950.00
17-Feb-2009	174532986	CITIZENS COMMUNITY BANK	164	DIVIDEND PAYMENT	21,666.67
17-Feb-2009	17462Q982	CITIZENS FIRST CORPORATION	339	DIVIDEND PAYMENT	68,281.11
17-Feb-2009	176682979	CITIZENS SOUTH BANKING CORPORATION	195	DIVIDEND PAYMENT	179,375.00
17-Feb-2009	178566972	CITY NATIONAL CORPORATION	25	DIVIDEND PAYMENT	4,666,666.67
17-Feb-2009	19041N985	COASTAL BANKING COMPANY, INC.	90	DIVIDEND PAYMENT	96,736.11
17-Feb-2009	190897967	COBIZ FINANCIAL INC.	166	DIVIDEND PAYMENT	501,277.78
17-Feb-2009	192025989	CODORUS VALLEY BANCORP, INC.	358	DIVIDEND PAYMENT	82,500.00
17-Feb-2009	19623P986	COLONY BANKCORP, INC.	259	DIVIDEND PAYMENT	140,000.00
17-Feb-2009	197236979	COLUMBIA BANKING SYSTEM, INC.	66	DIVIDEND PAYMENT	897,143.33
17-Feb-2009	200340206	COMERICA INC.	16	DIVIDEND PAYMENT	28,437,500.00
17-Feb-2009	202750964	COMMONWEALTH BUSINESS BANK	57	DIVIDEND PAYMENT	2,117.50
17-Feb-2009	202750980	COMMONWEALTH BUSINESS BANK	57	DIVIDEND PAYMENT	23,530.83
17-Feb-2009	203612981	COMMUNITY BANKERS TRUST CORPORATION	113	DIVIDEND PAYMENT	137,511.11
17-Feb-2009	20365L985	COMMUNITY FINANCIAL CORPORATION	194	DIVIDEND PAYMENT	98,334.44
17-Feb-2009	203719968	COMMUNITY INVESTORS BANCORP, INC.	284	DIVIDEND PAYMENT	1,690.00

(Continued)

Payment Date	CUSIP	QFI Name	Program ID	Payment Type	Amount
17-Feb-2009	203719984	COMMUNITY INVESTORS BANCORP, INC.	284	DIVIDEND PAYMENT	18,777.78
17-Feb-2009	204154967	COMMUNITY TRUST FINANCIAL CORPORATION	322	DIVIDEND PAYMENT	10,800.00
17-Feb-2009	204154983	COMMUNITY TRUST FINANCIAL CORPORATION	322	DIVIDEND PAYMENT	120,000.00
17-Feb-2009	204157986	COMMUNITY WEST BANCSHARES	82	DIVIDEND PAYMENT	121,333.33
17-Feb-2009	20716N961	CONGAREE BANCSHARES, INC.	384	DIVIDEND PAYMENT	1,476.00
17-Feb-2009	20716N987	CONGAREE BANCSHARES, INC.	384	DIVIDEND PAYMENT	16,425.00
17-Feb-2009	225744978	CRESCENT FINANCIAL CORPORATION	201	DIVIDEND PAYMENT	124,500.00
17-Feb-2009	227647963	CROSSTOWN HOLDING COMPANY	456	DIVIDEND PAYMENT	2,931.50
17-Feb-2009	227647989	CROSSTOWN HOLDING COMPANY	456	DIVIDEND PAYMENT	32,541.67
17-Feb-2009	253238968	DICKINSON FINANCIAL CORP. II	441	DIVIDEND PAYMENT	52,946.75
17-Feb-2009	253238984	DICKINSON FINANCIAL CORP. II	441	DIVIDEND PAYMENT	588,269.03
17-Feb-2009	268948981	EAGLE BANCORP, INC.	84	DIVIDEND PAYMENT	371,729.17
17-Feb-2009	27579R401	EAST WEST BANCORP, INC.	93	DIVIDEND PAYMENT	2,980,308.33
17-Feb-2009	29255V987	ENCORE BANCSHARES INC.	79	DIVIDEND PAYMENT	330,555.56
17-Feb-2009	293712972	ENTERPRISE FINACIAL SERVICES CORP./ ENTERPRISE BANK	135	DIVIDEND PAYMENT	272,222.22
17-Feb-2009	301227963	EXCHANGE BANK	177	DIVIDEND PAYMENT	30,100.00
17-Feb-2009	301227989	EXCHANGE BANK	177	DIVIDEND PAYMENT	334,444.44
17-Feb-2009	30242L967	FFW Corporation	8	DIVIDEND PAYMENT	5,096.00
17-Feb-2009	30242L983	FFW Corporation	8	DIVIDEND PAYMENT	56,692.22
17-Feb-2009	30245D962	FCB BANCORP, INC.	363	DIVIDEND PAYMENT	6,510.00
17-Feb-2009	30245D988	FCB BANCORP, INC.	363	DIVIDEND PAYMENT	72,286.67
17-Feb-2009	302520978	F.N.B. CORPORATION	306	DIVIDEND PAYMENT	500,000.00
17-Feb-2009	30254M978	FPB BANCORP, INC.	179	DIVIDEND PAYMENT	56,388.89
17-Feb-2009	30886Z967	FARMERS BANK, WINDSOR, VIRGINIA	406	DIVIDEND PAYMENT	2,409.00
17-Feb-2009	30886Z983	FARMERS BANK, WINDSOR, VIRGINIA	406	DIVIDEND PAYMENT	26,742.22
17-Feb-2009	315831982	FIDELITY BANCORP, INC.	261	DIVIDEND PAYMENT	61,250.00
17-Feb-2009	316144963	FIDELITY FINANCIAL CORPORATION	275	DIVIDEND PAYMENT	25,396.00

Payment Date	CUSIP	QFI Name	Program ID	Payment Type	Amount
17-Feb-2009	316144997	FIDELITY FINANCIAL CORPORATION	275	DIVIDEND PAYMENT	282,193.33
17-Feb-2009	316394980	FIDELITY SOUTHERN CORPORATION	178	DIVIDEND PAYMENT	374,888.89
17-Feb-2009	317585982	FINANCIAL INSTITUTIONS, INC.	234	DIVIDEND PAYMENT	270,941.67
17-Feb-2009	31866P987	THE FIRST BANCORP, INC.	186	DIVIDEND PAYMENT	125,000.00
17-Feb-2009	318672979	FIRST BANCORP	368	DIVIDEND PAYMENT	1,611,111.11
17-Feb-2009	318910981	FIRST BANCORP	368	DIVIDEND PAYMENT	325,000.00
17-Feb-2009	319287967	FIRST BANKS, INC.	446	DIVIDEND PAYMENT	166,162.50
17-Feb-2009	319287983	FIRST BANKS, INC.	446	DIVIDEND PAYMENT	1,846,250.00
17-Feb-2009	31929F968	FIRST BANKERS TRUSTSHARES, INC.	309	DIVIDEND PAYMENT	3,625.00
17-Feb-2009	31929F984	FIRST BANKERS TRUSTSHARES, INC.	309	DIVIDEND PAYMENT	40,277.78
17-Feb-2009	319395984	FIRST CALIFORNIA FINANCIAL GROUP, INC.	204	DIVIDEND PAYMENT	194,444.44
17-Feb-2009	319459988	FIRST CITIZENS BANC CORP	427	DIVIDEND PAYMENT	70,840.00
17-Feb-2009	319835989	FIRST COMMUNITY CORPORATION	78	DIVIDEND PAYMENT	132,416.67
17-Feb-2009	31983A970	FIRST COMMUNITY BANCSHARES INC.	26	DIVIDEND PAYMENT	484,166.67
17-Feb-2009	31985E988	FIRST COMMUNITY BANK CORPORATION OF AMERICA	296	DIVIDEND PAYMENT	77,169.44
17-Feb-2009	31986N987	1ST CONSTITUTION BANCORP	369	DIVIDEND PAYMENT	86,666.67
17-Feb-2009	32006W981	FIRST DEFIANCE FINANCIAL CORP.	108	DIVIDEND PAYMENT	359,722.22
17-Feb-2009	320209984	FIRST FINANCIAL BANCORP	46	DIVIDEND PAYMENT	577,777.78
17-Feb-2009	32022X989	1ST FINANCIAL SERVICES CORPORATION	2	DIVIDEND PAYMENT	206,885.97
17-Feb-2009	320239965	FIRST FINANCIAL HOLDINGS INC.	110	DIVIDEND PAYMENT	631,944.44
17-Feb-2009	320517980	FIRST HORIZON NATIONAL CORPORATION	27	DIVIDEND PAYMENT	10,952,102.78
17-Feb-2009	32076T967	FIRST MANITOWOC BANCORP, INC.	486	DIVIDEND PAYMENT	4,350.00
17-Feb-2009	32076T983	FIRST MANITOWOC BANCORP, INC.	486	DIVIDEND PAYMENT	48,333.33
17-Feb-2009	320867971	FIRST MIDWEST BANCORP, INC.	54	DIVIDEND PAYMENT	1,876,388.89
17-Feb-2009	33582V983	FIRST NIAGRA FINANCIAL GROUP	9	DIVIDEND PAYMENT	2,146,795.00
17-Feb-2009	33589V986	FIRST PACTRUST BANCORP, INC.	70	DIVIDEND PAYMENT	225,166.67
17-Feb-2009	336312962	FIRST SECURITY GROUP, INC.	374	DIVIDEND PAYMENT	165,000.00

(Continued)

Payment Date	CUSIP	QFI Name	Program ID	Payment Type	Amount
17-Feb-2009	33647C970	FIRST SOUND BANK	137	DIVIDEND PAYMENT	53,444.44
17-Feb-2009	336901988	1ST SOURCE CORPORATION	292	DIVIDEND PAYMENT	339,166.67
17-Feb-2009	33735L965	FIRST ULB CORP.	276	DIVIDEND PAYMENT	1,347.50
17-Feb-2009	33735L999	FIRST ULB CORP.	276	DIVIDEND PAYMENT	14,972.22
17-Feb-2009	337915987	FIRSTMERIT CORPORATION	51	DIVIDEND PAYMENT	625,000.00
17-Feb-2009	343873204	FLUSHING FINANCIAL CORPORATION	226	DIVIDEND PAYMENT	544,444.44
17-Feb-2009	360271977	FULTON FINANCIAL CORPORATION	263	DIVIDEND PAYMENT	2,719,166.67
17-Feb-2009	38141G997	GOLDMAN SACHS GROUP INC	17	DIVIDEND PAYMENT	148,611,111.00
17-Feb-2009	386627962	GRANDSOUTH CORPORATION	327	DIVIDEND PAYMENT	4,050.00
17-Feb-2009	386627988	GRANDSOUTH CORPORATION	327	DIVIDEND PAYMENT	45,000.00
17-Feb-2009	390905982	GREAT SOUTHERN BANCORP	102	DIVIDEND PAYMENT	563,888.89
17-Feb-2009	394361984	GREEN BANKSHARES, INC.	180	DIVIDEND PAYMENT	522,007.78
17-Feb-2009	40424G983	HMN FINANCIAL, INC.	295	DIVIDEND PAYMENT	187,777.78
17-Feb-2009	409321981	HAMPTON ROADS BANKSHARES, INC.	236	DIVIDEND PAYMENT	502,168.75
17-Feb-2009	420476970	HAWTHORNE BANCSHARES, INC.	264	DIVIDEND PAYMENT	235,316.67
17-Feb-2009	42234Q987	HEARTLAND FINANCIAL USA, INC.	326	DIVIDEND PAYMENT	635,428.89
17-Feb-2009	42722X981	HERITAGE FINANCIAL CORPORATION	69	DIVIDEND PAYMENT	280,000.00
17-Feb-2009	436893986	HOME BANCSHARES, INC.	86	DIVIDEND PAYMENT	201,388.89
17-Feb-2009	439734989	HOPFED BANCORP	109	DIVIDEND PAYMENT	161,000.00
17-Feb-2009	440407989	HORIZON BANCORP	176	DIVIDEND PAYMENT	194,444.44
17-Feb-2009	446150955	HUNTINGTON BANCSHARES	28	DIVIDEND PAYMENT	17,670,064.03
17-Feb-2009	450828975	IBERIABANK CORPORATION	81	DIVIDEND PAYMENT	875,000.00
17-Feb-2009	451126965	IDAHO BANCORP	396	DIVIDEND PAYMENT	2,501.25
17-Feb-2009	451126981	IDAHO BANCORP	396	DIVIDEND PAYMENT	27,791.67
17-Feb-2009	453836983	INDEPENDENT BANK CORP.	268	DIVIDEND PAYMENT	390,790.00
17-Feb-2009	453838948	INDEPENDENT BANK CORPORATION	182	DIVIDEND PAYMENT	630,000.00
17-Feb-2009	454674987	INDIANA COMMUNITY BANCORP	119	DIVIDEND PAYMENT	188,125.00

Payment Date	CUSIP	QFI Name	Program ID	Payment Type	Amount
17-Feb-2009	45881M985	INTERMOUNTAIN COMMUNITY BANCORP	62	DIVIDEND PAYMENT	210,000.00
17-Feb-2009	459044988	INTERNATIONAL BANCSHARES CORPORATION	136	DIVIDEND PAYMENT	1,560,000.00
17-Feb-2009	460927981	INTERVEST BANCSHARES CORPORATION	316	DIVIDEND PAYMENT	180,555.56
17-Feb-2009	49326A978	KEYCORP KEYBANK NATIONAL ASSOCIATION	30	DIVIDEND PAYMENT	31,597,222.22
17-Feb-2009	50181P985	LCNB CORP.	302	DIVIDEND PAYMENT	67,000.00
17-Feb-2009	502100209	LNB BANCORP, INC.	91	DIVIDEND PAYMENT	220,701.25
17-Feb-2009	50215P985	LSB CORPORATION	267	DIVIDEND PAYMENT	131,250.00
17-Feb-2009	52168W967	LEADER BANCORP, INC.	215	DIVIDEND PAYMENT	3,796.00
17-Feb-2009	52168W983	LEADER BANCORP, INC.	215	DIVIDEND PAYMENT	42,105.56
17-Feb-2009	530176940	LIBERTY BANCSHARES, INC.	454	DIVIDEND PAYMENT	15,812.50
17-Feb-2009	530176965	LIBERTY BANCSHARES, INC.	454	DIVIDEND PAYMENT	175,694.44
17-Feb-2009	53700P965	THE LITTLE BANK, INCORPORATED	150	DIVIDEND PAYMENT	4,875.00
17-Feb-2009	53700P981	THE LITTLE BANK, INCORPORATED	150	DIVIDEND PAYMENT	54,166.67
17-Feb-2009	55261F989	M&T BANK CORPORATION	160	DIVIDEND PAYMENT	4,333,333.33
17-Feb-2009	55264U975	MB FINANCIAL INC.	49	DIVIDEND PAYMENT	1,905,555.56
17-Feb-2009	55920M961	MAGNA BANK	278	DIVIDEND PAYMENT	8,970.00
17-Feb-2009	55920M987	MAGNA BANK	278	DIVIDEND PAYMENT	99,630.56
17-Feb-2009	56062Y987	MAINSOURCE FINANCIAL GROUP, INC.	423	DIVIDEND PAYMENT	229,583.33
17-Feb-2009	562754986	MANHATTAN BANCORP	80	DIVIDEND PAYMENT	16,527.78
17-Feb-2009	571599968	MARQUETTE NATIONAL FINANCIAL CORPORATION	167	DIVIDEND PAYMENT	24,850.00
17-Feb-2009	571599984	MARQUETTE NATIONAL FINANCIAL CORPORATION	167	DIVIDEND PAYMENT	276,111.11
17-Feb-2009	571837988	MARSHALL AND ILSLEY CORPORATION	39	DIVIDEND PAYMENT	21,675,694.44
17-Feb-2009	59540G982	MID PENN BANCORP, INC./MID PENN BANK	138	DIVIDEND PAYMENT	77,777.78
17-Feb-2009	597746965	MIDLAND STATES BANCORP, INC.	398	DIVIDEND PAYMENT	2,799.50
17-Feb-2009	597746981	MIDLAND STATES BANCORP, INC.	398	DIVIDEND PAYMENT	31,133.06
17-Feb-2009	598039980	MIDSOUTH BANCORP, INC.	370	DIVIDEND PAYMENT	100,000.00
17-Feb-2009	598251973	MIDWEST BANC HOLDINGS, INC.	45	DIVIDEND PAYMENT	824,288.89

(Continued)

Payment Date	CUSIP	QFI Name	Program ID	Payment Type	Amount
17-Feb-2009	605038983	MISSION COMMUNITY BANCORP	170	DIVIDEND PAYMENT	25,850.00
17-Feb-2009	608875969	Monadnock Bancorp, Inc.	227	Dividend Payment	1,288.00
17-Feb-2009	608875985	Monadnock Bancorp, Inc.	227	Dividend Payment	14,264.44
17-Feb-2009	617774963	Morrill Bancshares, Inc	532	Dividend Payment	4,712.50
17-Feb-2009	617774989	MORRILL BANCSHARES, INC	532	DIVIDEND PAYMENT	52,361.11
17-Feb-2009	619462963	MOSCOW BANCSHARES, INC.	401	DIVIDEND PAYMENT	1,710.50
17-Feb-2009	619462989	MOSCOW BANCSHARES, INC.	401	DIVIDEND PAYMENT	18,993.33
17-Feb-2009	62845B971	MUTUALFIRST FINANCIAL, INC.	290	DIVIDEND PAYMENT	233,870.00
17-Feb-2009	628794968	NCAL BANCORP	301	DIVIDEND PAYMENT	7,000.00
17-Feb-2009	628794984	NCAL BANCORP	301	DIVIDEND PAYMENT	77,777.78
17-Feb-2009	637138975	NATIONAL PENN BANCHSHARES, INC.	189	DIVIDEND PAYMENT	1,312,500.00
17-Feb-2009	644722985	NEW HAMPSHIRE THRIFT BANCSHARES, INC.	228	DIVIDEND PAYMENT	40,277.78
17-Feb-2009	64975C969	NEW YORK PRIVATE BANK & TRUST CORPORATION	524	DIVIDEND PAYMENT	120,276.00
17-Feb-2009	64975C985	NEW YORK PRIVATE BANK & TRUST CORPORATION	524	DIVIDEND PAYMENT	1,336,370.00
17-Feb-2009	65406E961	NICOLET BANKSHARES, INC.	216	DIVIDEND PAYMENT	9,724.00
17-Feb-2009	65406E987	NICOLET BANKSHARES, INC.	216	DIVIDEND PAYMENT	108,073.33
17-Feb-2009	658418983	NORTH CENTRAL BANCSHARES, INC.	336	DIVIDEND PAYMENT	51,000.00
17-Feb-2009	663904985	NORTHEAST BANCORP	191	DIVIDEND PAYMENT	36,986.25
17-Feb-2009	665859880	NORTHERN TRUST CORPORATION	4	DIVIDEND PAYMENT	19,918,888.91
17-Feb-2009	675234983	OCEANFIRST FINANCIAL CORP.	565	DIVIDEND PAYMENT	154,114.86
17-Feb-2009	680033966	OLD NATIONAL BANCORP	31	DIVIDEND PAYMENT	875,000.00
17-Feb-2009	680277985	OLD SECOND BANCORP, INC.	489	DIVIDEND PAYMENT	294,027.78
17-Feb-2009	68275Z990	ONE UNITED BANK	97	DIVIDEND PAYMENT	93,823.33
17-Feb-2009	693475964	THE PNC FINANCIAL SERVICES GROUP, INC.	32	DIVIDEND PAYMENT	47,370,000.00
17-Feb-2009	69404P986	PACIFIC CAPITAL BANCORP	53	DIVIDEND PAYMENT	2,107,396.67
17-Feb-2009	69406T960	PACIFIC CITY FINANCIAL CORPORATION	142	DIVIDEND PAYMENT	11,340.00
17-Feb-2009	69406T986	PACIFIC CITY FINANCIAL CORPORATION	142	DIVIDEND PAYMENT	126,000.00

Payment Date	CUSIP	QFI Name	Program ID	Payment Type	Amount
17-Feb-2009	694076969	PACIFIC COAST BANKERS' BANCSHARES	428	DIVIDEND PAYMENT	7,540.00
17-Feb-2009	694076985	PACIFIC COAST BANKERS' BANCSHARES	428	DIVIDEND PAYMENT	83,777.78
17-Feb-2009	694100967	PACIFIC COAST NATIONAL BANCORP	315	DIVIDEND PAYMENT	1,493.50
17-Feb-2009	694100983	PACIFIC COAST NATIONAL BANCORP	315	DIVIDEND PAYMENT	16,594.44
17-Feb-2009	700658982	PARK NATIONAL CORPORATION	174	DIVIDEND PAYMENT	722,222.22
17-Feb-2009	701492985	PARKVALE FINANCIAL CORPORATION	346	DIVIDEND PAYMENT	229,392.22
17-Feb-2009	70335a965	PATRIOT BANCSHARES, INC.	98	DIVIDEND PAYMENT	18,228.00
17-Feb-2009	70335a999	PATRIOT BANCSHARES, INC.	98	DIVIDEND PAYMENT	202,517.78
17-Feb-2009	704699974	PEAPACK-GLADSTONE FINANCIAL CORPORATION	125	DIVIDEND PAYMENT	143,425.00
17-Feb-2009	710577982	PEOPLES BANCORP OF NORTH CAROLINA, INC.	329	DIVIDEND PAYMENT	180,945.56
17-Feb-2009	720304963	PIERCE COUNTY BANCORP	430	DIVIDEND PAYMENT	1,870.00
17-Feb-2009	720304989	PIERCE COUNTY BANCORP	430	DIVIDEND PAYMENT	20,777.78
17-Feb-2009	72346q971	PINNACLE FINANCIAL PARTNERS, INC.	184	DIVIDEND PAYMENT	831,250.00
17-Feb-2009	733174973	POPULAR, INC.	117	DIVIDEND PAYMENT	9,090,277.78
17-Feb-2009	736233982	PORTER BANCORP INC	60	DIVIDEND PAYMENT	408,333.33
17-Feb-2009	743859308	PROVIDENT BANKSHARES CORP	13	DIVIDEND PAYMENT	1,914,791.67
17-Feb-2009	74531y967	PUGET SOUND BANK	424	DIVIDEND PAYMENT	1,631.25
17-Feb-2009	74531y983	PUGET SOUND BANK	424	DIVIDEND PAYMENT	18,125.00
17-Feb-2009	745548982	PULASKI FINANCIAL CORP.	507	DIVIDEND PAYMENT	131,055.83
17-Feb-2009	74824r968	THE QUEENSBOROUGH COMPANY	47	DIVIDEND PAYMENT	5,400.00
17-Feb-2009	74824r984	THE QUEENSBOROUGH COMPANY	47	DIVIDEND PAYMENT	60,000.00
17-Feb-2009	757903968	REDWOOD FINANCIAL, INC.	199	DIVIDEND PAYMENT	1,350.00
17-Feb-2009	757903984	REDWOOD FINANCIAL, INC.	199	DIVIDEND PAYMENT	14,975.00
17-Feb-2009	7591ep969	REGIONS BANK	19	DIVIDEND PAYMENT	44,236,111.11
17-Feb-2009	767644966	RISING SUN BANCORP	313	DIVIDEND PAYMENT	2,691.00
17-Feb-2009	767644982	RISING SUN BANCORP	313	DIVIDEND PAYMENT	29,915.00
17-Feb-2009	783859960	S&T BANCORP, INC.	347	DIVIDEND PAYMENT	437,722.78

(Continued)

Payment Date	CUSIP	QFI Name	Program ID	Payment Type	Amount
17-Feb-2009	78401V979	SCBT FINANCIAL CORPORATION	305	DIVIDEND PAYMENT	260,915.42
17-Feb-2009	78486Q986	SVB FINANCIAL GROUP	87	DIVIDEND PAYMENT	2,056,250.00
17-Feb-2009	800363988	SANDY SPRING BANCORP, INC.	89	DIVIDEND PAYMENT	807,858.33
17-Feb-2009	802235986	SANTA LUCIA BANCORP	168	DIVIDEND PAYMENT	31,111.11
17-Feb-2009	812502961	SEASIDE NATIONAL BANK & TRUST	212	DIVIDEND PAYMENT	1,562.00
17-Feb-2009	812502987	SEASIDE NATIONAL BANK & TRUST	212	DIVIDEND PAYMENT	17,346.39
17-Feb-2009	813903986	SECURITIY FEDERAL CORPORATION	208	DIVIDEND PAYMENT	140,000.00
17-Feb-2009	814124962	SECURITY BUSINESS BANCORP	143	DIVIDEND PAYMENT	2,610.00
17-Feb-2009	814124988	SECURITY BUSINESS BANCORP	143	DIVIDEND PAYMENT	29,015.00
17-Feb-2009	81412M962	SECURITY CALIFORNIA BANCORP	107	DIVIDEND PAYMENT	3,069.00
17-Feb-2009	81412M988	SECURITY CALIFORNIA BANCORP	107	DIVIDEND PAYMENT	34,075.00
17-Feb-2009	81811M985	SEVERN BANCORP, INC.	71	DIVIDEND PAYMENT	272,918.33
17-Feb-2009	825107980	SHORE BANCSHARES, INC.	394	DIVIDEND PAYMENT	125,000.00
17-Feb-2009	530176965	LIBERTY BANCSHARES, INC.	454	DIVIDEND PAYMENT	175,694.44
17-Feb-2009	53700P965	THE LITTLE BANK, INCORPORATED	150	DIVIDEND PAYMENT	4,875.00
17-Feb-2009	53700P981	THE LITTLE BANK, INCORPORATED	150	DIVIDEND PAYMENT	54,166.67
17-Feb-2009	55261F989	M&T BANK CORPORATION	160	DIVIDEND PAYMENT	4,333,333.33
17-Feb-2009	55264U975	MB FINANCIAL INC.	49	DIVIDEND PAYMENT	1,905,555.56
17-Feb-2009	55920M961	MAGNA BANK	278	DIVIDEND PAYMENT	8,970.00
17-Feb-2009	55920M987	MAGNA BANK	278	DIVIDEND PAYMENT	99,630.56
17-Feb-2009	56062Y987	MAINSOURCE FINANCIAL GROUP, INC.	423	DIVIDEND PAYMENT	229,583.33
17-Feb-2009	562754986	MANHATTAN BANCORP	80	DIVIDEND PAYMENT	16,527.78
17-Feb-2009	571599968	MARQUETTE NATIONAL FINANCIAL CORPORATION	167	DIVIDEND PAYMENT	24,850.00
17-Feb-2009	571599984	MARQUETTE NATIONAL FINANCIAL CORPORATION	167	DIVIDEND PAYMENT	276,111.11
17-Feb-2009	571837988	MARSHALL AND ILSLEY CORPORATION	39	DIVIDEND PAYMENT	21,675,694.44
17-Feb-2009	59540G982	MID PENN BANCORP, INC./MID PENN BANK	138	DIVIDEND PAYMENT	77,777.78
17-Feb-2009	597746965	MIDLAND STATES BANCORP, INC.	398	DIVIDEND PAYMENT	2,799.50

Payment Date	CUSIP	QFI Name	Program ID	Payment Type	Amount
17-Feb-2009	597746981	MIDLAND STATES BANCORP, INC.	398	DIVIDEND PAYMENT	31,133.06
17-Feb-2009	598039980	MIDSOUTH BANCORP, INC.	370	DIVIDEND PAYMENT	100,000.00
17-Feb-2009	598251973	MIDWEST BANC HOLDINGS, INC.	45	DIVIDEND PAYMENT	824,288.89
17-Feb-2009	605038983	MISSION COMMUNITY BANCORP	170	DIVIDEND PAYMENT	25,850.00
17-Feb-2009	608875969	MONADNOCK BANCORP, INC.	227	DIVIDEND PAYMENT	1,288.00
17-Feb-2009	608875985	MONADNOCK BANCORP, INC.	227	DIVIDEND PAYMENT	14,264.44
17-Feb-2009	617774963	MORRILL BANCSHARES, INC	532	DIVIDEND PAYMENT	4,712.50
17-Feb-2009	617774989	MORRILL BANCSHARES, INC	532	DIVIDEND PAYMENT	52,361.11
17-Feb-2009	619462963	MOSCOW BANCSHARES, INC.	401	DIVIDEND PAYMENT	1,710.50
17-Feb-2009	619462989	MOSCOW BANCSHARES, INC.	401	DIVIDEND PAYMENT	18,993.33
17-Feb-2009	62845B971	MUTUALFIRST FINANCIAL, INC.	290	DIVIDEND PAYMENT	233,870.00
17-Feb-2009	628794968	NCAL BANCORP	301	DIVIDEND PAYMENT	7,000.00
17-Feb-2009	628794984	NCAL BANCORP	301	DIVIDEND PAYMENT	77,777.78
17-Feb-2009	637138975	NATIONAL PENN BANCHSHARES, INC.	189	DIVIDEND PAYMENT	1,312,500.00
17-Feb-2009	644722985	NEW HAMPSHIRE THRIFT BANCSHARES, INC.	228	DIVIDEND PAYMENT	40,277.78
17-Feb-2009	64975C969	NEW YORK PRIVATE BANK & TRUST CORPORATION	524	DIVIDEND PAYMENT	120,276.00
17-Feb-2009	64975C985	NEW YORK PRIVATE BANK & TRUST CORPORATION	524	DIVIDEND PAYMENT	1,336,370.00
17-Feb-2009	65406E961	NICOLET BANKSHARES, INC.	216	DIVIDEND PAYMENT	9,724.00
17-Feb-2009	65406E987	NICOLET BANKSHARES, INC.	216	DIVIDEND PAYMENT	108,073.33
17-Feb-2009	658418983	NORTH CENTRAL BANCSHARES, INC.	336	DIVIDEND PAYMENT	51,000.00
17-Feb-2009	663904985	NORTHEAST BANCORP	191	DIVIDEND PAYMENT	36,986.25
17-Feb-2009	665859880	NORTHERN TRUST CORPORATION	4	DIVIDEND PAYMENT	19,918,888.91
17-Feb-2009	675234983	OCEANFIRST FINANCIAL CORP.	565	DIVIDEND PAYMENT	154,114.86
17-Feb-2009	680033966	OLD NATIONAL BANCORP	31	DIVIDEND PAYMENT	875,000.00
17-Feb-2009	680277985	OLD SECOND BANCORP, INC.	489	DIVIDEND PAYMENT	294,027.78
17-Feb-2009	68275Z990	ONE UNITED BANK	97	DIVIDEND PAYMENT	93,823.33
17-Feb-2009	693475964	THE PNC FINANCIAL SERVICES GROUP, INC.	32	DIVIDEND PAYMENT	47,370,000.00

(Continued)

Payment Date	CUSIP	QFI Name	Program ID	Payment Type	Amount
17-Feb-2009	69404P986	PACIFIC CAPITAL BANCORP	53	DIVIDEND PAYMENT	2,107,396.67
17-Feb-2009	69406T960	PACIFIC CITY FINANCIAL CORPORATION	142	DIVIDEND PAYMENT	11,340.00
17-Feb-2009	69406T986	PACIFIC CITY FINANCIAL CORPORATION	142	DIVIDEND PAYMENT	126,000.00
17-Feb-2009	694076969	PACIFIC COAST BANKERS' BANCSHARES	428	DIVIDEND PAYMENT	7,540.00
17-Feb-2009	694076985	PACIFIC COAST BANKERS' BANCSHARES	428	DIVIDEND PAYMENT	83,777.78
17-Feb-2009	694100967	PACIFIC COAST NATIONAL BANCORP	315	DIVIDEND PAYMENT	1,493.50
17-Feb-2009	694100983	PACIFIC COAST NATIONAL BANCORP	315	DIVIDEND PAYMENT	16,594.44
17-Feb-2009	700658982	PARK NATIONAL CORPORATION	174	DIVIDEND PAYMENT	722,222.22
17-Feb-2009	701492985	PARKVALE FINANCIAL CORPORATION	346	DIVIDEND PAYMENT	229,392.22
17-Feb-2009	70335A965	PATRIOT BANCSHARES, INC.	98	DIVIDEND PAYMENT	18,228.00
17-Feb-2009	70335A999	PATRIOT BANCSHARES, INC.	98	DIVIDEND PAYMENT	202,517.78
17-Feb-2009	704699974	PEAPACK-GLADSTONE FINANCIAL CORPORATION	125	DIVIDEND PAYMENT	143,425.00
17-Feb-2009	710577982	PEOPLES BANCORP OF NORTH CAROLINA, INC.	329	DIVIDEND PAYMENT	180,945.56
17-Feb-2009	720304963	PIERCE COUNTY BANCORP	430	DIVIDEND PAYMENT	1,870.00
17-Feb-2009	720304989	PIERCE COUNTY BANCORP	430	DIVIDEND PAYMENT	20,777.78
17-Feb-2009	72346Q971	PINNACLE FINANCIAL PARTNERS, INC.	184	DIVIDEND PAYMENT	831,250.00
17-Feb-2009	733174973	POPULAR, INC.	117	DIVIDEND PAYMENT	9,090,277.78
17-Feb-2009	736233982	PORTER BANCORP INC	60	DIVIDEND PAYMENT	408,333.33
17-Feb-2009	743859308	PROVIDENT BANKSHARES CORP	13	DIVIDEND PAYMENT	1,914,791.67
17-Feb-2009	74531Y967	PUGET SOUND BANK	424	DIVIDEND PAYMENT	1,631.25
17-Feb-2009	74531Y983	PUGET SOUND BANK	424	DIVIDEND PAYMENT	18,125.00
17-Feb-2009	745548982	PULASKI FINANCIAL CORP.	507	DIVIDEND PAYMENT	131,055.83
17-Feb-2009	74824R968	THE QUEENSBOROUGH COMPANY	47	DIVIDEND PAYMENT	5,400.00
17-Feb-2009	74824R984	THE QUEENSBOROUGH COMPANY	47	DIVIDEND PAYMENT	60,000.00
17-Feb-2009	757903968	REDWOOD FINANCIAL, INC.	199	DIVIDEND PAYMENT	1,350.00
17-Feb-2009	757903984	REDWOOD FINANCIAL, INC.	199	DIVIDEND PAYMENT	14,975.00
17-Feb-2009	7591EP969	REGIONS BANK	19	DIVIDEND PAYMENT	44,236,111.11

Payment Date	CUSIP	QFI Name	Program ID	Payment Type	Amount
17-Feb-2009	767644966	RISING SUN BANCORP	313	DIVIDEND PAYMENT	2,691.00
17-Feb-2009	767644982	RISING SUN BANCORP	313	DIVIDEND PAYMENT	29,915.00
17-Feb-2009	783859960	S&T BANCORP, INC.	347	DIVIDEND PAYMENT	437,722.78
17-Feb-2009	78401V979	SCBT FINANCIAL CORPORATION	305	DIVIDEND PAYMENT	260,915.42
17-Feb-2009	78486Q986	SVB FINANCIAL GROUP	87	DIVIDEND PAYMENT	2,056,250.00
17-Feb-2009	800363988	SANDY SPRING BANCORP, INC.	89	DIVIDEND PAYMENT	807,858.33
17-Feb-2009	802235986	SANTA LUCIA BANCORP	168	DIVIDEND PAYMENT	31,111.11
17-Feb-2009	812502961	SEASIDE NATIONAL BANK & TRUST	212	DIVIDEND PAYMENT	1,562.00
17-Feb-2009	812502987	SEASIDE NATIONAL BANK & TRUST	212	DIVIDEND PAYMENT	17,346.39
17-Feb-2009	813903986	SECURITIY FEDERAL CORPORATION	208	DIVIDEND PAYMENT	140,000.00
17-Feb-2009	814124962	SECURITY BUSINESS BANCORP	143	DIVIDEND PAYMENT	2,610.00
17-Feb-2009	814124988	SECURITY BUSINESS BANCORP	143	DIVIDEND PAYMENT	29,015.00
17-Feb-2009	81412M962	SECURITY CALIFORNIA BANCORP	107	DIVIDEND PAYMENT	3,069.00
17-Feb-2009	81412M988	SECURITY CALIFORNIA BANCORP	107	DIVIDEND PAYMENT	34,075.00
17-Feb-2009	81811M985	SEVERN BANCORP, INC.	71	DIVIDEND PAYMENT	272,918.33
17-Feb-2009	825107980	SHORE BANCSHARES, INC.	394	DIVIDEND PAYMENT	125,000.00
17-Feb-2009	82669G989	SIGNATURE BANK	104	DIVIDEND PAYMENT	1,050,000.00
17-Feb-2009	836068965	SOUND BANKING COMPANY	144	DIVIDEND PAYMENT	1,386.00
17-Feb-2009	836068981	SOUND BANKING COMPANY	144	DIVIDEND PAYMENT	15,350.00
17-Feb-2009	837841956	THE SOUTH FINANCIAL GROU INC.	99	DIVIDEND PAYMENT	3,373,611.11
17-Feb-2009	842632986	SOUTHERN COMMUNITY FINANCIAL CORP.	105	DIVIDEND PAYMENT	415,625.00
17-Feb-2009	843120965	SOUTHERN ILLINOIS BANCORP, INC.	491	DIVIDEND PAYMENT	1,375.00
17-Feb-2009	843120981	SOUTHERN ILLINOIS BANCORP, INC.	491	DIVIDEND PAYMENT	15,277.78
17-Feb-2009	843380981	SOUTHERN MISSOURI BANCORP, INC.	145	DIVIDEND PAYMENT	92,847.22
17-Feb-2009	844767970	SOUTHWEST BANCORP INC.	114	DIVIDEND PAYMENT	680,555.56
17-Feb-2009	846851988	TAYLOR CAPITAL GROUP	83	DIVIDEND PAYMENT	1,222,935.00
17-Feb-2009	855716205	STATE BANCORP, INC.	146	DIVIDEND PAYMENT	358,186.11

(Continued)

Payment Date	CUSIP	QFI Name	Program ID	Payment Type	Amount
17-Feb-2009	856577960	STATE BANKSHARES, INC.	477	DIVIDEND PAYMENT	18,125.00
17-Feb-2009	856577986	STATE BANKSHARES, INC.	477	DIVIDEND PAYMENT	201,388.89
17-Feb-2009	858907967	STERLING BANCSHARES, INC.	147	DIVIDEND PAYMENT	1,095,482.50
17-Feb-2009	859158966	STERLING BANCORP	299	DIVIDEND PAYMENT	303,333.33
17-Feb-2009	859319956	STERLING FINANCIAL CORPORATION	183	DIVIDEND PAYMENT	2,945,833.33
17-Feb-2009	861756963	STONEBRIDGE FINANCIAL CORP.	559	DIVIDEND PAYMENT	3,019.50
17-Feb-2009	861756989	STONEBRIDGE FINANCIAL CORP.	559	DIVIDEND PAYMENT	33,528.61
17-Feb-2009	866264989	SUMMIT STATE BANK	148	DIVIDEND PAYMENT	66,111.11
17-Feb-2009	86663B987	SUN BANCORP, INC.	188	DIVIDEND PAYMENT	446,550.00
17-Feb-2009	86806M304	SUPERIOR BANCORP	112	DIVIDEND PAYMENT	670,833.33
17-Feb-2009	86888W964	SURREY BANCORP	202	DIVIDEND PAYMENT	900.00
17-Feb-2009	86888W980	SURREY BANCORP	202	DIVIDEND PAYMENT	10,000.00
17-Feb-2009	869099986	SUSQUEHANNA BANCSHARES, INC.	95	DIVIDEND PAYMENT	2,625,000.00
17-Feb-2009	87161C972	SYNOVUS FINANCIAL CORP.	100	DIVIDEND PAYMENT	7,527,877.78
17-Feb-2009	87182V967	SYRINGA BANCORP	395	DIVIDEND PAYMENT	2,900.00
17-Feb-2009	87182V983	SYRINGA BANCORP	395	DIVIDEND PAYMENT	32,222.22
17-Feb-2009	872242961	TCB HOLDING COMPANY	218	DIVIDEND PAYMENT	4,255.75
17-Feb-2009	872242987	TCB HOLDING COMPANY	218	DIVIDEND PAYMENT	47,245.83
17-Feb-2009	872275987	TCF FINANCIAL CORPORATION	52	DIVIDEND PAYMENT	4,564,812.78
17-Feb-2009	87230P962	TCNB FINANCIAL CORP	213	DIVIDEND PAYMENT	1,300.00
17-Feb-2009	87230P988	TCNB FINANCIAL CORP	213	DIVIDEND PAYMENT	14,444.44
17-Feb-2009	872449988	TIB FINANCIAL CORP	152	DIVIDEND PAYMENT	359,722.22
17-Feb-2009	88043P983	TENNESSEE COMMERCE BANCORP, INC.	101	DIVIDEND PAYMENT	233,333.33
17-Feb-2009	88059U967	TENNESSEE VALLEY FINANCIAL HOLDINGS, INC.	350	DIVIDEND PAYMENT	1,950.00
17-Feb-2009	88059U983	TENNESSEE VALLEY FINANCIAL HOLDINGS, INC.	350	DIVIDEND PAYMENT	21,666.67
17-Feb-2009	88224Q974	TEXAS CAPITAL BANCSHARES, INC.	373	DIVIDEND PAYMENT	302,083.33

Payment Date	CUSIP	QFI Name	Program ID	Payment Type	Amount
17-Feb-2009	886374982	TIDELANDS BANCSHARES, INC.	246	DIVIDEND PAYMENT	112,373.33
17-Feb-2009	89214T309	TOWNEBANK	153	DIVIDEND PAYMENT	669,007.50
17-Feb-2009	89464P965	TREATY OAK BANCORP, INC	555	DIVIDEND PAYMENT	1,181.75
17-Feb-2009	89464P981	TREATY OAK BANCORP, INC	555	DIVIDEND PAYMENT	13,162.78
17-Feb-2009	89546L966	TRI-COUNTY FINANCIAL CORPORATION	75	DIVIDEND PAYMENT	10,878.00
17-Feb-2009	895461982	Tri-County Financial Corporation	75	DIVIDEND PAYMENT	120,866.67
17-Feb-2009	898402987	TRUSTMARK CORPORATION	77	DIVIDEND PAYMENT	2,508,333.33
17-Feb-2009	90262T506	UCBH HOLDINGS INC.	3	DIVIDEND PAYMENT	3,775,707.07
17-Feb-2009	902973981	US BANCORP	48	DIVIDEND PAYMENT	83,404,027.78
17-Feb-2009	905399986	UNION BANKSHARES CORPORATION	238	DIVIDEND PAYMENT	458,888.89
17-Feb-2009	90944L988	UNITED BANCORP, INC.	448	DIVIDEND PAYMENT	82,972.22
17-Feb-2009	90944R985	UNITED BANCORPORATION OF ALABAMA, INC.	272	DIVIDEND PAYMENT	74,388.89
17-Feb-2009	90984P980	UNITED COMMUNITY BANKS, INC.	59	DIVIDEND PAYMENT	1,750,000.00
17-Feb-2009	910305960	UNITED FINANCIAL BANKING COMPANIES, INC.	426	DIVIDEND PAYMENT	2,051.75
17-Feb-2009	910305986	UNITED FINANCIAL BANKING COMPANIES, INC.	426	DIVIDEND PAYMENT	22,789.17
17-Feb-2009	913290987	UNITY BANCORP, INC.	154	DIVIDEND PAYMENT	200,754.17
17-Feb-2009	918183963	UWHARRIE CAPITAL CORP	129	DIVIDEND PAYMENT	6,500.00
17-Feb-2009	918183989	UWHARRIE CAPITAL CORP	129	DIVIDEND PAYMENT	72,222.22
17-Feb-2009	918255985	VIST FINANCIAL CORP.	155	DIVIDEND PAYMENT	194,444.44
17-Feb-2009	919513945	VALLEY COMMUNITY BANK	254	DIVIDEND PAYMENT	2,475.00
17-Feb-2009	919513960	VALLEY COMMUNITY BANK	254	DIVIDEND PAYMENT	27,500.00
17-Feb-2009	919629980	VALLEY FINANCIAL CORPORATION	169	DIVIDEND PAYMENT	140,166.25
17-Feb-2009	919794966	VALLEY NATIONAL BANCORP	34	DIVIDEND PAYMENT	3,791,666.67
17-Feb-2009	92778Q976	VIRGINIA COMMERCE BANCORP	221	DIVIDEND PAYMENT	621,250.00
17-Feb-2009	929328987	WSFS FINANCIAL CORPORATION	514	DIVIDEND PAYMENT	160,798.61
17-Feb-2009	930705975	WAINWRIGHT BANK & TRUST COMPANY	156	DIVIDEND PAYMENT	171,111.11
17-Feb-2009	938824208	WASHINGTON FEDERAL S AND L ASSOCIATION	11	DIVIDEND PAYMENT	2,527,777.78

(Continued)

Payment Date	CUSIP	QFI Name	Program ID	Payment Type	Amount
17-Feb-2009	947890976	WEBSTER FINANCIAL CORPORATION	50	DIVIDEND PAYMENT	4,666,666.67
17-Feb-2009	949746978	WELLS FARGO AND COMPANY	36	DIVIDEND PAYMENT	371,527,777.78
17-Feb-2009	950810986	WESBANCO, INC.	68	DIVIDEND PAYMENT	729,166.67
17-Feb-2009	95123P981	WEST BANCORPORATION, INC.	270	DIVIDEND PAYMENT	225,000.00
17-Feb-2009	957638976	WESTERN ALLIANCE BANCORPORATION	44	DIVIDEND PAYMENT	1,633,333.33
17-Feb-2009	95801P964	WESTERN COMMUNITY BANCSHARES, INC.	280	DIVIDEND PAYMENT	4,745.00
17-Feb-2009	95801P980	WESTERN COMMUNITY BANCSHARES, INC.	280	DIVIDEND PAYMENT	52,650.00
17-Feb-2009	966612202	WHITNEY HOLDING CORPORATION	161	DIVIDEND PAYMENT	2,333,333.33
17-Feb-2009	971807201	WILMINGTON TRUST CORPORATION	94	DIVIDEND PAYMENT	2,887,500.00
17-Feb-2009	97650W975	WINTRUST FINANCIAL CORPORATION	222	DIVIDEND PAYMENT	1,944,444.44
17-Feb-2009	984314989	YADKIN VALLEY FINANCIAL CORPORATION	391	DIVIDEND PAYMENT	145,000.00
17-Feb-2009	989701966	ZIONS BANCORPORATION	37	DIVIDEND PAYMENT	17,694,444.44
18-Feb-2009	084680982	BERKSHIRE HILLS BANCORP, INC.	200	DIVIDEND PAYMENT	311,111.11
02-Mar-2009	46625H894	JPMORGAN CHASE AND CO	29	DIVIDEND PAYMENT	312,500,000.00
16-Mar-2009	857477897	STATE STREET CORPORATION	20	DIVIDEND PAYMENT	25,000,000.00
16-Mar-2009	867914608	SUNTRUST BANKS, INC.	5	DIVIDEND PAYMENT	43,750,000.00
16-Mar-2009	867914707	SUNTRUST BANKS, INC.	5	DIVIDEND PAYMENT	14,062,500.00
18-Mar-2009	605038983	MISSION COMMUNITY BANCORP	170	RETURN OF DIVIDEND OVER-PAYMENT	-270.00
20-Mar-2009	06426P982	BANK OF NEW YORK MELLON	15	DIVIDEND PAYMENT	37,500,000.00
31-Mar-2009	063425201	BANK OF MARIN BANCORP	127	FULL REDEMP-TION	28,000,000.00
31-Mar-2009	063425201	BANK OF MARIN BANCORP	127	DIVIDEND PAYMENT	178,888.89
31-Mar-2009	15234K986	CENTRA FINANCIAL HOLDINGS, INC.	257	DIVIDEND PAYMENT	95,833.33
31-Mar-2009	15234K986	CENTRA FINANCIAL HOLDINGS, INC.	257	FULL REDEMPTI ON	15,000,000.00
31-Mar-2009	316773407	FIFTH THIRD BANCORP	40	DIVIDEND PAYMENT	42,600,000.00

Payment Date	CUSIP	QFI Name	Program ID	Payment Type	Amount
31-Mar-2009	450828975	IBERIABANK CORPORATION	81	FULL REDEMP-TION	90,000,000.00
31-Mar-2009	450828975	IBERIABANK CORPORATION	81	DIVIDEND PAYMENT	575,000.00
31-Mar-2009	680033966	OLD NATIONAL BANCORP	31	DIVIDEND PAYMENT	638,888.89
31-Mar-2009	680033966	OLD NATIONAL BANCORP	31	FULL REDEMP-TION	100,000,000.00
31-Mar-2009	82669G989	SIGNATURE BANK	104	FULL REDEMP-TION	120,000,000.00
31-Mar-2009	82669G989	SIGNATURE BANK	104	DIVIDEND PAYMENT	766,666.67
					2,870,873,839.24
TIP					
17-Feb-2009	060505435	BANK OF AMERICA CORPORATION	38	DIVIDEND PAYMENT	128,888,888.89
17-Feb-2009	172967929	CITIGROUP INC	24	DIVIDEND PAYMENT	200,000,000.00
					328,888,888.89
					3,480,751,528.23

Source: Treasury, response to SIGTARP data call, 4/8/2009.

E. Cross-Reference of Report to the Inspector General Act of 1978

This appendix cross-references this report to the reporting requirements under the Inspector General Act of 1978 (P.L. 95-452), as amended, 5 **U.S.C. APP**.

Section	Statute (Inspector General Act of 1978)	SIGTARP Action	Report Reference
Section 5(a)(1)	"Description of signicant problems, abuses, and deciencies... "	List problems, abuses, and deciencies from SIGTARP audits and investigations.	Section 1: "The Ofce of the SIGTARP" Section 4: "Looking Forward"
Section 5(a)(2)	"Description of recommendations for corrective action…with respect to signicant problems, abuses, or deciencies... "	List recommendations from SIGTARP audits and investigations.	Section 1: "The Ofce of the SIGTARP" Section 4: "Looking Forward"
Section 5(a)(3)	"Identfication of each signicant recommend-dation described in	List all instances of inco-mplete corrective action from previous semiannual reports.	Section 4: "Looking Forward"

(Continued)

Section	Statute (Inspector General Act of 1978)	SIGTARP Action	Report Reference
	previous semiannual reports on which corrective action has not been completed..."		
Section 5(a)(4)	"A summary of matters referred to prosecutive authorities and the prosecutions and convictions which have resulted... "	List status of SIGTARP investigations referred to prosecutive authorities.	At press time, SIGTARP had not issued reportable investigations or audits. This field will be populated in later reports as appropriate.
Section 5(a)(5)	"A summary of each report made to the [Treasury Secretary] under section 6(b)(2)... " (instances where information requested was refused or not provided)	List TARP oversight reports by Treasury, FSOB, SEC, GAO, COP, OMB, CBO, Federal Reserve, FDIC, and SIGTARP.	At press time, SIGTARP had not issued reportable investingtions or audits. This field will be populated in later reports as appropriate.
Section 5(a)(6)	"A listing, subdivided according to subject matter, of each audit report issued..." showing dollar value of questioned costs and recommedations that funds be put to better use.	List SIGTARP audits.	At press time, SIGTRP had not issued reportable investingtions or audits. This field will be populated in later reports as appropriate.
Section 5(a)(7)	"A summary of each particularly signicant report... "	Provide a synopsis of signicant SIGTARP audits.	At press time, SIGTARP had not issued reportable investigations or audits. This field will be populated in later reports as appropriate.
Section 5(a)(8)	"Statistical tables showng the total number of audit reports and the total dollar value of questioned costs... "	Provide statistical tables showing dollar value of questioned cost from SIGTARP audits.	At press time, SIGARP had not issued reportable investigaions or audits. This field will be populated in later reports as appropriate.
Section 5(a)(9)	"Statistical tables showing the total number of audit reports and the dollar value of	Provide statistical tables showing dollar value of funds put to better use by management from SIGTARP audits.	At press time, SIGTRP had not issued reportable investingtions or audits. This field will be populated

	recommndations that funds be put to better use by management..."		in later reports as appropriate.
Section 5(a)(10)	"A summary of each audit report issued be-ore the commencement of the reporting period for which no management decision has been made by the end of reporting period, an explanation of the reasons such manag-ment decision has not been made, and a sta-ement concerning the desired timetable for achieving a management decision..."	Provide a synopsis of signicant SIGTARP audit reports in which recom-mendations by SIGTARP are still open.	At press time, SIGTRAP had not issued report-able investigations or audits. This field will be populated in later reports as appropriate.
Section 5(a)(11)	"A description and explanation of the reasons for any signicant revised management decision..."	Explain audit reports in which significant revisions have been made to management decisions.	At press time, SIGTARP had not issued reportable investigations or audits. This field will be populated in later reports as appropriate.
Section 5(a)(12)	"Information concerning any signicant manage-ment decision with whi-h the Inspector General is in disagreement..."	Provide information where management disagreed with a SIGTARP audit finding.	At press time, SIGT-RP had not issued reportable investing-tions or audits. This eld will be populated in later reports as appropriate.

F. Public Announcements of Audits

This appendix provides announcements of public audits by the following agencies:

A U.S. Department of Treasury Inspector General ("Treasury OIG")

B Federal Reserve Board Office of Inspector General ("Federal Reserve OIG")

C Government Accountability Office ("GAO")

D Federal Deposit Insurance Corporation Office of the Inspector General ("FDIC OIG")

A. Treasury OIG[21]

As reported in the Initial Report, Treasury OIG is currently performing one case study audit of Treasury's selection of City National Bank, Beverly Hills, California, to receive $400 million under the Capital Purchase Program. Treasury OIG issued the engagement letter on this audit on December 4, 2008, and held entrance conferences with Treasury of cials on December 11, 2008, and Office of the Comptroller of the Currency of cials on January 6, 2009. The work on this audit is ongoing.

Treasury OIG initiated an inquiry into the role, if any, and actions by the Treasury Department in the decision by American International Group ("AIG") to pay bonuses of more than $160 million to AIG employees. Treasury OIG plans to inquire into the activities of Treasury's Office of General Counsel ("OGC") and other Treasury of cials in reviewing the bonus contracts entered into by AIG and its employees, with a view to determining the particulars of the obligations incurred and the conclusions reached by OGC. The work on this inquiry is ongoing.

B. Federal Reserve OIG[22]

The Federal Reserve OIG is conducting an audit of the Board of Governors of the Federal Reserve System's ("Board") processing of Capital Purchase Program applications from Board-supervised financial institutions (fieldwork is ongoing).

C. GAO[23]

Leveraging and Deleveraging Financial Institutions

The purpose of this mandate is to determine the extent to which leverage and sudden deleveraging of financial institutions was a factor behind the current financial crisis. This study will:

1. examine to what extent large financial institutions have deleveraged since the financial crisis started, and how such actions, if at all, have contributed to the crisis
2. analyze how Federal regulators were overseeing the use of leverage by such institutions and what actions, if any, they have taken to limit the use of leverage
3. review the recommendations that have been made by regulators, market participants, and others to address concerns about leverage and deleverage
4. review the regulations under which the Federal Reserve regulates the extension of credit by banks and broker-dealers

Implications of Actions Taken in Response to Economic Slowdown/Financial Distress for Debt and Debt Management

GAO is seeking to answer the following questions:

1. What are Treasury's borrowing plans to finance asset and capital purchases through the Troubled Asset Relief Program ("TARP") and obtain the funds needed to increase Federal spending during a recession?
2. What are the scale and timing of borrowing decisions?
3. What cost-cutting borrowing options exist to fund TARP's capital purchases?
4. What Treasury securities would be most attractive to domestic and foreign buyers in the short run and medium run?
5. What debt management policies would reduce the possibility of stress in financial markets in the medium and long term?

Federal Assistance under Automotive Industry Financing Program

In December 2008, Treasury announced that it would provide about $18 billion to Chrysler and General Motors, and required that they submit restructuring plans by February 17, 2009. By the end of March 2009, the companies must report on their progress in implementing the plans.

GAO is seeking to answer the following questions:

1. What is the nature and purpose of the Federal assistance provided to the automakers under the Troubled Asset Relief Program?
2. What mechanisms did Treasury establish to protect the taxpayers' interests in providing Federal assistance to the automakers?
3. What steps have the automakers taken, or do they plan to take, to restructure their companies?

Troubled Asset Relief Program's ("TARP's") Fiscal Year 2009 Financial Statement Audit

The Emergency Economic Stabilization Act of 2008 (P.L. 110-343) established the Office of Financial Stability within the Department of Treasury and authorized the Troubled Asset Relief Program ("TARP"). The act requires TARP to annually prepare and issue audited financial statements prepared in accordance with U.S. Generally Accepted Accounting Principles, and GAO to annually audit such statements. GAO's objectives are to determine:

1. if TARP's financial statements are fairly presented in all material respects as of and for the period ended September 30, 2009
2. if TARP's internal controls related to the financial statements are effective as of September 30, 2009
3. if there is any reportable noncompliance with selected provisions of laws and regulations

CPP

GAO is seeking to:

1. evaluate Treasury's application review and approval process
2. evaluate how regulators and Treasury are applying criteria for institutions returning funds

Mortgage Mitigation

GAO is seeking to:

1. evaluate Treasury's internal control framework for the Home Affordable Modification Program ("HAMP")
2. assess Treasury's analytical and empirical basis for HAMP

D – FDIC OIG[24]

No ongoing audits have been announced.

G. Key Oversight Reports and Testimonies

U.S. Department Of The Treasury ("Treasury")

Roles and Mission
The mission of treasury is to serve the american people and strengthen national security by managing the U.S. government's finances effectively; promoting economic growth and stability; and ensuring the safety, soundness, and security of the u.s. and international financial systems. Treasury advises the president on economic and financial issues, encourages sustainable economic growth, and fosters improved governance in financial institutions.
Oversight Reports
Treasury, Section 105(a) Report, 12/5/2008, accessed 4/2/2009.
Treasury, Section 102 Report, 12/31/2008, accessed 4/2/2009.
Treasury, Section 105(A) Report, 1/6/2009, accessed 4/2/2009.
Treasury, Section 105(A) Report, 2/3/2009, accessed 4/2/2009.
Treasury, Transactions Report, accessed 4/2/2009 (released weekly).
Treasury, Section 105(A) Report, 3/6/2009, accessed 4/2/2009.
Treasury, Tranche Report, accessed 4/2/2009 (for every $50 billion committed).
Recorded Testimony
Treasury, "HP-1234 Neel Kashkari Testimony before the Senate Committee on Banking, Housing, and Urban Affairs," 10/23/2008, accessed 4/2/2009.
Treasury, "HP-1273 Testimony of Interim Assistant Secretary For Financial Stability Neel Kashkari before the House Committee on Oversight and Government Reform, Subcommittee For Domestic Policy," 11/14/2008, accessed 4/2/2009.
Treasury, "HP-1279 Testimony By Treasury Secretary Henry M. Paulson Jr. Before The House Committee On Financial Services," 11/18/2008, accessed 4/2/2009.
Treasury, "Joint Statement by Treasury, Federal Reserve and the Fdic on Citigroup," Press Release, 11/23/2008, accessed 4/2/2009.
Treasury, "HP-1301 Secretary Paulson Remarks on the Us Economy and Financial System," 12/1/2008, accessed 4/2/2009.
Treasury, "HP-1312 Neel Kashkari Testimony Before The Senate Appropriations Subcommittee on Financial Services and General Government," 12/4/2008, accessed 4/2/2009.
Treasury, "HP-1314 Interim Assistant Secretary for Financial Stability Neel Kashkari Remarks on Financial Markets and TARP Update," 12/5/2008, accessed 4/2/2009.
Treasury, "HP-1321 Interim Assistant Secretary for Financial Stability Neel Kashkari Update ON The TARP Program," 12/8/2008, accessed 4/2/2009.
Treasury, "HP 1322 Neel Kashkari Testimony before the U.S. House of Representatives Financial Services Committee," 12/10/2008, accessed 4/2/2009.
Treasury, "HP-1332 Secretary Paulson Statement on Stabilizing the Automotive Industry," 12/19/2008, accessed 4/2/2009.

Treasury, "HP-1347 Interim Assistant Secretary for Financial Stability Neel Kashkari Remarks at Brookings Institution," 1/8/2009, accessed 4/2/2009.
Treasury, "HP-1349 Interim Assistant Secretary for Financial Stability Neel Kashkari Review of the Financial Market Crisis and the Troubled Asset Relief Program," 1/13/2009, accessed 4/2/2009.
Treasury, "HP-1349 Neel Kashkari Review of the Financial Market Crisis & TARP," 1/13/2009, accessed 4/2/2009.
Treasury, "Secretary Tim Geithner Opening Statement—Delivery Senate Banking Committee Hearing," Press Release, 2/10/2009, accessed 4/2/2009.
Treasury, "Secretary Tim Geithner Opening Statement—Senate Budget Committee Hearing Policies to Address the Crises in Financial and Housing Markets," Press Release, 2/11/2009, accessed 4/2/2009.
Treasury, "U.S. Treasury Secretary Tim Geithner Written Testimony House Ways and Means Committee Hearing—as Prepared for Delivery," Press Release, 3/3/2009, accessed 4/2/2009.
Treasury, "Treasury Secretary Tim Geithner House Budget Committee Hearing Opening Statement—As Prepared for Delivery," Press Release, 3/5/2009, accessed 4/2/2009.
U.S. DEPARTMENT OF THE TREASURY ("TREASURY")
Treasury, "Interim Assistant Secretary for Financial Stability Neel Kashkari Testimony before the House Committee on Oversight And Government Reform, Subcommittee On Domestic Policy—As Prepared For Delivery," Press Release, 3/11/2009, accessed 4/2/2009.
Treasury, "Treasury Secretary Tim Geithner Senate Budget Committee Hearing Opening Statement," Press Release, 3/12/2009, accessed 4/2/2009.
Treasury, "Treasury Secretary Tim Geithner Written Testimony House Financial Services Committee Hearing," Press Release, 3/24/2009, accessed 4/2/2009.
Treasury, "Treasury Secretary Tim Geithner Remarks before the Council on Foreign Relations as Prepared Ffor Delivery," Press Release, 3/25/2009, accessed 4/2/2009.
Treasury, "Treasury Secretary Tim Geithner Written Testimony House Financial Services Committee Hearing," Press Release, 3/26/2009, accessed 4/2/2009.
Financial Stability Oversight Board ("FSOB")
Roles and Mission
FSOB is responsible for reviewing the exercise of authority under programs developed in accordance with EESA, including: • *Policies implemented by the secretary and the office of financial stability, including the appointment of financial agents, the designation of asset classes to be purchased, and plans for the structure of vehicles used to purchase troubled assets* • *The effect of such actions in assisting american families in preserving home ownership, stabilizing financial markets, and protecting taxpayers in addition, FSOB is responsible for making recommendations to the secretary on the use of the authority under EESA, as well as for reporting any suspected fraud, misrepresentation, or malfeasance to sigtarp or the U.S. attorney general.*
Oversight Reports
Fsob, Amended and Restated Bylaws
Fsob, Statement and Procedures Regarding Public Access to Records of the Financial Stability Board
FSOB, Minutes of the Financial Stability Oversight Board Meeting, October 7, 2008
FSOB, Minutes of the Financial Stability Oversight Board Meeting, October 13, 2008
FSOB, Minutes of the Financial Stability Oversight Board Meeting, October 22, 2008
FSOB, Minutes of the Financial Stability Oversight Board Meeting, November 9, 2008
FSOB, Minutes of the Financial Stability Oversight Board Meeting, December 10, 2008
FSOB, Minutes of Financial Stability Oversight Board Meeting, December 19, 2008
FOSB, First Quarterly Report to Congress pursuant to section 104(g) of the EESA, for quarter ending December 31, 2008
FSOB, Minutes of Financial Stability Oversight Board Meeting, January 8, 2009
FSOB, Minutes of Financial Stability Oversight Board Meeting, January 15, 2009
Recorded Testimony
None
SECURITIES AND EXCHANGE COMMISSION ("SEC")
Roles and Mission

(Continued)

SEC administers the federal securities laws, requires disclosure by public companies, and brings enforcement actions against violators of securities law. While other federal and state agencies are legally responsible for regulating mortgage lending and the credit markets, sec has taken these decisive actions to address the extraordinary caused by the current credit crisis: • *aggressively combating fraud and market manipulation through enforcement actions* • *taking swift action to stabilize financial markets* • *enhancing transparency in financial disclosure*
Oversight Reports
SEC, "Report and recommendations pursuant to section 133 of the emergency economic stabilization act of 2008: study on mark-to- market accounting," office of the chief accountant, division of corporation finance, 12/30/2008, accessed 1/22/2009.
Recorded Testimony
SEC, "Testimony concerning turmoil in U.S. Credit Markets: Recent Actions Regarding Government Sponsored Entities, Investment Banks and Other Financial Institutions," Chairman Christopher Cox, Sec, before The Committee on Banking, Housing, and Urban Affairs, U.S. Senate, 9/23/2008, accessed 1/22/2009.
Sec, "Testimony Concerning The Role Of Federal Regulators: Lessons from the Credit Crisis for the Future of Regulation," Chairman Christopher Cox, SEC, before the Committee on Oversight and Government Reform, U.S. House of Representatives, 10/23/2008, accessed 1/22/2009.
SEC, "Testimony Concerning Securities Law Enforcement in the Current Financial Crisis," Commissioner Elisse B. Walter, Sec, Before the United States House of Representatives Committee on Financial Services, 3/20/2009, accessed 3/23/2009.
GOVERNMENT ACCOUNTABILITY OFFICE ("GAO")
Roles and Mission
GAO is tasked with performing ongoing oversight of TARP's performance, including:
• *evaluating the characteristics of asset purchases and the disposition of assets acquired*
• *assessing TARP's efficiency in using the funds*
• *evaluating compliance with applicable laws and regulations*
• *assessing the efficiency of contracting procedures*
• *auditing TARP's annual financial statements and internal controls*
• *submitting reports to congress at least every 60 days*
Oversight Reports
GAO, "TARP: Additional Actions Needed to Better Ensure Integrity, Accountability, And Transparency" (GAO-09-161), 12/2/2008
GAO, "TARP: Status of Efforts to Address Defaults and Foreclosures in Mortgages" (GAO-09-231), 12/4/2008, accessed 4/8/2009.
GAO, "Troubled Asset Relief Program: Status of Efforts to Address Defaults and Foreclosures on Home Mortgages" (GAO-09-231t), 12/4/2008, accessed on 1/22/2009.
GAO, "Auto Industry: A Framework for Considering Federal Financial Assistance" (GAO-09-247t), 12/5/2008, accessed 1/22/2009.
GAO, "Troubled Asset Relief Program: Additional Actions Needed to Better Ensure Integrity, Accountability, and Transparency" (GAO-09-266t), 12/10/2008, accessed 1/22/2009.
GAO, "High-Risk Series: An Update" (Gao-09-271), 1/2009, accessed 4/8/2009.
GAO, "Troubled Asset Relief Program: Status Of Efforts to Address Transparency and Accountability Issues" (GAO-09-296), 1/2009, accessed 4/8/2009.
GAO, "Financial Regulation: A Framework for Craft and Assessing Proposals to Modernize the Outdated U.S. Financial Regulatory System" (GAO-09-216), 1/8/2009, accessed 1/22/2009.
GAO, "Small Business Administration: Additional Guidance on Documenting Credit Elsewhere Decisions Could Improve 7(A) Program Oversight" (GAO-09-228), 2/2009, accessed 3/23/2009.
GAO, "TARP: Status of Efforts to Address Transparency and Accountability Issues" (GAO-09-359), 2/5/2009, accessed 4/8/2009.
GAO, "TARP: Status of Efforts to Address Transparency and Accountability Issues" (GAO-09-417), 2/24/2009, accessed 4/8/2009.
GAO, "Status of Efforts to Address Transparency and Accountability Issues" (GAO-09-474), 2/24/2009, accessed 3/23/2009.
GAO, "Status of Efforts to Address Transparency and Accountability Issues" (GAO-09-474), 3/11/2009, accessed

3/23/2009.
GAO, "Preliminary Observations on Assistance Provided to Aig" (GAO-09-490), 3/18/2009, accessed 3/23/2009.
GAO, "Status of Efforts to Address Transparency And Accountability Issues" (GAO-09-484), 3/19/2009, accessed 3/23/2009.
GOVERNMENT ACCOUNTABILITY OFFICE ("GAO")
GAO, "Troubled Asset Relief Program: Capital Purchase Program Transactions for the Period October 28, 2008 Through March 20, 2009 and Information on Financial Agency Agreements, Contracts, and Blanket Purchase Agreements Awarded as of March 13, 2009" (GAO-09-522sp, An E-Supplement To Gao-09-504), 3/31/2009, accessed 3/31/2009.
GAO, "TARP: March 2009 Status of Efforts to Address Transparency and Accountability Issues" (GAO-09-522), 3/31/2009, accessed 4/8/2009.
GAO, "TARP: Status Of Efforts To Address Transparency And Accountability Issues" (GAO-09-539), 3/31/2009, accessed 4/8/2009.
Recorded Testimony
GAO, "Federal Financial Assistance, Preliminary Observations on Assistance Provided to AIG," Orice M. Williams, Director Financial Markets and Community Investment, 3/18/2009, accessed 3/23/2009."
GAO, "Relief Program: Status Of Efforts to Address Transparency and Accountability Issues," Gene L. Dodaro, Acting Comptroller General of the United States, before the Senate Committee on Finance, 3/31/2009, accessed 3/31/2009.
CONGRESSIONAL OVERSIGHT PANEL ("COP")
Roles and Mission
COP Is tasked with reviewing the current state of the financial markets and the regulatory system. As a by-product of these oversight activities, COP is required to produce the following reports to congress:
• *regular reports every 30 days that cover a variety of issues, including administration of the program, the impact of purchases on the financial markets/financial institutions, market transparency, and the effectiveness of foreclosure mitigation, minimization of long-term costs, and maximization of benefits for taxpayers*
• *a special report on regulatory reform, published no later than january 20, 2009, analyzing the current state of the regulatory system and its effectiveness at overseeing the participants in the financial system and protecting consumers. The report is to provide recommendations for improvement regarding whether any participants in the financial markets that are currently outside the regulatory system should become subject to the regulatory system, the rationale underlying such recommendation, and whether there are any gaps in existing consumer protections.*
Oversight Reports
COP, "Questions About The $700 Billion Emergency Economic Stabilization Funds," The First Report of the Congressional Oversight Panel for Economic Stabilization, 12/10/2008, on 1/22/2009.
COP, Regulatory Reform Hearing on December 16, 2008.
COP, "Special Report on Regulatory Reform," 1/2009.
COP, "Accountability for the Troubled Asset Relief Program," The Second Report of the Congressional Oversight Panel, 1/9/2009.
COP, Regulatory Reform Hearing On January 14, 2009.
COP, "Report to the Congressional Oversight Panel for Economic Stabilization Legal Analysis of the Investments By The U.S. Department of the Treasury in Financial Institutions under the Troubled Asset Relief Program," By Timothy G. Massad, Esq., 1/27/2009, accessed on 3/23/2009.
COP, "February Oversight Report, Valuing Treasury's Acquisitions," 2/6/2009, accessed on 3/23/2009.
Recorded Testimony
COP, "Learning from the Past—Lessons from the Banking Crises of the 20th Century," 3/19/2009, accessed on 3/23/2009.
OFFICE OF MANAGEMENT AND BUDGET ("OMB")
Roles and Mission
OMB's predominant mission is to assist the president in overseeing the preparation of the federal budget and to supervise its administration in executive branch agencies. in helping to formulate the president's spending plans, omb evaluates the effectiveness of agency programs, policies, and procedures, assesses competing funding demands among agencies, and sets funding priorities. OMB ensures that agency reports, rules, testimony, and proposed legislation are consistent with the president's budget and with administration policies. *In addition, OMB oversees and coordinates the administration's procurement, financial management, information, and regulatory policies. In each of these areas, OMB's role is to help improve administrative management, to develop better performance measures and coordinating mechanisms, and to reduce any unnecessary burdens on the public.*
Oversight Reports
OMB, "OMB Report under the Emergency Economic Stabilization Act, Section 202," 2/5/2008, accessed 1/19/09.

(Continued)

Recorded Testimony
None
CONGRESSIONAL BUDGET OFFICE ("CBO")
Roles and Mission
CBO's mandate is to provide the congress with objective, nonpartisan, and timely analyses to aid in economic and budgetary decisions on the wide array of programs covered by the federal budget, and the information and estimates required for the congressional budget process. *CBO assists the house and senate budget committees, and the congress more generally, by preparing reports and analyses. in accordance with the CBO's mandate to provide objective and impartial analysis, CBO's reports contain no policy recommendations.*
Oversight Reports
CBO, "The Troubled Asset Relief Program: Report on Transactions Through December 31, 2008," 1/2009, accessed 1/22/2009.
CBO, "Estimated Costs Of Additional Debt Service That Would Result From Enacting H.R.1, The American Recovery and Reinvestment Act of 2009," 1/27/2009, accessed 3/23/2009.
Cbo, "Estimated Macroeconomic Impacts of H.R.1 As Passed By The Senate and the House," 2/11/2009, accessed 3/23/2009.
Recorded Testimony
None
FEDERAL RESERVE BOARD ("FEDERAL RESERVE")
Roles and Mission
Federal Reserve's duties fall into four general areas:
• *Conducting the nation's monetary policy by influencing the monetary and credit conditions in the economy in pursuit of maximum employment, stable prices, and moderate long-term interest rates* • *Supervising and regulating banking institutions to ensure the safety and soundness of the nation's banking and financial system and to protect the credit rights of consumers* • *Maintaining the stability of the financial system and containing systemic risk that may arise in financial markets* • *Providing financial services to depository institutions, the U.S. government, and foreign official institutions, including playing a major role in operating the nation's payments system*
Oversight Reports
No report issued to date
Recorded Testimony
Federal Reserve, "Economic Outlook and Financial Markets," Chairman Ben S. Bernanke, Testimony before the Committee on the Budget, U.S. House of Representatives, 10/20/2008, accessed 1/22/2009.
Federal Reserve, "Foreclosure Prevention Efforts And Market Stability," Governor Elizabeth A. Duke, Testimony before the Committee on Banking, Housing, and Urban Affairs, U.S. Senate, 10/23/2008, accessed 1/22/2009.
Federal Reserve, "TARP and The Federal Reserve's Liquidity Facilities," Chairman Ben S. Bernanke, Testimony before the Committee on Financial Services, U.S. House Of Representatives, 11/18/2008, accessed 1/22/2009.
Federal Reserve, "Effects of the Financial Crisis on Small Business," Governor Randall S. Kroszner, Testimony Before The Committee on Small Business, U.S. House of Representatives, 11/20/2008, accessed 1/22/2009.
Federal Reserve, "The Crisis and The Policy Response," Chairman Ben S. Bernanke, Stamp Lecture, London School of Economics, 1/13/2009, accessed 1/22/2009.
Federal Reserve, "Troubled Asset Relief Program," Vice Chairman Donald L. Kohn, Testimony before the Committee on Financial Services, 1/13/2009, accessed 1/22/2009.
Federal Reserve, "Federal Reserve Programs To Strengthen Credit Markets and the Economy," Chairman Ben S. Bernanke , Testimony before the Financial Services, U.S. House of Representatives, 2/10/2009, accessed 3/23/009.
Federal Reserve, "Federal Reserve Programs to Strengthen Credit Markets and the Economy," Chairman Ben S. Bernanke, Testimony before the Committee on Financial Services, U.S. House Of Representatives, 2/10/2009, accessed 4/2/2009.
Federal Reserve, "American International Group," Vice Chairman Donald L. Kohn, Testimony Before The Committee on Banking, Housing, and Urban Affairs, 3/5/2009, accessed 4/2/2009.
Federal Reserve, "American International Group," Vice Chairman Donald L. Kohn, Testimony before the Committee on Banking, Housing, and Urban Affairs, U.S. Senate, 3/5/2009, accessed 3/23/2009.
FEDERAL RESERVE BOARD ("FEDERAL RESERVE")
Federal Reserve, "American International Group," Chairman Ben S. Bernanke, Testimony before the Committee on Financial Services, U.S. House of Representatives, 3/24/2009, accessed 4/2/2009.
Federal Reserve, "Credit Availability and Prudent Lending Standards," Governor Elizabeth A. Duke, Testimony

before the Committee on Financial Services, U.S. House of Representatives, 3/25/2009, accessed 4/2/2009.
FEDERAL DEPOSIT INSURANCE CORPORATION (FDIC)
Roles And Mission
FDIC is an independent agency created by congress that maintains the stability and public confidence in the nation's financial system by insuring deposits, examining and supervising financial institutions, and managing receiverships.
Oversight Reports
None
Recorded Testimony
FDIC, U.S. Senate, "Statement of Sheila C. Bair, Chairman, Fdic, on Turmoil in the U.S. Credit Markets: Examining Recent Regulatory Responses," Committee on Banking, Housing And Urban Affairs, 10/23/2008, accessed 1/22/2009.
FDIC, U.S. House of Representatives, "Statement of Sheila C. Bair, Chairman, FDIC, on Oversight of Implementation of the Emergency Economic Stabilization Act Of 2008 and of Government Lending And Insurance Facilities," Committee on Financial Services, 11/18/2008, accessed 1/22/2009.
FDIC, U.S. Senate, "Statement Of Michael H. Krimminger, Special Advisor for Policy, Office of the Chairman; FDIC on Oversight Of Implementation of the Eesa Of 2008 and Efforts to Mitigate Foreclosures," Subcommittee on Financial Services And General Government Committee On Appropriations, 12/4/2008, accessed 1/22/2009.
FDIC, U.S. House Of Representatives, "Statement of John F. Bovenzi, Deputy To The Chairman and Coo, FDIC, On Priorities for the Next Administration: Use of TARP Funds under The EESA Of 2008," Committee On Financial Services, 1/13/2009, accessed 1/22/2009.
FEDERAL DEPOSIT INSURANCE CORPORATION OFFICE OF THE INSPECTOR GENERAL (FDIC OIG)
Roles and Mission
The Office of Inspector General Promotes The Economy, Efficiency, and Effectiveness of FDIC Programs And Operations, and Protects Against Fraud, Waste, and Abuse, to Assist and Augment The FDIC's Contribution to Stability and Public Confidence in the Nation's Financial System.
Oversight Reports
FDIC OIG, "Controls Over The FDIC's Processing of Capital Purchase Program Applications From FDIC-Supervised Institutions," 3/20/2008, accessed 3/30/2009.
Recorded Testimony
None
SPECIAL INSPECTOR GENERAL FOR THE TROUBLED ASSET RELIEF PROGRAM ("SIGTARP")
Roles and Mission
SIGTARP is responsible for conducting, supervising, and coordinating audits and investigations of the purchase, management, and sale of by the Secretary of the Treasury under any program established by the Secretary under EESA. SIGTARP shall also establish, maintain, and oversee such systems, procedures, and controls as the Special Inspector General considers appropriate. *SIGTARP's mission is to advance economic stability by promoting the efficiency and effectiveness of TARP management, through transparency, through coordinated oversight, and through robust enforcement against those, whether inside or outside of Government, who waste, steal, or abuse TARP funds.*
Oversight Reports
SIGTARP, "Use of Funds Letter," 2/5/2009, accessed 3/23/09.
SIGTARP, "Initial Report to Congress," 2/6/2009, accessed 3/23/09.
SIGTARP, "Questions and Answers Regarding the February 6, 2009 SIG TARP Letter," 2/6/2009
SIGTARP_Initial_Report_to_the_Congress.pdf, accessed 3/23/09.
Recorded Testimony
SIGTARP, Letter to Chairmen and Ranking Members of Congressional Committees Reported to by SIGTARP, 1/7/2009. (See SIGTARP Initial Report to Congress, Appendix G)
SIGTARP, Letter to Chairmen and Ranking Members of Congressional Committees Reported to by SIGTARP, 1/22/2009. (See SIGTARP Initial Report to Congress, Appendix G)
SIGTARP, Testimony Before the Senate Committee on Banking, Housing, and Urban Affairs, Special Inspector General Neil Barofsky, 2/5/2009, accessed on 3/23/2009.
SIGTARP, Testimony Before the Senate Committee on the Judiciary, Special Inspector General Neil Barofsky, 2/11/2009

(Continued)

SIGTARP, Testimony Before the House Committee on Financial Services Subcommittee on Oversight and Investigations, Special Inspector General Neil Barofsky, 2/24/2009, accessed on 3/23/2009.
SIGTARP, Testimony Before the House Committee on Oversight and Government Reform Subcommittee on Domestic Policy, Special Inspector General Neil Barofsky, 3/11/2009, accessed on 3/23/2009.
SIGTARP, Testimony Before the House Committee on Ways and Means Subcommittee on Oversight, 3/19/2009, Special Inspector General Neil Barofsky, accessed on 3/23/2009.
SIGTARP, Testimony Before the United States Senate Finance Committee, Special Inspector General Neil Barofsky, 3/31/2009, accessed on 4/2/2009.

Note: Italics style indicates verbatim narrative taken from source documents.

Sources: Treasury, accessed 4/2/2009; Treasury Inspector General, accessed 4/2/2009; Financial Stability Oversight Board, accessed 4/2/2009; SEC, accessed 4/2/2009; GAO, accessed 4/2/2009; COP, accessed 4/2/2009; OMB, accessed 4/2/2009; CBO, accessed 4/2/2009; Federal Reserve Board, accessed 4/2/2009; FDIC, accessed 4/2/2009; FDIC OIG, accessed 4/10/2009.

H. Warrants

When a warrant's exercise price is lower than the current market price of the stock, the warrants are "in the money." When the strike price (exercise price) is above the stock's market price, it is "out of the money." It is important to note that even warrants that are "out of the money" have value; this value is based on the possibility that the share price will eventually rise above the strike price. It is not unusual that warrants are "out of the money" when they are issued. The following table contains the current status of the warrants that Treasury obtained under CPP, SSFI, TIP, AIFP, and AGP (for publicly traded companies).

As of March 31, 2009, Treasury continued to hold the warrants received from the four publicly traded financial institutions and the single private financial institution that repurchased preferred shares from the Government. On March 31, 2009, Iberiabank Corporation, Bank of Marin Bancorp, Old National Bancorp, Signature Bank, and Centra Financial Holdings, Inc./Centra Bank, Inc. repurchased their preferred shares. Upon repurchase of their preferred shares, institutions have a right to purchase their Government-held warrants before they are offered for sale to a third party. Only the private financial institution, Centra Financial Holdings, Inc./Centra Bank, Inc., had notified Treasury of its intention to repurchase its warrant preferred shares at their aggregate liquidation preference. If the four publicly traded financial institutions choose not to exercise this right within 15 calendar days of repurchase, Treasury has stated that it will liquidate the warrants. Treasury has stated that it will receive a profit from the sale of these assets, regardless of the final purchaser, since Treasury did not incur any additional cost to acquire them. Details of these share repurchases and their corresponding impact on Treasury's warrant portfolio will be provided in SIGTARP's next quarterly report.

Status of Warrants Treasury Obtained Under CPP, SSFI, TIP, AIFP, and AGP

Participant	Transaction Date	Ticker Symbol	Stock Price as of Transaction Date	Exchange	Program	Number of Warrants Received	Strike Price as Stated in the Agreements	Stock Price as of 3/31/2009	In or Out of the Money?	Amount "In the Money" or "Out of the Money" as of 3/31/2009
1st Constitution Bancorp	12/23/2008	FCCY	$8.81	NASDAQ	CPP - Public	200,222	$8.99	$6.25	OUT	(2.74)
1st FS Corporation	11/14/2008	FFIS	$7.50	OTC BB	CPP - Public	276,815	$8.87	$4.75	OUT	(4.12)
1st Source Corporation	1/23/2009	SRCE	$17.43	NASDAQ	CPP - Public	837,947	$19.87	$18.05	OUT	(1.82)
AB&T Financial Corporation	1/23/2009	ABTO	$6.90	OTC BB	CPP - Public	80,153	$6.55	$6.00	OUT	(0.55)
AIG	11/25/2008	AIG	$1.77	NYSE	SSFI	53,798,766	$2.50	$1.00	OUT	(1.50)
Alaska Pacific Bancshares, Inc.	2/6/2009	AKPB	$4.15	OTC BB	CPP - Public	175,772	$4.08	$3.60	OUT	(0.48)
Alliance Financial Corporation	12/19/2008	ALNC	$23.00	NASDAQ	CPP - Public	173,069	$23.33	$17.94	OUT	(5.39)
American Express Company	1/9/2009	AXP	$19.23	NYSE	CPP - Public	24,264,129	$20.95	$13.63	OUT	(7.32)
Ameris Bancorp	11/21/2008	ABCB	$9.21	NASDAQ	CPP - Public	679,443	$11.48	$4.71	OUT	(6.77)
AmeriServ Financial, Inc.	12/19/2008	ASRV	$1.85	NASDAQ	CPP - Public	1,312,500	$2.40	$1.67	OUT	(0.73)
Anchor BanCorp Wisconsin, Inc.	1/30/2009	ABCW	$2.02	NASDAQ	CPP - Public	7,399,103	$2.23	$1.35	OUT	(0.88)
Annapolis Bancorp, Inc.	1/30/2009	ANNB	$2.10	NASDAQ	CPP - Public	299,706	$4.08	$2.72	OUT	(1.36)
Associated Banc-Corp	11/21/2008	ASBC	$17.10	NASDAQ	CPP - Public	3,983,308	$19.77	$15.45	OUT	(4.32)
Bancorp Rhode Island, Inc.	12/19/2008	BARI	$19.55	NASDAQ	CPP - Public	192,967	$23.32	$18.07	OUT	(5.25)
BancTrust Financial Group, Inc.	12/19/2008	BTFG	$11.01	NASDAQ	CPP - Public	730,994	$10.26	$6.33	OUT	(3.93)
Bank of America Corporation	1/16/2009	BAC	$7.18	NYSE	TIP	150,375,940	$13.30	$6.82	OUT	(6.48)
Bank of America Corporation	10/28/2008	BAC	$23.02	NYSE	CPP - Public	73,075,674	$30.79	$6.82	OUT	(23.97)
Bank of America Corporation	1/9/2009	BAC	$12.99	NYSE	CPP - Public	48,717,116	$30.79	$6.82	OUT	(23.97)
Bank of Commerce Holdings	11/14/2008	BOCH	$5.25	NASDAQ	CPP - Public	405,405	$6.29	$5.04	OUT	(1.25)
Bank of Marin Bancorp1	12/5/2008	BMRC	$23.15	NASDAQ	CPP - Public	154,242	$27.23	$21.51	OUT	(5.72)
Bank of New York Mellon Corporation	10/28/2008	BK	$31.80	NYSE	CPP - Public	14,516,129	$31.00	$28.25	OUT	(2.75)
Bank of North Carolina	12/5/2008	BNCN	$7.97	NASDAQ	CPP - Public	543,337	$8.63	$6.05	OUT	(2.58)
Bank of the Ozarks, Inc.	12/12/2008	OZRK	$27.02	NASDAQ	CPP - Public	379,811	$29.62	$23.08	OUT	(6.54)
Banner Corporation	11/21/2008	BANR	$9.17	NASDAQ	CPP - Public	1,707,989	$10.89	$2.91	OUT	(7.98)

(Continued)

Participant	Transaction Date	Ticker Symbol	Stock Price as of Transaction Date	Exchange	Program	Number of Warrants Received	Strike Price as Stated in the Agreements	Stock Price as of 3/31/2009	In or Out of the Money?	Amount "In the Money" or "Out of the Money" as of 3/31/2009
Bar Harbor Bankshares/ Bar Harbor Bank & Trust	1/16/2009	BHB	$23.70	AMEX	CPP - Public	104,910	$26.81	$23.30	OUT	(3.51)
BB&T Corp.	11/14/2008	BBT	$28.05	NYSE	CPP - Public	13,902,573	$33.81	$16.92	OUT	(16.89)
BCSB Bancorp, Inc.	12/23/2008	BCSB	$7.75	NASDAQ	CPP - Public	183,465	$8.83	$8.75	OUT	(0.08)
Berkshire Hills Bancorp, Inc.	12/19/2008	BHLB	$28.53	NASDAQ	CPP - Public	226,330	$26.51	$22.92	OUT	(3.59)
Blue Valley Ban Corp.	12/5/2008	BVBC	$15.25	OTC BB	CPP - Public	111,083	$29.37	$12.00	OUT	(17.37)
Boston Private Financial Holdings, Inc.	11/21/2008	BPFH	$5.65	NASDAQ	CPP - Public	2,887,500	$8.00	$3.51	OUT	(4.49)
Bridge Capital Holdings	12/23/2008	BBNK	$4.40	NASDAQ	CPP - Public	396,412	$9.03	$4.50	OUT	(4.53)
Broadway Financial Corporation	11/14/2008	BYFC	$5.85	NASDAQ	CPP - Public	183,175	$7.37	$5.24	OUT	(2.13)
C&F Financial Corporation	1/9/2009	CFFI	$18.93	NASDAQ	CPP - Public	167,504	$17.91	$14.45	OUT	(3.46)
Cadence Financial Corporation	1/9/2009	CADE	$5.15	NASDAQ	CPP - Public	1,145,833	$5.76	$4.42	OUT	(1.34)
Capital Bank Corporation	12/12/2008	CBKN	$7.05	NASDAQ	CPP - Public	749,619	$8.26	$4.56	OUT	(3.70)
Capital One Financial Corporation	11/14/2008	COF	$31.19	NYSE	CPP - Public	12,657,960	$42.13	$12.24	OUT	(29.89)
Carolina Bank Holdings, Inc.	1/9/2009	CLBH	$6.30	NASDAQ	CPP - Public	357,675	$6.71	$4.20	OUT	(2.51)
Carolina Trust Bank	2/6/2009	CART	$6.00	NASDAQ	CPP - Public	86,957	$6.90	$4.80	OUT	(2.10)
Carrollton Bancorp	2/13/2009	CRRB	$6.10	NASDAQ	CPP - Public	205,379	$6.72	$5.12	OUT	(1.60)
Associated Banc-Corp	11/21/2008	ASBC	$17.10	NASDAQ	CPP - Public	3,983,308	$19.77	$15.45	OUT	(4.32)
Bancorp Rhode Island, Inc.	12/19/2008	BARI	$19.55	NASDAQ	CPP - Public	192,967	$23.32	$18.07	OUT	(5.25)
BancTrust Financial Group, Inc.	12/19/2008	BTFG	$11.01	NASDAQ	CPP - Public	730,994	$10.26	$6.33	OUT	(3.93)
Bank of America Corporation	1/16/2009	BAC	$7.18	NYSE	TIP	150,375,940	$13.30	$6.82	OUT	(6.48)
Bank of America Corporation	10/28/2008	BAC	$23.02	NYSE	CPP - Public	73,075,674	$30.79	$6.82	OUT	(23.97)
Bank of America Corporation	1/9/2009	BAC	$12.99	NYSE	CPP - Public	48,717,116	$30.79	$6.82	OUT	(23.97)
Bank of Commerce Holdings	11/14/2008	BOCH	$5.25	NASDAQ	CPP - Public	405,405	$6.29	$5.04	OUT	(1.25)
Bank of Marin Bancorp1	12/5/2008	BMRC	$23.15	NASDAQ	CPP - Public	154,242	$27.23	$21.51	OUT	(5.72)
Bank of New York Mellon Corporation	10/28/2008	BK	$31.80	NYSE	CPP - Public	14,516,129	$31.00	$28.25	OUT	(2.75)
Bank of North Carolina	12/5/2008	BNCN	$7.97	NASDAQ	CPP - Public	543,337	$8.63	$6.05	OUT	(2.58)
Bank of the Ozarks, Inc.	12/12/2008	OZRK	$27.02	NASDAQ	CPP - Public	379,811	$29.62	$23.08	OUT	(6.54)

(Continued)

Participant	Transaction Date	Ticker Symbol	Stock Price as of Transaction Date	Exchange	Program	Number of Warrants Received	Strike Price as Stated in the Agreements	Stock Price as of 3/31/2009	In or Out of the Money?	Amount "In the Money" or "Out of the Money" as of 3/31/2009
Banner Corporation	11/21/2008	BANR	$9.17	NASDAQ	CPP - Public	1,707,989	$10.89	$2.91	OUT	(7.98)
Bar Harbor Bankshares/ Bar Harbor Bank & Trust	1/16/2009	BHB	$23.70	AMEX	CPP - Public	104,910	$26.81	$23.30	OUT	(3.51)
BB&T Corp.	11/14/2008	BBT	$28.05	NYSE	CPP - Public	13,902,573	$33.81	$16.92	OUT	(16.89)
BCSB Bancorp, Inc.	12/23/2008	BCSB	$7.75	NASDAQ	CPP - Public	183,465	$8.83	$8.75	OUT	(0.08)
Berkshire Hills Bancorp, Inc.	12/19/2008	BHLB	$28.53	NASDAQ	CPP - Public	226,330	$26.51	$22.92	OUT	(3.59)
Blue Valley Ban Corp.	12/5/2008	BVBC	$15.25	OTC BB	CPP - Public	111,083	$29.37	$12.00	OUT	(17.37)
Boston Private Financial Holdings, Inc.	11/21/2008	BPFH	$5.65	NASDAQ	CPP - Public	2,887,500	$8.00	$3.51	OUT	(4.49)
Bridge Capital Holdings	12/23/2008	BBNK	$4.40	NASDAQ	CPP - Public	396,412	$9.03	$4.50	OUT	(4.53)
Broadway Financial Corporation	11/14/2008	BYFC	$5.85	NASDAQ	CPP - Public	183,175	$7.37	$5.24	OUT	(2.13)
C&F Financial Corporation	1/9/2009	CFFI	$18.93	NASDAQ	CPP - Public	167,504	$17.91	$14.45	OUT	(3.46)
Cadence Financial Corporation	1/9/2009	CADE	$5.15	NASDAQ	CPP - Public	1,145,833	$5.76	$4.42	OUT	(1.34)
Capital Bank Corporation	12/12/2008	CBKN	$7.05	NASDAQ	CPP - Public	749,619	$8.26	$4.56	OUT	(3.70)
Capital One Financial Corporation	11/14/2008	COF	$31.19	NYSE	CPP - Public	12,657,960	$42.13	$12.24	OUT	(29.89)
Carolina Bank Holdings, Inc.	1/9/2009	CLBH	$6.30	NASDAQ	CPP - Public	357,675	$6.71	$4.20	OUT	(2.51)
Carolina Trust Bank	2/6/2009	CART	$6.00	NASDAQ	CPP - Public	86,957	$6.90	$4.80	OUT	(2.10)
Carrollton Bancorp	2/13/2009	CRRB	$6.10	NASDAQ	CPP - Public	205,379	$6.72	$5.12	OUT	(1.60)
Cascade Financial Corporation	11/21/2008	CASB	$4.89	NASDAQ	CPP - Public	863,442	$6.77	$2.50	OUT	(4.27)
Cathay General Bancorp	12/5/2008	CATY	$20.48	NASDAQ	CPP - Public	1,846,374	$20.96	$10.43	OUT	(10.53)
Cecil Bancorp, Inc.	12/23/2008	CECB	$6.25	OTC BB	CPP - Public	261,538	$6.63	$5.10	OUT	(1.53)
Center Bancorp, Inc.	1/9/2009	CNBC	$8.00	NASDAQ	CPP - Public	173,410	$8.65	$7.22	OUT	(1.43)
Center Financial Corporation	12/12/2008	CLFC	$7.08	NASDAQ	CPP - Public	864,780	$9.54	$2.82	OUT	(6.72)
Centerstate Banks of Florida, Inc.	11/21/2008	CSFL	$15.02	NASDAQ	CPP - Public	250,825	$16.67	$11.01	OUT	(5.66)
Central Bancorp, Inc.	12/5/2008	CEBK	$5.88	NASDAQ	CPP - Public	234,742	$6.39	$4.74	OUT	(1.65)
Central Federal Corporation	12/5/2008	CFBK	$3.10	NASDAQ	CPP - Public	336,568	$3.22	$2.90	OUT	(0.32)
Central Jersey Bancorp	12/23/2008	CJBK	$6.00	NASDAQ	CPP - Public	268,621	$6.31	$6.50	IN	0.19
Central Pacific Financial Corp.	1/9/2009	CPF	$7.92	NYSE	CPP - Public	1,585,748	$12.77	$5.60	OUT	(7.17)

(Continued)

Participant	Transaction Date	Ticker Symbol	Stock Price as of Transaction Date	Exchange	Program	Number of Warrants Received	Strike Price as Stated in the Agreements	Stock Price as of 3/31/2009	In or Out of the Money?	Amount "In the Money" or "Out of the Money" as of 3/31/2009
Central Valley Community Bancorp	1/30/2009	CVCY	$5.07	NASDAQ	CPP - Public	158,133	$6.64	$4.67	OUT	(1.97)
Central Virginia Bankshares, Inc.	1/30/2009	CVBK	$5.34	NASDAQ	CPP - Public	263,542	$6.48	$3.95	OUT	(2.53)
Centrue Financial Corporation	1/9/2009	1	$6.50	NASDAQ	CPP - Public	508,320	$9.64	$5.38	OUT	(4.26)
CIT Group, Inc.	12/31/2008	CIT	$4.54	NYSE	CPP - Public	88,705,584	$3.94	$2.85	OUT	(1.09)
Citigroup, Inc.	12/31/2008	C	$6.71	NYSE	AGP	254,476,909	$10.61	$2.53	OUT	(8.08)
Citigroup, Inc.	1/16/2009	C	$3.50	NYSE	TIP	188,500,000	10.61	$2.53	OUT	(8.08)
Citigroup, Inc.	10/28/2008	C	$13.41	NYSE	CPP - Public	210,084,034	$17.85	$2.53	OUT	(15.32)
Citizens & Northern Corporation	1/16/2009	CZNC	$18.78	NASDAQ	CPP - Public	194,794	$20.36	$18.49	OUT	(1.87)
Citizens First Corporation	12/19/2008	CZFC	$4.00	NASDAQ	CPP - Public	254,218	$5.18	$4.00	OUT	(1.18)
Citizens Republic Bancorp, Inc.	12/12/2008	CRBC	$2.33	NASDAQ	CPP - Public	17,578,125	$2.56	$1.55	OUT	(1.01)
Citizens South Banking Corporation	12/12/2008	CSBC	$6.52	NASDAQ	CPP - Public	428,870	$7.17	$5.08	OUT	(2.09)
City National Corporation	11/21/2008	CYN	$35.64	NYSE	CPP - Public	1,128,668	$53.16	$33.77	OUT	(19.39)
Coastal Banking Company, Inc.	12/5/2008	CBCO	$5.75	OTC BB	CPP - Public	205,579	$7.26	$6.00	OUT	(1.26)
CoBiz Financial, Inc.	12/19/2008	COBZ	$9.59	NASDAQ	CPP - Public	895,968	$10.79	$5.25	OUT	(5.54)
Codorus Valley Bancorp, Inc.	1/9/2009	CVLY	$9.00	NASDAQ	CPP - Public	263,859	$9.38	$8.06	OUT	(1.32)
Colony Bankcorp, Inc.	1/9/2009	CBAN	$8.50	NASDAQ	CPP - Public	500,000	$8.40	$6.39	OUT	(2.01)
Columbia Banking System, Inc.	11/21/2008	COLB	$8.85	NASDAQ	CPP - Public	796,046	$14.49	$6.40	OUT	(8.09)
Comerica, Inc.	11/14/2008	CMA	$21.95	NYSE	CPP - Public	11,479,592	$29.40	$18.31	OUT	(11.09)
Commerce National Bank	1/9/2009	CNBF	$6.00	OTC BB	CPP - Public	87,209	$8.60	$6.10	OUT	(2.50)
Community Bankers Trust Corporation	12/19/2008	BTC	$3.00	AMEX	CPP - Public	780,000	$3.40	$3.40	OUT	0.00
Community Financial Corporation	12/19/2008	CFFC	$4.00	NASDAQ	CPP - Public	351,194	$5.40	$4.00	OUT	(1.40)
Community Partners Bancorp	1/30/2009	CPBC	$3.98	NASDAQ	CPP - Public	288,462	$4.68	$3.35	OUT	(1.33)
Community West Bancshares	12/19/2008	CWBC	$3.81	NASDAQ	CPP - Public	521,158	$4.49	$2.64	OUT	(1.85)
Crescent Financial Corporation	1/9/2009	CRFN	$4.50	NASDAQ	CPP - Public	833,705	$4.48	$3.60	OUT	(0.88)
CVB Financial Corp.	12/5/2008	CVBF	$11.04	NASDAQ	CPP - Public	1,669,521	$11.68	$6.63	OUT	(5.05)
Discover Financial Services	3/13/2009	DFS	$6.23	NYSE	CPP - Public	20,500,915	$8.96	$6.31	OUT	(2.65)

(Continued)

Participant	Transaction Date	Ticker Symbol	Stock Price as of Transaction Date	Exchange	Program	Number of Warrants Received	Strike Price as Stated in the Agreements	Stock Price as of 3/31/2009	In or Out of the Money?	Amount "In the Money" or "Out of the Money" as of 3/31/2009
DNB Financial Corporation	1/30/2009	DNBF	$5.99	NASDAQ	CPP - Public	186,311	$9.46	$7.52	OUT	(1.94)
Eagle Bancorp, Inc.	12/5/2008	EGBN	$6.15	NASDAQ	CPP - Public	770,867	$7.44	$6.25	OUT	(1.19)
East West Bancorp	12/5/2008	EWBC	$15.64	NASDAQ	CPP - Public	3,035,109	$15.15	$4.57	OUT	(10.58)
Eastern Virginia Bankshares, Inc.	1/9/2009	EVBS	$9.81	NASDAQ	CPP - Public	373,832	$9.63	$8.39	OUT	(1.24)
ECB Bancorp, Inc./East Carolina Bank	1/16/2009	ECBE	$15.93	NASDAQ	CPP - Public	144,984	$18.57	$15.30	OUT	(3.27)
Emclaire Financial Corp.	12/23/2008	EMCF	$23.50	OTC BB	CPP - Public	50,111	$22.45	$21.50	OUT	(0.95)
Encore Bancshares, Inc.	12/5/2008	EBTX	$13.23	NASDAQ	CPP - Public	364,026	$14.01	$8.87	OUT	(5.14)
Enterprise Financial Services Corp.	12/19/2008	EFSC	$14.46	NASDAQ	CPP - Public	324,074	$16.20	$9.76	OUT	(6.44)
F.N.B. Corporation	1/9/2009	FNB	$12.08	NYSE	CPP - Public	1,302,083	$11.52	$7.67	OUT	(3.85)
Farmers Capital Bank Corporation	1/9/2009	FFKT	$24.41	NASDAQ	CPP - Public	223,992	$20.09	$15.67	OUT	(4.42)
Fidelity Bancorp, Inc.	12/12/2008	FSBI	$6.75	NASDAQ	CPP - Public	121,387	$8.65	$10.07	IN	1.42
Fidelity Southern Corporation	12/19/2008	LION	$3.18	NASDAQ	CPP - Public	2,266,458	$3.19	$2.40	OUT	(0.79)
Fifth Third Bancorp	12/31/2008	FITB	$8.26	NASDAQ	CPP - Public	43,617,747	$11.72	$2.92	OUT	(8.80)
Financial Institutions, Inc.	12/23/2008	FISI	$13.34	NASDAQ	CPP - Public	378,175	$14.88	$7.62	OUT	(7.26)
First Bancorp	1/9/2009	FBNC	$15.74	NASDAQ	CPP - Public	616,308	$15.82	$11.97	OUT	(3.85)
First BanCorp	1/16/2009	FBP	$8.59	NYSE	CPP - Public	5,842,259	$10.27	$4.26	OUT	(6.01)
First Busey Corporation	3/6/2009	BUSE	$6.15	NASDAQ	CPP - Public	1,147,666	$13.07	$7.76	OUT	(5.31)
First California Financial Group, Inc.	12/19/2008	FCAL	$5.55	NASDAQ	CPP - Public	599,042	$6.26	$4.20	OUT	(2.06)
First Citizens Banc Corp.	1/23/2009	FCZA	$6.56	NASDAQ	CPP - Public	469,312	$7.41	$7.51	IN	0.10
First Community Bank Corporation of America	12/23/2008	FCFL	$5.13	NASDAQ	CPP - Public	228,312	$7.02	$4.10	OUT	(2.92)
First Community Bankshares Inc.	11/21/2008	FCBC	$24.88	NASDAQ	CPP - Public	176,546	$35.26	$11.67	OUT	(23.59)
First Community Corporation	11/21/2008	FCCO	$8.50	NASDAQ	CPP - Public	195,915	$8.69	$6.60	OUT	(2.09)
First Defiance Financial Corp.	12/5/2008	FDEF	$7.67	NASDAQ	CPP - Public	550,595	$10.08	$6.08	OUT	(4.00)
First Federal Bancshares of Arkansas, Inc.	3/6/2009	FFBH	$3.86	NASDAQ	CPP - Public	321,847	$7.69	$4.70	OUT	(2.99)
First Financial Bancorp	12/23/2008	FFBC	$12.26	NASDAQ	CPP - Public	930,233	$12.90	$9.53	OUT	(3.37)

(Continued)

Participant	Transaction Date	Ticker Symbol	Stock Price as of Transaction Date	Exchange	Program	Number of Warrants Received	Strike Price as Stated in the Agreements	Stock Price as of 3/31/2009	In or Out of the Money?	Amount "In the Money" or "Out of the Money" as of 3/31/2009
First Financial Holdings, Inc.	12/5/2008	FFCH	$20.65	NASDAQ	CPP - Public	483,391	$20.17	$7.65	OUT	(12.52)
First Financial Service Corporation	1/9/2009	FFKY	$12.58	NASDAQ	CPP - Public	215,983	$13.89	$11.10	OUT	(2.79)
First Horizon National Corporation	11/14/2008	FHN	$9.35	NYSE	CPP - Public	12,743,235	$10.20	$10.74	IN	0.54
First Litchfield Financial Corporation	12/12/2008	FLFL	$7.10	OTC BB	CPP - Public	199,203	$7.53	$7.00	OUT	(0.53)
First M&F Corporation	2/27/2009	FMFC	$6.23	NASDAQ	CPP - Public	513,113	$8.77	$6.12	OUT	(2.65)
First Merchants Corporation	2/20/2009	FRME	$11.12	NASDAQ	CPP - Public	991,453	$17.55	$10.79	OUT	(6.76)
First Midwest Bancorp, Inc.	12/5/2008	FMBI	$18.48	NASDAQ	CPP - Public	1,305,230	$22.18	$8.59	OUT	(13.59)
First Niagara Financial Group	11/21/2008	FNFG	$14.37	NASDAQ	CPP - Public	1,906,191	$14.48	$10.89	OUT	(3.59)
First Northern Community Bancorp	3/13/2009	FNRN	$4.05	OTC BB	CPP - Public	352,977	$7.39	$4.99	OUT	(2.40)
First PacTrust Bancorp, Inc.	11/21/2008	FPTB	$8.80	NASDAQ	CPP - Public	280,795	$10.31	$6.75	OUT	(3.56)
First Place Financial Corp.	3/13/2009	FPFC	$2.38	NASDAQ	CPP - Public	3,670,822	$2.98	$3.36	IN	0.38
First Security Group, Inc.	1/9/2009	FSGI	$5.00	NASDAQ	CPP - Public	823,627	$6.01	$3.37	OUT	(2.64)
First Sound Bank	12/23/2008	FSWA	$6.01	OTC BB	CPP - Public	114,080	$9.73	$3.00	OUT	(6.73)
First United Corporation	1/30/2009	FUNC	$12.15	NASDAQ	CPP - Public	326,323	$13.79	$8.38	OUT	(5.41)
Firstbank Corporation	1/30/2009	FBMI	$6.50	NASDAQ	CPP - Public	578,947	$8.55	$5.01	OUT	(3.54)
FirstMerit Corporation	1/9/2009	FMER	$18.51	NASDAQ	CPP - Public	952,260	$19.69	$18.20	OUT	(1.49)
Flagstar Bancorp, Inc.	1/30/2009	FBC	$0.60	NYSE	CPP - Public	64,513,790	$0.62	$0.75	IN	0.13
Flushing Financial Corporation	12/19/2008	FFIC	$12.01	NASDAQ	CPP - Public	751,611	$13.97	$6.02	OUT	(7.95)
FNB United Corp.	2/13/2009	FNBN	$3.00	NASDAQ	CPP - Public	2,207,143	$3.50	$2.60	OUT	(0.90)
FPB Bancorp, Inc.	12/5/2008	FPBI	$4.10	NASDAQ	CPP - Public	183,158	$4.75	$2.50	OUT	(2.25)
Fulton Financial Corporation	12/23/2008	FULT	$8.76	NASDAQ	CPP - Public	5,509,756	$10.25	$6.63	OUT	(3.62)
General Motors Corporation	12/29/2008	GM	$3.60	NYSE	AIFP	1,733,068	$5.02	$1.94	OUT	(3.08)
GMAC LLC	12/29/2008	GJM	$9.00	NYSE	AIFP	250,002	$0.01	$7.46	IN	7.45
Great Southern Bancorp	12/5/2008	GSBC	$8.15	NASDAQ	CPP - Public	909,091	$9.57	$14.01	IN	4.44

(Continued)

Participant	Transaction Date	Ticker Symbol	Stock Price as of Transaction Date	Exchange	Program	Number of Warrants Received	Strike Price as Stated in the Agreements	Stock Price as of 3/31/2009	In or Out of the Money?	Amount "In the Money" or "Out of the Money" as of 3/31/2009
Green Bankshares, Inc.	12/23/2008	GRNB	$14.00	NASDAQ	CPP - Public	635,504	$17.06	$8.80	OUT	(8.26)
Guaranty Federal Bancshares, Inc.	1/30/2009	GFED	$5.50	NASDAQ	CPP - Public	459,459	$5.55	$5.30	OUT	(0.25)
Hampton Roads Bankshares, Inc.	12/31/2008	HMPR	$8.73	NASDAQ	CPP - Public	1,325,858	$9.09	$7.79	OUT	(1.30)
Hawthorn Bancshares, Inc.	12/19/2008	HWBK	$16.13	NASDAQ	CPP - Public	245,443	$18.49	$11.75	OUT	(6.74)
HCSB Financial Corporation	3/6/2009	HCFB	$11.01	OTC BB	CPP - Public	91,714	$21.09	$11.01	OUT	(10.08)
Heartland Financial USA, Inc.	12/19/2008	HTLF	$21.33	NASDAQ	CPP - Public	609,687	$20.10	$13.54	OUT	(6.56)
Heritage Commerce Corp.	11/21/2008	HTBK	$11.00	NASDAQ	CPP - Public	462,963	$12.96	$5.25	OUT	(7.71)
Heritage Financial Corporation	11/21/2008	HFWA	$12.06	NASDAQ	CPP - Public	276,074	$13.04	$10.45	OUT	(2.59)
Heritage Oaks Bancorp	3/20/2009	HEOP	$4.25	NASDAQ	CPP - Public	611,650	$5.15	$4.15	OUT	(1.00)
HF Financial Corp.	11/21/2008	HFFC	$12.00	NASDAQ	CPP - Public	302,419	$12.40	$12.75	IN	0.35
HMN Financial, Inc.	12/23/2008	HMNF	$3.99	NASDAQ	CPP - Public	833,333	$4.68	$3.10	OUT	(1.58)
Home Bancshares, Inc.	1/16/2009	HOMB	$21.76	NASDAQ	CPP - Public	288,129	$26.03	$19.97	OUT	(6.06)
HopFed Bancorp	12/12/2008	HFBC	$11.25	NASDAQ	CPP - Public	243,816	$11.32	$9.75	OUT	(1.57)
Horizon Bancorp	12/19/2008	HBNC	$13.00	NASDAQ	CPP - Public	212,104	$17.68	$11.10	OUT	(6.58)
Huntington Bancshares	11/14/2008	HBAN	$7.79	NASDAQ	CPP - Public	23,562,994	$8.90	$1.66	OUT	(7.24)
Iberiabank Corporation[1]	12/5/2008	IBKC	$50.82	NASDAQ	CPP - Public	276,980	$48.74	$45.94	OUT	(2.80)
Independent Bank Corp.	1/9/2009	INDB	$25.29	NASDAQ	CPP - Public	481,664	$24.34	$14.75	OUT	(9.59)
Independent Bank Corporation	12/12/2008	IBCP	$2.01	NASDAQ	CPP - Public	3,461,538	$3.12	$2.34	OUT	(0.78)
Indiana Community Bancorp	12/12/2008	INCB	$12.81	NASDAQ	CPP - Public	188,707	$17.09	$13.00	OUT	(4.09)
Integra Bank Corporation	2/27/2009	IBNK	$1.00	NASDAQ	CPP - Public	7,418,876	$1.69	$1.89	IN	0.20
Intermountain Community Bancorp	12/19/2008	IMCB	$5.30	OTC BB	CPP - Public	653,226	$6.20	$4.60	OUT	(1.60)
International Bancshares Corporation	12/23/2008	IBOC	$20.65	NASDAQ	CPP - Public	1,326,238	$24.43	$7.80	OUT	(16.63)
Intervest Bancshares Corporation	12/23/2008	IBCA	$3.76	NASDAQ	CPP - Public	691,882	$5.42	$2.15	OUT	(3.27)
JPMorgan Chase & Co.	10/28/2008	JPM	$37.60	NYSE	CPP - Public	88,401,697	$42.42	$26.58	OUT	(15.84)
KeyCorp	11/14/2008	KEY	$9.60	NYSE	CPP - Public	35,244,361	$10.64	$7.87	OUT	(2.77)

(Continued)

Participant	Transaction Date	Ticker Symbol	Stock Price as of Transaction Date	Exchange	Program	Number of Warrants Received	Strike Price as Stated in the Agreements	Stock Price as of 3/31/2009	In or Out of the Money?	Amount "In the Money" or "Out of the Money" as of 3/31/2009
Lakeland Bancorp, Inc.	2/6/2009	LBAI	$7.82	NASDAQ	CPP - Public	949,571	$9.32	$8.03	OUT	(1.29)
Lakeland Financial Corporation	2/27/2009	LKFN	$17.45	NASDAQ	CPP - Public	396,538	$21.20	$19.19	OUT	(2.01)
LCNB Corp.	1/9/2009	LCNB	$9.20	OTC BB	CPP - Public	217,063	$9.26	$9.50	IN	0.24
LNB Bancorp, Inc.	12/12/2008	LNBB	$5.60	NASDAQ	CPP - Public	561,343	$6.74	$5.00	OUT	(1.74)
LSB Corporation	12/12/2008	LSBX	$13.92	NASDAQ	CPP - Public	209,497	$10.74	$8.94	OUT	(1.80)
M&T Bank Corporation	12/23/2008	MTB	$53.90	NYSE	CPP - Public	1,218,522	$73.86	$45.24	OUT	(28.62)
MainSource Financial Group, Inc.	1/16/2009	MSFG	$11.70	NASDAQ	CPP - Public	571,906	$14.95	$8.04	OUT	(6.91)
Manhattan Bancorp	12/5/2008	MNHN	$8.00	OTC BB	CPP - Public	29,480	$8.65	$4.75	OUT	(3.90)
Marshall & Ilsley Corporation	11/14/2008	MI	$14.70	NYSE	CPP - Public	13,815,789	$18.62	$5.63	OUT	(12.99)
MB Financial, Inc.	12/5/2008	MBFI	$26.00	NASDAQ	CPP - Public	1,012,048	$29.05	$13.60	OUT	(15.45)
MetroCorp Bancshares, Inc.	1/16/2009	MCBI	$6.13	NASDAQ	CPP - Public	771,429	$8.75	$2.79	OUT	(5.96)
Mid Penn Bancorp, Inc.	12/19/2008	MPB	$22.00	NASDAQ	CPP - Public	73,099	$20.52	$19.00	OUT	(1.52)
Middleburg Financial Corporation	1/30/2009	MBRG	$11.00	NASDAQ	CPP - Public	208,202	$15.85	$11.47	OUT	(4.38)
MidSouth Bancorp, Inc.	1/9/2009	MSL	$11.90	AMEX	CPP - Public	208,768	$14.37	$10.24	OUT	(4.13)
Midwest Banc Holdings, Inc.	12/5/2008	MBHI	$2.26	NASDAQ	CPP - Public	4,282,020	$2.97	$1.01	OUT	(1.96)
Monarch Community Bancorp, Inc.	2/6/2009	MCBF	$3.00	NASDAQ	CPP - Public	260,962	$3.90	$3.46	OUT	(0.44)
Monarch Financial Holdings, Inc.	12/19/2008	MNRK	$6.86	NASDAQ	CPP - Public	264,706	$8.33	$5.10	OUT	(3.23)
Morgan Stanley	10/28/2008	MS	$15.20	NYSE	CPP - Public	65,245,759	$22.99	$22.77	OUT	(0.22)
MutualFirst Financial, Inc.	12/23/2008	MFSF	$6.75	NASDAQ	CPP - Public	625,135	$7.77	$4.80	OUT	(2.97)
Nara Bancorp, Inc.	11/21/2008	NARA	$7.52	NASDAQ	CPP - Public	1,042,531	$9.64	$2.94	OUT	(6.70)
National Penn Bancshares, Inc.	12/12/2008	NPBC	$14.23	NASDAQ	CPP - Public	1,470,588	$15.30	$8.30	OUT	(7.00)
New Hampshire Thrift Bancshares, Inc.	1/16/2009	NHTB	$7.00	NASDAQ	CPP - Public	184,275	$8.14	$7.25	OUT	(0.89)
NewBridge Bancorp	12/12/2008	NBBC	$2.60	NASDAQ	CPP - Public	2,567,255	$3.06	$2.11	OUT	(0.95)
North Central Bancshares, Inc.	1/9/2009	FFFD	$10.50	NASDAQ	CPP - Public	99,157	$15.43	$12.25	OUT	(3.18)
Northeast Bancorp	12/12/2008	NBN	$7.24	NASDAQ	CPP - Public	67,958	$9.33	$7.51	OUT	(1.82)

(Continued)

Participant	Transaction Date	Ticker Symbol	Stock Price as of Transaction Date	Exchange	Program	Number of Warrants Received	Strike Price as Stated in the Agreements	Stock Price as of 3/31/2009	In or Out of the Money?	Amount "In the Money" or "Out of the Money" as of 3/31/2009
Northern States Financial Corporation	2/20/2009	NSFC	$3.14	NASDAQ	CPP - Public	584,084	$4.42	$7.45	IN	3.03
Northern Trust Corporation	11/14/2008	NTRS	$44.92	NASDAQ	CPP - Public	3,824,624	$61.81	$59.82	OUT	(1.99)
Oak Ridge Financial Services, Inc.	1/30/2009	BKOR	$6.41	NASDAQ	CPP - Public	163,830	$7.05	$3.90	OUT	(3.15)
Oak Valley Bancorp	12/5/2008	OVLY	$5.68	NASDAQ	CPP - Public	350,346	$5.78	$3.75	OUT	(2.03)
OceanFirst Financial Corp.	1/16/2009	OCFC	$14.83	NASDAQ	CPP - Public	380,853	$15.07	$10.22	OUT	(4.85)
Old Line Bancshares, Inc.	12/5/2008	OLBK	$7.50	NASDAQ	CPP - Public	141,892	$7.40	$5.90	OUT	(1.50)
Old National Bancorp[1]	12/12/2008	ONB	$15.48	NYSE	CPP - Public	813,008	$18.45	$11.17	OUT	(7.28)
Old Second Bancorp, Inc.	1/16/2009	OSBC	$9.01	NASDAQ	CPP - Public	815,339	$13.43	$6.35	OUT	(7.08)
Pacific Capital Bancorp	11/21/2008	PCBC	$13.31	NASDAQ	CPP - Public	1,512,003	$17.92	$6.77	OUT	(11.15)
Pacific International Bancorp	12/12/2008	PIBW	$5.01	OTC BB	CPP - Public	127,785	$7.63	$3.50	OUT	(4.13)
Park National Corporation	12/23/2008	PRK	$63.95	AMEX	CPP - Public	227,376	$65.97	$55.75	OUT	(10.22)
Parke Bancorp, Inc.	1/30/2009	PKBK	$6.50	NASDAQ	CPP - Public	299,779	$8.15	$7.00	OUT	(1.15)
Parkvale Financial Corporation	12/23/2008	PVSA	$12.48	NASDAQ	CPP - Public	376,327	$12.66	$10.98	OUT	(1.68)
Peapack-Gladstone Financial Corporation	1/9/2009	PGC	$22.89	NASDAQ	CPP - Public	143,139	$30.06	$18.03	OUT	(12.03)
Peninsula Bank Holding Co.	1/30/2009	PBKH	$9.75	OTC BB	CPP - Public	81,670	$11.02	$10.00	OUT	(1.02)
Peoples Bancorp of North Carolina, Inc.	12/23/2008	PEBK	$9.31	NASDAQ	CPP - Public	357,234	$10.52	$5.75	OUT	(4.77)
Pinnacle Financial Partners, Inc.	12/12/2008	PNFP	$26.37	NASDAQ	CPP - Public	534,910	$26.64	$23.71	OUT	(2.93)
Plumas Bancorp	1/30/2009	PLBC	$6.97	NASDAQ	CPP - Public	237,712	$7.54	$5.99	OUT	(1.55)
Popular, Inc.	12/5/2008	BPOP	$5.85	NASDAQ	CPP - Public	20,932,836	$6.70	$2.16	OUT	(4.54)
Porter Bancorp, Inc.	11/21/2008	PBIB	$15.51	NASDAQ	CPP - Public	299,829	$17.51	$11.33	OUT	(6.18)
PremierWest Bancorp	2/13/2009	PRWT	$3.91	NASDAQ	CPP - Public	1,038,462	$5.98	$4.02	OUT	(1.96)
Princeton National Bancorp, Inc.	1/23/2009	PNBC	$19.17	NASDAQ	CPP - Public	155,025	$24.27	$14.00	OUT	(10.27)
PrivateBancorp, Inc.	1/30/2009	PVTB	$14.58	NASDAQ	CPP - Public	1,290,026	$28.35	$14.46	OUT	(13.89)
Provident Bancshares Corp.	11/14/2008	PBKS	$8.99	NASDAQ	CPP - Public	2,374,608	$9.57	$7.05	OUT	(2.52)
Provident Community Bancshares, Inc.	3/13/2009	PCBS	$2.49	NASDAQ	CPP - Public	178,880	$7.77	$2.65	OUT	(5.12)

(Continued)

Participant	Transaction Date	Ticker Symbol	Stock Price as of Transaction Date	Exchange	Program	Number of Warrants Received	Strike Price as Stated in the Agreements	Stock Price as of 3/31/2009	In or Out of the Money?	Amount "In the Money" or "Out of the Money" as of 3/31/2009
Pulaski Financial Corp.	1/16/2009	PULB	$7.52	NASDAQ	CPP - Public	778,421	$6.27	$5.00	OUT	(1.27)
QCR Holdings, Inc.	2/13/2009	QCRH	$10.00	NASDAQ	CPP - Public	521,888	$10.99	$8.04	OUT	(2.95)
Regions Financial Corp.	11/14/2008	RF	$9.67	NYSE	CPP - Public	48,253,677	$10.88	$4.26	OUT	(6.62)
Royal Bancshares of Pennsylvania	2/20/2009	RBPA.A	$3.00	NASDAQ	CPP - Public	1,104,370	$4.13	$2.10	OUT	(2.03)
S&T Bancorp	1/16/2009	STBA	$29.14	NASDAQ	CPP - Public	517,012	$31.53	$21.21	OUT	(10.32)
Salisbury Bancorp, Inc.	3/13/2009	SAL	$22.65	AMEX	CPP - Public	57,671	$22.93	$24.55	IN	1.62
Sandy Spring Bancorp, Inc.	12/5/2008	SASR	$19.36	NASDAQ	CPP - Public	651,547	$19.13	$11.16	OUT	(7.97)
Santa Lucia Bancorp	12/19/2008	SLBA	$15.50	OTC BB	CPP - Public	37,360	$16.06	$11.50	OUT	(4.56)
SCBT Financial Corporation	1/16/2009	SCBT	$29.49	NASDAQ	CPP - Public	303,083	$32.06	$20.90	OUT	(11.16)
Seacoast Banking Corporation of Florida	12/19/2008	SBCF	$7.41	NASDAQ	CPP - Public	1,179,245	$6.36	$3.03	OUT	(3.33)
Security Federal Corporation	12/19/2008	SFDL	$16.00	OTC BB	CPP - Public	137,966	$19.57	$15.50	OUT	(4.07)
Severn Bancorp, Inc.	11/21/2008	SVBI	$4.95	NASDAQ	CPP - Public	556,976	$6.30	$3.15	OUT	(3.15)
Shore Bancshares, Inc.	1/9/2009	SHBI	$20.75	NASDAQ	CPP - Public	172,970	$21.68	$16.75	OUT	(4.93)
Signature Bank[1]	12/12/2008	SBNY	$25.60	NASDAQ	CPP - Public	595,829	$30.21	$28.23	OUT	(1.98)
Somerset Hills Bancorp	1/16/2009	SOMH	$6.62	NASDAQ	CPP - Public	163,065	$6.82	$6.16	OUT	(0.66)
South Financial Group, Inc.	12/5/2008	TSFG	$4.02	NASDAQ	CPP - Public	10,106,796	$5.15	$1.10	OUT	(4.05)
Southern Community Financial Corp.	12/5/2008	SCMF	$3.50	NASDAQ	CPP - Public	1,623,418	$3.95	$3.56	OUT	(0.39)
Southern First Bancshares, Inc.	2/27/2009	SFST	$5.82	NASDAQ	CPP - Public	330,554	$7.85	$5.61	OUT	(2.24)
Southern Missouri Bancorp, Inc.	12/5/2008	SMBC	$11.00	NASDAQ	CPP - Public	114,326	$12.53	$10.80	OUT	(1.73)
Southwest Bancorp, Inc.	12/5/2008	OKSB	$12.57	NASDAQ	CPP - Public	703,753	$14.92	$9.38	OUT	(5.54)
State Bancorp, Inc.	12/5/2008	STBC	$10.00	NASDAQ	CPP - Public	465,569	$11.87	$7.70	OUT	(4.17)
State Street Corporation	10/28/2008	STT	$41.81	NYSE	CPP - Public	5,576,208	$53.80	$30.78	OUT	(23.02)
StellarOne Corporation	12/19/2008	STEL	$17.04	NASDAQ	CPP - Public	302,623	$14.87	$11.91	OUT	(2.96)
Sterling Bancorp	12/23/2008	STL	$12.27	NYSE	CPP - Public	516,817	$12.19	$9.90	OUT	(2.29)
Sterling Bancshares, Inc.	12/12/2008	SBIB	$5.68	NASDAQ	CPP - Public	2,615,557	$7.18	$6.54	OUT	(0.64)

(Continued)

Participant	Transaction Date	Ticker Symbol	Stock Price as of Transaction Date	Exchange	Program	Number of Warrants Received	Strike Price as Stated in the Agreements	Stock Price as of 3/31/2009	In or Out of the Money?	Amount "In the Money" or "Out of the Money" as of 3/31/2009
Sterling Financial Corporation	12/5/2008	STSA	$5.75	NASDAQ	CPP - Public	6,437,677	$7.06	$2.07	OUT	(4.99)
Stewardship Financial Corporation	1/30/2009	SSFN	$11.00	NASDAQ	CPP - Public	127,119	$11.80	$8.14	OUT	(3.66)
Summit State Bank	12/19/2008	SSBI	$5.00	NASDAQ	CPP - Public	239,212	$5.33	$4.60	OUT	(0.73)
Sun Bancorp, Inc.	1/9/2009	SNBC	$7.19	NASDAQ	CPP - Public	1,543,376	$8.68	$5.19	OUT	(3.49)
SunTrust Banks, Inc.	11/14/2008	STI	$33.52	NYSE	CPP - Public	11,891,280	$44.15	$11.74	OUT	(32.41)
SunTrust Banks, Inc.	12/31/2008	STI	$29.54	NYSE	CPP - Public	6,008,902	$33.70	$11.74	OUT	(21.96)
Superior Bancorp Inc.	12/5/2008	SUPR	$4.30	NASDAQ	CPP - Public	1,923,792	$5.38	$3.98	OUT	(1.40)
Susquehanna Bancshares, Inc.	12/12/2008	SUSQ	$14.30	NASDAQ	CPP - Public	3,028,264	$14.86	$9.33	OUT	(5.53)
SVB Financial Group	12/12/2008	SIVB	$32.82	NASDAQ	CPP - Public	708,116	$49.78	$20.01	OUT	(29.77)
Synovus Financial Corp.	12/19/2008	SNV	$7.95	NYSE	CPP - Public	15,510,737	$9.36	$3.25	OUT	(6.11)
Taylor Capital Group	11/21/2008	TAYC	$8.92	NASDAQ	CPP - Public	1,462,647	$10.75	$4.45	OUT	(6.30)
Sandy Spring Bancorp, Inc.	12/5/2008	SASR	$19.36	NASDAQ	CPP - Public	651,547	$19.13	$11.16	OUT	(7.97)
Santa Lucia Bancorp	12/19/2008	SLBA	$15.50	OTC BB	CPP - Public	37,360	$16.06	$11.50	OUT	(4.56)
SCBT Financial Corporation	1/16/2009	SCBT	$29.49	NASDAQ	CPP - Public	303,083	$32.06	$20.90	OUT	(11.16)
Seacoast Banking Corporation of Florida	12/19/2008	SBCF	$7.41	NASDAQ	CPP - Public	1,179,245	$6.36	$3.03	OUT	(3.33)
Security Federal Corporation	12/19/2008	SFDL	$16.00	OTC BB	CPP - Public	137,966	$19.57	$15.50	OUT	(4.07)
Severn Bancorp, Inc.	11/21/2008	SVBI	$4.95	NASDAQ	CPP - Public	556,976	$6.30	$3.15	OUT	(3.15)
Shore Bancshares, Inc.	1/9/2009	SHBI	$20.75	NASDAQ	CPP - Public	172,970	$21.68	$16.75	OUT	(4.93)
Signature Bank1	12/12/2008	SBNY	$25.60	NASDAQ	CPP - Public	595,829	$30.21	$28.23	OUT	(1.98)
Somerset Hills Bancorp	1/16/2009	SOMH	$6.62	NASDAQ	CPP - Public	163,065	$6.82	$6.16	OUT	(0.66)
South Financial Group, Inc.	12/5/2008	TSFG	$4.02	NASDAQ	CPP - Public	10,106,796	$5.15	$1.10	OUT	(4.05)
Southern Community Financial Corp.	12/5/2008	SCMF	$3.50	NASDAQ	CPP - Public	1,623,418	$3.95	$3.56	OUT	(0.39)
Southern First Bancshares, Inc.	2/27/2009	SFST	$5.82	NASDAQ	CPP - Public	330,554	$7.85	$5.61	OUT	(2.24)
Southern Missouri Bancorp, Inc.	12/5/2008	SMBC	$11.00	NASDAQ	CPP - Public	114,326	$12.53	$10.80	OUT	(1.73)
Southwest Bancorp, Inc.	12/5/2008	OKSB	$12.57	NASDAQ	CPP - Public	703,753	$14.92	$9.38	OUT	(5.54)
State Bancorp, Inc.	12/5/2008	STBC	$10.00	NASDAQ	CPP - Public	465,569	$11.87	$7.70	OUT	(4.17)

(Continued)

Participant	Transaction Date	Ticker Symbol	Stock Price as of Transaction Date	Exchange	Program	Number of Warrants Received	Strike Price as Stated in the Agreements	Stock Price as of 3/31/2009	In or Out of the Money?	Amount "In the Money" or "Out of the Money" as of 3/31/2009
State Street Corporation	10/28/2008	STT	$41.81	NYSE	CPP - Public	5,576,208	$53.80	$30.78	OUT	(23.02)
StellarOne Corporation	12/19/2008	STEL	$17.04	NASDAQ	CPP - Public	302,623	$14.87	$11.91	OUT	(2.96)
Sterling Bancorp	12/23/2008	STL	$12.27	NYSE	CPP - Public	516,817	$12.19	$9.90	OUT	(2.29)
Sterling Bancshares, Inc.	12/12/2008	SBIB	$5.68	NASDAQ	CPP - Public	2,615,557	$7.18	$6.54	OUT	(0.64)
Sterling Financial Corporation	12/5/2008	STSA	$5.75	NASDAQ	CPP - Public	6,437,677	$7.06	$2.07	OUT	(4.99)
Stewardship Financial Corporation	1/30/2009	SSFN	$11.00	NASDAQ	CPP - Public	127,119	$11.80	$8.14	OUT	(3.66)
Summit State Bank	12/19/2008	SSBI	$5.00	NASDAQ	CPP - Public	239,212	$5.33	$4.60	OUT	(0.73)
Sun Bancorp, Inc.	1/9/2009	SNBC	$7.19	NASDAQ	CPP - Public	1,543,376	$8.68	$5.19	OUT	(3.49)
SunTrust Banks, Inc.	11/14/2008	STI	$33.52	NYSE	CPP - Public	11,891,280	$44.15	$11.74	OUT	(32.41)
SunTrust Banks, Inc.	12/31/2008	STI	$29.54	NYSE	CPP - Public	6,008,902	$33.70	$11.74	OUT	(21.96)
Superior Bancorp Inc.	12/5/2008	SUPR	$4.30	NASDAQ	CPP - Public	1,923,792	$5.38	$3.98	OUT	(1.40)
Susquehanna Bancshares, Inc.	12/12/2008	SUSQ	$14.30	NASDAQ	CPP - Public	3,028,264	$14.86	$9.33	OUT	(5.53)
SVB Financial Group	12/12/2008	SIVB	$32.82	NASDAQ	CPP - Public	708,116	$49.78	$20.01	OUT	(29.77)
Synovus Financial Corp.	12/19/2008	SNV	$7.95	NYSE	CPP - Public	15,510,737	$9.36	$3.25	OUT	(6.11)
Taylor Capital Group	11/21/2008	TAYC	$8.92	NASDAQ	CPP - Public	1,462,647	$10.75	$4.45	OUT	(6.30)
Tennessee Commerce Bancorp, Inc.	12/19/2008	TNCC	$6.89	NASDAQ	CPP - Public	461,538	$9.75	$7.68	OUT	(2.07)
Texas Capital Bancshares, Inc.	1/16/2009	TCBI	$11.11	NASDAQ	CPP - Public	758,086	$14.84	$11.26	OUT	(3.58)
The Bancorp, Inc.	12/12/2008	TBBK	$4.06	NASDAQ	CPP - Public	1,960,405	$3.46	$4.24	IN	0.78
The Bank of Kentucky Financial Corporation	2/13/2009	BKYF	$18.99	NASDAQ	CPP - Public	274,784	$18.56	$19.00	IN	0.44
The Connecticut Bank and Trust Company	12/19/2008	CTBC	$4.60	NASDAQ	CPP - Public	175,742	$4.65	$3.25	OUT	(1.40)
The Elmira Savings Bank, FSB	12/19/2008	ESBK	$9.80	NASDAQ	CPP - Public	116,538	$11.70	$10.75	OUT	(0.95)
The First Bancorp, Inc.	1/9/2009	FNLC	$18.09	NASDAQ	CPP - Public	225,904	$16.60	$15.86	OUT	(0.74)
The First Bancshares, Inc.	2/6/2009	FBMS	$7.60	NASDAQ	CPP - Public	54,705	$13.71	$9.82	OUT	(3.89)
The Goldman Sachs Group, Inc.	10/28/2008	GS	$93.57	NYSE	CPP - Public	12,205,045	$122.90	$106.02	OUT	(16.88)
The PNC Financial Services Group Inc.	12/31/2008	PNC	$49.00	NYSE	CPP - Public	16,885,192	$67.33	$29.29	OUT	(38.04)
TIB Financial Corp.	12/5/2008	TIBB	$4.88	NASDAQ	CPP - Public	1,063,218	$5.22	$2.88	OUT	(2.34)

(Continued)

Participant	Transaction Date	Ticker Symbol	Stock Price as of Transaction Date	Exchange	Program	Number of Warrants Received	Strike Price as Stated in the Agreements	Stock Price as of 3/31/2009	In or Out of the Money?	Amount "In the Money" or "Out of the Money" as of 3/31/2009
Tidelands Bancshares, Inc	12/19/2008	TDBK	$2.88	NASDAQ	CPP - Public	571,821	$3.79	$3.05	OUT	(0.74)
Timberland Bancorp, Inc.	12/23/2008	TSBK	$7.45	NASDAQ	CPP - Public	370,899	$6.73	$5.16	OUT	(1.57)
TowneBank	12/12/2008	TOWN	$21.69	NASDAQ	CPP - Public	538,184	$21.31	$16.33	OUT	(4.98)
Trustmark Corporation	11/21/2008	TRMK	$17.90	NASDAQ	CPP - Public	1,647,931	$19.57	$18.38	OUT	(1.19)
U.S. Bancorp	11/14/2008	USB	$26.30	NYSE	CPP - Public	32,679,102	$30.29	$14.61	OUT	(15.68)
UCBH Holdings, Inc.	11/14/2008	UCBH	$3.99	NASDAQ	CPP - Public	7,847,732	$5.71	$1.51	OUT	(4.20)
Umpqua Holdings Corp.	11/14/2008	UMPQ	$14.35	NASDAQ	CPP - Public	2,221,795	$14.46	$9.06	OUT	(5.40)
Union Bankshares Corporation	12/19/2008	UBSH	$23.34	NASDAQ	CPP - Public	422,636	$20.94	$13.85	OUT	(7.09)
United Bancorp, Inc.	1/16/2009	UBCP	$9.08	NASDAQ	CPP - Public	311,492	$9.92	$9.45	OUT	(0.47)
United Bancorporation of Alabama, Inc.	12/23/2008	UBAB	$15.50	OTC BB	CPP - Public	104,040	$14.85	$15.50	IN	0.65
United Community Banks, Inc.	12/5/2008	UCBI	$12.33	NASDAQ	CPP - Public	2,132,701	$12.66	$4.16	OUT	(8.50)
Unity Bancorp, Inc.	12/5/2008	UNTY	$4.50	NASDAQ	CPP - Public	764,778	$4.05	$3.19	OUT	(0.86)
Valley Financial Corporation	12/12/2008	VYFC	$6.20	NASDAQ	CPP - Public	344,742	$6.97	$4.76	OUT	(2.21)
Valley National Bancorp	11/14/2008	VLY	$17.55	NYSE	CPP - Public	2,297,090	$19.59	$12.37	OUT	(7.22)
Virginia Commerce Bancorp	12/12/2008	VCBI	$5.45	NASDAQ	CPP - Public	2,696,203	$3.95	$3.79	OUT	(0.16)
VIST Financial Corp.	12/19/2008	VIST	$9.31	NASDAQ	CPP - Public	364,078	$10.30	$7.00	OUT	(3.30)
Wainwright Bank & Trust Company	12/19/2008	WAIN	$7.33	NASDAQ	CPP - Public	390,071	$8.46	$6.48	OUT	(1.98)
Washington Banking Company/ Whidbey Island Bank	1/16/2009	WBCO	$7.84	NASDAQ	CPP - Public	492,164	$8.04	$6.80	OUT	(1.24)
Washington Federal, Inc.	11/14/2008	WFSL	$15.22	NASDAQ	CPP - Public	1,707,456	$17.57	$13.29	OUT	(4.28)
Webster Financial Corporation	11/21/2008	WBS	$11.70	NYSE	CPP - Public	3,282,276	$18.28	$4.25	OUT	(14.03)
Wells Fargo & Company	10/28/2008	WFC	$34.46	NYSE	CPP - Public	110,261,688	$34.01	$14.24	OUT	(19.77)
Wesbanco Bank, Inc.	12/5/2008	WSBC	$25.07	NASDAQ	CPP - Public	439,282	$25.61	$22.83	OUT	(2.78)
West Bancorporation, Inc.	12/31/2008	WTBA	$12.25	NASDAQ	CPP - Public	474,100	$11.39	$7.45	OUT	(3.94)
Westamerica Bancorporation	2/13/2009	WABC	$45.52	NASDAQ	CPP - Public	246,640	$50.92	$45.56	OUT	(5.36)
Western Alliance Bancorporation	11/21/2008	WAL	$10.17	NYSE	CPP - Public	1,574,213	$13.34	$4.56	OUT	(8.78)

(Continued)

Participant	Transaction Date	Ticker Symbol	Stock Price as of Transaction Date	Exchange	Program	Number of Warrants Received	Strike Price as Stated in the Agreements	Stock Price as of 3/31/2009	In or Out of the Money?	Amount "In the Money" or "Out of the Money" as of 3/31/2009
Whitney Holding Corporation	12/19/2008	WTNY	$15.11	NASDAQ	CPP - Public	2,631,579	$17.10	$11.45	OUT	(5.65)
Wilmington Trust Corporation	12/12/2008	WL	$21.69	NYSE	CPP - Public	1,856,714	$26.66	$9.69	OUT	(16.97)
Wilshire Bancorp, Inc.	12/12/2008	WIBC	$8.36	NASDAQ	CPP - Public	949,460	$9.82	$5.16	OUT	(4.66)
Wintrust Financial Corporation	12/19/2008	WTFC	$20.06	NASDAQ	CPP - Public	1,643,295	$22.82	$12.30	OUT	(10.52)
WSFS Financial Corporation	1/23/2009	WSFS	$28.54	NASDAQ	CPP - Public	175,105	$45.08	$22.36	OUT	(22.72)
Yadkin Valley Financial Corporation	1/16/2009	YAVY	$11.77	NASDAQ	CPP - Public	385,990	$13.99	$7.45	OUT	(6.54)
Zions Bancorporation	11/14/2008	ZION	$32.69	NASDAQ	CPP - Public	5,789,909	$36.27	$9.83	OUT	(26.44)

Note:

[1] Participant repurchased shares on 3/31/2009. As of 3/31/2009, Treasury was still waiting to see if the four participants would invoke their rights to repurchase the warrants.

Sources: Participants and Transaction Date: Treasury, *Transactions Report*, 3/30/2009, Stock Price: Capital IQ, Inc. (a division of Standard & Poor's), accessed 3/12/2009 at 11:00 am EST and 4/2/2009 at 2:00 pm EST (except 3/31/2009 market price data for United Bancorporation of Alabama, Inc., HCSB Financial Corporation, and DNB Financial Corporation, and 12/12/2008 and 3/31/2009 market price data for Pacific International Bancorp., which were collected from Yahoo Finance website, Number of Warrants Received and Strike Price: Treasury, response to SIGTARP data call, 4/1/2009; Repurchases: Treasury, response to SIGTARP data call, 4/8/2009.

I. Correspondence With Treasury Regarding TALF

This appendix provides a copy of the March 4, 2009, letter from SIGTARP to Neel Kashkari, Interim Assistant Secretary for Financial Stability, regarding information about the Term Asset-Backed Securities Loan Facility ("TALF"), as well as the March 9, 2009, response letter. It also contains a Treasury memo on the same subject, dated April 14, 2009.

OFFICE OF THE SPECIAL INSPECTOR GENERAL
TROUBLED ASSET RELIEF PROGRAM
1500 Pennsylvania Ave., NW, Suite 1064
Washington, D.C. 20220

March 4, 2009

Neel Kashkari
U.S. Department of the Treasury
1500 Pennsylvania Ave., NW
Washington, D.C. 20220

Dear Mr. Kashkari:

The Office of the Special Inspector General for the Troubled Asset Relief Program requests explanations from the Department of the Treasury ("Treasury") with respect to two issues relating to the Term Asset-Backed Securities Loan Facility ("TALF").

First, please describe what information Treasury, whether itself or in conjunction with the Federal Reserve Bank of New York ("FRBNY"), intends to release about TALF transactions. In particular, please specify what information will be disclosed publicly with respect to all loans made by the FRBNY and, if different, what information will be disclosed upon surrender of collateral and purchase of such collateral by the Special Purpose Vehicle ("SPV"), such as, without limitation, (1) a listing of any securities that the SPV purchases from the FRBNY and the price paid by the SPV; (2) the borrowers who abandon any securities that the SPV purchases; (3) the amounts borrowed and the securities that are pledged as collateral to the FRBNY irrespective of whether they are abandoned; and (4) the identities of borrowers irrespective of whether the collateral has been abandoned.

Second, please describe Treasury's position on how the TALF program is consistent with the executive compensation provision of the Emergency Economic Stabilization Act, as amended.

Because the Special Inspector General will be testifying before Congress next week, please provide a response to these questions no later than Monday, March 9, 2009. Thank you in advance for your prompt response.

Very truly yours,

NEIL M. BAROFSKY
Special Inspector General

By: [signature]
KEVIN R. PUVALOWSKI
Chief of Staff

cc: Bernard Knight, Esq.
Paul Wolfteich, Esq.

DEPARTMENT OF THE TREASURY
WASHINGTON, D.C.

ASSISTANT SECRETARY

March 9, 2009

Neil M. Barofsky
Special Inspector General
U.S. Department of the Treasury
1500 Pennsylvania Avenue, N.W.
Washington, D.C., 20220

Dear Mr. Barofsky:

I am responding to your letter of March 4, 2009, requesting information about the Term Asset-Backed Securities Loan Facility ("TALF").

As you know, the TALF is a Federal Reserve credit facility authorized under section 13(3) of the Federal Reserve Act. The Federal Reserve Bank of New York (FRBNY) will make available up to $200 billion in loans, secured by eligible collateral. These are not Treasury loans, and the funds used to make these loans are not appropriated under the Emergency Economic Stabilization Act of 2008 (EESA). If a borrower does not repay a loan, the FRBNY will sell the collateral to a special purpose vehicle (SPV) established specifically to manage these assets. Treasury supports the TALF by investing funds in the SPV to purchase collateral that has been forfeited.

Treasury is committed to making its investment in the TALF transparent. Treasury posted program guidelines and other information about the TALF on the new website, www.financialstability.gov, and on the current site, http://www.treasury.gov/initiatives/eesa/, including a transaction report showing Treasury's $20 billion investment in the facility. Treasury negotiated provisions in the Credit Agreement with the FRBNY giving Treasury, the GAO, and SIGTARP access to personnel and books, papers, records or other data for the purpose of ascertaining compliance with the terms and conditions of the loan documents. Treasury has also ensured that the Department will receive regular reports about TALF activities, which will be made available to your office and the GAO. We are working with FRBNY to design these reports, and we invite you to provide input from an oversight perspective. Our agreement with the FRBNY does not give us access to the identity of individual borrowers, but we can receive demographic information about borrowers and detailed information, such as the amount, type, and CUSIP number, for collateral purchased by the SPV.

When the TALF begins making loans, Treasury will post other information on our web site about how TARP funds are being used. We will post information in our monthly reports and in our tranche reports issued under EESA section 105. Once the TALF becomes operational and the reporting requirements are defined, Treasury will decide what additional information will be posted. At a minimum, Treasury anticipates posting information about the securities purchased by the SPV, including the price, when the TALF begins making loans. We will not post information about the identity of individual borrowers, which is not available to Treasury under its agreement with the Federal Reserve Bank of New York.

You also requested information about how EESA's executive compensation requirements apply to the TALF. As previously explained in a letter to you dated January 16, 2009, from the Treasury Office of the General Counsel, Treasury determined that under the original executive compensation standards established in EESA section 111, the statutory limitations did not apply to the private parties participating in TALF. However, the FRBNY in consultation with Treasury made a preliminary policy decision to require sponsors of ABS to adopt certain executive compensation and corporate governance requirements as a condition of participation. After EESA section 111 was amended by the American Recovery and Reinvestment Act of 2009, Treasury re-evaluated the new executive compensation standards and reached the same conclusion -- that the standards did not apply to TALF participants. Treasury and FRBNY also re-evaluated the preliminary decision to, nonetheless, apply executive compensation limitations to ABS sponsors, and determined that such a policy would not enhance the effectiveness of the TALF in restoring consumer credit markets. Therefore, it was decided to remove those voluntary executive compensation provisions. In its forthcoming regulations implementing the amended executive compensation standards, as required under EESA section 111(h), Treasury will determine whether and to what extent its counterparty in the TALF transaction, the FRBNY SPV, is subject to the new standards.

Please let us know if you need additional information.

Sincerely,

Neel Kashkari
Interim Assistant Secretary for
Financial Stability

GENERAL COUNSEL

DEPARTMENT OF THE TREASURY
WASHINGTON, D.C.

APR 14 2009

MEMORANDUM TO FILE

Under the original Emergency Economic Stabilization Act of 2008 (EESA), the executive compensation provisions in section 111 applied to any financial institution that "sells troubled assets" to the Secretary. In the context of the Term Asset Backed Securities Loan Facility (TALF), these original executive compensation provisions only applied to the special purpose vehicle (SPV) created by the Federal Reserve Bank of New York (FRBNY), because the FRBNY SPV was the entity selling the subordinated debt to the Troubled Asset Relief Program (TARP). It was determined that other participants in TALF, such as sponsors of securities pledged as collateral or the institutions receiving loans directly from TALF, were not covered because they were not selling troubled assets to TARP. Nonetheless, Treasury and FRBNY originally proposed as a matter of policy to apply certain executive compensation restrictions to sponsors of TALF eligible securities. These provisions would have been implemented through contractual terms between FRBNY and its counterparties.

EESA Sec. 111, as amended by the American Recovery and Reinvestment Act of 2009 (ARRA), now contains provisions on executive compensation that apply to "TARP Recipients." The amended statute defines this term as "an entity that has received or will receive financial assistance under the financial assistance provided under TARP." This new standard contains more ambiguity than the prior standard, and therefore requires agency interpretation in many instances. Treasury will be further defining the terms "TARP Recipient" and "financial assistance" in the implementing regulations for the new section 111, as required in section 111(h). In advance of the regulations, Treasury determined that the relationship between TALF participants and the TARP program was not sufficiently direct to conclude that the TALF participants were receiving "financial assistance" from TARP, particularly when compared to TARP recipients that receive funds directly from TARP through the CPP, SSFI or TIP programs. Thus, even though the standard for application of executive compensation restrictions changed with the section 111 amendments, the legal determination regarding the applicability of these provisions to third party TALF participants did not change. With that background, when implementing the TALF program, a policy decision was made between Treasury and FRBNY to no longer require the contractual executive compensation restrictions on the sponsors.

In its regulations, Treasury will clarify the ambiguity in section 111, as amended, regarding whether its counterparty in the TALF transaction, FRBNY, may be deemed to be receiving "financial assistance" from the TARP. Treasury will be evaluating, among other things, FRBNY's status as a non-profit governmental instrumentality, the treatment of dividends from FRBNY flowing back to the Treasury as provided for in the Federal Reserve Act, and the existing statutory basis under the Federal Reserve Act for compensation decisions regarding employees of Federal Reserve Banks.

J. Responses to SIGTARP Recommendations

This appendix provides copies of letters to SIFTARP in response to SIGTARP recommendations:

Responses to SIGTARP Recommendations

Date	**Respondednt**	**Regarding**
4/7/2009	Treasury	Recommendations in SIGTARP's 2/6/2009 Initial Report to Congress
4/10/2009	Federal Reserve Bank of New York	Recommendations in SIGTARP's Draft 4/21/2009 Quarterly report to Congress
4/14/2009	Treasury	Recommendations in SIGTARp's Draft 4/21/2009 Quarterly Report to Congress

The U.S. Treasury Department
Summary Response to February 6, 2009 Recommendations of SIGTARp

April 7, 2009

Introduction:

The Treasure Department (Treasury) welcomes the recommendations made by the Special Inspector General for the Troubled Asset Relief Program (SIGTARP), including the recent recommendations set forth in SIGTTARP's February 6, 2009 report.

This document is Treasury's Summary Response to the SIGTARP'S recommendations in that report. This Summary Response provides a written, high level summary of Treasury's progress in implementing the SIGTARP recommendations and identifies the next steps that Treasury plans to take in these areas.

This report is structured as follows:

- **Identification of each SIGTARP recommendation**
- **Summary of the status of the matter to which that recommendation pertained as of the time of the February 6, 2009 SIGTARP Report**
- **Discussion of Treasury's progress in implementing the recommendation as of the date of this response**
- **Identification of Treasury's next steps**

<u>SIGTARP Recommendation1:</u> All TARP agreements should contain oversight-related language that (a) acknowledges explicitly the jurisdiction and authority of SIGTARP and other oversight bodies, as relevant, to oversee compliance of the conditions contained in the agreement in question; (b) for each contagion imposed, the participant should be required to establish internal controls with respect to that condition, report periodically to OFS Compliance regarding the implementation of those controls and its compliance with the condition and provide signed certification from an appropriate senior official to OFS Complaince that such report is accurate; and (c) the participant should be required to use best efforts to account for the use of TARP funds, to set up internal controls to comply with such accounting, and to report periodically to OFS Compliance on the results, with appropriate certification, in the manner discussed above.

<u>Status at time of previous report:</u>

As of February 6, 2009, transactional documents for TARP programs contained varying oversight and compliance provisions. In general, those provisions were more robust in the program documents for the Systemically Significant Failing Institution Program, the Targeted Investment Program, and the Automotive Industry Financing Program then for the Capital Purchase Program.

<u>Summary of Progress Since Previous Report:</u>

Two programs have been fully documented since February 6, 2009: the Term Asset-Based Securities Lending Facility (TALF) and the Auto Suppliers Support Program. Oversight-related and compliance provisions have been incorporated into documentation for these programs, as follows:

- **-Term Asset-Backed Securities Lending Facility (TALF):**
    - **-<u>Inspection rights</u> – Section 9.18 of the Credit Agreement among the Treasury, Federal Reserve Bank of New York (FRBNY), and TALF LLC contains specific language allowing SKTARP, GAO and the Treasury access to personnel and information regarding TALF borrowers to ascertain compliance with the agreement's terms and conditions.**
    - **-<u>Internal Controls</u> – Section 6 of the Credit Agreement specifically requires that TALF LLC maintain evidence of compliance with requirements under the Credit Agreement. The Federal Reserve will monitor internal controls for TALF, as the program administrator, and Treasury will have access in these reports.**
    - **-<u>Use of TARP Funds</u> – Section 4.01 _ of the Credit Agreement targets the use of TALF loan proceeds solely for specific financing asset acquisitions.**
- **Auto Suppliers Support Program:**
    - **<u>Inspection Rights</u> – Section 9.17 of the credit agreement between the Treasury and each special purpose vehicle established by the automobile manufacturers (the "OEM SFVs") to fund the program specifically contains language giving SKITARP, GAO and the Treasury access to personnel and information regarding compliance with the agreement's terms and conditions. Further, Section 30 of the pledge agreement provides the same inspection rights with respect to the automobile manufacturers and Section 9.16 of the servicing agreement provides the same with respect to the servicer of the program.**
    - **<u>Internal Controls</u> – Section 6 of the credit agreement requires that each OEM SPV borrower maintain evidence of compliance with requirements**

under the credit agreement. Treasury will receive certifications related to compliance from the borrowed in periodic borrowing requests. As set forth in the servicing agreement, the program services will also monitor compliance with certain program requirements and will deliver monthly servicing reports and periodic payment collaboration reports to Treasury. Under Section 3.3 of the Servicing Agreement, Treasury will also receive a certification on a monthly basis from the program servicer regarding its compliance with requirements of the servicing agreement.

- Use of TARP Funds – Funds drawn under the loan agreement may be used only to purchase automotive supplies receiveables that meet criteria specified by Treasury as part of its program to assist General Motors and Chrysler in restructuring.

In addition, the folliwng steps have been taken with respect to programs that were operational prior to SIGTARP's February 6, 2009 report:

- Capital Purchase Program Treasury has launched a monthly lending survey of the 21 largest recipients of funds under the Capital purchase Program (CPP). The Snapshot contains quantitative information on those major categories of lending – consumer, commercial, and other activities – tested on banks' internal reporting, as well as commentary to explain changes in lending levels for each category. Treasury has already published 2 Snapshots that are available on our web site at http://www.financialstability.gov/impact/surveys.htm, and will publish the next one in mid-April. Treasury plans to expand the monthly lending survey to all CPP participants. The expanded CPP monthly lending report is expected to be published by mid-May.
- Targeted Investment Program/Assed Guarantee Program – Under existing agreements, participants under the Targeted Investment Program and Asset Guarantee Program are required to report and certify internal controls established to ensure compliance with certain terms and conditions under the securities purchase agreement and participant's use of funds received under these programs.
- Automotive Industry Financing Program – Treasury currently requires extensive reporting from the auto companies on program operation requirements in their respective agreements. Funds received by auto companies are specifically targeted to bridge cash shortfalls as identified and described in these reports.

Treasury's Next Steps:

- Systemically Significantly Failing Institutions Program – Treasury is currently drafting agreements for additional investments in AIG. These agreements will include the inspection rights and internal control provisions. In addition, the agreements will require AIG to provide a plan, both on the closing date and when funds are drawn from the capital facility, on how capital received will be utilized.
- New programs in the process of being documented: Treasury is in the process of drafting program agreements for the programs announced since SIGTARP's initial Congressional report published on February 6, 2009. Treasury is committed to include inspection rights and internal control requirements in the appropriate agreements for each of the new programs.

<u>SIGTARP Recommendation 2:</u> Treasury needs to begin developing a more complete strategy on what to do with the very substantial portfolio that it now manages on behalf of the American people. In particular, Treasury needs to develop effective evaluation methodologies to value the preferred shares and warrants that it holds and on overall investment strategy to manage the equality portfolio it holds.

<u>Status at time of previous report:</u>

On November 7, 2008, Treasury issued a notice soliciting interested institutions to serve as financial agents to manage the portfolio of securities from Treasury by public and private Financial Institutions participating in the Capital Purchas Program (CPP) and other similar programs that may be established under the Act. The notice set forth a variety of portfolio management and asset evaluation services sought by Treasury.

<u>Summary of programs since previous report:</u>

- **Over several months, Treasury thoroughly evaluated the 205 submissions received in response to its notice for asset management services, and has identified but not yet engaged a cadre of potential managers best suited to the portfolio.**
- **Treasury has drafted provisions for formal investment policies and asset manager guidelines to govern administration of the portfolio, and coordinate the development of its investment policy approach with Federal banking agencies.**
- **Treasury has hired experienced personnel in portfolio management, who have developed internal models for the valuation of preferred shares and warrants, and evaluated a variety of commercial tools and software products to assist in warrant valuations.**
  - **The valuation methods will be based on observable market prices for securities with similar characteristics, a set of well-studied financial models (such as discounted cash flow, regression analysis, binomials, and Black-Scholes pricing), fundamental analysis of each Financial Institution's assets, capital, credit and cash flow, and on the input of outside consultants with independent models.**
  - **For Financial Institutions with publicly traded preferred stock of subordinated debt, the valuation method for preferred shares will incorporate yields on comparable securities and estimations of the timing of repayment for each Financial Institution. For Financial Institutions without publicly traded preferred stock or subordinated debt, the valuation method will incorporate estimated timing of repayment and an appropriate discount rate applied to the schedule of cash floors**
- **Pending selection of the asset managers, Treasury tasked its custodian Bank of New York Mellon (BNY Mellon) to provide initial market valuations for the portfolio. BNY Mellon engaged Gifford Fong Associates to assist with these initial variations.**
- **Treasury and BNY Mellon have implemented policies and procedures to monitor and respond to the Financial Institutions corporate actions and other counterparty events that may have an impact on the value of holdings.**
- **Treasury has hired additional dedicated staff to develop models for credit reform subsidies and accounting, following the new administration's policy decision to reflect assets in the portfolio consistent with the Federal Credit Reform Act.**

Treasury's next steps:

- Treasury will shortly engage its initial asset managers and will assign each with investment positions in the portfolio.
- After collective consultation with and input from the chosen asset managers, Treasury will adjust its investment policies and asset manager guidelines, to include instructions on portfolio posts and strategy asset valuation asset monitoring and management portfolio

SIGTARP Recommendation 3: Treasury should consider requiring that some baseline fraud prevention standards be adopted.

Status at time of previous report:

As of February 6, 2009, the Federal Reserve Bank of New York (FRBNY) and the Board of Governors of the Federal Reserve System (the Fed) were still developing the specific details of TALF, including broad baseline fraud prevention measures.

Summary of progress since previous report:

Treasury, in collaboration with FRBNY and the Fed, has put in place an extensive set of requirements that address both fraud and credit loss prevention. Treasury believes these measures (listed below) are consistent with achieving TALF's purpose of encouraging lending to consumers and small businesses. These guidelines include:

- Fraud Prevention requirements:
    - A borrower acceptance standard and an assurance program related to borrower eligibility requirements
    - Co-side inspection rights cover borrowers and the right to reject a borrower for any reason.
    - The right to review all loan files held by the custodian pertaining to each borrower.
    - A telephone and internet-based hotline for reporting of fraudulent conduct of activity associated with the TALF.
    - The ABS issuer must provide a certification in connection with the prospectus that the ABS is TALF eligible, that a nationally recognized certified independent accounting firm has certified that the4 ABS is TALF eligible, and that the issuer has not made any untrue statements of material fact to an NRSR to obtain the credit rating of the ABS.
    - The ABS issuer and ABS sponsor must provide an indemnity certification which acts as an additional determent for fraudulent behavior. This indemnity also protects Treasury.
    - If a borrower who has participated in the program is found to be ineligible or is found to have knowingly broached a representation related to the eligibility of the collateral, the non-recounts feature of the loan becomes inapplicable and the borrower must repay the loan.
    - To assist FRBNY in screening borrowers, primary dealers are required to apply their internal customer identification program and due diligence procedures to each borrower and escalate information relating to those borrowers assessed at high risk to FRBNY.
- Credit Loss Protection Requirements:

- **Investors are required to supply risk capital in the form of haircuts that will provide the first loss position in front of the U.S. Government. Investors therefore have significant incentive to conduct due diligence about the quality of the underlying securities and underwriting standards.**
- **TALF haircut methodology is risk-sensitive across asset classes and maturities. Rigorous analytical studies (by both FRBNY and Treasury's outside advisor) project minimal credit loss even under highly stressed scenarios.**
- **TALF only accepts collateral that has received two credit ratings in the highest investment-grade rating category of AAA (and no rating below that category) or that is fully U.S. Government-guaranteed.**

- **Fraud Prevention and Credit Loss Protection at the Disposition SPV Level**
  - **With respect to the Disposition SPV (TALF LLC) to which the U.S. Treasury will be providing a $20 billion subordinated loan, additional credit loss protection, fraud prevention and compliance mechanisms have been put in place which will fover the Treasury's relationship with TALF and TALF LLC, including:**
    - **Loan-spread interest will pass to the SPV and accumulate to provide the first loss cash cushion to any potential losses that may occur if collateral is put to the SPV.**
    - **UST will retain the right to refuse any changes in the TALF loan haircuts or loan fee charged to borrowers.**
    - **UST will have access to information and reports regarding TALF loans outstanding and underlying collateral in addition to SPV financial reporting and notices.**
    - **UST will have the rights to monitor the FRBNY's internal controls and compliance measures for TALF.**

Treasury's Next Steps:

- **UST is continuing to build out its team dedicated to monitoring all aspects of the program and working with FRBNY and UST's Office of Financial Stability oversight and compliance personnel.**
- **Treasury will exercise its rights to receive information regarding collateral not yet "put" to TALF LLC in order to fully assess the likelihood of ABS reaching TALF LLC.**
- **Treasury has met, and will continue to meet with SIGTARP, to determine the best financial metrics to use in tracking the performance of collateral that could be put to TALF LLC.**
- **As new classes of securities are added to TALF, Treasury will work with fraud-prevention professionals and SIGTARP to identify appropriate measures for fraud prevention and credit loss protection.**
- **UST plans to add fraud-prevention expertise to the TARP team**

SIGTARP Recommendation 4:

Treasury should consider, before committing TARP funds, requiring that beneficiaries of TALF sign an agreement that includes oversight-enabling provisions.

Status at time of previous report:

As of February 6, 2009, FRBNY and the Fed were still developing the specific details of TALF.

Summary of Progress since previous report:

- **Treasury required that SIGTARP and the Government Accountability Office (GAO) be given specific oversight rights with regard to TALF LLC and FRBNY. See Section 9.18 of the Credit Agreement by and running TALF LLC, FRBNY and Treasury.**
- **Treasury also required that SIGTARP and GAO be given access rights to the ABS sponsors in the event that any ABS collateral of that sponsor used deemed to be ineligible. This access right governs all aspects of the ineligibility of the ABS**

Treasury's next steps:

As new classes of securities are added to TALF, Treasury will work with SIGTARP to identify appropriate oversight standards.

SIGTARP Recommendations 5 and 6:

Treasury should give careful consideration before agreeing to the expansion of TALF to include mortgage-backed securities ("MBS") without further review. (4) TALF should not be expanded to existing "legacy" MBS in its current format.

Status at time of previous report:

As of February 6, 2009, FRBNY and the Fed were still developing the specific details of TALF. Neither asset class has yet been included in TALF.

Summary of progress since previous report:

The asset-backed securities (ABS) markets historically have finished a substantial share of credit to home owners, customers and businesses. Continued disruption of these markets could significantly limit the availability of credit to households and businesses of all sizes and thereby contribute to further weakening of U.S. economic activity. TALF is designed to increase credit availability and support economic activity by facilitating renewed assistance of consumer and business ABS at more normal interest rate spreads. We have begun to see some of the first few signs of success from TALFs first subscription in stimulating new demand and issuance for consumer and business loans.

The Federal Reserve and the Treasury are currently analyzing the appropriate terms and conditions for accepting commercial mortgage-backed securities, including acceptable sponsor haircuts and other protections. In addition, the Federal Reserve and the Treasury have been evaluating expanding TALF to residential mortgage-backed securities, both newly attained and possibly 'legacy' ABS. Our goal is to include securities that will have the greatest macroeconomic impact and that could most efficiently be added at a low and manageable risk to the government. The TALF facility will cease making loans on December 31, 2009, unless the Board of Governors of the Federal Reserve Board extends the facility.

Treasury's next steps:

- **Treasury will continue to explore the expansion of TALF as noted above. In connection with the proposed expansion, Treasury will work closely with fraud-**

prevention professionals and SIGTARP to structure appropriate safeguards and compliance measures.

SIGTARP Recommendation 7:

Treasury should establish a compliance protocol with the Federal Reserve before TALF is put into effect.

Status at time of previous report:

As of February 6, 2009, FRBNY and the Fed were still developing the specific details of TALF

Summary of progress since previous report:

- **Compliance protocol put into effect included extensive eligibility requirements, collateral eligibility requirements, issuer assurances, auditor attestation, conflicts of interest guidelines, collateral sufficiency tests, and know Your Customer ("KYC") standards. The requirements can be found at:** http://www.newyorkfed.org/markets/talf_docs.html.
- **Treasury required specific representations, warranties, covenants and certifications from TALF LLC prior to closing the initial version of TALF.**
- **Treasury has specific and extensive information rights with regard to TALF LLC and FRBNY**
- **Treasury has the right to receive all compliance certificates (spender, issuer, auditor) received by FRBNY in connection with the loans made by FRBNY.**
- **As there are not ongoing compliance functions at the SPV-level for an SPV owned and controlled by FRBNY, it is not anticipated that Treasury will receive periodic compliance certificates. Treasury will, however, receive extensive informational reports with regard to the ABS used as collateral for FRBNY loans.**

Treasury's next steps:

Treasury will study whether the expansion of TALF creates new compliance concerns and will adjust the compliance regime accordingly.

Our objective is to design effective programs that restart these markets and help clear banks' balance sheets in order to restore the flow of credit, while protecting taxpayers. We have structured our programs to attract the very best private sector expertise, both to select and price assets and to share in the risks and rewards of the programs. Given the severity of the crisis, Treasury must take these unprecedented actions to stabilize our financial system. Our actions must be in the long-term best interest of taxpayers, considering both the potential risks to taxpayers of action and also the potential risks to taxpayers of inaction. We believe our programs strike the right balance, and we appreciate your team's efforts to help us make them better.

Sincerely,

Neel Kashkari
Interim Assistant Secretary
For Financial Stabiliy

K. ORGANIZATIONAL CHART

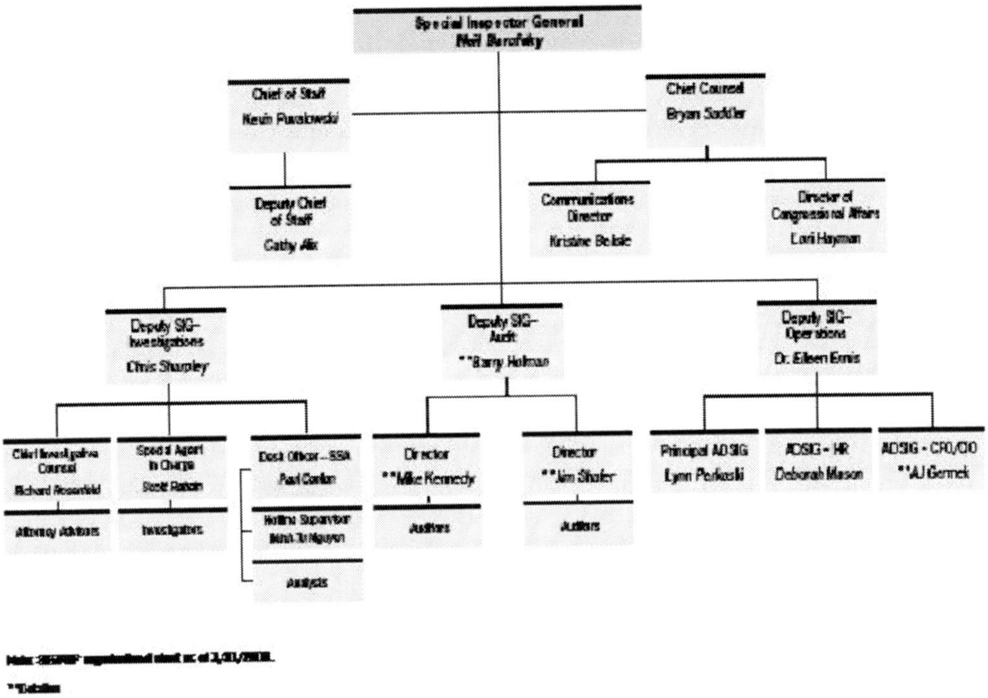

L. Use of Funds Request Letter

This appendix contains a copy of the February 5, 2009, letter from SIGTARP sent to TARP recipients requesting information on their usage of TARP funds.

OFFICE OF THE SPECIAL INSPECTOR GENERAL
TROUBLED ASSET RELIEF PROGRAM
1500 Pennsylvania Ave., N.W., Suite 1064
Washington, D.C. 20220
February 5, 2009

(Addressee)

The Emergency Economic Stabilization Act of 2008 ("EESA") that established the Troubled Asset Relief Program (TARP) also created the Office of the Special Inspector General Troubled Asset Relief Program (SIGTARP). SIGTARP is responsible for coordinating and conducting audits and investigations of any program established by the Secretary of the Treasury under the act. As part of an audit into TARP recipients' use of funds and their compliance with EESA's executive compensation requirements,

I am requesting that you provide my office, within 30 days of this request, the following information:

(1) A narrative response specifically outlining (a) your anticipated use of TARP funds; (b) whether the TARP funds were segregated from other institutional funds; (c) your actual use of TARP funds to date; and (d) your expected use of unspent TARP funds. In your response, please take into consideration your anticipated use of TARP funds at the time that you applied for such funds, or any actions that you have taken that you would not have been able to take absent the infusion of TARP funds.

(2) Your specific plans, and the status of implementation of those plans, for addressing executive compensation requirements associated with the funding. Information provided regarding executive compensation should also include any assessments made of loan risks and their relationship to executive compensation; how limitations on executive compensation will be implemented in line with Department of Treasury guidelines; and whether any such limitations may be offset by other changes to other, longer-term or deferred forms of executive compensation.

In connection with this request:

(1) We anticipate that responses might well be quantitative as well as qualitative in nature regarding the impact of having the funds, and we encourage you to make reference to such sources as statements to the media, shareholders, or others concerning your intended or actual use of TARP funds, as well as any internal email, budgets, or memoranda describing your anticipated use of funds. We ask that you segregate and preserve all documents referencing your use or anticipated use of

TARP funds such as any internal email, budgets, or memoranda regarding your anticipated or actual use of TARP funds.

(2) Your response should include copies of pertinent supporting documentation (financial or otherwise) to support your response.

(3) Further, I request that, your response be signed by a duly authorized senior executive officer of your company, including a statement certifying the accuracy of all statements, representations, and supporting information provided, subject to the requirements and penalties set forth in Title 18, United States Code, Section 1001.

(4) Responses should be provided electronically within 30 days to SIGTARP at SIGTARP.response@do.treas.gov with an original signed certification and any other supporting documentation mailed to: Special Inspector General – TARP; 1500 Pennsylvania Avenue, NW; Suite 1064; Washington, D.C. 20220.

We think this initiative is vital to providing transparency of the TARP program, and to the ability of SIGTARP and others to assess the effectiveness of TARP programs over time. If you have any questions regarding this initiative, please feel free to contact Mr. Barry W. Holman, my Deputy Inspector General for Audit at (202) 927-9936.

Very truly yours,

Neil M. Barofsky
Special Inspector General
OMB Control No. 1505-0212
(Expires August 2009)

An agency is not authorized to conduct, and persons are not required to respond to, an information collection request unless it displays a valid control number. Response is mandatory for all selected participants in the TARP program

End Notes

1 Treasury, Programs webpage, 3/30/2009, www.financialstability.gov, accessed 4/9/2009.
2 Treasury, response to SIGTARP data call, 4/8/2009.
3 Treasury, Programs webpage, 3/30/2009, www.financialstability.gov, accessed 4/9/2009.
4 Treasury, Programs webpage, 3/30/2009, www.financialstability.gov, accessed 4/9/2009.
5 Treasury, Programs webpage, 3/30/2009, www.financialstability.gov, accessed 4/9/2009.
6 Treasury, Programs webpage, 3/30/2009, www.financialstability.gov, accessed 4/9/2009.
7 Treasury, Programs webpage, 3/30/2009, www.financialstability.gov, accessed 4/9/2009.
8 Treasury, Programs webpage, 3/30/2009, www.financialstability.gov, accessed 4/9/2009.
9 Treasury, "Treasury Announces Auto Supplier Support Program; Program Will Aid Critical Sector of American Economy," 3/19/2009, www.treas.gov, accessed 3/19/2009.
10 Treasury, "Obama Administration's New Warranty Commitment Program," 3/30/2009, www.treas.gov, accessed 3/30/2009.
11 Treasury, Section 105(a) Report, www.financialstabiliy.gov, 12/5/2009, accessed 4/10/2009.

[12] Treasury, "Fact Sheet: Financial Stability Plan," 2/10/2009, www.financialstability.gov, accessed 4/10/2009.
[13] Treasury, Office of Financial Stability, Chief of Compliance and CFO, SIGTARP interview, 3/30/2009.
[14] Treasury, Programs webpage, 3/30/2009, www.financialstability.gov, accessed 4/9/2009.
[15] Treasury, Programs webpage, 3/30/2009, www.financialstability.gov, accessed 4/9/2009.
[16] Treasury, Programs webpage, 3/30/2009, www.financialstability.gov, accessed 4/9/2009.
[17] Treasury, response to SIGTARP data call, 4/8/2009.
[18] Treasury, response to SIGTARP data call, 3/31/2009. According to Treasury, information on EARNEST Partners is based on representations by the company received by OFS and from the company website.
[19] Treasury, response to SIGTARP data call, 4/8/2009.
[20] Treasury, response to SIGTARP data call, 4/8/2009.
[21] Treasury OIG, response to SIGTARP data call, 4/1/2009.
[22] Federal Reserve OIG, response to SIGTARP data call, 4/9/2009.
[23] GAO, response to SIGTARP data call, 4/8/2009.
[24] FDIC OIG, response to SIGTARP data call, 3/30/2009.

INDEX

F

G

H

I

J

K

L

M

N

O

P

R

S

T

U

V

W